European Constitutional Law Network-Series

edited by Prof. Dr. Dr. h.c. Ingolf Pernice,
Walter Hallstein-Institute for European Constitutional Law (WHI)

Vol. 9

Lina Papadopoulou/Ingolf Pernice
Joseph H.H. Weiler (eds.)

Legitimacy Issues of the European Union in the Face of Crisis

Dimitris Tsatsos in memoriam

HART
PUBLISHING

Nomos

The Deutsche Nationalbibliothek lists this publication in the Deutsche Nationalbibliografie; detailed bibliographic data are available on the Internet at http://dnb.d-nb.de

ISBN: HB (Nomos) 978-3-8487-4107-6
ePDF (Nomos) 978-3-8452-8416-3

British Library Cataloguing-in-Publication Data
A catalogue record for this book is available from the British Library.

ISBN: HB (Hart) 978-1-5099-1821-8

Library of Congress Cataloging-in-Publication Data
Papadopoulou, Lina / Pernice, Ingolf / Weiler, Joseph H.H.
Legitimacy Issues of the European Union in the Face of Crisis
Dimitris Tsatsos in memoriam
Lina Papadopoulou / Ingolf Pernice / Joseph H.H. Weiler (eds.)
432 p.

ISBN 978-1-5099-1821-8 (hardcover Hart)

1. Edition 2017

Table of Contents

Introduction: Legitimacy Issues of the European Union

Ingolf Pernice

The European Constitutional Law Network (ECLN) met in Thessaloniki (Greece) on the 19 and 20 May 2015 to discuss '*Legitimacy Issues of the European Union. Lessons from the Financial Crisis*'. Even today the financial crisis of the EU is not yet over – it is still hitting our polities, societies and markets. Economic growth is still at the bottom,[1] while the rates of "sovereign" debts[2] and unemployment, in particular of young people, remain unacceptable high.[3] Some indications of hope, however, that the bottom had been reached, and some signs that the situation was improving seemed to be visible at the time of the Thessaloniki conference. Unfortunately, these signs have meanwhile disappeared, and the problems of the Economic and Monetary Union continue to plague us, while the European Union is facing new challenges, from within as well as from without. The concept of legitimacy in the EU itself would deserve a special conference and far more study in the European context,[4] but given the need for con-

---

1 According to Eurostat date the average was 1.9 % for the 28 Member States in 2016, see Eurosstat at: http://ec.europa.eu/eurostat/tgm/table.do?tab=table&init=1&language=en&pcode=tec00115&plugin=1 (accessed 11 April 2017).

2 The rate for the EU 28 decreased from 2014 to 2015 from 86,7 % to 85 %, compared to 57,5 % in 2007 and 83,8 % in 2012, see: Eurostat at: http://ec.europa.eu/eurostat/tgm/table.do?tab=table&plugin=1&language=de&pcode=tsdde410 (accessed 11 April 2017).

3 For the youth unemployment rates, the highest were recorded in Greece (45.2 % in December 2016), Spain (41.5 %) and Italy (35.2 %). See Eurostat figures indicating a slight decrease, however, in the year from 2016 to 2017, at: http://ec.europa.eu/eurostat/statistics-explained/index.php/Unemployment_statistics (accessed 11 April 2017): The EU-28 unemployment rate was 8.0 % in February 2017, down from 8.1 % in January 2017 and from 8.9 % in February 2016.

4 See, however, the stimulating ideas of Joseph H.H. Weiler, 'Europe in Crisis – on "political messianism", "legitimacy" and the "rule of law"', *Singapore Journal of Legal Studies* (2012), pp 248-68, at: http://law.nus.edu.sg/sjls/articles/SJLS-Dec-12-248.pdf (accessed 23 August 2016).

structive reform ideas in times of looming disintegration,[5] discussing legitimacy issues of the EU in context and from different perspectives proved extremely useful and stimulating.

Inside the EU, the most worrying new development is the British referendum on Brexit.[6] There may be many approaches to explaining the 'leave' outcome. Internal problems like the position of Scotland as well as constitutional questions may have given rise to doubts as to whether or not the notice under Article 50 TEU would be sent to Brussels. New developments show that it has been filed in March 2017. It is yet an open question, what the outcome of the negotiations on the agreement on the conditions of the exit will be, or whether after a period of time, negotiation and reflection, the notice may even be withdrawn. The Brexit-vote of 23 June 2016, at least, came as a surprise to British and other people in Europe, and it raises a number of questions regarding the present state of the European Union and its constitution.

One of these questions regards democratic legitimacy. It is coupled with the wide variety of difficulties the Union is actually facing: how to overcome the economic crisis in most of the southern countries, and the unacceptable level of unemployment that is about to destroy the future of a whole generation of young people in this part of Europe. Where is the solidarity among the member states and peoples as promised and hoped to govern our mutual relationships in the Union?[7] What are we, each of us citizens of the Union, ready to invest in our common future, founded in

---

5 See already Lenz Jacobsen, 'There's No Plan B for Europe's Future', in: *Zeit Online* 9 July 2015 available at: http://www.zeit.de/politik/ausland/2015-07/european-union-integration-disintegration-crisis (accessed 29 August 2016). See also Georges Soros, 'Ver une disintegration de l'Europe', in: *Les Echos.fr* 26 June 2016, at: http://www.lesechos.fr/idees-debats/cercle/cercle-158357-le-brexit-et-lavenir-de-leurope-2009687.php (accessed 29 August 2016); Franz C. Mayer, 'Of Blind Men, Elephants and European Disintegration – What could and what should legal academics do against the "disintegration" of Europe?', in *Verfassungsblog* 26 March 2015, at: http://verfassungsblog.de/von-blinden-maennern-und-elefanten-was-kann-und-sollte-die-rechtswissenschaft-gegen-die-desintegration-europas-tun/ (accessed 29 August 2016).

6 See Paul Craig, Brexit. A Drama in Six Acts, *ELRev.* 41(2016) pp 447-468; Ingolf Pernice, European Constitutionalism and the National Constitutions of the Member States – Implications for Brexit, WHI-paper 1/2017, at: http://www.whi-berlin.eu/tl_files/WHI-Papers%20ab%202013/WHI-Paper_01_2017.pdf.

7 For some thoughts about solidarity in the EU see Ingolf Pernice, 'Solidarität in Europa. Eine Ortsbestimmung im Verhältnis zwischen Bürger, Staat und Europäischer

the values laid down in Article 2 TEU, a future of peace, liberty and welfare in Europe and beyond? Nationalism and the belief in national sovereignty has proven not to be the recipe. This deep historical insight, based upon the experience of hundreds of years of war among European peoples, is what drove Altiero Spinelli back in 1941, and Jean Monnet, Walter Hallstein, Alcide de Gasperi and the other fathers of European Integration in the early 50's to design a new political arrangement beyond the state, for shaping a better future for post-war generations. It produced more than seventy years of peace among former competing nations and enemies, a longer period of peace than we have ever had across this continent. It allowed the unification of post-war Europe and – what for many Germans seemed to remain a hopeless dream – the reunification of Germany. The latter was possible 'under the roof of Europe': integration instead of the awkward insistence on national sovereignty. But the devil of national sovereignty is not dead. Populists like Nigel Farage with his UKIP in Britain and similar movements in other Member States like the 'Front National' of Marine Le Pen, prefer solving problems the way we hoped to have left behind. Brexit might never happen, as we can read in an article published by 'Deutsche Welle' on 15 August 2016.[8] So we may still hope. Would it need a second referendum in Britain?[9] Would an agreement under Article 50 TEU for being ratified by the EU need a referendum in the other Member States, or a European-wide referendum – for the status of all EU citizens being affected? What the 'leave' movement

Union', in: Christian Calliess (ed), *Europäische Solidarität und nationale Identität – Überlegungen im Kontext der Krise im Euroraum* (Tübingen, Mohr Siebeck, 2013) pp 25-56, also available as WHI-Paper 01/2013 at: http://www.whi-berlin.eu/tl_files/documents/WHI-Paper%201-13-Solidarita%CC%88t.pdf (accessed 29 August 2016).

8 Bernd Rieger, 'Wait and see: Theresa May is in no hurry on Brexit', DW of 15 August 2016: 'the Brexit will take longer than British voters imagined in the June referendum – and there's a good chance it will never happen. DW looks at key questions and answers.',http://www.dw.com/en/wait-and-see-theresa-may-is-in-no-hurry-on-brexit/a-19476195 (accessed 22 August 2016).

9 See Pavlos Eleftheriadis, 'A New Referendum is a Constitutional Requirement', Oxford Business Law Blog, 4 July 2016, at: https://www.law.ox.ac.uk/business-law-blog/blog/2016/07/new-referendum-constitutional-requirement (last accessed 27 August 2016).

celebrated as 'independence day',[10] if implemented, would mean is that Britain would leave the EU-framework, a framework that was understood by Jacques Delors and others to guarantee that Germany —even if unified — would never again become a threat to other European peoples. What the 'leavers' are celebrating as 'independence' is, in fact, the loss of Britain's voice in Europe and of any control it still has, through the EU system of mutual constitutional stabilisation[11], also on Germany.

At least in order to have the benefits of the internal market even after Brexit, i.e. like Norway or Switzerland, Britain would have to adapt to EU legislation without having a voice.[12] If this is what the 'leave' campaign was looking at, the underlying concept of sovereignty may be quite different from the traditional understanding of this term. Another open question of legitimacy concerns the constitutional requirements for a government to proceed under Article 50 TEU. Given the legal consequences, including the loss for the national citizens of their status as citizens of the Union and the loss, for the citizens of the other Member States, of their respective rights in the withdrawing Member State, the exit of one of the Member States is far from being just an act of 'foreign' policy. Notwithstanding the principle of voluntariness of membership,[13] the EU is not a golf club people join or leave without further ado. In the case of Britain, acting without

---

10 See: BBC 24 June 2016: 'Nigel Farage says Leave win marks UK "independence day"', at: http://www.bbc.com/news/uk-politics-eu-referendum-36613238 (accessed 22 June 2016). For critical comments see: Independent Voices 24 June 2016: 'It's offensive to call Brexit an "Independence Day" – the EU wasn't an enslaving colonial power like Britain': 'Calling for a British Independence Day is wounding to all the nations that revolted and fought hard against British colonial rule. This kind of language is contributing to real incidents of xenophobia across the UK', at: http://www.independent.co.uk/voices/its-offensive-to-call-brexit-an-independence-day-the-eu-wasnt-a-colonial-power-enslaving-your-nation-a7104286.html (accessed 22 August 2016).

11 For the limits on national constitutional autonomy through the system of mutual constitutional stabilisation as provided for by the Treaties and, in particular, Articles 2 and 7 TEU see already Ingolf Pernice, 'Bestandssicherung der Verfassungen: Verfassungsrechtliche Mechanismen zur Wahrung der Verfassungsordnung', in: Roland Bieber and Pierre Widmer (eds), *L'espace constitutionnel européen. Der Europäische Verfassungsraum. The European Constitutional Area* (Zürich, Schulthess, 1995) pp 225, 261-4.

12 See already Paul Craig, 'Brexit: A Drama in Six Acts', *ELRev.* (2016) pp 447, 456.

13 This is – apart from additionality and open democracy – one of the three fundamental principles of European integration: see Ingolf Pernice, 'The EU – A Citi-

express parliamentary authorisation would have been difficult to reconcile with the sovereignty of the British Parliament,[14] and so was the decision of the UK Supreme Court of 24 January 2017 in the *Miller*-case.[15] Last but not least, if in accordance with the principle of subsidiarity, the EU is made to achieve, for the benefit of the citizens, what a single Member State cannot achieve, does Brexit not result in a loss of sovereignty for the UK instead of regaining sovereignty, as the Brexiters pretend to pursue?[16]

The present disintegration movements and increasing nationalism in several Member States may have different causes and explanations, yet they seem to be nourished by a feeling, among people, that European politics made in Brussels are not 'our' politics, not a matter of the citizens of the Union. But who, if not 'we, the people' —or in our case, the Union's citizens— should have ownership of European politics? This points to our attitude towards the EU and, thus, the question of legitimacy.

Among the challenges from without, first of all the crises of Ukraine and Syria raise questions about the institutional setting and efficiency of

---

zens' Joint Venture. Multilevel Constitutionalism and Open Democracy in Europe', in: José M Magone (ed), *Routledge Handbook of European Politics* (Routledge 2015) pp 184-201.

14 For some thoughts thus far see Ingolf Pernice, 'Brexit im Europäischen Verfassungsverbund', in: *Verfassungblog on matters constitutional*, 27 June 2016, at: http://verfassungsblog.de/author/ingolf-pernice/ (accessed 14 August 2106). The new British Prime Minister, Theresa May, seems to have accepted, meanwhile, that the notice under Article 50 TEU cannot be given without authorization by an Act of Parliament, as she has announced the "A Great Repeal Bill to get rid of the European Communities Act – introduced in the next Parliamentary session" in her speech to the Conservative Party Conference 2016, October 2, 2016, at https://www.youtube.com/watch?v=OuH3zgz_1xQ, for the text of the speech see: The Independent, 5.10.16: Theresa May's keynote speech at Tory conference in full, http://www.independent.co.uk/news/uk/politics/theresa-may-speech-tory-conference-2016-in-full-transcript-a7346171.html.

15 Judgment of 24 January 2017 of the Supreme Court at: https://www.supremecourt.uk/cases/docs/uksc-2016-0196-judgment.pdf; see already the High Court judgment of 3 November 2016,R (Miller) -v- Secretary of State for Exiting the European Union at: https://www.judiciary.gov.uk/judgments/r-miller-v-secretary-of-state-for-exiting-the-european-union/. Meanwhile, the UK has triggered the procedure under Article 50 TEU.

16 In this vein see Ingolf Pernice, European Constitutionalism and the National Constitutions of the Member States. Implications of Brexit, WHI-Pater 01/2017, at: http://www.whi-berlin.eu/tl_files/WHI-Papers%20ab%202013/WHI-Paper_01_2017.pdf.

the CFSP. Secondly, not only refugees from Africa, but also from Afghanistan and, even more drastically, from Syria, challenge the unity of, and the (remaining) solidarity within the European Union: an unexpected and —for too long— largely underestimated threat. The refugee crisis and diverging views among the Member States on the integration of immigrants are becoming a new factor of disintegration in Europe. The right of free movement and the openness of the internal borders has been under pressure since the openness of the external borders of the EU was tested successfully by refugees from third countries: people under political or economic pressure having been misled by trafficking gangs. Our citizens expect the Union to quickly find adequate solutions, based upon our common values as well as on the powers that have been conferred to the Union under Articles 67-80 TFEU. This concerns output legitimacy. The capacity to act effectively, and to agree rapidly on urgent measures in times of need is a condition for the continuing support of the European Union by its citizens. Failure to act in common according to the provisions of the Treaties, necessarily affects legitimacy. It is a challenge to the legitimacy of the Union system as a whole.

The contributions to the present volume, presented and discussed at the ECLN-conferences in New York (October 2012)[17] and Thessaloniki (May 2015)[18], cannot cover all these issues, and particularly not the more recent events. The primary background and focus of the Thessaloniki conference were the financial crisis and the measures taken to avoid the bankruptcy of Member States, European policies that hit Greece in particular. This topic is delicate, for there are no 'real' competences of the EU for economic and fiscal policies. Deficits and failures are thus attributed to a creature without real powers: Articles 119-121 TFEU repeatedly talk about 'the close coordination of Member States' economic policies', the fact that Member States are bound to 'conduct *their* economic policies with a view to contributing to the achievement of the objectives of the Union', or to 'regard *their* economic policies as a matter of common concern…'. Only the monetary policies are a matter of —exclusive— competence of the Union.

17 ECLN Conference New York 2012: '*Retheorizing European Integration and its Public Space'*, New York University School of Law, October 11-12, 2012, at: http://www.ecln.net/new-york-2012.html. (accessed 21 April 2017).

18 ECLN Conference Thessaloniki 2015: ‚Challenging the Legitimacy of Europe. Makedonia Palace Hotel, May 21-22, 2015, at: http://www.ecln.net/thessaloniki-2015.html (accessed 21 April 2017).

While EU institutions do play an active role in the coordination of these policies, and are given responsibilities regarding their implementation regardless of the constitutional asymmetry of the construction of the Economic and Monetary Union, the measures taken to deal with the crisis ultimately remain the responsibility of the national governments, which are accountable only to their respective parliaments and peoples. To qualify this as 'executive federalism' enhancing the democratic deficit of the EU,[19] sounds like a euphemism, for there is little in place of what 'federalism' would require. Nevertheless, legitimacy is rightly questioned in an arrangement that mainly places power over national budgets and fiscal policies in the hands of executives sitting behind closed doors and taking decisions without direct parliamentary control. Parliaments at both levels need to be given more direct control of the budgetary policies of the Union and the European framework and guidance established for the Member States' economic, fiscal and social policies.[20]

The present volume consists of an introduction, fifteen substantive chapters and an epilogue. It offers an analysis of EU legitimacy issues, ranging from more theoretical fundamentals to concrete policy recommendations. The issues are studied against the background of the financial crisis since 2009 and the attempts made by national governments and the European Union to avoid a financial disaster in Greece and other countries, and the breakdown of the Euro-system. As constitutional law and courts not only set the general framework of political action but also determine the concrete limits that should be respected by governments and parliaments, the role of the judges and the legitimacy of their contributions take a central place in the discussion. This includes some reflection on the fundamental rights of the citizens and new instruments available for enhancing participative democracy and legitimacy in a 'digital Europe'.

I. Part One of the present volume is devoted to the search for '*Appropriate Concepts: Legitimacy and European Democracy*'.

---

19 Jürgen Habermas, *The Crisis of the European Union* (Cambridge, Polity Press, 2012) 12, 52, with solutions developed on pp 119-32.

20 See Ingolf Pernice, 'Financial Crisis, National Parliaments and EMU Reform', in: Davor Jancic & Damian Chalmers (eds), *Resilience or Resignation: National Parliaments and the EU* (Oxford, Oxford University Press, 2017), p 115-139. With important observations on the difficulties and perspectives of setting up better interparliamentary cooperation in the EU see Ian Cooper, The Emerging Order of Interparliamentary Cooperation in the Post-Lisbon EU, in: ibid., p. 227-246.

George Gerapetritis develops a theoretical background of deliberative democracy and explains that in a multilevel system deliberative democracy ought to be developed not only as a conceptual instrument of political philosophy but mostly as a set of applied constitutional mechanisms to supplement existing institutional safeguards in order to fulfil its potential as a factor of constitutional legitimacy.

Lina Papadopoulou more specifically questions the existing attempts to construct democratic legitimacy in the European Union as a 'double legitimacy'. With a view to the status and role the Treaties are reserving for the citizens of the Union she proposes that the suitable 'democratic' legitimacy in the present historical and political phase is rather a triple one, based on states, peoples and citizens alike.

Giacinto della Cananea adopts a more practical perspective on legitimacy and claims that the most important condition for enhanced democratic legitimacy in the EU is based upon an old and broadly recognised principle: 'no taxation without representation', which should be reversed into '*no representation without taxation*'. He explains why European taxes are a necessary element of democratic legitimacy and argues that more attention for duties, particularly in the fiscal domain, can be matched with a renewed attention for public goods, such as infrastructures for European society.

In the final chapter of the first part Tom Eijsbouts suggests a new understanding of the sources of democratic legitimacy. He argues for a better construction of the notions (plural) of 'people', 'peoples' etc. in EU law, and so fights against populist simplifications attracted to a singular and fundamental legal notion of People in general. He distinguishes two distinct meanings of people: that of the 'original' people, founder of the constitution, and that of the 'electoral' people, which functions inside the constitution, e.g. as the electorate; with an emphasis on the essential plurality of the notion of 'people', he thus strives to 'debunk' the *no demos*-thesis of the German Federal Constitutional Court and others.

II. *Looking at the Economic Measures and European Courts in Times of Crisis.* Part Two of the volume is devoted to the causes of and remedies to the financial crisis, with a particular focus on the role of the judges as part of the system established for the management of the financial crisis in Europe.

Mattias Kumm presents a thorough analysis of the causes of the financial crisis and their current misinterpretations. He suggests that the central cause of the crisis in Europe is not an undisciplined spending by profligate states, but the asymmetric structural symbiosis between states and banks. For him the reforms undertaken in recent years gesture in the right direction but often remain ineffectual or cosmetic at best. He sees the public costs of bank bailouts as genuinely European risks, for which it would be appropriate to hold the European Union as a whole accountable. This money should be paid, he argues, by genuinely European funds, raised by European taxes or levies. To some extent, this conclusion supports the more general claim of Giacinto della Cananea for European taxation as a condition of legitimacy.

George Karavokyris gives a fascinating analysis of how the constitutionality of the austerity measures in Greece and their conventionality in the framework of the European Convention of Human Rights were mainly decided through the test of the standards of necessity and proportionality; given the great flexibility and judicial restraint proper to this approach, he demonstrates that the limited —judicial— claim of authority of the courts lies in an epistemic and political matter of competence.

A certain amount of flexibility and judicial restraint also seems to qualify the European Court of Justice (ECJ), which had to decide upon the referral made by the German Federal Constitutional Court (GFCC). This court submitted its view that the OMT program of the European Central Bank was unconstitutional and clearly violated the European Treaties. Jean-Victor Louis presents a profound analysis of the preliminary ruling in which the ECJ stated that with certain conditions the OMT program was in conformity with EU law. As the GFCC has meanwhile given its final judgment on the case —in accordance with the ruling of the ECJ, though with great emphasis on strict conditions for the implementation of the program— Louis concludes that quite diverse logics were confronted here but in the end a realistic and conciliatory solution was adopted. National constitutional identity has played a particular role in the referral of the OMT question to the ECJ by the GFCC.

Against this background Jirí Zemanek gives an analysis of these terms from a comparative perspective. He argues that any constitutional change should respect certain basic limits defined by a common core of European constitutionalism. This is an important condition for legitimacy. Within the multilevel constitutional system of the EU national constitutional identities do not suggest, in his view, an anti-thesis to the Union constitutional foundations rather they are specific emanations intensifying a common constitutional core. He also argues that the ECJ should contribute to the convergence of material cores within the Member States′ constitutions based on shared values, ultimately amounting to a European constitutional identity.

Part Two concludes with another perspective on the developments particularly in Greece: in the light of the Greek constitutional jurisprudence Antonis Manitakis observes a surprising resilience of the constitution itself. The resilience of the *Greek constitutional order* to the shock waves of the 'crisis', he finds, coincides with, and is manifested in, the equally striking *ability* of this constitutional order to *adapt* to both the multiple demands of the *European integration process* and the 'real' coercive forces of the globalised market economy. The case law does not rely on an exception from constitutional imperatives dictated by emergency but, as he concludes, creates a new constitutional normality which, compared with the past, is characterised by a greater regulatory 'plasticity or flexibility'.

III. *Citizens, Rights and New Techniques for Enhancing Legitimacy* is the title of Part Three of the present volume focussing human rights, citizenship and legitimacy by digitisation.

Ana Maria Guerra Martins discusses the very important opinion of the ECJ on the European Union's accession to the European Convention on Human Rights (ECHR). Her analysis of the opinion contrasts other critiques and looks for a stimulating theoretical perspective. Her question is whether an adequate constitutional theory, which includes the multilevel protection of fundamental rights in Europe as one among other factors of legitimacy, could have led the Court to other conclusions. On an understanding of multilevel constitutionalism 'in which the different components —EU law, national laws and ECHR law— need to work together towards a major objective, namely a higher level of protection of fundamental rights', she concludes that the outcome of the ECJ's analysis would have been different. In her opinion, only the respect for the principles of cooperative judicial dialogue, of sincere cooperation and of mutual trust between all players makes it possible to avoid jurisdictional conflicts and to reinforce the protection and enforcement of fundamental rights in Europe with a view to enhancing legitimacy of the EU.

An analysis of a very specific jurisprudence of the Court by Anna-Maria Konsta concerns the notion of the citizen of the Union and the right to care as a citizenship right. She suggests that a broader interpretation of the concept of 'care' in accordance with the notion of social family, which is connected to bonds of affection among its members, regardless of their gender, could lead to the proper institutionalisation of an autonomous right to care and, at least from the gender perspective, to a more adequate concept of citizenship: a 'new era in reconceiving family relations and law' as a matter of legitimacy.

A particular perspective on the citizen's ownership and participation in the political processes of the EU is taken by Ingolf Pernice who explores the potential of the internet serving as an instrument for enhancing legitimacy at European level. Using the concepts of input-, output- and throughput-legitimacy, he explains how two separately existing discourses of digitisation (digital agenda and e-government) and of legitimacy (democratic procedures and accountability) in the Union can be merged so to allow for ensuring more transparency of, and citizen's participation in the exercise of public authority in the EU. The internet could bring the institutions closer to the citizen, enhance deliberative and participatory democracy and, thus, help overcoming legitimacy deficits in a digital Europe.

IV. Practical proposals for enhancing legitimacy in Europe and some fundamental thoughts on EU democracy are developed in Part Four titled: *Re-organising Legitimacy in the European Union: Reform Perspectives.*

Federico Fabbrini follows a rather institutional path for addressing the legitimacy problem of the EU. In his view, the lack of transparency and accountability in the Union's decision-making processes is due to an opaque functioning of the Council. His proposal is to revise the EU Treaties, by explicitly making the European Council, rather than the Council of Ministers, the EU upper legislative house. Both, the dual nature of the Union and the allocation of legislative and executive responsibilities in the EU would thus be made clearer to the citizen.

Miguel Poires Maduro observes that the future governance of the EU must be based upon a revised justification of the project of European integration, a justification that focuses on the democratic and social challenges faced by the States and the EU value in responding to them. The EU is not a challenge to national democracy but, instead, an entity offering renewed possibilities for democracy and social justice where States can no longer offer them. With a democratic explanation for the crisis and the Union's failure to successfully address it to date, he demonstrates why the existing model based upon the Stability Compact and instruments of financial solidarity and debt mutualisation cannot function. Financial solidarity in the EU must be detached from transfers between states and related, instead, to the wealth generated by the process of European economic integration. He therefore argues in favour of a EU budget capable of providing the Union with the necessary financial muscle to address and prevent future crises. In addition, the EU would need to change the nature of its policies so as to improve the way in which the institutions 'communicate' with citizens and increase their capacity to induce real systemic reforms in the States.

With a very deep and forward-looking analysis of the developments in the EU Joseph Weiler, finally, describes the current circumstances as "a loss of *heimat*". He explains the long-term processes in the EU as a "depletion of legitimacy resources of Europe and the Union" and uses Brexit and the current responses to it as "a prism to examine the reaction to the crisis". So he develops some ideas on how "to arrest the decline and even possible demise" of the EU. It starts with reminding the "nobel side" of patriotism, that is part of "the republican form of democracy", an appeal to the civic responsibility of each citizen for the politics of his homeland – taking ownership– as I understand, not only of one's state but also of the EU. Valéry Giscard d'Estaing, in his great Humboldt-Speech on Europe, 2006, has explained patriotism by two sources: "fierté et appartenance" (pride and belonging), the latter arising from an emotional pulse ("pulsation affective") encompassing both, that we belong to Europe and that Europe belongs to us.[21] Losing this belonging means losing *heimat*. Also the emphasis only on rights, the mistake that we understand ourselves as a "rights generation" contributes to this loss; and so does the insistence upon human dignity as uniqueness only, leaving aside that as humans we are also social beings, that we are part of a collective and have duties. For Weiler, the current concepts of (input-, output- and telos-) legitimacy are "exhausted, inoperable in the current European circumstance", and democracy "still feels like a foreign implant": it was not part of the "original DNA of European Integration", and the "collabse" of all the legitimacy resources of the EU comes in a moment when the Union would need them all. Finally, the loss of leadership in the EU is explained as another – "fear inducing" – loss of *heimat*. Weiler uses the response to Brexit as an illustration for this. His proposal is to look for a status of the UK as comfortable as possible, "even perhaps a form of Associate Membership". This could result in a win-win situation.

21 Valéri Giscard d'Estaing, Peut-on créer un patriotisme europeén? Speech of 9 November 2006, in: Ingolf Pernice (ed.), Europa-Visionen (Berliner Wissenschafts-Verlag, 2007), p. 199, 202, also available at: https://plone.rewi.hu-berlin.de/de/lf/oe/whi/humboldt-reden-zu-europa/archiv-humboldt-reden/reden/hre-giscard-destaing.pdf (accessed 11 April 2017).

In the present introduction it is not possible to give more than a faint idea of the richness and thoroughness of the contributions made at the conference. Its only purpose is to whet the reader's appetite to go through the following chapters and develop his/her own views and initiatives for enhancing the legitimacy of the EU. They may be encouraged to develop their own – critical – views by the comments made by Joseph H.H. Weiler on a number of contributions in his "Dialogical Epilogue" concluding the volume, and on the reactions and explanations of the authors of the contributions. This dialogue is an attempt to giving more life to the debate of one of the most crucial problems of the European Union. It shall contribute to an open deliberative process of critical thinking and creativity on the financial crisis, on Brexit and on a reform of the EU with a view to find a solution which is overdue if the process of integration is to be driven forward in a way acceptable to those who are the real owners of the Union: the citizens.

The Thessaloniki conference would not have been possible without the generous support of the Friedrich-Ebert-Foundation and Christos Katsioulis, the head of the Foundation's office in Athens. We also owe a lot to the friendly support of the Goethe Institute in Thessaloniki, represented by Mr. Peter Panes and Aris Kalogiros, for regaling the participants with a most enjoyable Greek working dinner. And we are extremely grateful to the Jean Monnet Chair for Constitutional Law and Culture of the Law School of the Aristotle University of Thessaloniki for generous support both with human resources and funding and, in particular, to Professor Lina Papadopoulou and her team who made this conference happen —and an unforgettable event for all those attending.

The conference was organised *in memoriam Dimitris Tsatsos*, and this volume is dedicated to the *Dimitris Tsatsos*, founding member of the ECLN whose personality unforgettably combined the best of Greek culture and unlimited devotion to —and creative political and legal thinking for— our common project, which is the European Union.

Berlin, 11 April 2017 *Ingolf Pernice*

Part One
Looking for appropriate concepts: Legitimacy and European Democracy

1 Deliberative Democracy
Within and beyond the State

George Gerapetritis

Abstract

Deliberative democracy provides the framework for a new vision of constitutional legitimacy as a response to the shortcomings of conventional sources of formal legitimacy and accountability. This deficit has become broader and deeper due to the augmented powers conferred on, or assumed by, supranational entities, especially the European Union, and the vertical and horizontal interplay between various institutional actors both at national and at international level. In order to realise its potential as a factor of constitutional legitimacy, deliberative democracy ought to be developed not only as a conceptual instrument of political philosophy but mostly as a set of applied constitutional mechanisms to supplement existing institutional safeguards. The paper examines both the theoretical background and the constitutional implementation of deliberative democracy.

I. Introduction

Deliberative democracy constitutes the most contemporary and most intense form of the debate on democracy. David Held considered it as a new (ninth) version of democracy in the 3rd edition of his authoritative *Models of Democracy*.[1] As a term, it first appeared in Joseph Bessett's work in 1980[2] and was expanded in his later works.[3] Distinguished scholars world-

1 D Held, *Models of Democracy*, 3rd edn (Cambridge/Malden, Polity Press, 2006) 231-58.

2 J Bessett, 'Deliberative Democracy: The Majority Principle in Republican Government' in L Goldwin and D Shambra (eds), *How Democratic is the Constitution?* (Washington DC, American Enterprise Institute, 1980).

3 J Bessett, *The Mild Voice of Reason: Deliberative Democracy and American National Government* (Chicago, University of Chicago Press, 1994).

wide have ever since elaborated upon the theme, such as Joshua Cohen, Claus Offe and Ulrich Preuss, James Fishkin, Jon Elster, John Dryzek, Philip Petit and James Bohman. Further, fundamental aspects of deliberativism in democratic decision-making have been treated by leading figures of political philosophy, such as Jürgen Habermas, John Rawls, James Madison, Karl Marx and Plato himself. In his seminal contribution, bridging ancient Athens with contemporary representative democracy, Habermas set out the idea of the public sphere as a (virtual) community where people gather together as a public, articulating the needs of society and generating opinions and arguments that guide the state in a rational discourse in which all participate on an equal basis. Accordingly, in a state of 'ideal speech situation', everyone should be allowed to take part in a discourse, to introduce and question any assertion whatever and to express their attitudes, desires and needs; on the other hand, no one should be prevented, by internal or external coercion, from exercising the above rights.[4]

As of the 1990s there has been a deliberative turn, which stands for a wider reflection on the qualities of deliberative democracy as a response to the inherent deficiencies of democracy, mostly from the standpoint of political science and philosophy. This turn culminated in the 2000s with a further shift from a purely theoretical assessment of political behaviour to an implied constitutional demand for further deliberative techniques within the framework of constitutional legitimacy. Thus, deliberativism has developed as a condition for state legitimacy, political justice and equality. In Rawls' view, a liberal political conception of justice and a reasonably just constitutional democracy must ensure sufficient all-purpose means to enable everyone to make intelligent and effective use of their freedoms. This requires a basic structure preventing social and economic inequalities from becoming excessive: 'The guaranteed constitutional liberties taken alone are properly criticized as purely formal. By themselves, without … [the

4 J Habermas, *Strukturwandel der Öffentlichkeit. Untersuchungen zu einer Kategorie der bürgerlichen Gesellschaft*, 5. Auflage (Darmstadt/Neuwied, Hermann Luchterhand Verlag, 1962) 176-85; translated into English by Th Burger with the assistance of F Lawrence under the title *The Structural Transformation of the Public Sphere: An Inquiry into a Category of Bourgeois Society* (Boston MA, Massachusetts Institute of Technology, 1989).

means to use the freedoms] they are an impoverished form of liberalism – indeed not liberalism at all but libertarianism'.[5]

II. Definition of 'deliberative democracy'

Although there are significant conceptual varieties of the doctrine, deliberative democracy stands for the process of opinion convergence through wide and equal participation and the reasoned and elaborate exchange of arguments so as to produce legitimate outcomes, i.e. ethical and justifiable grounds for regular obedience to power. Accordingly, no judgment can claim correctness and validity unless it constitutes the product of a deliberative process that makes it justified and reasoned. Therefore, deliberativism does not need to establish a single pattern of reason that ought to dominate the deliberative process. Although participants must be in a position to properly assess the evidence provided in the context of interplay and fair play procedures, by placing emphasis on the future political community interest, a fact-regarding, future-regarding and others-regarding process of reasoning, as Offe and Preuss suggest,[6] there is no manual of reason. According to deliberative theory, when the decision-making process employs the required conditions precedent, the outcome is bound to be reasoned, without the need to have recourse to setting a standard of reason in order to assess the outcome itself. By way of contrast, if no deliberative process is followed, the outcome may still be, as a matter of coincidence, reasonable, or even optimal, but it cannot be reasoned. It is, in that view, the deliberative process that will adduce reason and not the opposite. In that abstract sense, the deliberative process resembles Rawls' 'pure procedural justice' (as opposed to perfect and imperfect procedural justice), in which if there is a correct or fair procedure, the outcome is likewise correct or fair, whatever it is, provided that the procedure has been properly followed.[7]

---

5 J Rawls, *The Law of Peoples with the Idea of Public Reason Revisited* (Cambridge MA, Harvard University Press, 1999) 49.

6 C Offe and U Preuss, 'Democracy Institutions and Moral Resources' in D Held (ed), *Political Theory Today* (Cambridge, Polity, 1991) 156-57.

7 J Rawls, *A Theory of Justice* (Cambridge MA, Harvard University Press, 1971) 118-41.

Deliberation semantically surpasses both reflection and dialogue. It surpasses reflection, which is a solipsistic exercise, by involving at least two people or deliberative bodies or entities; one person, irrespective of the level of his/her intelligence, is not in a position to enter into a deliberative process of argumentation and exchange.[8] It also surpasses dialogue, in that it emphasises not only the procedural mechanics of speech-making, to which dialogue is basically restricted, but also the scope of participation (the maximum possible of all stakeholders) and the actual outcome of the deliberative process, i.e. the achievement of an optimum result for the political community. It essentially stresses the importance of public discourse, beyond the conventional static concepts of constitutional pluralism and civil multi-culturalism, which are founded merely upon the idea of participation and tolerance and call for more elaborate and more legitimate techniques of decision-making.

Deliberative democracy can take two different forms. First, it can take the form of an internal, deliberative decision-making process. In this respect, deliberative democracy sets out deliberative rules of procedural propriety for any multi-member decision-making body, either institutional, such as a constitutional assembly, parliament, cabinet or court, or non-institutional, such as a family assembly (internal deliberativism). Second, it can take the form of an external deliberative technique that assists and substantiates the decision-making process. Thus, in order for a deciding body to take a decision it might establish various consultative deliberative techniques, such as deliberative assemblies, polls and referenda. In turn, these collective bodies must themselves abide by the standards of deliberative decision-making (external deliberativism).

Deliberativism applies both to direct democracy and to representative democracy. Contrary to the Athenian ideals of direct democracy through the continuing expression of the will of the people, representative democracy places emphasis predominantly on a predetermined public process that guarantees the free and equal expression of competing social and political values, as a form of societal conflict resolution based on reason. Therefore, deliberativism, requiring both wide participation and deliberative procedures, might equally be compatible with either type of democracy. Accordingly, in direct democracy the participation test is by definition

8 I Shapiro, 'Optimal Deliberation?' (2002) 10 *Journal of Political Philosophy* 196, 196-97.

satisfied and it remains for the deliberation test to be tested, whereas in representative democracy both the participation and the deliberation tests ought to be satisfied.

In the same way, deliberativism applies equally to procedural and instrumental democracy.[9] Procedural democracy values political participation for its own sake as a fundamental mode of self-realisation, thus restricted to guaranteeing global participation in periodic elections and the free expression of all citizens. Procedural democracy focuses on the actual significance of the process of political participation in the election of representatives and, at a later stage, on the one-off mandate granted to them through the constitutional process of election. In this case, deliberativism serves as an additional tool to ease the potentially adverse effects of both the majoritarian nature of democratic processes and the defects of the instant (as opposed to on-going) expression of a people's will. Instrumental democracy has tended to become a means for protecting citizens from authoritarian choices, thus going over and beyond mere elections and majority rule and broadly embracing the salient notion of the rule of law. Instrumental democracy aspires to safeguard the rights of citizens on an on-going basis and to prevent potential arbitrariness on the part of the rulers. Accordingly, deliberativism operates so as to define at any given time the limits of government as a form of reflective civil attitude towards political choices that may be motivated by the government's own interests or do not, at the end of the day, serve the interests of the political community. In the light of the above, deliberative democracy aspires to bring together the two seemingly antithetical poles of procedural and instrumental democracy by cherry-picking the best qualities of both models. From the first it enhances the quality of procedural propriety as a means to produce legitimate results; from the second it enhances the quality of good cause as a way of producing reasoned results.

Since no single reasonableness test exists, it is of no avail to consider whether it should be a judicial- or political-like decision-making process, which eventually turns to the discussion on legal and political constitutionalism respectively. Although, admittedly, there is a different perspective and scope in each debate, as there is in any other forum (professional, family etc.), the standards of deliberativism remain the same. The deliberative process is not more akin to a judicial decision-making context be-

9 D Held, *Models of Democracy* (n 1) 231.

cause the latter needs to adhere more to a deductive pattern of reasoning. For the tools of reasoning, irrespective of how flexible or strict they are, remain outside the necessary components of the deliberative process. A political entity aspires to make the optimum decisions for the benefit of the political society it represents by using its discretion within the boundaries of the law and the constitution, whereas a judicial organ is mandated to apply the law and the constitution so as better to serve the spirit and letter of the rule, which in turn is supposed to advance the welfare of the political community. In both cases, however, the deliberative process can equally apply and, if so, the outcome will be deemed reasoned and, therefore, legitimate.

III. Purpose of deliberative democracy

Deliberative democracy serves a threefold purpose in the decision-making process: the dogmatic purpose of legitimacy, the instrumental purpose of participation and the substantive purpose of reason.

The *dogmatic* purpose of legitimacy suggests that deliberativism serves to invest with legitimacy the decisions taken by authorities (the dogmatic purpose). This is particularly the case when the deciding entities do not enjoy a satisfactory level of legitimacy or need their legitimacy to be updated or upgraded. The underlying idea is that, as John Dryzek, Professor in Social and Political Theory at the Australian National University and a great proponent of deliberative democracy, sees it, the outcomes are legitimate to the extent that they receive reflective assent through participation in authentic deliberation by all those subject to the decision in question.[10] In this, deliberativism purports to bridge the potential gap between legality and legitimacy. A decision may well conform to the law in its traditional sense of a system of legality, but might lack legitimacy either because it comes from an authority without or with only limited legitimacy (the organic factor), such as might be the case of an expert committee established by the executive or the legislature to settle a difficult technical issue, or because it runs contrary to the people's will or reason, such as might be

10 JS Dryzek, *Deliberative Democracy and Beyond: Liberals, Critics, Contestations* (Oxford, Oxford University Press, 2000) 651.

the case of a parliamentary decision that undervalues or ignores the outcomes of polls or consultative referenda (the substantive factor).

The *instrumental* purpose of participation suggests that deliberativism improves the level of citizens' involvement. This is not, however, equivalent to the essence of participatory democracy. For participatory democracy resembles direct democracy inasmuch as the outcomes are deemed to be legitimate through the mere act of participation, which might take the form of voting or signing, irrespective of the level of deliberation preceding the participation. However, there is no direct causal link between participation and reason. Even direct democracy does not necessarily produce reasonable outcomes, as reality often shows. Thus, participation is achieved in an artificial manner by calling citizensto formally take part in the political community in a context that does not favour genuine interaction of the various arguments. As Fishkin puts it, contemporary democracy appears as a forced choice between politically equal but relatively incompetent masses and politically unequal but powerful elites; in either case people are uninterested, debate is superficial and dominated by personalities as opposed to reason, and politics is dominated by a media-saturated world.[11]

Deliberative democracy overall constitutes a step beyond participatory democracy and a response to its inadequacies. It is not, therefore, crucial to broaden participation, although this is as a matter of principle desirable, but to introduce added-value procedures resulting in the formulation of 'carefully considered, consistent, situationally abstract, socially validated and justifiable preferences'.[12] Deliberativism not only suggests that quality procedures ought to apply outside an unconstructive yes/no context, but also raises public awareness of issues falling into political discourse. It manages to achieve this mainly because through deliberative democracy people develop faith in democratic procedures and can exercise a genuine influence on the formation of the will of the political community.

The *substantive* purpose of deliberativism aspires to implement a democracy of reason. A democracy of reason reflects the aspiration to achieve optimum outcomes through rational decisions that will necessarily involve all potential arguments and all sustainable solutions. Reason, including beliefs about the means and the ends, is a salient feature in collec-

---

11 JS Fishkin, *Democracy and Deliberation: New Directions for Democratic Reform* (New Haven, Yale University Press, 1991) 1-3.

12 Offe and Preuss, 'Democracy Institutions' (n 5) 167.

tive decision-making, serving to eliminate the force of other hidden or revealed incentives, such as interest and passion.[13] Further, reason operates as a counterbalance to majoritarianism, which constitutes a reflection of liberal democracy. Majoritarianism, within the bounds of the constitutional restraints upon government, is somehow indifferent towards the achievement of optimal outcomes. For there is a presumption that either the majority holds the wisdom to advance what is best for the political community (and therefore for the majority itself) or that the interests of the majority are equivalent to the interest of the political community as a whole. Irrespective of the obvious counter-arguments that one may raise against these premises either on the basis of political ideology or on the basis that such collective wisdom can never exist, the argument that optimal outcomes stem from majoritarian processes is challenged on a variety of narrative grounds. The majority outcome is not necessarily tested against any other alternatives, either because all the arguments may not be in place (due to a lack of information), or because arguments might not have been given their relative value (due to inadequate or false procedures), or because those suggesting arguments are not on an equal footing when it comes to the formation of the majority will (due to the influential role of political elites and media or people's apathy towards issues affecting the political community). By bringing reason into the discussion, deliberative democracy departs from the arena of market-oriented political competition and adopts a forum-oriented approach where reason dominates public discourse.

IV. Conditions precedent

The conditions precedent to the implementation of a deliberative decision-making process are inclusiveness, endorsement, evidence, interplay and fair play and transparency. These requirements are complementary and

---

13 J Elster, 'Forces and Mechanisms in the Constitution-Making Process' (1995) 45 *Duke Law Journal* 364; idem, '*Arguing* and Bargaining in Two Constituent Assemblies' (2000) 2 *University of Pennsylvania Journal of Constitutional Law* 345. In his later work the author made a partial retraction by acknowledging there was some good in interest and passion in the public discourse: idem, 'Clearing and Strengthening the Channels of Constitution Making' in T Ginsburg (ed), *Comparative Constitutional Design* (Cambridge, Cambridge University Press, 2012).

ought in principle to apply cumulatively (with the exception of the transparency requirement in certain instances).

A. *Inclusiveness*

The first condition of deliberativism is the enhancement of all interests involved in or affected by the outcome of the decision-making. In global participatory processes the condition of inclusiveness by definition does not apply, since everyone is entitled to participate and express an opinion. This is the case, for example, in large-scale or local —physical or electronic— referenda, where all citizens participate in the voting. These participatory processes, however, do not by themselves qualify as deliberative because they do not necessarily fulfil the remaining criteria of deliberativism. In fact, in most cases of referenda, a very low level of evidence is supplied and an even lower level of authentic deliberative interplay is set in place. In most cases, when issues are set in a yes/no form, society is more or less polarised, thus lacking the embracement criterion, which, in turn, blurs the whole process of deliberation prior to the referendum. In the eyes of deliberative lawyers this preceding procedure is equally, if not more, important than the voting itself.

Obviously, if not all interests are represented, there will most likely be a shortage in the arguments presented to the deliberative body. Furthermore, the arguments set out in the course of the deliberative process need not only be presented but also elaborated, refined and enriched when interacting with other contrary or concurring —in part or in whole— arguments, so that all participants may reflect on the qualities of each argument and reach a reasoned conclusion. Therefore, both arguments and those originally advancing each set of arguments ought to be present and active in the deliberative process. Of course, the need to embrace all arguments in the deliberative process does not imply that there must be an algorithm securing proportionate representation of all those affected by the prospective decision, which is an issue relating to the diversity question. It suffices that the arguments are set in place and open to authentic deliberation.

In particular, inclusiveness in deliberative processes requires:

1. identification of all interests relevant and/or subject to and/or affected by the forthcoming decision (collectively referred to as 'the interested parties');

2. discernment of those amongst the interested parties whose interest is causally linked to the forthcoming decision (collectively referred to as 'the stakeholders');
3. identification of all stakeholders (if possible) or the most representative individuals / bodies of each of the stakeholders (in cases where the deliberative process operates as a representative model), and
4. establishment of a deliberative process tailor-made to address peculiarities of the subject-matter and the number and idiosyncrasies of the stakeholders.

Identifying all the interested parties (a) is an extremely complex intellectual process. This is because a decision might exercise influence upon a variety of people or groups, directly or indirectly. At various times in the past, it was considered that producing income, or having a family, or possessing property, or paying taxes constituted an irrefutable presumption that one had vested interests in the well-being of the political community and conditions precedent for granting political rights. This notion has clearly become outdated since there can be no interest in a particular issue of public concern that can be associated with such vague and remote criteria. On the other hand, the increasing significance of group politics has reduced the influence that an individual may exercise by claiming his/her own private interest. Accordingly, the composition of a deliberative body will most probably embrace group interests, which will be represented by members of the respective groups.

A process of narrowing down the list of interested parties might reasonably occur at the stage of discerning the stakeholders (b). This process broadly resembles the discussion concerning standing before a court of law and the legitimate interest required to proceed with a legal action, although it clearly entails more political and social rather than legally formalistic considerations. Inclusiveness in deliberative processes must address a twofold problem, which has been presented in the relevant literature as the 'scale problem'. In direct democracy all interests are by definition present or ought to be present if proper diffusion of information has occurred; the scale problem in this case concerns the necessarily cumbersome procedures created by the large number of people present and active. In representative democracy, procedures are easier to conduct because of the limited number of participants, the problem being the actual, reflective and effective participation and expression of all relevant interests. In the latter case, there is an inherent danger of over-inclusiveness (thus including participants that are not widely affected by the prospective decision) and under-inclusiveness (thus excluding participants that are deeply, though not necessarily directly, affected by the prospective decision). Economic analysis, especially in the form of economics of participation and econometry, might provide a ground upon which to build the forum of stakeholders. Further, municipalities and regions, in matters of local or regional interest are presumed to be stakeholders in the context of polycentric governance. At any rate, smaller groups of individuals can more easily adopt deliberative modules, in the sense that participants become more involved and self-conscious knowing that proportionately they are in a position to exercise more influence upon the body and their opinion is not diluted within large-scale groups. Following the economic model of voter participation, which has been developed with extreme mathematical rigour by Riker and Ordeshook, it appears that the level of voter participation in any voting procedure is largely determined by the subjective probability of affecting the election results, i.e. the closer the citizens believe the election will be.[14] Therefore, it is of acute importance that the electors believe that their opinion can be effective and might succeed in overturning a prevailing view or that the vote might be a crucial one. This political behaviour is empirically substantiated when one compares the turn-out in parliamentary elections with that in municipal or local elections, when these two sets of elections do not coincide.[15] In smaller-scale electorates, citizens are more likely to participate, knowing that mathematically their vote will be more influential than in large-scale electorates. Accordingly, the upper house of a parliament (normally of smaller size) is more inclined to engage in deliberative processes than the lower house, as are parliamentary committees compared with the plenary of the house, neighbourhood committees compared with municipal or regional bodies, and juries compared with whole electorate bodies.

The identification of all stakeholders (c, first case) is not difficult as such, especially when the issues at stake are of significance for the totality of the citizenry. The situation becomes gradually more complex in cases where deliberative processes operate at a representative level and there must be some criteria to facilitate selection from a wide pool of potentially

14 WH Riker and PC Ordeshook, 'A Theory of the Calculus of Voting' (1968) 62 *The American Political Science Review* 25.

15 T Darvish and J Rosenberg, 'The Economic Model of Voter Participation. A Further Test' (1988) 56 *Public Choice* 185.

interested stakeholders (c, second case). In the latter case, there can conceivably be three criteria for selecting individuals to participate in the process: intelligence/expertise among the members of the stakeholders' group; a high level of representation, i.e. agreement with the position and argumentation of the majority of the particular stakeholders' group; and proximity to the case, i.e. which members of the stakeholders will be more affected by the prospective decision.

Personal intelligence or expertise cannot be a relevant criterion, not only because this might render the deliberative body an elitist forum, but also because the underlying principle is that deliberative communication, enhancing proper information and elaborate techniques of exchange of arguments, could make up for potential perception deficits in the participants. This anti-elitist approach, running contrary to Plato's *alogon*, places emphasis on deliberativism as a self-reliant and self-correcting mechanism of human communication. Still, it remains as a truism that a skilful individual is *par excellence* in a position to draw out hidden arguments or aspects of a particular case and further elaborate upon existing arguments that might prove to be conclusive in the context of a deliberative process. Representatives of the stakeholders' group could be summoned, through an election process or otherwise, for the deliberative process. Yet again, this process might result in a small-scale representative system that could resemble a parliament, with all corresponding deficiencies, especially polarisation and lack of 'retraction predilection', because representatives are, or feel, bound by their mandate. At any rate, in group politics there is always the problem that those representing the group will not eventually set out the arguments in favour of the group's view for a variety of reasons. The idea that participation of different groups within a body will by itself make it diverse renders diversity a rather formalistic goal. Accordingly, it is mainly perceived as a means to formally bring together various bodies and not as a substantive principle requiring true expression of the various social groups. By assimilating the goal with the means, the doctrine becomes rather circular in its argumentation: instead of the goal legitimising the means, the inverse is accepted. To achieve genuine diversity, it is necessary that the members of groups participating in a body, irrespective of how proportionate this representation is, contribute their own experience and social understanding.[16] In other words, the essence of diversity in deliberation is not achieved if the participants representing a stakeholder's group do not themselves bear the typical characteristics of this group. In group membership debate, entitativity (i.e. the degree and mode by which groups are perceived as having the nature of an entity) and similarity (the issue of the arguably common characteristics of the members of any specific group in terms of goals, beliefs and behaviour) are extremely difficult issues which touch upon the fields of sociology and social psychology. An element of similarity exists by definition in order to give rise to entitativity (e.g. race, religion, ethnicity, family liaison, sports club), but groups may in fact share no further characteristics. However, the basic perception of a group lies in the common core similarity that broadly relates to a prototypical composition. Limited similarity, nevertheless, might imply that society at large assumes that common features are held by the group, even if these features do not largely exist. Both entitativity and similarity are necessary components of a debate on stereotyping since this pathology arises precisely from the common properties of membership and the social perception of the constitution and cohesion of a group. Finally, the establishment of a deliberative process that is tailor-made to deal with each issue in question (d) depends largely upon the numbers of the participants in the deliberative process and their ability to be physically present.

B. Endorsement

Deliberativism is essentially trying to set out some procedural ground rules in order to accommodate and render constructive the implications of disagreement in public discourse. As Popper convincingly suggests in the context of critical rationalism, seeking to replace allegedly justificatory methods with critical ones, disagreement goes hand in hand with open societies.[17] In this, it presupposes two subjective perceptions of the participants. First, all solutions and arguments presented in the course of the process must be presumed and treated by the participants as valid, without

---

16 G Gerapetritis, 'Affirmative Action Policies and Judicial Review Worldwide' (2016) 47 *Ius Gentium: Comparative Perspectives on Law and Justice* 66.

17 K Popper, (1976a). 'The Logic of the Social Sciences' (1976) in T Adorno (ed.), *The Positivist Dispute in German Sociology* (New York, Harper & Row 1976) 87; idem, 'Reason or Revolution?', ibid. 288.

any prejudice as to their sustainability (unconditional validity). In this sense, no solutions or arguments are considered by definition as false or trivial and they are all subject to deliberative scrutiny. Second, the participants in the deliberative process must be ready and inclined to accept the validity and soundness of any view or argument and retract from their original position (retraction predilection).

Unconditional validity and retraction predilection jointly constitute the normative psychological aspect of what Offe and Preuss more objectively suggest are 'reflecting preferences', namely end-results based on the conscious confrontation of one's own point of view with an opposing point of view or multiplicity of viewpoints, in contrast to spontaneous and context-contingent choices.[18] This means that the participants, although they may have a strong view on the issue in question, not only accept that their views might be changed but are in fact expected to change them in the light of convincing counter-arguments. This retraction predilection constitutes a psychological state that allows the participants to depart from their original position without undue frustration, sentiments of defeat or the need to justify their retraction to themselves or to any other stakeholder in the deliberative process or outsider.

It is essential to point out at this point that unconditional validity and retraction predilection indicate that the deliberative process does not imply a forum of negotiation or bargaining where rival interests compete and a fair balance is sought. Deliberative processes intend to reach optimal decisions through reason, which might mean employing one out of many possible alternatives. In fact, there is no winning party in the outcome of a deliberation but merely a justifiable and legitimate outcome which has successfully passed the deliberation test. Negotiation can only be part of the process to the extent that it might serve to qualify some of the proposed alternatives in search of the optimal course of action. Thus, in conceptual terms, the deliberative process entails neither negotiation nor bargaining. This is why unconditional validity and retraction predilection are *sine qua non* conditions for the effective development of any deliberative forum.

On the basis of the above reservations, it appears that there are two problems relating to the inherent subjectivity of any human judgment, which inexorably affect the effectiveness of the premises of unconditional validity and retraction predilection. The most important point is whether

18 Offe and Preuss, 'Democracy Institutions' (n 5) 169-70.

all disagreements are akin to a deliberative process or whether there are subject-matters which ought to be excluded due to the value or perplexity associated with them (the scope issue). The next point is whether unconditional validity and retraction predilection entail the impartiality of the participants as a condition for the implementation and effectiveness of a deliberative process or whether, on the other hand, there is no need to pursue such a task (the impartiality issue).

As for the main point (the scope issue), a legitimate objection to a deliberative process with a wide participation of stakeholders is that certain issues are not suited to it. This might be particularly true of moral or ethical arguments associated with the protection of fundamental rights. Given that fundamental rights do operate as a safeguard for individuals against authoritarian governance but also as a defence against the majoritarian will and force, they are not subject to argumentation and/or negotiation. The problem lies at the heart of the classic debate between positivists, such as Hart and McCormick, and natural law philosophers such as Fuller and Dworkin. If primary rights exist before their expression in the form of rules and develop in the legal system through the shaping of political morality, scholars of the latter school of thought invariably suggest that there is no room for deliberation since these rights are subject to qualifications. In this respect, there can be no discussion, irrespectively of whether it might satisfy the deliberative criteria concerning basic liberties such as civil, social and political equality or people's dignity and value. For these rights cannot be weighed against any other public purpose or utilitarian expectations. In this view, in the case of refugees there can be no discussion concerning their right to establishment in any territory in order to escape the violent consequences of domestic conflicts or the entitlement to be granted a residence permit or asylum status. An outcome of a deliberative process that could reduce the level of protection for these individuals, which is not to be excluded due to the general level of fear and stereotyping that obviously reduces the efficacy of retraction predilection (if any), would be in this view unacceptable as a matter of principle. Accordingly, the process can by definition produce no useful result.

Albeit at a different level, the same vein of criticism on the scope and ambit of deliberative processes occurs in issues of high politics, such as diplomacy. These issues are publicly non-negotiable because, technically, they entail a multi-dimensional analysis that cannot be performed by people at large due to a lack of relevant knowledge or expertise and because, psychologically, people tend to decide such matters more on the basis of emotion and less so on reason. In this, not only is the retraction predilection low but also the key feature of deliberativism, a reasoned exchange of arguments to reach an optimal outcome, is by definition unreachable.

This type of objection has been raised in relation to the unconditional validity premise by the seminal authors in the field, Amy Gutmann and Dennis Thompson. They claim that the key factors determining a deliberative process are justification and reciprocity of the furnished grounds, together meaning a reason-giving process based on premises mutually accepted by the participants. The authors thus limit the ambit of the grounds that are permissible in a deliberative process in that not all reasons are reciprocal, but merely those founded upon basic democratic principles.[19] The argument entails a substantive qualification of the grounds set forth in the process that must satisfy fundamental freedoms, such as equality, and widely accepted moral values that are essential to the welfare of a political community ('principles morally and politically provisional'). This thesis, however, seems to be somewhat self-contradicting in that it undermines the predominantly procedural nature of the deliberative process and sets not merely procedural but also substantive ground rules as a benchmark of success. Nevertheless, the more one departs from the functional basics of deliberation and moves towards a set of principles that are *a priori* upheld (i.e. without having themselves been subjected to a deliberative scrutiny), the process becomes much more subjective and loses its main legitimising feature, the reasoned process.

Obviously, the arguments against deliberativism on the scope theme are to some extent sustainable. However, they tend to underestimate in pragmatic terms the basic presupposition upon which a deliberative process relies, i.e. that participants do possess the skill of reasoning, shaped and strengthened by the retraction predilection. In this respect, this argumentation places very little faith in the human factor of deliberativism and in the consciousness and awareness that such procedures will add to humans' decision-making skills. In this, there is an underlying paternalistic suggestion that people are not in a position to take proper care of issues affecting them and ought not to be left alone to decide by themselves. In its extreme form, the argument goes as far as to deprive people of 'the ability to express their views, through elections, on highly complex moral or political

19 A Gutmann and D Thompson, *Why Deliberative Democracy?* (Princeton, Princeton University Press, 2004) 95-124.

matters, thus approaching Plato's elitist view of rule by the learned, dismissing democracy as a process in which political judgment is reduced to the level of the lowest common denominator of the participating citizens. Disturbing as it may sound, people must participate in relevant decision-making processes with the implicit understanding that a decision against fundamental rights or against a proper course of international action will be to the detriment of the political community and, in turn, to their own detriment. It all depends on the faith and reliance we place in the power and persuasiveness of argument and reason. Anyhow, a deliberative process cannot by definition produce results that run contrary to the human rights enshrined in the constitution, which therefore form the basic counter-balance to potential extreme eventualities. Still, extreme results in a reasoned exchange of arguments will be in principle unsustainable.

As for the minor point (the impartiality issue), although there is no consensus on the matter among advocates of deliberative democracy and there is an oft-invoked narrative argument against it by its opponents, it appears more in line with the essence of the theory that participants do not have to be in a state of absolute impartiality, in the sense that they ought to be deprived of any prior personal views on the matter before entering the deliberative forum. This type of Rawlsian veil of ignorance cannot in practice exist in a society of multi-complex interests and abundant information, which renders reflective equilibrium an implausible solipsistic experiment. Instead, it is more plausible and arguably more expedient to try and curb potential partiality by allowing all the interested parties to appeal to their respective self-interests.[20] Participants in deliberative bodies ought to be directly involved in the process, not simply as outsiders to the issue in question (e.g. as a jury member) or as an arbitrator but as a stakeholder himself/herself. In this, members of deliberative assemblies must be eager to reach the optimal result by means of reasoned discourse. In a political community where people tend to imagine themselves in the position of various other people and take decisions on the presumption of what they would do, Goodin suggests a model of 'democratic deliberation within' where, through provided evidence, people are reflective by themselves and expansive across time and distance.[21]

20 J Mansbridge, 'The Place of Self-Interest and the Role of Power in Deliberative Democracy' (2010) 18 *Journal of Political Philosophy* 64.

21 RE Goodin, 'Democratic Deliberation Within' (2000) 29 *Philosophy & Public Affairs* 81.

On the other hand, a deliberative forum needs a diversity of opinions to be presented and discussed thoroughly, even passionately, and this can only be achieved if the participants have an opinion on the issue in question. The participants may or may not have an original position but in either case they must be ready to change their original position or the position they developed in the course of the deliberative process; the retraction predilection, properly applied, will in this regard compensate for the lack of an originally impartial attitude towards the matter in question. In this respect, the deliberative process does not resemble a court/moot court or a conventional parliamentary procedure but more a jury procedure. This is because in the former case participants do have an original position, which they try to convey to the opposite members of the body with the aim of changing their rivals' views. An attorney in court or an MP in a parliamentary process are in principle indifferent to the optimal result of the issue in question and try to build up their own case. Accordingly, the level of retraction predilection is rather low. On the other hand, in jury proceedings, members may have an original position, shaped by their own convictions, before the hearing of the case in court, during which their position is shaped (strengthened, challenged or modified) further, but behind closed doors they enter into a process of testing their view against those of all their fellow jurors. Given the size of the body and the nature of the proceedings (especially the requirement for consensus), jury members normally have a high level of retraction predilection.

Substantive legitimacy furnished by the deliberative process, in conjunction with the retraction predilection of the participants, constitutes the basis for the establishment of an understanding that the eventual result is presumed to be optimal. This is not to indicate that minority opinion proponents are subject to and bound by the majority outcome. For in the latter case the legitimacy of the decision stems from the eventual outcome as such, i.e. the end result, irrespective of the procedural quality resulting in the outcome, whereas in deliberativism it is the process that legitimises the outcome. In fact, in the majoritarian approach, it is of no importance whether the outcome is indeed the optimal one, whereas in the deliberative process the outcome is presumed to be just so.

C. Evidence

A significant aspect of the deficit of contemporary democracy is that the masses are not well informed about public affairs.[22] Despite living in an era where data transmission is quick and easy, people by and large are still not very well informed. Evidence, however, constitutes a key element in any deliberative process, in the sense that public information on matters of policy is made available so as to allow people to make rational choices.[23] There can be no reasoned exchange of views and arguments if the deliberative body does not possess a critical mass of relevant information required to produce a full and accurate assessment. This information includes physical evidence or expert opinions on the technical and political aspects of the issue in question, including the social implications of the adoption of each possible alternative.

There are three questions relating to the evidence in a deliberative process. The first is how much information is required (the quantity question), the second is if the evidence is subject to qualifications (the quality question) and the third is the relevant value to be attributed to the information (the value question).

As regards the *quantity* question, a deliberative process presupposes the collection of all relevant evidence. A lack of relevant information results in an unsubstantiated decision. A deliberative decision might eventually be the correct decision, but this will happen only accidentally if relevant information has not been part of the deliberative process. On the other hand, if all the relevant information is produced before the deliberative body, the decision might still be mistaken, but this will not be a fault of the deliberative process but ought to be attributed mainly to the inability of the members of the deliberative body to properly assess the evidence adduced. Even in the absence of broad and proper representation, if the relevant information is made available, groups can effectively deliberate about the public good if the participants are willing and able to engage in such deliberation.[24] Elster argues in this respect that smaller assemblies might be better at acquiring information, whereas larger assemblies might be bet-

22 D Held, *Models of Democracy* (n 1) 231.

23 J Rawls, *The Law of Peoples with the Idea of Public Reason Revisited* (Cambridge MA, Harvard University Press 1999) 49-50.

24 H Kong, 'The Deliberative City' (2010) 28 *Windsor Yearbook of Access to Justice* 411.

ter at processing information. This is because the motivation to acquire information to form rational beliefs about how to realise the public good will, in principle, be diluted when the size of the assembly increases. Having established this, Elster argues that there is no stable point between the underproduction of information, leading to bad decisions, and the overproduction of information, leading to costly redundancy.[25]

As regards the *quality* question, a clear-cut response would be that all relevant evidence should be produced and all irrelevant evidence should be discarded. Such a simplistic schema cannot, however, be effectuated. First of all, what is relevant or not is not a judgement devoid of subjectivity. In complex value judgement questions there is a series of secondary implications that lie in the grey zone of relevancy, depending on everyone's perception of morality and/or social and political beliefs. It is, thus, questionable on moral or ethical grounds whether evidence relating to the public cost of holding convicted offenders in prisons should be provided and evaluated when deciding on the abolition of the death penalty. In the same vein of argument, it is questionable on social and political grounds whether evidence relating to foreign investments should be provided and assessed when deciding on tax layers and burdens (the value problem). Secondly, one might reasonably argue that by furnishing all relevant evidence in the context of a particular case, decision-making becomes cumbersome if all the evidence is to be properly assessed (the procedural problem). And, thirdly, in an era when information circulates at high speed, the easiest way to miss a critical piece of information is to place it in a huge mass of other relevant or irrelevant and crucial or trivial evidence (the bulk problem). However, these concerns cannot justify prohibitions on the freedom of expression on grounds of misleading information, for this would seriously hamper the openness of the deliberative process and could potentially lead to the improper manufacturing of public information with the purpose of achieving specific-end results. All three problems raised in the context of the quality question —value, procedural and bulk problems — are of significant value and can only be treated if members of the deliberative bodies are educated and trained to deal with potential malfunctions in the course of the evidentiary process and possess the analytical capacity to discern what is of significance in the deliberative process.

---

25 J Elster, 'Clearing and Strengthening' (n 13) 20-22.

As regards the *value* question, it is obviously for the deliberative body to assess the evidence produced. This judgement is not a technical judgement but is, in fact, a policy choice that reflects a cost-benefit analysis of the implications for society and its members. Of course, given that deliberative bodies are composed of individuals who do not normally possess the expertise to deal with the specificities of each case (be they technical, economic, legal or social), all the relevant evidence is required to form an opinion and uphold or dismiss possible outcomes. This, however, does not mean that the deliberative result will have to conform to the options suggested by the evidence. Deliberative bodies are not courts of law, which have to apply a specific jurisdictional narrative, but decision-making entities that use variable standards when evaluating the relevant information. This is why deliberative bodies are not composed of experts but basically of interested parties and stakeholders. In deliberative procedures, experts and expert opinions are indeed welcomed and expedient but external experts ought not to participate in deliberative decision-making processes, so that the coherence of the deliberative prerequisites can be safeguarded and the formation of an elitist colloquial environment can be prevented. Deliberative fora are composed not of independent experts who are outsiders to the contextual basis of the problem, but mostly of stakeholders who have every right to defend a position that is presumed to affect their lives. This is why deliberativism is in principle incompatible with the idea of an experts' comitology polity where all decisions are taken by establishing a forum of technical experts in the field that will decide on the basis of their respective knowledge. Useful as it might be, technical expertise does not guarantee optimal results by mere reference to the alleged impartiality of the participants. Blank impartiality cannot exist and is not useful for the deliberative process. This is because neutrality does not by itself guarantee a valid argument, unless this argument is subject to effective deliberative scrutiny by a genuine deliberative body. Further, experts normally hold a predetermined opinion on issues relating to their expertise in a way that makes them less likely to change their original opinion, either because of professional vanity or because they do not want to be seen as being defeated in a professional arena, thus losing prestige in the eyes of their potential clientele. John Dryzek effectively dismisses instrumental rationality and objectivism in political institutions and public policy through technocracies and experts, claiming that they are not well equipped to deal with complex social problems.[26]

D. Interplay and fair play

Setting up a proper deliberative process requires effective interplay and fair play. Interplay essentially stems from the maxim *audi altera partem,* whose meaning becomes significantly enhanced in the context of a deliberative process. Since reason and persuasion constitute the basic tools of the process, there must be an unqualified condition that any argument should be subject to counter-argumentation by anyone involved in the process. This requirement does not follow as a matter of moral or divine obligation, as early criminal law jurisprudence in England might suggest.[27] It is a reflection of the rationalism that substantiates the legitimising factor of reason in the deliberative process. This process goes beyond the basic mainstays of common dialogue, which normally refers to an interplay of parallel monologues by the participants. Again, the traditional state fora, courts and parliaments, have to a large extent adopted a dialogic model, which falls short of the requirements of authentic deliberation. In these fora, participants may present counter-arguments but there is not a direct interplay with all other opinions, as normally happens with jury procedures. Fair play, on the other hand, requires a set of deliberative rules securing equality of arms among the participants so that all stakeholders may have an equal chance to exercise influence upon the body and be influenced by other fellow members. This set of rules ought not to be technical, in the sense of parliamentary or court regulations, which are beset by requirements of formalism and vulnerable to all sorts of potential legal annulments, but must reflect the necessarily colloquial and reflective spirit with which the deliberative process is endowed and which is reasonably required by the retraction predilection of the participants. Further, the partic-

26 J Dryzek, *Discursive Democracy: Politics, Policy, and Political Science* (Cambridge, Cambridge University Press, 1990) 151-200.

27 'The laws of God and man both give the party an opportunity to make his defence, if he has any. I remember to have heard it observed by a very learned man, upon such an occasion, that even God himself did not pass sentence upon Adam before he was called upon to make his defence', Justice Fortescue in *The King v. The Chancellor, Master and Scholars of the University of Cambridge*, 1 Str. 557 at 567, (1748) EngR 223, (1748 Fort 202, 92 ER 818).

ipants must always be at the centre of the deliberative process and they must genuinely and extensively interact with each other; there can be no process of deliberation with participants partly absent or when sub-groups or individuals are not interacting among each other. The exchange of written arguments cannot constitute a deliberative process because it lacks the necessarily adversarial flow of arguments and solutions and significantly isolates the necessary interplay.

Two, to some extent interconnected, issues still remain unanswered. The first question is where the end-point of a deliberative process is to be found, i.e. where the adequate convergence threshold lies; and the second question is if the deliberative body ought to furnish reasons for its decisions.

The convergence issue reflects on whether consensus should be achieved or whether majority agreement suffices, and if so what type of majority. This is a complex issue which also becomes crucial when deliberative bodies are vested with decisive powers. If, as it is conceded they do, the members of a deliberative assembly possess the quality of retraction predilection on the ground of reason, as a matter of logic all personal views will turn to the optimal and best substantiated opinion. If, after a proper deliberative process, there is still a divergence of opinion, even by a single dissenting opinion, the process has by definition failed to perform its basic function and reason has not ruled over the process as presumed. Still, when deliberative bodies, having completed proper deliberative processes, are still sharply divided, this harms the general persuasiveness of the process itself. In any event, as a matter of political psychology, one might reasonably argue that in cases where no unanimity is required participants in the collective bodies are less likely to moderate their views and eventually shift positions. By way of contrast, consensus seems to be at odds with the conventional concept of democracy, where disagreement is essential to the opposition and excessive agreement may hamper the envisaged democratic discourse,[28] while it may also be at odds with the relativist objection that there is not a single, let alone manifest, truth.[29] Both these approaches, however, underestimate the essence of deliberativism,

---

28 FM Watkins, *The Political Tradition of the West: a Study in the Development of Modern Liberalism* (Cambridge MA, Harvard University Press, 1948).

29 On the institutional role of the opposition in parliament as a forum of democratic disagreement, see the 2010 Report of the Council of Europe's European Commission for Democracy through Law (Venice Commission) to the Parliamentary As-

which suggests a process of argumentation in which the participants converge on the best substantiated argument which is *presumed* to be the optimal one – it is of no consequence whether it actually is or not.

Empirical evidence shows that in a limited number of cases where deliberative juries were put in place in the US with a view to achieving unanimity, there were some spectacular results, contrasting with those achieved by the elected representatives.[30] Indeed, irrespective of the pragmatic truth of the above statement, a strict requirement for unanimity would, in any case, necessarily be a micro-sample, as opposed to a mega-sample, since in the latter case the process would probably end up being unsuccessful and potentially frustrating, as well as very time-consuming. In this respect, the scale of the deliberative body is linked to the decision-making threshold: a micro-sample could function properly on the basis of unanimity, whereas a mega-sample would naturally lower the required threshold. This is clearly a matter of choice upon which deliberative scholars may well disagree. At any rate, if the latter view prevails, a collateral question arises as to where the decision-making threshold should be set: should the process depend on a golden vote, essentially transferring to the deliberative process the practice of parliamentary democracy, or should a higher threshold apply in order to preserve the integrity of the background theory of deliberativism (aspiring unanimity by reason) and the legitimacy thereof? The question obviously touches upon the very essence of deliberativism.

As for the reasons that must or must not be given, a preliminary position is that deliberativism is justified not on the basis of the end-result (i.e. whether the result is in fact the optimal one) or the reasons provided to justify the choice made (i.e. the persuasiveness of the reasons given to substantiate the end-result), but by the process of deliberation itself (irrespective of the quality of the actual expediency or persuasiveness of the end-result, which is nevertheless deemed to be the optimal one as per the process followed). In this sense, deliberativism is not tantamount to the legal requirement imposed on administrative authorities to provide reasons for those decisions of theirs that have adverse effects upon individuals. This legal requirement might be partly aimed in the same direction as deliberativism, i.e. at enhancing a culture of reason in decision-making on

sembly, CDL-AD(2010)025, at www.venice.coe.int/webforms/documents/?pdf=CDL-AD(2010)025-e.

30 D Held, *Models of Democracy* (n 1) 248-49.

public affairs, but it is much more formal. This is so because an administrative decision based on granted discretion can be substantiated by having recourse to a number of reasons. However, it might well be that there are adequately good reasons to substantiate other course(s) of action, in such a way that giving reasons becomes a mere formality. Eventually, the legal duty to give reasons does not result in better administrative practices but serves to enable a court in an application for judicial review to assess the legality and/or external reasonableness of the impugned act. In this, this legal duty is disassociated from deliberativism, which mostly focuses on the process rather than the end-result. Given that the deliberative process requires the production of full evidence, fair procedures for the exchange of all relevant arguments (considered equally valid) and transparency, the process, if followed properly, seems to provide by itself adequate legal reasons without the need to further elaborate upon the selection of one alternative over another.

E. Transparency

Transparency is not by itself an inherent element of deliberativism. However, it is a salient feature of deliberative *democracy* which highly values the openness of decision-making insofar as this open process renders the body accountable and legitimate, if such legitimacy does not stem directly from electoral representation.[31] Accordingly, deliberative bodies ought to perform their role in a state of transparency, which provides the setting for an appropriate testing of the degree of persuasion involved in the relevant argumentative process (so as to satisfy the substantive test of reason) and provides the decision with the necessary persuasiveness that elicits regular obedience (the institutional test of legitimacy).

Having established the formal value of openness in deliberative processes, the level of the said transparency is not an easy question to deal with. There are two reasons in particular why this is so. First, public proceedings often result in a more theatrical and less rational discourse. The members of collective bodies very often seem to appeal to the audience in order to draw their sympathy (on psychological or utilitarian grounds), in-

31 A Gutmann and D Thompson, *Democracy and Disagreement* (Cambridge MA, Harvard University Press, 1996) 105-27.

stead of presenting their arguments and reflecting upon the counter-arguments. This can be substantiated by the different attitudes of speakers in parliamentary processes which are broadcast by the media, as opposed to more closed procedures in parliamentary committees. In the former case, MPs address their electorate or the nation overall; in the latter, they address the arguments set out in the course of the relevant proceedings. Second, open procedures render members of collective bodies vulnerable to external pressure. Even though members of deliberative bodies are not supposed to be disassociated from their broader community environment, from which they essentially form their original view which they are requested to contribute to the forum, psychological stress or frustration due to outside burdens might reasonably affect either their concentration on the merits of the deliberative process or the level of their retraction predilection. This could inevitably hamper the quality of the deliberative process. Still, on balance, these risks ought to be subsumed into the imperative of the substantive and institutional tests, without which the deliberative process loses its rationalistic and legitimising qualities respectively. Jury processes normally qualify as satisfactory deliberative processes but they lack substantive legitimacy not only because of their largely unrepresentative character but also because proceedings take place behind closed doors. In contrast, parliamentary processes in democratic regimes do enjoy wide formal legitimacy because of the representative nature of the participants and the proceedings, which are open to public scrutiny, thus elevating the level of MPs' individual accountability. Nevertheless, parliamentary processes rank low in terms of deliberative legitimacy, in that there is normally no authentic interplay and fair play and deputies operate under the pressure of their parties and electorates, which significantly reduces their retraction predilection.

V. Deliberativism beyond the state

Multi-level deliberative democracy includes the element beyond the state and the element within the state. Deliberativism beyond the state needs to address a set of distinct issues of supranational organisations, especially the European Union, relating to the levels of their legitimacy (the legitimacy factor), the relationship vis-à-vis the Member States (the vertical factor), the relations developed among the supranational authorities (the horizontal factor) and the nature and procedures on a supranational level (the instrumental factor).

At the level of the EU, the *legitimacy* factor relates to the low level of legitimacy of the Union, the so-called democratic deficit. An elaborate analysis of this issue, which has spawned a huge bibliography, goes far beyond the purpose of the present analysis. Suffice it to say that, although there have been significant steps towards a more legitimate Union, basically through the empowerment of the European Parliament and the involvement of domestic parliaments and the embracement of specific aspects of indirect legitimacy of the Commission through a vote of confidence by the European Parliament, resulting in European party elections, the Union still lacks a sufficient level of legitimacy. There are three reasons why this is so: first, the key actors in EU decision-making remain in the Member States themselves, operating through the intergovernmental method, with the exception of the ministers when acting in the Council in a supranational manner; second, in areas where the EU has no competence to act following the Community method, there is a clear political hegemony in the form of a core of national executives from the most powerful states who take crucial decisions on major issues, such as the financial crisis or the future of Europe, in small round-tables; and, third, there is a wide involvement of non-legitimate expert fora established *ad hoc* or on a semi-permanent basis, which is addressed as the comitology issue. The round table and comitology methods obviously fall short on the level of accountability, their procedures are to a great extent obscure and, eventually, they harm the Union's overall level of legitimacy. In this context, the European Union needs to have recourse to alternative modes of legitimacy to make up for the existing deficit. To this end, the Preamble of the TEU expresses the desire 'to enhance further the democratic and efficient functioning of the institutions so as to enable them better to carry out, within a single institutional framework, the tasks entrusted to them'. From an instrumental point of view, deliberativism as a legitimising factor in the EU context seems to supplement the deficiencies of the principle of subsidiarity, which functioned in order to set up a balance between efficiency and legitimacy, albeit not always on a satisfactory level.

The *vertical* factor relates to nation-state involvement. In the course of decision-making, there is an underlying principle that there is an optimal solution for the participants in a global community, thus essentially presupposing the existence of a political community. In the case of supranational orders, it is doubtful whether this political community exists in the sense of the conventional *demos* and, in any case, the multi-layer structure of the decision-making, involving both the supranational authorities and the national states, seriously impedes the idea of a *single* optimal solution. The problem is reflected in the bipolar ambition of the European Union to enhance integration ('desiring to continue the process of creating an ever closer union among the peoples of Europe [...] in view of further steps to be taken in order to advance European integration': TEU Preamble), while respecting the national (constitutional) identities of the Member States ('the Union shall respect the equality of Member States before the Treaties as well as their national identities, inherent in their fundamental structures, political and constitutional', TEU Article 4 para 2). Given the multiplicity of national identities, which vary significantly depending on the historical and regulatory idiosyncrasies of each state, it becomes genuinely cumbersome to seek optimal solutions, if any. The situation becomes even more blurred in the light of the existing legal structures in Europe, i.e. the autonomy, supremacy and direct effect of European Union law combined with constitutional and international pluralism (including the European Convention on Human Rights), the involvement of domestic parliaments in safeguarding the principle of subsidiarity, the respect of regional and local self-government (TEU Article 4 para 2), the enhancement of the 'process of creating an ever closer union among the peoples of Europe, in which decisions are taken as closely as possible to the citizen', TEU Preamble) and the cultural diversity of multiple layers in Europe.

The landscape becomes even more complex if one adds to the above polycentric institutional labyrinth the fragile social and economic conditions and the sharp divisions between nations. John Dryzek, building upon the premises of a divided world and divided societies (the concept of the clash of civilisations, originally conceived by Bernard Lewis and developed and diffused by Samuel Huntington, arguing that on an international level cultural disputes would constitute the starting-point of world crisis in the future), and discarding the restrictive vision of neoconservativism and cosmopolitanism, suggests that global deliberative politics constitute the most reliable model of thorough democratic government.[32] A boost to Dryzek's idea of global deliberative politics was, rather unexcitingly, provided by the 2015 United Nations Climate Change Conference

32 J Dryzek, *Deliberative Global Politics: Discourse and Democracy in a Divided World* (Cambridge, Polity, 2006) 148-64..

held in Paris late that year. The conference negotiated the Paris Agreement, a global agreement on the reduction of climate change. The Agreement reflected an astonishing consensus of the representatives of 196 parties to set a goal of limiting global warming to less than 2 degrees Celsius compared to pre-industrial levels.[33]

The *horizontal* factor relates to the relationships (allocation of competence, composition of authorities, accountability between each other and reciprocal dependencies) developed among the authorities of supranational organisations where considerations of political, cosmopolitan and technocratic visions of government co-exist. The most complex landscape is that of the European Union where shared competences exist when at the same time the executive (Commission) and the legislature (Parliament and Council) are politically subject to the European Council.

The *instrumental* factor relates to the particular proceedings within the supranational orders. Basically, it refers both to the modes of decision-making and the unanimity required to achieve decisions at the level of conventional international treaties. In the context of the European Union this reflects the Community method of unanimity in the crucial aspects of EU regulation.

Multi-level deliberativism within the state suggests that deliberativism should apply at all levels of domestic governance, including central, regional and local government. In fact, decentralised layers of government are essential in the implementation of an effective model of deliberative democracy. This is so, on a practical level, primarily because the size of regional and local authorities allows for a more substantial involvement of participants and interaction of arguments on particular issues and eases the basic scale problem encountered by all proponents of deliberativist theories. On a theoretical level, decision–making at a level closer to the citizens provides further legitimacy through participation, in the broader context of the discussion on the benefits of subsidiarity in the allocation of

33 The conference was the 21st annual session of the Conference of the Parties (COP) to the 1992 United Nations Framework Convention on Climate Change (UNFCCC) and the 11th session of the Meeting of the Parties to the 1997 Kyoto Protocol. The Agreement will become legally binding if joined by at least 55 countries which together represent at least 55% of global greenhouse emissions. Such parties will need to sign the agreement in New York between 22 April 2016 (Earth Day) and 21 April 2017, and also incorporate it within their own legal systems.

state competences and in the state governance overall. This is particularly true when the issues in question relate mostly to matters of local interest, which are presumably more appropriately treated at a regional or local level. By referring to applied and effective local-level deliberative fora in Canada, Hoi Kong argues that the civic republican conception of legitimate state action offers the best justification for municipal regulation and provides the best normative foundation for developments in municipal consultation processes.[34]

If deliberative techniques were developed at the lower level of governance, not only in relation to matters of national interest but also for supranational competences, especially EU powers, not only could the allegation of an increasing democratic deficit be allayed but also the citizens' frustration that their opinions are being undervalued at a higher level could be significantly reduced. Consequently, citizens' participation, through awareness, could be significantly upgraded so as to combat the disappointing phenomenon of increasing civilian apathy towards matters relating to the political community. Thus, all identities in Europe, be they of a national kind or otherwise, could be adequately expressed. In September 2003 the late Neil MacCormick, an emblematic figure in the field of legal theory, in his capacity as alternate member of the European Convention (Convention on the Future of Europe), under the chairmanship of former French President Valéry Giscard d'Estaing, submitted a contribution entitled *Democracy at Many Levels: European Constitutional Reform,* in which he claimed the following:

> In drawing a Constitution, or Constitution-treaty for the European Union, the Convention ought to direct attention to the manifest truth that European Democracy must operate at many levels, and that a concern for subsidiarity cannot be exhausted by reflection merely on relations between member states and union institutions [...] Europe should have a constitution does not imply that Europe is or ought to become a state, far less a "super-state". It is a supranational union of a unique kind that acknowledges shared and divided sovereignty rather than its concentration, and that accommodates at least four significant levels of government (Union level, member state level, internal territorial level, and local authorities, themselves very varied in kind and scope of action). It needs an adequate constitution suited to its special charac-

34 H Kong, 'The Deliberative City', *Windsor Yearbook of Access to Justice* 28 (2), 411-33.

ter, so that its structure is readily intelligible to its citizens and empowers them to have their full and proper say at all levels.[35]

EU primary law, through the Committee of Regions and its jurisdictional standing before the Court of Justice of the European Union, indirectly renders the European regions shareholders: Article 8 of Protocol (No 2) on the application of the principles of subsidiarity and proportionality, annexed to the Treaty on European Union and the Treaty on the Functioning of the European Union by the Treaty of Lisbon of 13 December 2007, stipulates that the Court of Justice of the European Union shall have jurisdiction in actions on grounds of infringement of the principle of subsidiarity by a legislative act, brought in accordance with the rules laid down in Article 263 of the Treaty on the Functioning of the European Union by the Committee of the Regions against legislative acts for the adoption of which the Treaty on the Functioning of the European Union provides that it should be consulted.

On the other hand, it is imperative that lower levels of local communities of the member States become involved mostly in domestic but also in Union processes in matters affecting their well-being. This would require a restructuring of national and community decision-making and a better networking between local government authorities at a European level so that local interests can be heard.[36]

VI. Structuring deliberative democracy

A. Deliberative modules

Deliberative polls, juries and assemblies constitute the main means of deliberative democracy. Polls indicate the process where emphasis is given to the evidence provided to substantiate various approaches on the issue in

35 Conv 298/02 of 24 September 2002, available at http://european-convention.europa.eu/pdf/reg/en/02/cv 00/cv 00298.en02.pdf (accessed 9 August 2016).

36 These structures do exist to some extent at the domestic level, mostly in federal states. In Germany, for example, the *Länder* have a say, under Article 23 of the Basic Law, on the will formation of the German minister in the Council for all matters within the *Länder*-competence. In some regard, therefore, their governments and parliaments, like the German Bundestag, bear and exercise a 'European' responsibility.

question and not to the actual interplay between members of a voting body (an assembly in a proper sense), provided that the body is constituted properly, the process is transparent and the electors uphold the process and possess a retraction predilection. Juries indicate the process where emphasis is given to the actual interplay of members of a voting body with a view to achieving unanimity, provided that the evidence furnished to substantiate various approaches on the issue in question is at an appropriate level, the body is constituted properly and the electors uphold the process and possess a retraction predilection. Assemblies broadly resemble juries, the only difference being that no unanimity is required as a matter of principle, but the outcome is legitimate if an adequate majority is achieved.

Citizens' polls and assemblies constitute the most common feature of deliberative democratic modes. They include either all citizens, if the scope of the matter vis-à-vis the relevant scale of the community so allows, like in ancient Athens, or representatives of the stakeholders. In order to qualify as deliberative, such an assembly must abide by the basic rules of deliberativism as presented here above, i.e. inclusiveness, endorsement, evidence, interplay and fair play and transparency. Global polls and assemblies operate at the present time in Switzerland, whereas experiments of deliberative micro-bodies at a representative level have been launched in many parts of the world, especially at regional and local levels, with diverse results. One characteristic example is that which occurred in Canada's metropolitan region of British Columbia, where in 2004 the provincial government created an assembly of 160 near-randomly selected citizens to assess and effectively decide on the re-designation of the province's electoral system. The experiment has been reported to have had immense success, gave rise to a significant amount of academic literature and was exported to other metropolitan regions of Canada and abroad.[37]

The outcome of the deliberative polls and assemblies might be either decisive, when the deciding state authority ought to abide by the citizens' view, or consultative if it may depart from that view. Irrespective of the discretion enjoyed in the latter case, the competent authority must state explicit and specific reasons for neglecting the deliberative end-result and of course bear the significant political cost of ignoring the popular will,

37 ME Warren and H Pearse (eds), *Designing Deliberative Democracy.* The British Columbia Citizens' Assembly (Cambridge, Cambridge University Press, 2008).

which would normally have serious implications in the course of the democratic political process. The deliberative result, which by definition enjoys high legitimacy if the conditions precedent are adhered to, ought to be disseminated in order to make it widely known, raise the political awareness of the deciding authority and create a leverage of the respective level of accountability.

Finally, Fishkin argues that there is another crucial indicator apart from the outcome itself of the process of the deliberative assembly, namely the difference that has been produced from the original position held by its members. This indicator is established, according to Fishkin, through a process of comparing pre- and post-deliberative process results with the genuine deliberative process taking place in-between.[38] Indeed, the variation that has been produced between the starting- and end-points is of some importance, for it proves the merits of the deliberative process and the operational role of the applicable criteria, above all the retraction predilection of the members of the assembly. Still, the variable indicator is not by itself conclusive because members of the assembly might have had the optimal view even at the start of the process (either as a matter of quality information and reason or by mere intuition), in which case adherence to this approach does not hamper the normative validity of the deliberative process.

B. Deliberative education and financing

From a normative point of view, any decision suffers from a certain degree of subjectivity given that it is humans that take this decision. Deliberativism purports to minimise the adverse effects of subjectivity by establishing a rational process of decision-making, although it cannot altogether abolish the human factor which is at the root of subjectivity. Therefore, deliberative processes ought to be supplemented by a long vision of deliberative education that could raise the level of awareness of deliberative processes and help individuals become more effective at dealing with relevant challenges. This pedagogical responsibility of states and supranational entities should extend, first, to the establishment of a proper deliberative

38 JS Fishkin, Democracy and Deliberation: New Directions for Democratic Reform (New Haven, Yale University Press 1991) 81.

curriculum at all levels of education that must familiarise students with the benefits and techniques of deliberative democracy in order to reduce apathy towards public affairs and to establish a public benefit mentality within a communitarian context. Second, it should extend to the use of distant technologies to promote the advantages of deliberative democracy, to call for the broader participation of citizens through experimental polls and to disseminate information concerning issues of public interest. The project obviously entails financing deliberative education projects, originating both from the states and international organisations and from civic societies through private entities, aiming at a more efficient participation of citizens in public life.[39]

VII. Epilogue

Deliberative democracy constitutes a necessary complement of both participatory democracy and political equality. Participatory democracy introduces a quantitative dimension which is important in the context of constitutional representation. However, it is still not enough. Participation needs to be accomplished through deliberative features which possess a qualitative dimension that strengthens and supplements the democratic process. Quantity and quality in democracy jointly constitute an upgraded legitimating perspective that not only deals with the conceptual deficits of contemporary democracy, especially beyond the state, but above all produce better results in democratic decision-making for the benefit of the people.

Although this process may admittedly hamper the immediate efficiency of decision-making, since additional time will most probably be required to adduce evidence and enter into a genuine process of deliberation on all the relevant arguments, given the circumstances of the widespread crisis in constitutional democracy and the dominance of extra-institutional sources of power, and above all the instruments of fiscalism, one might reasonably argue in favour of a positive-sum gain in relation to the legitimacy and accountability versus efficiency debate, where democratic and managerial concepts become complementary and mutually reinforcing.[40]

---

39 JA Flammang, 'Symposium, *Democracy: Direct, Representative, and Deliberative' (2001) 41 Santa Clara Law Review* 1085, 1091.

40 I Bache and M Flinders, (2004). 'Multi-level Governance: Conclusions and Implications' in I Bache and M Flinders (eds), *Multi-Level Governance* (Oxford, Ox-

From the point of view of substantive equality, deliberativism subverts the imbalance inherent in a differentiated society, where politically, economically or spiritually powerful groups or individuals can dominate public discourse and subordinate the remaining part of society. The same is true at supranational level, where the inequalities among the states threaten the community since they essentially render fellow Member States competitors. In this, deliberativism not only bridges the existing gap between the participants in a political process but shapes a political agenda where there are no adverse externalities for the citizens (since the product of the deliberative process will, at the end of the day, be beneficial to everyone, either directly or by reflection) and no transaction costs will exist since it is the community itself that decides on a rational basis for the sake of the community. As Habermas notes in his concept of the 'ideal speech situation', there is no oppression in the decision-making process apart from that of the optimal solution, which cannot be rationally refuted. Error can only be rectified through reasoning.

---

ford University Press, 2004) 195, 206; B Jessop, 'The Rise of Governance and the Risk of Failure' (1998) 50 *International Social Science Journal* 29, 42.

2 'All good things come in threes': from a double to a triple democratic legitimacy of the European Union

Lina Papadopoulou

Abstract

The European Union claims independent legal authority and thus political power. The latter, in order to be effective, needs to be legitimated. It is a common topos that legitimation need not necessarily be procedural; however, the main claim of the democratic theory is that political power does have to be 'democratically' legitimated. But what does 'democratically' mean in the 'postnational constellation'?

This paper traces the theories that have developed concerning the democratic legitimacy of the European Union and acknowledges the progress that has been achieved with the adoption of the theory of double legitimacy, according to which the EU is not merely an international organisation, based only on the will of the 'high contracting parties', the Member States, but a '*Sympolity*'[1] of states and peoples. At the same time, the study discards the arguments for assessing the legitimacy of the EU as a regulatory regime whose legitimacy should be assessed exclusively in terms of its results. It contends, however, that the theory of double democratic legitimacy is no longer sufficient for the present state of Union affairs. It also challenges the view that the only 'pure' type of democratic legitimacy would be that emanating from a single 'European demos', which would transform the Union into a state. It rather proposes that the most suitable type of 'democratic' legitimacy at the present historical and political conjuncture is a triple one, based on states, peoples and citizens alike.

The triple legitimacy theory aims both to describe the state-of-the-art of the Union today and also to serve as a normative yardstick for future de-

1 See D Tsatsos, The European Sympolity, Towards a New Democratic Discourse (Brussels: Bruylant, 2009).

velopments: As for the former, triple legitimacy is already enshrined in some EU Treaty provisions, especially Articles 10, 11 and 12 TEU, newly inserted by the Lisbon Treaty, and the provision concerning the composition of the Convention (Art 48 par 3 TEU). These provisions have yet to be put into effect. As for the latter, further steps towards a more enhanced citizens' approval of the Union law and politics need to be taken in accordance with the triple legitimacy theory, given a number of specific limitations: the particularity of European citizenship and sentiment of (non-) belonging, the asymmetry in the federal structure which follows from the flexibility clause, and the notion of sovereignty, which is conceptually deeply flawed and rather absent in pragmatic terms. Nevertheless, it remains popular as a discursive claim in favour of state-centrism, which preserves the particular status of states and nations.

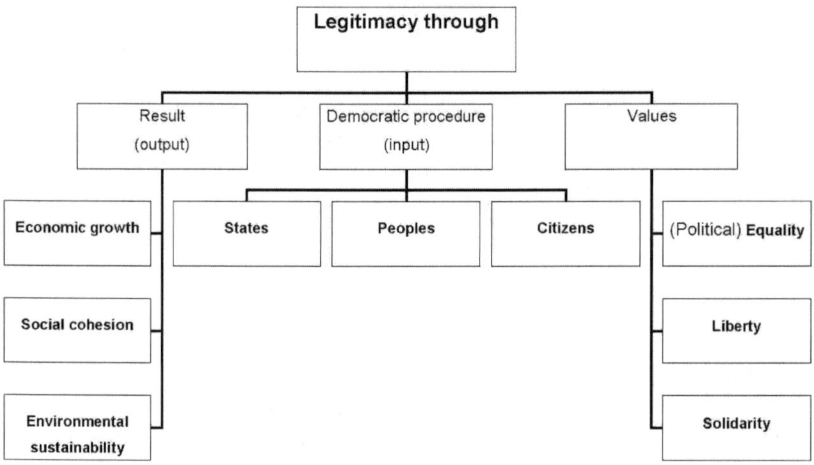

I. Three Modes of 'Translation'

Normative talks about constitutional phenomena necessarily presuppose subjective or at least inter-subjective political evaluations. Such talks about the constitutional setting of the European Union, a flexible and dynamic mode of co-exercising political power as the Euro-crisis becomes more evident than ever, presuppose a similarly politically biased evaluation of what the EU *is and should be*. One cannot but recognise 'the necessity to avoid being tempted by a kind of naturalist fallacy or the translation of the description of empirical reality as a normative ideal'.[2] It can hardly be denied, however, that often estimations of what the European Union *is* and *should be* are inextricably bound up with what the person making the estimation *wants* it to be. Hence, the question 'what is the European Union?' and the related question 'how is EU political power or legal authority to be legitimated?' are usually answered not on the basis of empirical observation alone, but also on the basis of political and normative preferences. Epistemological honesty thus obliges everybody to reveal not only their 'pre-hermeneutic perceptions'[3] but also the political choices which guide them to their hermeneutic conclusions. The point of departure for the present paper is the adoption of the Habermasian political scheme for Europe, according to which, '...the challenge before us is not to *invent* anything but to *conserve* the great democratic achievements of the European nation-state, beyond its own limits'. [4]

Moreover, the transition from *Sein* to *Sollen* and vice versa reveals the inevitable subjectivity involved in the observation of social phenomena and their description through the use of empirical or normative terms. Depending on one's own personal vision of the EU, one 'sees' in the EU what one wishes to see and thereby confirms one's preferences. Thus we often tend to 'translate' our political choices into a normative judgement, concealed under the cloak of empirical observation. The same necessarily applies to our judgements concerning the issue of legitimacy that applies and/or should apply to the political power of the EU. What is more, being ready to talk about legitimacy reveals a political (in the broadest sense of the word) bias: a human-centred approach and an individual-empowering agenda, which lie at the heart of constitutionalism. This is so as 'the effort to create and maintain legitimacy ... leads institutions to have a focus upon those who are being led, and their conceptions of jus-

2 C Closa, "The Implicit Model of Constitution in the EU Constitutional Project', in Eo Eriksen EO, IE Fossum, and AJ Menendez (eds) *Constitution Making and Democratic Legitimacy*, Arena Report, No. 5/2002, 9.

3 D Tsatsos, *Constitutional Law, Theoretical Foundation* (Athens: Ant. Sakkoulas, 1994, in Greek) 278.

4 J Habermas, 'Why Europe Needs a Constitution' (2001) 11 *New Left Review* 5: 6, the same, 'Democracy in Europe: Why the Development of the EU into a Transnational Democracy Is Necessary and How It Is Possible', 21 (2015) *European Law Journal* 546 (553).

tice and fairness. ... This suggests that a focus on legitimacy empowers the members of organizations and societies'.[5]

The difficulties of discussing the democratic legitimacy of the European Union are multiplied by yet another two processes of 'translation': the 'translation' of the constitutional terms used – which already have a different meaning in different national contexts – from the 'source language' of the nation state to the target language of a *sui generis* entity, namely the European Union;[6] this is a case of the well-known and vividly expressed problem of describing 'oranges with a botanical vocabulary developed for apples'.[7]

Last but not least, we have the translation of the theoretical model to a specified constitutional settlement. Schematically, agreements or disagreements by consent and *in camera* reflect the intergovernmental model; control by national parliaments corresponds to a form of 'demoi-cracy' and to the 'Union of peoples'; the reinforcement of the European Parliament and an increase in the political character of its decisions based on supranationally built majorities introduce the citizens' dimension; an engaging Charter of Fundamental Rights echoes unity on the basis of common values; a greater number of common political rights for all European citizens entails the establishment of a common European 'demos'; and, finally, the supremacy of EU law in relation to the law of the Member States exudes the air of a federal state. It is not then a coincidence that we, as the participants in the public political or scientific discourse, often find ourselves lost in the mazes of this multiple act of translation: from '*sein*' to '*sollen*' through '*wollen*', from the national to the supranational, from the theoretical model to a normative arrangement.

5 T Tyler, 'Psychological Perspectives on Legitimacy and Legitimation', (2006) 57 *Annual Review of Psychology* 375 (392).

6 N Walker 'Flexibility within a Metaconstitutional Frame: Reflections on the Future of Legal Authority in Europe', (1999) *Harvard Jean Monnet Working Paper* 12/99, available at: http://www.jeanmonnetprogram.org/archive/papers/99/991202.html and the same, 'Postnational Constitutionalism and the Problem of Translation' in JHH Weiler and M Wind (eds) *European Constitutionalism Beyond the State* (Cambridge University Press, 2003) 27.

7 JHH Weiler *The Constitution of Europe* (Cambridge University Press, 1999) 268ff.

II. Three Modes of Legitimacy

A. Talking about legitimacy

Legitimacy is 'the belief that authorities, institutions, and social arrangements are appropriate, proper, and just'.[8] Legitimacy facilitates the exercise of power by enhancing the probability that certain or all commands will be obeyed by a given group of persons.[9] The internalisation of specific justifications by the people allows a political system, its legal texts and its personal authorities, to be viewed 'as normatively or morally appropriate by the people within the system'.[10] As a result, 'control by others is replaced by self-control, as social norms and values are internalized and become part of the individual's own desires concerning how to behave'.[11]

Weber[12] outlines three major ideal types of legitimate domination: traditional (deference to customs and values), charismatic (devotion to the actions or character of an authority), and legal or rational (linked to the process of rule creation and interpretation). As a political system proceeds to adopt this third, rational form of authority, the latter takes on a legal form. Those who govern or rule either have, or appear to have, a legitimate legal right to do so – and those who are governed accept such a right. Constitutions, written legal texts, political offices, institutionalised modes of representation through elections and political parties are connected with this type of legitimacy, as opposed to the other two systems.

In the West, and within the latter type of legitimate exercising of power, it is possible to distinguish a further three forms of legitimacy: functional (output- or results-based), value-based[13] and procedural (input or democratic) legitimacy. Output legitimacy is often called 'government for the

---

8 Tyler, 'Psychological Perspectives on Legitimacy and Legitimation' (n 6), 376.

9 M Weber, *Economy and Society*, Vol. I (Berkeley / CA, University of California Press, 1968) 212.

10 Tyler, 'Psychological Perspectives on Legitimacy and Legitimation' (n 6) 378.

11 M Hoffman, 'Moral Internalization', (1977) *Adv. Exp. Soc. Psychol* 85.

12 Weber, *Economy and Society*, (n 10) 263.

13 A different *tertium* has been proposed), the so-called '*throughput* legitimacy', which focuses on accountability (policy-makers are responsive and can be held responsible for output decisions), transparency (citizens have access to information) and openness to 'civil society' (citizens organised in interest-based organisations have access to and influence over the decision-making process) see V Schmidt 'Democracy and Legitimacy in the European Union Revisited: Output, Input and

people' since it stems from the fact that adopted policies present effective solutions to the common problems of the governed, while input legitimacy is called 'government by the people' aiming to ensure that the governing processes are generally responsive to the manifest preferences of the governed.[14]

B. *Running out of output legitimacy*

The 'postnational constellation'[15] requires supranational and international structures in order to face the challenges posed by globalisation and so that citizens' needs for peace, security and prosperity can be sufficiently met. Functional legitimacy has for a long time been the main strategy employed by the Union, based on the well-known neo-functional axiom that

> 'the public is… concerned with income, price stability, better working conditions, cleaner air, more recreational facilities … [and] does not greatly care whether these are provided by national government or by Brussels'.[16]

For some commentators this kind of legitimacy remains the main field of play for the Union for several reasons: firstly, because there is apparently no demos and therefore no common identity or sufficiently shared values

---

Throughput', (2010) *Kolleg-Forschergruppe (KFG) Working Paper Series*, No. 21, 'The Transformative Power of Europe', Freie Universität Berlin, available: userpage.fu-berlin.de/kfgeu/kfgwp/wpseries/WorkingPaperKFG_21.pdf. This should be seen as a 'functional representation' through interest groups and, as such, as an additional form of democratic legitimisation in the EU, as suggested by Kohler-Koch and Kröger, see B Kohler-Koch, 'The Organization of Interests and Democracy in the E'U in B Kohler-Koch and B Rittberger (eds) *Debating the Democratic Legitimacy of the European Union* (Lanham, Maryland Rowman & Littlefield, 2007) 255 and S Kröger, 'Nothing but Consultation: The Place of Organized Civil Society in EU Policy-making across Policies', (2008) *European Governance Papers* (EUROGOV) No. C-08-03, at: connex-network.org/eurogov/pdf/egp-connex-C-08-08.pdf..

14 F Scharpf, 'Problem-Solving Effectiveness and Democratic Accountability in the EU', (2003) *MPIfG Working Paper* (Max Planck Institute for the Study of Societies) 03/1, 2 available at: www.mpifg.de/pu/workpap/wp03-1/wp03-1.html.

15 J Habermas, 'Die postnationale Konstellation und die Zukunft der Demokratie', in Die postnationale Konstellation, Politische Essays, (1998), 91.

16 E Haas, *The Obsolescence of Regional Integration Theory* (Berkeley CA, University of California Press, 1975), 79-80.

to guide institutional and political action;[17] secondly, it is considered the most suitable one for a 'regulatory state', such as the EU, since it ensures 'expertocracy' which produces effective policies serving the people;[18] thirdly, it is thought to be adequate enough since the Union has the ability to serve an 'efficiency promoting function' by doing things for the Member States that they cannot do on their own.[19]

In contrast to the input type of legitimacy, output legitimacy does not presuppose the existence of either a single demos or multiple 'demoi', based on social or political identity grounds. Instead, it is enough if the citizens have common interests. In this way, the decisions within the EU could be legitimated because they are improving economic efficiency for the citizens. Peace and personal security, social welfare and cohesion through reducing great inequalities in wealth and political power, and the environmental sustainability of economic development are to be identified as goals to be achieved by both national and European polities and whose achievement serves to generate output legitimacy for the Union.

In order for functional legitimacy to be effective, however, enough resources must be available for the system to deliver, and in this way it rewards people for their compliance. Lack of resources, during periods of scarcity, leads to the collapse of legitimacy.[20] This scarcity of resources may explain why the 'permissive consensus' of the early years, in which citizens silently accepted the EU and its policies, has been replaced by a 'constraining dissensus' along with a rise in Euro-scepticism.[21] In such cases, as in today's Europe, other sources of legitimacy need to be employed so that the public continues to view European governance as legitimate.

17 F Scharpf 'Legitimacy in the Multilevel European Polity', (2009) European Political Science Review 173.

18 G Majone, 'Europe's Democratic Deficit', (1998) 4 European Law Journal 5.

19 A Menon, and S Weatherill, 'Transnational Legitimacy in a Globalising World: How the European Union Rescues its States', (2008) West European Politics 397.

20 Tyler, 'Psychological Perspectives on Legitimacy and Legitimation' (n 6) 376.

21 L Hooghe and G Marks, 'A Postfunctionalist Theory of European Integration: From Permissive Consensus to Constraining Dissensus', (2009) British Journal of Political Science 1.

C. Values-based legitimacy

Such alternative sources of legitimacy may be found either in values shared by the majority of the population or a process guaranteeing popular involvement in decision-taking. In a constitutional state, it is possible to name (at least) three fundamental values which (must) normatively guide state action: personal autonomy and dignity (enshrined in civil rights and protecting minorities), political equality (enshrined in the political rights of free and equal citizens participating in a democratically governed polity) and solidarity (aiming at social equalisation, reflected in the social state's ethos and enshrined in social rights). These shared values are incorporated in the constitutional state as a liberal and social state ruled by law.

Constitutional democracy is thus not only procedural but also possesses a material character bearing fundamental values, which means that it is not conceivable without the preservation of citizens' fundamental rights. Values – and obligation as their core aspect – are vital since they may be internalised and lead to voluntary deference to the directives of legitimate authorities and rules.[22] These values are also enshrined in constitutional charters.[23] Under these conditions, democratic legitimacy presupposes that the citizens, as principal political subjects forming a 'demos', accompany the political choices either with their consent or tolerance, and participate, in this manner, in the development of the value system.[24]

These values are common to both the European and national constitutional settings. Thus, the value triplet functions as a 'roadmap' for the EU's policies and as a criterion for its political legitimacy. The European Union also draws its legitimacy from the belief that unification is neces-

---

22 Tyler, 'Psychological Perspectives on Legitimacy and Legitimation' (n 6) 378.

23 D Tsatsos, *Η έννοια της δημοκρατίας στην ευρωπαϊκή Συμπολιτεία* (The notion of democracy in the European Sympolity) (Athens: Polis, 2007, in Greek), 44, and the same, *The European Sympolity, Towards a New Democratic Discourse* (Brussels: Bruylant, 2009).

24 P Häberle, Europäische Verfassungslehre, 4th edn (Baden-Baden, Nomos, 2006), 301; D Tsatsos,, Ευρωπαϊκή Συμπολιτεία, Για μια Ευρωπαϊκή Ένωση των κρατών, των λαών, των πολιτών και του ευρωπαϊκού συνταγματικού πολιτισμού (European Sympolity. For a European Union of states, peoples, citizens and the European constitutional culture) (Athens, Livanis, 2007, in Greek), 46.

sary in order to safeguard these values —maybe the concomitant of what Weiler[25] calls 'political messianism'.

When oriented towards the value-based perception of democracy, the notion of 'a people' acquires a new dimension: pre-political homogeneity is abandoned and substituted with an attachment to a common-value universe with a minimalist content constituting the source of legitimacy. The European people are thus characterised by the fact that they share the same values under a European seal (see Preamble[26] and Art 2 TEU[27]). The realisation of these values is expected to produce social legitimacy for the European project and enhance the engaging nature of the decisions taken by non-nationals at European level. This presupposes a 'social contract' between the citizens of those states, who are in this way united in a wider political society. This view, as Weiler[28] has early enough emphasised, while preserving both the boundaries (the Self and the Other), also attempts to educate the '*I*' to approach the '*Other*'. Not only is the European Demos non-organic but we should not even attempt to make it such. Hence we share common basic values and that is exactly what makes us accept the subordination of some fields of our social co-existence to a political community that normatively consists of 'Others'.

The inability to deliver, however —especially in times of crisis— which renders the output type of legitimacy inadequate is often closely related to dissatisfaction concerning the degree to which the fundamental values served by European integration are realised. The social state, and thus the principle of solidarity, is just one case in point, but the most

---

25 JJH Weiler,'The political and legal culture of European integration: An exploratory essay' (2011) 9 *International Journal of Constitutional Law* 678, 682.

26 [27] Preamble of the TEU (Consolidated Version after the Treaty of Lisbon): 'Confirming their attachment to the principles of liberty, democracy and respect for human rights and fundamental freedoms and of the rule of law, Confirming their attachment to fundamental social rights as defined in the European Social Charter signed at Turin on 18 October 1961 and in the 1989 Community Charter of the Fundamental Social Rights of Workers, Desiring to deepen the solidarity between their peoples while respecting their history, their culture and their traditions… '.

27 Article 2 TEU (Lisbon Treaty) – The Union's values: 'The Union is founded on the values of respect for human dignity, freedom, democracy, equality, the rule of law and respect for human rights, including the rights of persons belonging to minorities. These values are common to the Member States in a society in which pluralism, non-discrimination, tolerance, justice, solidarity and equality between women and men prevail.'.

28 The Constitution of Europe, (n 8) 347.

prominent victim of problems arising from the current public debt crisis that obliges Europe to turn to democratic basics and seek its legitimacy at its very roots —recourse to input legitimacy (democratic procedure)— needs to be addressed more urgently than ever.

D. *Procedural, democratic legitimacy*

Procedural legitimacy refers to the 'participatory quality of the process leading to laws and rules'.[29] It may generate the belief that the distribution of resources is carried out in accordance with justice, fairness and the interests of the majority concerned since the latter are involved in free and equal deliberation and decision processes.[30] The need to enhance input, that is procedural and especially democratic, legitimacy is thus now more than ever the result of the inadequacy of output legitimacy in today's public debt crisis, which undermines the effectiveness of the post-war European social state. However, it has always been, and still is, a matter of principle —due to 'the importance of treating individuals as responsible agents'— to solve 'reasonable disagreements' and choose between numerous alternative and potentially equally valid points of view, while at the same time ensuring that all positions obtain an equal hearing and make rulers accountable and responsive to the ruled.[31]

In contrast to the above, European integration has meant the transposition of many important decisions from the national to the European level and thus an increase in executive power and a decrease in national parliamentary control. As a result, input legitimacy has always been weak, causing what has been called 'policy without politics'[32] at EU level, leaving at

29 Th Risse, 'Transnational Governance and Legitimacy' in Benz, A / Papadopoulos, I (eds) Governance and Democracy. Comparing National, European and International Experiences (London, Routledge, 2006) 179.

30 B Major, 'From Social Inequality to Personal Entitlement: The Role of Social Comparisons Legitimacy Appraisals, and Group Membership', (1994) *Advances in Experimental Social Psychology* 293, 304.

31 R Bellamy, 'Democracy without Democracy? Can the EU's Democratic "Outputs" be Separated from the Democratic "Inputs" Provided by Competitive Parties and Majority Rule?' (2010) *Journal of European Public Policy* 2.

32 V Schmidt, 'Re-Envisioning the European Union: Identity, Democracy, Economy', (2009) *Journal of Common Market Studies, Annual Review*, 17.

the same time the national arena with 'politics without policy'.[33] European citizens, both in their national and supranational capacity as such, have been deprived of a great part of their competence to participate in and influence political decisions. Demobilisation, euro-scepticism and radicalisation[34] may be seen as a result of this deprivation. Again, a matter of principle can be seen to lead to pragmatic threats, not only to the project of European integration itself but also to social integration as a whole.

Under these circumstances, arguments that more politicisation may undermine the EU's governing effectiveness[35] (and 'lead to stalemates that would only increase citizens' disaffection from and dissatisfaction with the EU'[36] sound less convincing than in earlier times. It is thus no surprise that since the breakdown of the 'permissive consensus' in the early 1990s, an 'input turn' in the debate on the EU's legitimacy deficit has taken place.[37] This turn becomes even more convincing in the light of recent research evidence showing that 'measures aimed at increasing the input legitimacy of the EU also hold the promise of increasing its output legitimacy'.[38] Last but not least, it should not be forgotten that the democratic principle is one of the common values of all the Member States of the Union, on which the latter is based (art 2 TEU). Nevertheless, the particularities of the Union construct, as a multilevel system of government, make it necessary to adapt the national model of democracy to the new factors of the wider territory, multilingualism and multinationality.

---

33 Schmidt 'Democracy and Legitimacy in the European Union Revisited' (n 14) 17.

34 P Mair, 'Political Parties and Party Systems' in P Graziano and MP Vink (eds) Europeanization: New Research Agendas (Basingstoke, Palgrave Macmillan, 2006) 303.

35 Majone, 'Europe's Democratic Deficit' (n 19), see also Fr Scharpf 'Reflections on Multilevel Legitimacy', (2007) MPIfG Working Paper 07/3, available at: www.mpifg.de/pu/workpap/wp07-3.pdf.

36 Schmidt 'Democracy and Legitimacy in the European Union Revisited' (n 14) 17.

37 B Finke 'Civil Society Participation in EU Governance', (2007) 2 *Living Reviews in European Governance*, available at www.livingreviews.org/lreg-2007-2.

38 K-O Lindgren and Th Persson, 'Input and Output Legitimacy: Synergy or Trade-Off? Empirical Evidence from an EU survey', (2010) 17 *Journal of European Public Policy* 449.

III. Models of EU Democratic Legitimacy

A. Unitary models

1. States as the single source of legitimacy

According to the original and long-held view of the EU, the Union constitutes no more than an intergovernmental organisation. The political prehermeneutic choice behind this intergovernmental doctrine is a vision of a Europe of nation states, as clearly expressed in the following declaration:

> Europe is a Europe of free, independent sovereign nations who choose to come together in pursuit of their own interests and the common good, achieving more together than one can alone (…) that is the Europe I want: a Europe of nations that in its economic and political strength is that superpower; but in its constitution and organisation, is not a superstate.[39]

This vision goes hand in hand with the state-centric perception of democracy, according to which the source of power and its legitimised exercise lies in the unit of a 'people' or 'nation', the uniformity of which is not grounded in a legal order, but exists prior to that.[40] Europe lacks such a political unit, a European demos —the argument goes— and that is why it can neither be a democracy, nor enjoy an autonomous democratic legitimacy.[41] This ethnocentric model denies any possibility of 'translating' concepts linked with representation and democracy in a context other than that of the nation-state.

Owing to the above, sovereign states and their respective 'peoples' remain the only possible source of legitimisation for the Union.[42] Being a mere international organisation, the Union is no worse than other democ-

---

39 T Blair (2000), *Superpower – not Superstate?* (London, The Federal Trust, European Essay No 12), available at: http://fedtrust.co.uk/wp-content/uploads/2014/12/Essay_12.pdf.

40 E-W Böckenförde, *Staat, Nation, Europa* (Frankfurt a/Main, Suhrkamp, 1999) 110ff.

41 P Kirchhof, *Brauchen wir ein erneuertes Grundgesetz? Motive-Texte-Materialien (MTM)*, (Bayerische Landeszentrale für Politische Bildungsarbeit, Band 61, Heidelberg, 1992) 38; D Grimm (1995) 'Braucht Europa eine Verfassung?' *Juristenzeitung* 581, 590.

42 H Lübbe, Abschied vom Superstaat, die Vereinigten Staaten von Europa Wird es nicht Geben (Berlin: Siedler, 1994) 100.

racies in terms of output legitimacy.[43] Internal decision-making is subject to national democratic rules, whereas negotiating between the states is a matter of naked power based on national interests.[44] Any other source of legitimacy leads to anti-democratic results, since democracy is only possible within a nation-state.[45]

2. *The European people as the single source of EU legitimacy*

The preceding theory is the other side of the coin from the so-called 'Eurocratic' view, which claims that Europe should be transformed into a federal state, wherein the single source of legitimacy of the common European sovereignty would be a politically united European people. Democracy, and thus a European Constitution, is conceivable only under this condition.[46]

The argument is not only principled but also functional: only a European state could possibly influence the international market and help safeguard citizens' social rights and thus strengthen the core of values and the confidence of the citizens in the public power, which is undergoing a serious crisis. Consequently, the 'translation' of concepts such as 'demos', 'constitution', 'democracy', 'representation' and 'legitimacy' from the national to the transnational level is simple, linear and automatic and only presupposes a change of degree.

This constitutional reading reflects a political vision of a united Europe where national states have surrendered their national interests and obey a common European interest under a Constitution that allows less flexibility than the current Treaty. But this political vision —regrettably or not— is not to be found either in the political practice or in the legal texts that make today's Union what it is — or what it can become in the foreseeable

---

43 A Moravcsik, 'In Defence of the "Democratic Deficit": Reassessing Legitimacy in the European Union', (2002) 40 Journal of Common Market Studies 603.

44 A Moravcsik, 'Preferences and Power in the European Community: A Liberal Intergovernmentalist Approach', (1993) 31 *Journal of Common Market Studies* 473, 481ff.

45 P Kirchhof 'The Balance of Powers Between National and European Institutions', (1999) 5 *European Law Journal* 225, 230, 238; German Federal Constitutional Court 89, 155, 186.

46 GF Mancini, 'Europe: The Case for Statehood', (1998) 4 *European Law Journal* 29, 40.

future. Even if Europe decides to respond to the challenges of a globalised debt crisis through federalising further its financial system and economic governance, the total resignation of their sovereignty rights by national states is still up in the air.

A more refined and developed unitary model is to be found in the theory of multilevel constitutionalism and governance,[47] in which the EU is envisaged as a system calibrated into different grades of social integration and different levels of action which are originally legitimised by the people and are included in a united constitutional system.[48] Consequently, the EU constitutes a system of different levels characterised by different degrees of integration. An additional public power level is created through the Union, drawing its legitimacy directly from all those who are subject to its policies.[49] As a multilevel constitutional system, the EU directly refers to its citizens for legitimacy purposes, follows the same discipline of representation as the state —even if it does not constitute a state— and may have a Constitution, as constitutionalism may be detached from the nation-state. Despite its attractiveness due to its straightforward constitutional logic, this model is neither borne out by the Treaties nor is it accepted by major political forces. As will be shown later in this paper, the Union's legitimacy does not directly depend on its subjects; their consent is rather mediated through states and national parliaments.

---

47 I Pernice, 'Constitutional Law Implications for a State Participating in a Process of Regional Integration. German Constitution and "Multilevel Constitutionalism"' in E Riedel (ed), *German Reports on Public Law*, Presented to the XV. International Congress on Comparative Law, Bristol, 26 July to 1 August 1998 (Baden-Baden, Nomos, 1998) 40; the same, 'The Treaty of Lisbon: Multilevel Constitutionalism in Action', (2009) 15 *Columbia Journal of European Law* 349 and the same, 'Multilevel Constitutionalism and the Crisis of Democracy in Europe', (2015) 11 *European Constitutional Law Review* 541.

48 I Pernice 'Multilevel Constitutionalism in the European Union', WHI Paper 5/2002, 7 and (2002) 27 *European Law Review* 511.

49 I Pernice, 'Rethinking the Methods of Dividing and Controlling the Competencies of the Union' in European Commission (ed), Europe 2004. Le Grant Debat. Setting the Agenda and Outlining the Options (Brussels, 2002) 95 (available at: ec.europa.eu/governance/whats_new/europe2004_en.pdf) 107.

B. *The double legitimacy: states and peoples*

Compared to the dominant view held until two decades ago, according to which the EU was complacently content with mere functional output legitimacy, the later view that European peoples, in their plurality, could be seen as a second source of legitimacy has presented a welcome step forward in terms of democracy. This view[50] would emphasise the twofold nature of the European Union as a union of both peoples and states. It encompasses the belief that the European political culture is based on values, but it also highlights the significance of parity among the states as a result of the democratic principle, which within its rights constitutes a fundamental principle of primary Union law. The European Parliament endorsed the Tsatsos proposal on the double nature of the Union as a union of states and peoples on multiple occasions[51] as an '*acqui democratique*'.

Based on similar reasoning, Nicolaïdis[52] contends that the European Union constitutes something more than a confederation; it constitutes not only a society of states but also a society of peoples, 'a Union of peoples, understood both as states and as citizens, who govern together but not as one',[53] given that the European peoples, who are organised in states, are interconnected through the European Parliament (EP). The element that unites the EU is not a common identity, but common projects. Conse-

---

50 D Tsatsos, Ευρωπαϊκή συμπολιτεία, Για μια ένωση λαών με ισχυρές πατρίδες (European Sympolity, For a Unification of peoples with strong homelands) (Athens, Kastaniotis, 2001, in Greek) 35.

51 See, for example, EP Resolution of 19.11.1997 on the Amsterdam Treaty (OJ C 371, 8.12.1997, p 99, rapporteurs: Iñigo Méndez de Vigo and Dimitris Tsatsos, A4-0347/1997); Resolution of 18.11.1999 on the preparation of the reform of the Treaties and the next Intergovernmental Conference (OJ C 189, 7.7.2000, p 222, rapporteurs: Giorgos Dimitrakopoulos and Jo Leinen, Doc. A5-0058/1999); Resolution of 13.4.2000 containing the European Parliament's proposals for the Intergovernmental Conference (OJ C 40, 7.2.2001, p 409, rapporteurs: Giorgos Dimitrakopoulos and Jo Leinen, Doc. A5 -0086/2000, A5-0086/2000, § 34); EP Report on the draft Treaty establishing a Constitution for Europe and the European Parliament's opinion on the convening of the Intergovernmental Conference (IGC), 10.9.2003, 11047/2003–C5-0340/2003–2003/0902 (CNS), Committee on Constitutional Affairs, Rapporteurs: José María Gil-Robles Gil-Delgado / Dimitris Tsatsos, A5-0299/2003.

52 K Nicolaïdis, '"We, the peoples of Europe…"', (2004) 83 *Foreign Affairs* 83, 110.

53 K Nicolaïdis, 'European Democracy and Its Crisis', (2013) 51 *Journal of Common Market Studies* 351, 353.

quently, Europe does not need an integrated European public space, but has to respect the different identities and cultures of the constituent peoples. Power is shared at a horizontal level and the European 'demoi-cracy' has to remain polycentric and to request not the harmonisation but the mutual recognition of national law, orders and legislation —and to ensure fair competition among them.

This constitutional reading is the 'translation' of a political choice to keep pace with history, preserve the separate states and acknowledge the distinct national identities which are a product of European history. In the same vein, Habermas[54] finds the basis for a European democracy that is a supranational federation but at the same time respects the heterarchical relationship between the latter and the Member States in the idea of the EU constituted by a 'doubled' sovereign —the European citizens and the European peoples (the States).

This reading is borne out both by the rhetoric of the Treaty[55] and by specific institutional arrangements, as will be shown in the next section. Although the theory of the double legitimacy basis of the Union presents a more democratic account compared to the intergovernmental model, it does not sufficiently cover the need to take the principles of political equality seriously and does not respond to the democratic axiom, read through the subsidiarity lens, according to which political decisions must be taken —in immediate or mediated terms— by those concerned. It also undermines the dynamic nature of European integration by sticking too much to historical developments, which themselves transformed what was perceived as 'reality' in ethnic terms through the formation of modern nations and nation-states.

---

54 J Habermas (2015) 'Democracy in Europe: Why the Development of the EU into a Transnational Democracy Is Necessary and How It Is Possible', *European Law Journal* 546, 554.

55 Article 1 [1] Treaty of EU (TEU) – Establishment of the Union: 'By this Treaty, the High Contracting Parties establish among themselves a European Union … on which the Member States confer competences to attain objectives they have in common. This Treaty marks a new stage in the process of creating an ever closer union among the peoples of Europe, in which decisions are taken as openly as possible and as closely as possible to the citizen'.

C. From double to triple legitimacy: adding citizens to states and peoples

In an attempt to respond to the abovementioned needs and remarks, the theory of the triple legitimacy of the European Union stresses the fact that the entities united and collaborating in the European scheme are not only states and peoples but also the European citizens themselves. This theoretical approach aims both to describe the 'state-of-the-legal-art' of the Union today and serve as a normative yardstick for future developments. It is also a critique of procedures that either preserve or enhance only the intergovernmental legitimacy pillar, thus justifying accusations speaking of an 'executive federalism'.[56] This accusation also concerns the ongoing process of economic integration that has been boosted since and as a result of the recent Euro-crisis. It implies the critical point that the measures which have been taken, such as the Fiscal Compact, the European Stability Mechanism and the so-called Two and Six Packs, reflect only the intergovernmental legitimacy pillar and ignore both the second (peoples) and the third pillar (citizens). This may be a further reason why they lack not only input but also social legitimacy, despite their functionality (output legitimacy).

Responding to Tsatsos' and Habermas' implied idea that equates peoples with their states ('peoples organised in / as states'), and thus results in the double sovereign thesis (states and peoples taken together as the first pillar and citizens as the second), the theoretical approach presented here argues that this equation fails to acknowledge the political minorities represented in the national parliaments. While states are represented by their heads of state or governments —and rightly so—, it is highly probable that a large minority —if not majority in non-linearly proportional electoral systems— is excluded. The people's diverse political views are rather reflected in the national parliaments.

The 'triple democratic legitimacy' theory embraces and utilises the theory of 'multiple demoi' of variable geometry[57], since it is also based on the view that nationality and citizenship are independent entities, as well as the conceptualisation of the latter in civic and political rather than ethno-cultural terms. It also recognises the value of national demoi as entities which have a stronger sense of belongingness while, at the same time, it

56 J Habermas, *The Crisis of the European Union: A Response* (Cambridge, Polity Press, 2012) 12.

57 The Constitution of Europe (n 8) 344.

relativises national identities as products of a historical trajectory of the European nation-states[58] and underlines the commitment to the European project as a sine-qua-non component of the national plan.[59] Within this context it acknowledges the historical possibility of advancing new common ties between Europeans based not on organic grounds of language and religion, but on commonly shared values and interests that transcend national and ethnic diversity and enable the formation of a sense of '*Wir-gefühl*'—even if weaker than the national sense—, given the fact that democratic citizenship 'establishes an abstract, legally mediated solidarity between strangers'.[60] By acknowledging this, the 'triple democratic legitimacy' theory also presupposes the values-based type of legitimacy and the added value of output legitimacy. Lastly, but most importantly, it reflects the voluntaristic approach that the democratic authority and constitutional embodiment of such a transnational demos does not presuppose —the development by the citizens of a subjective consciousness of belongingness; on the contrary, it is for the constitutional settlement to generate the bonds of loyalty of this constitutional demos.[61]

By emphasising the place of European citizens in the third pillar of EU legitimacy, the philosophy behind this theory is that if the European Union has been established to solve citizens' problems, these same problems, and the alternative solutions proposed for them, unite citizens on the basis of their political preferences rather than their national attachments. The recognition of the plurality of alternative policies as a response to citizens' needs brings politics into the fore and enhances the need for majoritarian decisions to be taken over and above national barriers.

This ideal type of legitimation is not totally idealistic; it is rather partially reflected in the Treaties. What is at stake both at the level of the everyday functioning of the Union and at the macro-level of its legally enshrined institutional design —that is to say, the 'constitution of the Union' — is the dynamics and the equilibrium between the three different sources of democratic legitimacy. In other words, how the ideal type of legitimacy is 'translated' to institutional settings and the functioning of the institutions in those settings. Next we will explore to what extent citizens' in-

58 Habermas, 'Why Europe Needs a Constitution', (n 5) 15.

59 Weiler (n 8).

60 Habermas, 'Why Europe Needs a Constitution', (n 5)16.

61 JHH Weiler, 'A Constitution for Europe? Some Hard Choices', (2002) 40 *Journal of Common Market Studies* 563, 566.

volvement is foreseen in the Treaties, in parallel with the indisputable involvement of states and the recently enhanced involvement of peoples (through their national representations).

IV. Constitutional Arrangements and Political Legitimacy

A. Institutions and procedures reflecting the triple legitimacy of the Union

All the aforementioned views regarding the source(s) of EU legitimacy may be 'translated' into different organisational schemes, bodies, institutions, and procedures. It is a common topos that EU institutions might be divided into those of an intergovernmental type (the European Council, the Council of Ministers) and those of a supranational type (the European Parliament, the Commission and the ECJ); however, this is not a precise division since the composition and functions of these institutions do not necessarily reflect only one source of legitimacy. Some paradigmatic examples are given below.

1. The European Council and the Council

The European Council and the Council constitute the intergovernmental institutions *par excellence*, representing the Member States (art 10, para 2b TEU). Decisions are prepared by a diplomatic body (COREPER) and are made mainly by consensus (art 15 para 4 TEU) and *in camera*. Heads of States or Governments and Ministers are not controlled at a European level; they are only accountable to their national constituencies (art 10 para 2b TEU) so that their control is only possible within the frame of the national political arena and through national elections, to the —practically minimal— extent that the political view they support is known.

The intergovernmental character of these institutions is relativised, however, when the European Council elects its President by a qualified majority (art 15 para 5 TEU), or when the Council decides by (qualified) majority: the 'weighted vote' (as long as it was in force, see art 3 Protocol No 36 to the Lisbon Treaty on Transitional Provisions), as well as the new (art 16 para 4 TEU) qualified majority (from 1.11.2014, defined as at least 55 per cent of the members of the Council, comprising at least fifteen of them and representing Member States comprising at least 65 per cent of the population of the Union) undermine the intergovernmental doctrine of equality between the States and reflect, even in a distorted manner, the relationship between the sizes of the national peoples. Moreover, the dissenting states accept the binding character of decisions made in an institution which consists of 'Others'.

2. The European and the national Parliaments

The enhancement of the European Parliament's role was for a long time considered to be a direct compensation for the reduced competences of the national parliaments.[62] Through the Lisbon Treaty, its role in the law-making process is enhanced and new powers have emerged concerning the EU budget and international agreements — thus the classic strategy of 'democratisation through parliamentarisation' continues.[63]

Despite the declaration by art 14 para 2 TEU ('The European Parliament shall be composed of representatives of the Union's citizens') and art 10 para 2 TEU ('Citizens are directly represented at Union level in the European Parliament'), the Parliament is still seen as the expression of a legitimacy based mainly on the distinct peoples of Europe, and citizens forming national peoples, and less on the European citizens as such. This evaluation stems from the non-unitary character of the electoral system, the national agenda in the pre-election periods and the absence of genuine pan-European political parties with individual membership.[64] The degressive proportionality of the Parliament (art 14 para 2c) is another expression of the peoples' size.

On the other hand, the representation of European citizens is reflected in the Parliament's functioning, given that the latter decides by majority, in most cases based upon political preferences expressed by supranational parliamentary groups corresponding to the ideological and political fami-

62 S Hix 'The End of Democracy in Europe? How the European Union (as Currently Designed) Restricts Political Competition', (2003) LSE Unpublished Research Paper, available at: personal.lse.ac.uk/hix/Working_Papers/Hix-End_of_Democracy_in_Europe.pdf.

63 V Cuesta Lopez 'The Lisbon Treaty's Provisions on Democratic Principles: A Legal Framework for Participatory Democracy', (2010) 16 *European Public Law* 123, 129.

64 T Papadopoulou, Politische Parteien auf europäischer Ebene, Auslegung und Ausgestaltung von Artikel 191 (ex 138a) EUV (Baden Baden, Nomos, 1999).

lies. This dimension is closely related to the politicisation of the Union. However, one can hardly deny that 'it is impossible to link in any meaningful way the results of elections to the European Parliament to the performance of the political groups within the preceding parliamentary session, in the way that is part of the mainstay of political accountability within the member states'.[65] This is the outcome of the confluence of two political deficits, of a government and of genuine political parties representing the European citizens. Enhancing the European Parliament (e.g. through the recognition of its legislative initiative) would enhance both the peoples' and the citizens' participation in the Union's governance but would in no way worsen the democratic deficit, as some commentators imply.[66]

The national parliaments, on their part, clearly represent the peoples which are organised in states. Having been considered as the main losers in the integration process due to the transfer of their competences, the national parliaments have seen their role grow at least nominally (art 12 TEU, Protocol No 1 and Protocol No 2 on the Application of the Principles of Subsidiarity and Proportionality). This means an enhancement of legitimacy through the national peoples, which is endowed with the support of those who invoke the parliamentary principle while at the same time identifying this principle with the national state.

3. The European Commission

The Commission (and similarly the Court of Justice), although consisting of members nominated by the national governments —a provision which reflects the intergovernmental ratio and parity between the states (art 17 paras 4-5 TEU)—, does not represent the national governments but is regarded as a supranational institution *par excellence*, given that it is intended to promote and uphold the Union's interests. At the same time, by drawing its legitimisation from the vote of consent of the European Parliament, the Commission borrows the latter's double legitimacy basis. In this

65 JHH Weiler, 'Van Gend en Loos: The Individual as Subject and Object and the Dilemma of European Legitimacy', (2014) 12 International Journal of Constitutional Law 94, 101.

66 D Grimm, 'Die Stärke der EU liegt in einer klugen Begrenzung' (The strength of the EU lies in prudent limitation), *Frankfurter Allgemeine Zeitung* 11.08. 2014, 11.

sense one could say that the Commission acquires its triple legitimation from the states (nominations), the peoples (the Parliament's consent) and the citizens (functional legitimisation, as it functions on the basis of the common European interest and with due respect to fundamental rights, see art 17 para 1 TEU). The same applies for the motion of censure (art 17 para 8 TEU and art 234 TFEU) which the Parliament may pass against the Commission. Thus, the introduction into the European Union of some seeds of the principle of parliamentarianism, in which the executive is responsible and accountable to the legislative, is quite manifest, a fact that signifies a tendency towards a more political character of the European executive. It is, however, certain that the evaluation of these provisions greatly depends on their application, i.e. the 'real' constitution.

The presentation by the European political parties of 'Spitzenkandidaten' as candidates for the presidency of the Commission in the 2014 European elections and their pan-European debates have been a noteworthy step in this direction. A new form of election campaign was introduced featuring debates between the candidates nominated by the European political parties. The winner of the elections was named by the Council, although article 17 para 7 TEU is not straightforward in its normative meaning and there were objections to this nomination by national heads. However, the observance of this mild rule was a precondition for the Parliament's election of the candidate proposed by the Council. This has been a parliamentary and political victory and a step full of symbolism within the context of the dynamic fluidity that exists in the equilibrium between intergovernmental, nation-based and supranational elements in the European governance. It may also be a first step towards the establishment of a constitutional convention leading to a more pronounced parliamentarisation, in which it will be the Parliament, or the elected Commission's President, and not the European Council that selects the Commission's members.[67] Only via this process would it be possible to achieve the accountability[68] that is missing from a (quasi) European government.

67 A Jakab, 'Full Parliamentarisation of the EU without Changing the Treaties, Why We Should Aim for It and How Easily It Can be Achieved', (2012) *NYU Jean Monnet Working Paper* 03/12, available at: http://jeanmonnetprogram.org/paper/full-parliamentarisation-of-the-eu-without-changing-the-treaties-why-we-should-aim-for-it-and-how-easily-it-can-be-achieved/.

68 Weiler,'The political and legal culture of European integration' (n 26), 679-80.

4. *The procedure to amend the Treaties*

An evaluating criterion of the legitimacy enjoyed by the Union lies in the amendment procedure for its constituent treaties. This procedure requires the unanimous agreement of all the Member States, which is one of the manifestations —in fact, the most important— of what is called 'the federalist deficit'.[69] As Weiler[70] observes, 'unanimity embodying the principle of sovereign equality and consent is typically a hallmark of internationalism, not constitutionalism', thus amendment by majority is not, a 'mere' political issue but is of profound constitutional and social significance: it represents a move towards a polity.

Nowadays, states —represented by their Heads or Heads of Government or the Intergovernmental Conference— are still the only decisive bearers of both the ordinary and the simplified revision procedures. National parliaments or/and peoples (through referenda) are only involved in the ordinary revision procedure, on the basis of national constitutional stipulations. Nevertheless, there are four developments that allow for a differentiated view since they constitute a retrogression of the pure intergovernmental method towards a more supranational 'constitutionalisation' of the revision procedure.

Firstly, in the course of the ordinary revision procedure not only the Commission and the Member State governments, but also the European Parliament can take the initiative to submit an amendment proposal, while national parliaments should also be notified (article 48 para 2 TEU). Neither of these provisions was present in the Treaty of Nice (art 48); they were only inserted by the ECT and preserved by the Lisbon Treaty. The involvement and reinforced role of both the European and the national parliaments reflects a higher degree of politicisation of the revision procedure and constitutes a token of a greater democratic control of the content of the revision. It is to be regretted, however, that the European Parliament (and the Commission) are only to be consulted by the European Council before the latter adopts —significantly by a simple majority— a decision in favour of examining the proposed amendments (art 48 para 3).

Secondly, and perhaps most importantly, in the preparatory phase of the ordinary revision procedure the Intergovernmental Conference has now

69 A Trechsel, 'How to Federalise the European Union … and Why Bother', (2005) 12 *Journal of European Public Policy* 401 (406).

70 'A Constitution for Europe? Some Hard Choices' (n 62) 565.

been legally replaced (art 48 para 3 TEU) by a representative Convention composed of representatives of the national parliaments (representing the European peoples), the heads of states or governments (representing the states), the European Parliament (representing the peoples and citizens) and the Commission (which promotes the general interest of the EU). This composition clearly reflects the double legitimacy of the Union (according to Tsatsos,[71] based on states and citizens organised in peoples) or, according to the view presented here, the Union's triple legitimacy. Tsatsos himself, however, recognises[72] that the enactment of a Convention is 'a significant step towards the philosophy of the Europe of Citizens'.[73]

The historic turning-point will be reached when this Convention acquires the decisive power to revise the Constitution now enjoyed by the 'representatives of the governments of the Member States' (art 48 para 4 TEU). The European Parliament's competence to vote, on a per article basis, on amendments proposed by the Convention would complete the idea of European parliamentarianism and allow closer political integration, triggering the formation of political majorities through alliances and undermining the current consensus model which rests upon comprehensive negotiations ('nothing is agreed before everything is agreed'), which are characteristic of the international political arena.

Thirdly, there is the possibility of a simplified revision procedure (art 48 paras 6-7 TEU) regarding the provisions of Part Three of the Treaty on the Functioning of the European Union, in order to replace the Council's stipulated unanimity with a qualified majority. The simplification lies in the fact that there is no longer any requirement to convoke an Intergovernmental Conference or/and Convention, but the revision may be carried out by the European Council unanimously. This differentiation of the two revision procedures implies a different ranking of the TEU and the first two parts of the TFEU on the one hand and the third part of the TFEU on the other. If a more difficult amendment procedure is characteristic of a formal Constitution, the abovementioned differentiation in the amendment procedures may be thought of as elevating the TEU and the first two parts of the TFEU to a constitutional level, leaving the third part of the TFEU at

71 The notion of democracy in the European Sympolity (n 24) 313.

72 European Sympolity (n 24) 313.

73 See also C Closa, 'The Convention Method and the Transformation of EU Constitutional Politics' in EO Eriksen, E Fossum, and A Menéndez (eds), *Developing a Constitution for Europe*, (London and New York, Routledge, 2004) 184.

an intermediate level between the Union Constitution and secondary law. In other words, the differentiation of the revision procedures may bestow the character of a formal constitution to that part of the Treaties which may also be seen as constitutional in material terms.

Last but not least, art 48 para 5 TEU,[74] however vague it may be, contains a transformative dynamism. No one knows yet and no one can actually predict if and how this article is going to be implemented. In any case, this provision constitutes an alternative to the oppressive intergovernmental method that involves the approval of each revision by all Member States.[75]

These changes entail a reinforcement of the 'union of peoples and citizens' element, as opposed to the currently prevailing 'union of states' element, a reinforcement which would be applauded by moderate federalists, while the transposition of the preparatory procedure to the public sphere increases the possibility of discussion and transparency, which is pursued by republicans, thus leaving more room for a greater incorporation of value choices than the harsh intergovernmental bargaining behind closed doors.

B. The Lisbon Treaty architecture of democracy

On a rhetorical level, the Lisbon Treaty followed the Treaty of Nice and not the Constitutional Treaty which solemnly declared the double legitimacy theory (art I-1 CT: 'Reflecting the will of the citizens and States of Europe to build a common future, this Constitution establishes the European Union ...'). In the current Treaty the 'high contracting parties' remain the subjects who establish among themselves a European Union; the move from the will of 'the high contracting parties', i.e. the states, to a concept including both states *and* citizens has not survived the defeat of the Constitutional Treaty: art 1 EC and its Preamble, according to which the Union was established by the Constitution 'reflecting the will of the

74 'If, two years after the signature of a treaty amending the Treaties, four fifths of the Member States have ratified it and one or more Member States have encountered difficulties in proceeding with ratification, the matter shall be referred to the European Council.'.

75 Trechsel, 'How to Federalise the European Union', (n 70) 413.

citizens and States of Europe to build a common Future', as a new double source of EU legitimisation, has been omitted in the Treaty of Lisbon.

The second title of the Lisbon TEU, however, partially renders title VI, 'The Democratic Life of the Union', of the 'Treaty establishing a Constitution for the European Union', (known as the 'Constitutional Treaty' – henceforth CT), which has never been put into force, and includes a series of provisions designed to enhance the democratic legitimacy of the Union. Article 10 of the TEU sets out the principle of representation, while article 11 endorses the parliamentary and participatory dimension of EU democracy. Although this title has been critically characterised as a 'heterogeneous normative mass',[76] it is worth looking at it more closely in order to focus on the democracy model adopted by the current quasi-constitution of the Union. At the same time, by combining articles 10 and 11 of the TEU (representative democracy along with provisions concerning means of consultation and participation) and article 12 (on the role of national Parliaments) an attempt is made in the Treaties to refute the allegations claiming a democratic deficit.

1. Representative democracy

Art 10 TEU declares that the Union rests on a system of representative democracy. This seems to be in accordance with the German Constitutional Court's judgment on the Lisbon Treaty, which holds that representative democracy is central to any democratic system.[77] Needless to say, this declaration of representative democracy is not enough to guarantee its quality, which is undermined by both the inadequate parliamentary input in the law-making process at European level and also the lost competences at a national and regional level.[78]

In the Treaty, representative democracy seems to be based on two pillars; the states, on the one hand, represented by the European Council, and the Council and the citizens on the other, represented directly in the European Parliament (remainder of art I-46 CT). The CT expressly states (art 1

---

76 R Streinz, Chr Ohler, and Cr Herrmann, *Die neue Verfassung für Europa* (Munich, C. H. Beck-Verlag, 2005), 57.

77 BVerfGE, 2 BvE 2/08, *Gauweiler v Treaty of Lisbon*, 30.6.2009, para 211.

78 D Chalmers, G Davies, and G Monti, *European Union Law* (Cambridge, CUP, 2010, 2nd edn) 125.

para 1 CT) that the Constitution establishes the EU, 'reflecting the will of the citizens and States of Europe', thus shifting the second pillar of legitimacy from the peoples to the citizens. As has already been made apparent, this shift is a fallacy, since the increase of powers granted to both the European and the national Parliaments means an enhancement of the peoples' legitimacy and less of the citizens'. European citizens are referred to as a source of EU legitimacy neither as an integrated European people nor as individuals,[79] but rather as citizens organized in peoples, as Tsatsos puts it in his monograph on the '*European Sympolity*'.[80]

Thus equality of the citizens, as described in art 9 of the TEU ('In all its activities, the Union shall observe the principle of the equality of its citizens,…'), in no way implies an equivalence with voting at Union level, which would undermine the first legitimacy pillar of the Union, the equality of the Member States. Under this limitation, the democratic principle is to be understood as going hand in hand with the federal principle, as revealed in the principle of degressive proportionality (art 14 of the TEU), which results in the under-representation of the citizens of smaller states compared with the citizens of larger ones; hence the political equality of the citizens and the equality of the states undermine each other, converting democracy at Union level to an *aliud* compared with democracy at the national level. Such a disproportion is inevitable, given that in the opposite case, the citizens of smaller states would not be represented at all unless the number of Parliament members was dramatically increased.[81]

2. *Enhancing the citizens' Europe*

a. Participatory democracy

The direct participation and involvement of citizens in the decision-making process is likely to enhance their trust in the outcomes and enhance their readiness to comply. Moreover, through participation, public deliber-

79 J Schwarze, (ed), *EU-Kommentar*, (Baden-Baden: Nomos, 2009, 2nd edn) 81-2, § 6.

80 The European Sympolity (n 2).

81 R Geiger, in R Geiger, D-E Khan and M Kotzur, EUV/AEUV, Vertrag über die Europäische Union und Vertrag über die Arbeitsweise der Europäischen Union, Kommentar (München, Verlag C.H. Beck, 2010) 54, 57, Rn 6.

ation is enriched with new arguments presented by those directly affected by political decisions. Civic participation is thus considered to produce 'better' results, since the involvement of societal groups in the decision-making process will probably expand the knowledge base and make public administration accountable to society as a whole.[82]

Art 11 TEU, a new provision introduced by the Lisbon Treaty (partly copying art I-47 CT) aims to promote what is usually termed as 'participative' democracy and brings about a normative turn in the 'regime' of the European Union. Participation as an element of governance, a means of achieving the better resolution of certain problems and the greater efficacy of regulatory decisions within the frame of complex governance structures has now become a fundamental principle of EU democracy and a fundamental citizen's right.

Art 11 TEU foresees the political right of every citizen to participate in the democratic life of the Union and complements the fundamental principle of representative democracy proclaimed in the previous article with elements of consultation and direct citizen participation in decision-making processes. The right to participate also aims to establish a sense of belonging to a political community. Although the only institutional innovation introduced by the present articles is the legislative citizens' initiative (para 4) —while the other paragraphs formalise at the level of primary Union law provisions which to a great extent had already been introduced by the Commission with the White Paper on the Governance of the Union (COM2001-428, final on 25-07-2001)— the additional constitutional and symbolic value is significant, as it is the very first time that democracy at a Union level is connected with its citizens and semi-direct democratic instruments have been inserted.[83]

In this way participatory democracy functions as a normative foundation and as a legitimacy criterion for Union law,[84] posing a challenge to the case-law of the Union's courts, according to which the right to be heard cannot be conceived within the framework of the Union's legislative

82 Kohler-Koch, 'The Organization of Interests and Democracy in the EU' (n 14) 257.

83 J Mendes, 'Participation and the Role of Law after Lisbon: A Legal View on Article 11 TEU', (2011) 48 *Common Market Law Review* 1849, 1850, 1857.

84 A von Bogdandy, 'Founding Principles' in A von Bogdandy and J Bast (eds), *Principles of European Constitutional Law* (Oxford, Hart / Beck / Nomos, 2009, 2nd edn) 11.

process[85] and the participation of the Parliament is sufficient to democratically legitimise legislation.[86]

Not only individuals but also 'representative associations', 'civil society' and 'parties concerned' are mentioned in art 11 TEU; while these terms may be used interchangeably and undermine the normative clarity of the provision,[87] the inclusion of both individual and collective subjects can help to enhance the Union's legitimacy. Art 11 para 1 imposes on the Union's institutions the obligation to 'give citizens and representative associations the opportunity to make known and publicly exchange their views in all areas of Union action'. This may be achieved either by legal or other means, such as electronic deliberation.[88] Furthermore, 'the European Commission shall carry out broad consultations with parties concerned in order to ensure that the Union's actions are coherent and transparent' (art 11 para 3), including interested NGOs. Despite the lack of a regulatory framework for NGOs at EU level, these organisations try to organise themselves in each sector, while many of them are present in Brussels, in order to participate more effectively in the deliberation processes.[89] Special forms of participation by European citizens in the political process are foreseen in art 24 paras 2-4 TFEU, including the right to petition the European Parliament (art 227 TFEU), apply to the Ombudsman (art 228 TFEU) and write to any of the institutions or bodies referred to in article 24 TFEU or 13 TEU. Citizens also have the right to receive an answer in the same language as that used in their original letters (see also arts 20 para 2d and 342 TFEU).

---

85 See CFI Case T-521/93 Atlanta AG and Others v Council and Commission[1996], II-1707, paras 70-74 and Case C-104/97 P *Atlanta AG and Others v Commission of the European Communities and Council of the European Union* [1999] I-6983, paras 35-38.

86 T-135/96 *UEAPME* v *Council* [1998] ECR II-2335, para 88.

87 Mendes, 'Participation and the Role of Law after Lisbon (n 84), 1854.

88 A Fischer-Hotzel 'Democratic Participation? The Involvement of Citizens in Policy-making at the European Commission' 6 *Journal of Contemporary European Research* (2010), 335, 341, 343.

89 F-X Priollaud and D Siritzky, Le traité de Lisbonne. Commentaire, article par article, des nouveaux traités européens (TUE et TFUE) (Paris, La Documentation Française, 2008) 57.

b. The citizens' initiative

The most important —if not the only— innovation of art 11 TEU is the legislative citizens' initiative (para 4). Any proposal needs to be signed by at least 'one million citizens who are nationals of a significant number of Member States', which is approx. 0.2 per cent of the total citizenry of the EU, a percentage that may be seen as rather low.[90] Regulation 211/2011 of the European Parliament and the Council of 6.2.2011 (OJ L65/1/11-03-2011) foresees that the signatories (citizens of a MS) need to come from at least one fourth of the Member States (MS). Through this initiative, citizens have the competence to invite 'the European Commission, within the framework of its powers, to submit any appropriate proposal on matters where citizens consider that a legal act of the Union is required for the purpose of implementing the Treaties' (art 11 para 4).

Although —especially in the case of a major proposal— the European Commission is highly likely to respond, no sanctions are provided for in the opposite case. This means that the citizens' initiative of Art 11 TEU is only of a 'mild' character,[91] since it does not necessarily lead to either legislation or a referendum, but its continuation remains under the discretion of the Commission, and the adoption of the proposal falls within the competence of the ordinary legislative institutions (Council and Parliament). It may thus not undermine the prominent position of the states in the constitutional edifice of the Union.[92] Nevertheless, the initiative is expected to help in mobilising and integrating European citizens, even if it is used merely to counteract policies chosen by the EU institutions.

V. Loyal to the God of Small Steps

Incrementalism has always been the way forward for the European Union and nothing but a colossal economic disaster could alter this, as the recent debt crisis has proven. Thus, the proposals set forth are nothing but the logical implementation of the principles mentioned above, most —if not

90 V Robertson 'Elemente der direkten Demokratie im Vertrag von Lissabon. Eine Analyse mit rechtsvergleichendem Blick nach Deutschland, Österreich und in die Schweiz', (2010) 18 *Journal für Rechtspolitik* 133, 139.

91 Robertson, 'Elemente der direkten Demokratie' (n 91) 140.

92 Schwarze, EU-Kommentar (n 80) 82, § 6.

all— of which have already been widely discussed. These proposals are based on the belief that enhancing the third source of legitimacy, the European citizens as such and not only organised in peoples —'taking the citizens seriously', as Pernice[93] suggests— would be a way out —or would facilitate a way out— of the crisis. In other words, the way towards a 'veritable European citizenship', which is 'about the ability of citizens to "own" the polity', should continue to be followed if Europe wants to overcome the current crisis and continue to play a role as a positive player in the global arena.[94]

A first step should be taken in order for the European Parliament to live up to its new role as a representative institution of the citizens: a uniform electoral system and the formation of pan-European parties with greater cohesion is a sine qua non prerequisite for this to happen. Its more energetic involvement in the revision procedure —for example, through voting on the amendment of each article— would also be advisable and would enhance the peoples' and the people's constitutional position.

A second element that would signal the 'translation' of the supranational approaches and the upgrading of the citizens to a source of legitimacy would be the introduction of a direct democratic procedure at EU level, such as the holding of a pan-European referendum approving a new Treaty on the basis of the axiom 'one person-one vote'. As Weiler[95] has pointed out in the case of the Constitutional Treaty, this is something that is pragmatically and historically possible. The same is also conceivable for the election of the President of the Union (combining what is now the President of the Commission and the President of the Council). In such a hypothetical case the very same process of the Treaty's approval or the President's election would constitute a first step towards the creation of a 'European demos' under a normative and constitutional concept. Such a referendum or election would additionally serve as an opportunity and impetus for a pan-European public forum of discussion and for the densification of the European public sphere.

---

93 Pernice, 'Multilevel Constitutionalism and the Crisis of Democracy in Europe', (n 48).

94 G Amato, E Guigou, V Vike-Freiberga, V and JHH Weiler, 'Towards a "New Schuman Declaration"', (2015) 13 *Int J Constitutional Law* 339.

95 Weiler, 'A Constitution for Europe? Some Hard Choices' (n 62) 566.

This would also be the most suitable procedure for the introduction of a European Constitution. As Habermas[96] has observed, the constituent process is by itself a unique means of achieving a form of communication that is above and beyond national borders. It has the potential of a self-fulfilling prophecy. The fact is that this single and united 'demos' would be accompanied for several years to come by the existence of many national peoples, realising the historical possibility of the parallel existence of 'multiple demoi'.

No constitutional or legal doctrine could, however, exclude the possibility of the next Treaty (especially those parts that are now subject to the ordinary and not the simplified revision procedure —as could have happened to the Constitutional Treaty) being adopted through a pan-European referendum, in the same way that no legal doctrine could either impose or ban the convocation of a real constituent 'Convention'. The fact that such a constituent process has not yet been stipulated does not prove that it is impossible; it merely shows that there has not been enough political will to do it. The preference for a 'Europe of Home–Countries' and national demoi has prevailed over a 'Europe of Citizens'. It lies in the hands of politicians to 'take out of the dustbin' of history proposals discarded after the failure of the Constitutional Treaty that concern a more participative equilibrium between the Union's three sources of legitimacy, i.e. states, peoples and citizens, in order to reduce the 'federalist deficit' by introducing an amendment procedure based on a qualified majority of states (Heads of States or Governments' signatures) and peoples (national referenda or decisions by national parliaments) and a simple majority of citizens (pan-European referendum).

What remains a paradox is the marriage between legal federalism —based on the doctrine that federal law should have primacy over national law— and 'constitutional intergovernmentalism' (with the internal controversy that this term implies). One might justifiably argue that there are constraints to the extent to which the third pillar, citizens, can be developed as a source of democratic legitimacy for the EU. Since not only good things come in threes, the following can be considered as the main obstacles: first, the particularity of European citizenship and the sentiment of non-belongingness, or the so-called 'no-demos' thesis (which is appropriately commented on in this volume by Professor Tom Eijsbouts). The

96 Habermas, 'Why Europe Needs a Constitution', (n 5).

second obstacle seems to be an institutional asymmetry in the federal structure which follows mainly but not only from the flexibility clause. The latter also causes an asymmetry not only in the states' but also in the citizens' governance, which is incompatible with a constitutional system. Thirdly, at a rhetorical and ideological level, sovereignty as a discursive claim remains very popular, although it is conceptually a hollow notion. As such a claim it favours state centrism and defends democracy as an exclusively national endeavour. Together, all the above form an explosive mixture, especially in view of the triple crisis of the Euro, the European Union and democracy itself.[97]

Fighting this kind of false patriotism, namely nationalism, requires the construction of a European political identity. The debt crisis has been a good opportunity to do so, although in fact it has been utilised for the opposite purpose. More recent challenges, such as the flood of refugees and migrants and the terrorist attacks by Islamic extremists present fresh opportunities to either construct the notion of European citizens' solidarity or destroy it even further.

97 ^Ph Schmitter 'The Triple Crisis: The Euro, the European Union and Democracy in Europe' (2013) Konrad Adenauer Stiftung Online Publication, available at: http://www.kas.de/wf/doc/9914-1442-2-30.pdf.

3 No Representation Without Taxation in the European Union

Giacinto della Cananea

Abstract

Questions such as 'who gets what?' and 'who pays?' are crucial in any system of government. They are particularly relevant in the context of the European Union (EU), for two reasons that are discussed in this paper: the EU is not characterised by the association of representation with taxation that lies at the heart of Western constitutionalism and, consequently, its Parliament has just spending powers, notwithstanding the emphasis put on the 'own resources' of the EU. The paper argues that an attention for duties, particularly in the fiscal domain, can be matched with a renewed attention for public goods, such as infrastructures for European society. In other and shorter words, representation should be associated with taxation.

Introduction: 'Old' Democratic Principles Revisited

Questions such as 'who gets what?' and 'who pays?' are crucial in any system of government because they shed light on the functioning of that system, in addition to clarifying its relations with those who are directly or indirectly affected by the choices concerning getting and spending.[1] Raising such questions, therefore, does not require a particular justification. The title of this paper, however, which inverts the main elements of the famous maxim 'no taxation without representation' in the context of the European Union (EU), does require a preliminary clarification.

---

1 See both of the following early German public lawyers: R Gneist, Gesetz und Budget. Constitutionelle Streitfragen aus der preussischen Ministerkrisis vom März 1878 (Berlin, Springer, 1879), and M Weber, Parliament and Government in Germany Under a New Political Order (1918, R. Speirs transl., Cambridge, Cambridge University Press, 1994), 131.

Let us begin with the EU. Two basic strands of thought have dominated public law thought about the legitimacy of the Community, later transformed into the Union.[2] The first strand of thought, which emphasises output legitimacy, finds its bases not only in ideas and theories about law and government, but also in important legal realities. Consider, for example, the 'foundational' act of European integration (1950), the Schuman Plan, with its strong emphasis on legitimacy based on output legitimacy, that is to say the two 'public goods' promised by Monnet and Schuman: peace and prosperity.[3] The other strand of thought, which has increasingly gained consent in academic and political circles, is based on the assumption that the institutions of the EU should be accountable in much the same manner as the institutions of government to which we are more used to living with, those of the individual Member States. Precisely because this line of reasoning gives much weight to input legitimacy, it points out the importance of the European Parliament. A variant of this strand, which is largely veined by a sort of nostalgia for the lost paradise of national constitutionalism, brings this argument further and thus criticises the 'democratic deficit' from which the EU suffers.

My aim in this short essay is not to discuss these strands of thought. It is, rather, to show that they fail to provide adequate answers not only to a fundamental question of Western constitutionalism, that concerning the association of representation with taxation, but also to the question of what EU institutions should do in order to strengthen their legitimacy in the future. Moreover, the second strand of thought fails to appreciate the contribution that a modern vision of public law can receive from a greater attention for fiscal duties. I have no doubts that others will hold different views, not only on the answers given to the issues raised here, but also on the nature of the issues that need to be addressed. However, since the issues that will be addressed here are less frequently considered than others, I think

---

2 This distinction coincides neither with that between the international and the supranational approaches, nor with that between functionalists and federalists. For an *outline* of these, and other approaches, see A von Bogdandy, 'A Bird's Eye View on the Science of European Law, Structures, Debates and Development Prospects of Basic Research on the Law of the European Union in a German Perspective' (2000) 3 *European Law Journal* 20.

3 *For* this thesis, see JHH Weiler, *The Constitution of Europe* (Cambridge, Cambridge University Press, 1999).

that they can be helpful in stimulating discussion and reflection on a topic that has both theoretical and practical importance.

The paper is divided into three parts. In Part I, my analysis will focus on the principle expressed by the maxim '*No Taxation Without Representation*'. In Part II, an attempt will be made to argue that the EU deviates from this principle and that many of its current problems derive from this. This line of reasoning is brought one step further in Part III, where an attempt will be made to argue that an attention for duties, particularly in the fiscal domain, can be matched with a renewed attention for public goods. Finally, some conclusions will be set out.

I. 'No Taxation Without Representation'

A. Origins of the Principle

Although the principle expressed by the maxim '*no taxation without representation*' is more or less universally known, it can be helpful to sketch its origins and subsequent history.

First of all, we need to take a position in the debate concerning English constitutional history, more precisely as to whether the *Magna Charta* really was the great liberating document portrayed by Whiggism or such a role only has later and instrumentally, as a pillar of the ancient constitution, been illustrated by Blackstone[4] Whatever the importance of *Magna Charta*'s norms concerning *scutage* (from *scutum*, shield in Latin, a form of taxation which was used in lieu of military service) and 'aid' for which the 'general consent of the realm' was required,[5] there is evidence that erecting a shield against unjustified taxation was a seventeenth-century endeavour culminating in 1688.[6] The following year the Bill of Rights provided that no taxes should be levied without the authority of Parliament.[7]

---

4 *See* M Loughlin, *Public Law and Political Theory* (Oxford, Clarendon, 1992), 144.

5 *Magna Charta*, §§ 12 and 14.

6 See D Millar, 'Parliamentary Control of Taxation in Britain', in D Coombes (ed), *The Power of the Purse* (London, P.E.P., 1971), 198.

7 The Bill of Rights provided that 'levying money for or to the use of the Crown by pretence of prerogative, without grant of Parliament, for longer time, or in other manner than the same is or shall be granted, is illegal'.

It was to that tradition that, one century later, the American colonies referred when they contested stamp taxes and other measures. The absence of representatives from those Colonies in the English Parliament implied a lack of control over the distant and powerful government, which was regarded as arbitrary and fearsome. As James Otis wrote,'the British colonists ... are, by Magna Charta, as well entitled to have a voice in their taxes, as the subjects within the realm'[8] *He was thus associated* with the phrase 'taxation without representation is tyranny', which appeared for the first time a few years later.

The necessity of some consent to taxation was by no means unknown in the rest of Europe. Limits to taxation already existed, in particular, in France. In *L'ancien régime et la Révolution* Tocqueville emphasised that the aristocracy always insisted that no tax bill or edict could be approved without the consent of the '*états-généraux*'.[9] This was a medieval institution including representatives of the clergy, the nobility, and the third estate. When the *ancien régime* was close to financial collapse, a broad reform of taxation was proposed by the King's Minister of Finances, Calonne, in 1787.[10] A natural, though perhaps not inevitable, measure was thus to apply a tradition that had gradually faded during the rise of the absolutist State. But the King's attempt to focus solely on taxes, in order to avoid the issue of representation, failed completely. A few years later, Article 14 of the Declaration of 1789 affirmed that all citizens had the right to express, either directly or through their representatives, their consent to taxation and to check the use of public resources.[11] In sum, the association of representation and taxation lies at the roots of European Constitutionalism, ancient and modern.

8 J Otis, *Rights of British Colonies Asserted (Boston, Almon, 1764).*

9 Tocqueville, *L'ancien régime et la Révolution* (1856; edited by JP Mayer, Paris, Gallimard, 1967), 364.

10 VR Gruder, '"No Taxation Without Representation": The Assembly of Notables of 1787 and Political Ideology in France', (1982) 7 *Legislative Studies Quarterly* 263.

11 See E Garcia de Enterria, *La lengua de los derechos* (Madrid, Civitas, 1994), 179 (examining the Napoleonic Constitution of the Year VIII).

B. A Common Constitutional Tradition

In the nineteenth century, sooner or later the monarchs were forced to cede some of their authority to representative institutions. Parliamentary consent to taxation was affirmed, for example, by the Belgian Constitution (1831). The constitution of the Kingdom of Sardinia did the same and recognised the primacy of the lower house.[12] The necessity of parliamentary consent was more controversial in Prussia in the years 1862-66, but even Paul Laband and his school recognised that an (*ex post*) act of consent was needed.[13]

Two aspects of this development are particularly important for our purposes. First, the association of taxation with representation became a sort of commonplace in a century in which a form of 'rate-payer democracy' emerged in the whole of Europe. It was, more precisely, a common constitutional tradition. Second, the existence of such a common tradition did not depend on hierarchy or domination. It depended, rather, on the fact that a specific value was shared by European peoples.

During the twentieth century, despite the gradual replacement of the 'rate-payer democracy' in the context of the widening of electoral rights, the necessity of parliamentary consent to taxation has been preserved. Not only the constitutions of France, Germany and Italy, but also those of other founders of the EC have kept this principle. Consider, for example, Article 104 of the Dutch Constitution, according to which 'Taxes imposed by the State shall be levied pursuant to Act of Parliament'. Consider also the provisions established by members of the Community, such as Greece, Spain and Portugal.[14] Consider, finally, the new constitutions enacted after 1989, such as that of Poland.[15] It is precisely because of the existence of this common constitutional tradition that it is important to see whether and

12 V Onida, 'The Historical and Constitutional Foundations of the Budgetary System in Italy', in D Coombes (ed), *The Power of the Purse* (1971), 215.

13 For a critique, see R Gneist, *Gesetz und Budget* (1879) (n 1), § IV.B.1.

14 See Article 78.1 of the Greek Constitution ('No tax shall be levied without a statute enacted by Parliament') and Article 103.2 of the Portuguese Constitution ('Taxes shall be created by laws').

15 See Articles 84 ('Everyone shall comply with his responsibilities and public duties, including the payment of taxes, as specified by statute') and 273 ('the imposition of taxes, as well as other public imposts, ..., shall be by means of statute').

to what extent this is not only a tradition shared by the Member States of the EU but also one that is relevant for the latter.[16]

II. The Finances of the EU: A Politically Incorrect View

A. A Limited Budget?

For our purposes, there is no need to consider in detail the vexed question of whether the Union's resources, and more specifically those included in its general budget, are too limited to sustain the joint (i.e. together with its Member States) promotion of articulated policies.

A recurring critique —dating back to the MacDougall Report (1977)— is precisely that the size of the finances of the EU is too limited. It is small if compared with those of the Member States, as well as with the finances of existing federations. It follows from this that a necessary condition for economic and political integration is that the current amount of the budget, equivalent to something less than 1 per cent of the Union's gross domestic product, should be raised significantly.

Whatever the intellectual soundness and political expediency of this respectable opinion, from a legal point of view at least three elements should not be neglected. First, the Union's financial activities have grown, though they are still far from those of existing federations, and permit its institutions to spend significant amounts of public money.[17] Secondly, those amounts of money allow a direct financing of some actions and policies carried out by the EU, some of which have —at least potentially— redistributive effects, especially between the richer and poorer regions of Europe, through the Structural Funds and the Cohesion Fund.[18] Thirdly, by virtue of the principle of additionality, the financial resources of which the Union disposes are very often managed together with those made avail-

16 My argument is about Europe, without any claim to universality. In this respect, see ML Ross, 'Does Taxation Lead to Representation?' (2004) 34 *Brit. J. Pol. Sc.* 229 (arguing that 'most research on contemporary democratization says little or nothing about the effects of taxation').

17 According to the Commission, in 2013 the size of the EU budget was approx 6,400 bn Euros, about 1% of the Union's gross national product, smaller than that of Austria or Belgium: http://ec.europa.eu/budget/explained/myths/myths_en.cfm.

18 For further remarks, see CJ Carrubba, 'Net Financial Transfers in the European Union: Who Gets What and Why?' (1997) 59 *Journal of Politics* 469.

able by its Member States. The relevance of the finances of the EU is, therefore, higher than current figures would seem to suggest.

It ought to be made clear that this argument differs from that concerning the capacity of EU institutions to influence national budgetary policies in the context of the EMU: whether the current union of fiscal discipline can be turned into a fiscal union[19] is another question. What my argument is about is not the size of the Union's budget but the connection between revenue and expenditure, more specifically between taxation and capital investment.

B. Ambiguity of the 'Own Resources'

An aspect which is more directly connected to my main argument is that, when considering the legal order of the EU from the perspective of the connection between taxation and representation, a certain ambiguity emerges. It concerns both the concept of 'own resources' and the role of the European Parliament.

Ambiguity is, first of all, a feature of the political decisions taken with regard to the resources of the EU. Of particular importance here is the difference between the current treaties and the first one, the Treaty of Paris establishing the Coal and Steel Community (1952). At the heart of that institutional framework there was the High Authority. It was entrusted with wide powers of regulation and adjudication. It was also entrusted with the power 'to procure the funds necessary to the accomplishment of its mission'. The powers enjoyed by the High Authority were of two kinds: first, the placing of levies on the production of coal and steel and, second, borrowing.[20]

Even a quick look at the current treaties reveals that the situation is quite different from that which was originally envisaged in the context of the ECSC. There is, first, an explicit prohibition of borrowing, because annual expenditure must be completely covered by annual revenue. As a result, there is no room for the Union to run up a deficit in the way that national governments do, apart from the loans granted by the European In-

19 See C Joerges, 'Europas Wirtschaftverfassung in der Krisis', (2012) 51 *Der Staat*, 357,.

20 See Article 49 ECSC. The provision that followed, Article 50, indicated the expenses that those resources were intended to cover.

vestment Bank (EIB) and, more recently, by the European Stability Mechanism (ESM).

Secondly, the Union's revenue differs from that of federal systems of government. Initially, Community financial activities were based on national contributions and direct revenue-raising was postponed. This feature was changed at the beginning of the 1970's, when the system of 'own resources' was introduced. The main pillars of this system are: i) custom duties on imports from outside the EU and sugar levies; ii) a uniform rate of 0.3 per cent of value added tax, and iii) an additional transfer based on gross national income, the largest source of revenue.[21] However, a further specification is needed. Although duties and levies are exacted by national authorities, they are regulated by EU norms in a way that leaves no discretionary powers to them. The VAT element of the current own resources is, instead, a national rather than an EU tax.[22] National governments may, accordingly, take different decisions with regard to the VAT charged and the goods affected by it. In sum, although the own resources of EU institutions obviously differ from the contributions made by national governments, some of them can be varied by the latter and even the others are not exacted by the former. This implies, according to some observers, that the finances of the EU still 'derive' from the finances of its Member States.[23]

C. The European Parliament: A Spending Authority

Ambiguity is also a feature of the role played by the European Parliament (EP). Its members, it is punctually observed, can cast a vote on the candidates for the Commission and censure its conduct. They can enact legislation in a wide range of policy areas, including —in addition to agricultural policy— a cohesion policy, with financial transfers. They can also amend most lines in the general budget proposed by the Commission, including compulsory expenditure. The Council, therefore, is no longer the sole budgetary authority.

21 Other revenue includes deductions from EU staff salaries and interests on fines.

22 H Wallace, Budgetary Politics. The Finances of the European Communities (London, Allen & Unwin, 1980), 57.

23 See JP Jacqué, *Droit institutionnel de l'Union européenne* (Paris, Dalloz, 2013), 211.

However, even after the disputes of the 1980's and the constitutional amendments of the last few decades, the EP does not take decisions concerning both sides of the budget, that is to say revenue and expenditure. The same provision of the TFEU (Article 311), according to which 'the Union shall pursue its objectives by appropriate means commensurate with the competences which are conferred upon it in the Treaties', provides that the Council alone should decide about existing and new revenue and the decision must be unanimous. The EP must only be consulted. Moreover, the Member States must approve every new decision on revenue and in most cases such decision must be ratified by national parliaments. This is explicitly recognised by the 2014 new own resources decision, which is founded on the premise that the decision 'should enter into force only once it has been approved by all Member States in accordance with their respective constitutional requirements, thus fully respecting national sovereignty'[24] In sum, the European Parliament does not have a voice on which revenue should go to the Union.[25]

Nothing in what I have just said should be seen as aiming to deny or diminish the importance of the role that the EP can play. However, unlike national parliaments, it does not take decisions concerning both sides of the budget, that is to say revenue and expenditure. It is, therefore, a spending authority[26] and, consequently, it is not based on the same kind of association between taxation and representation that was identified earlier as a main pillar of Western constitutionalism.

D. *Rights Dissociated from Duties*

Some consequences of the conclusion just reached ought to be mentioned. We may, first, ask ourselves what is the real meaning of the provision laid down by Article 3.6 TEU, as well as by Article 311 TFEU, according to which 'The Union shall pursue its objectives by appropriate means com-

24 Council Decision 2014/335/EU, Euratom of 26 May 2014 on the system of own resources of the European Union (not yet entered into force), point 2 in Preamble.

25 H Wallace, *Budgetary Politics* (1980), 56 (pointing out the French influence).

26 See JHH Weiler (n 3) 266 (for the remark that, while the formal powers of the EP have increased, there has been a decreasing popular participation in its elections). See also his remarks about the widespread underestimation of the absence of a truly European party system (268).

mensurate with the competences which are conferred upon it in the Treaties', a point I will return to later.

More importantly, we may ask ourselves whether, without the type of legitimacy which derives from taxation, the EU is inevitably induced to put an excessive emphasis on rights, as separate from duties. It is not just a matter of symbols, which have a certain importance in the public sphere; it is a matter of balance between rights and duties. The Union has not simply one bill of rights, but several. Retrospectively, the ECHR was the first bill of rights for the Community, though the reception of its norms was more similar to the reception of Roman law in modern Europe than the formal methods envisaged by legal positivism.[27] National constitutions, as noted earlier, were regarded as being another source of rights which the Court had to ensure were respected. Finally, the Charter of Fundamental Rights of the EU has been 'solemnly' adopted and, after Lisbon, has been given the same legal value as the treaties.

There is no doubt that the rights provided by the Charter can make the EU more attractive to its citizens. However, not only does it not strengthen their empowerment[28], but it also accentuates the dissociation —which in modern Western societies has a plurality of causes— between rights and duties. What emerges is, thus, a vision of the political community in which the EU recognises or grants a variety of rights, which individuals can exercise without being called to assume any basic duty: neither that to 'defend' the Union, nor that to pay any sort of tax established by the EP.

III. Prolegomena for a 'Just' European Taxation

While the two main arguments set out in Parts II and III are essentially normative, to the extent that they have defined a standard for assessing the mechanism adopted in any system of government (in the tradition of Western constitutionalism) to handle public finance, with specific regard to revenue, and have applied it to the current system of government of the EU, respectively, Part III follows a different approach. It argues that a neces-

27 Modern studies have argued that a reception does not mean only a reception of norms, that is, the transfer of a legal norm or a body of norms, but also of method, because legal doctrines and theories play an important role.

28 See JHH Weiler (n 3) 333 (criticising the 'bread-and-circus vision' that Maastricht offered).

sary condition for European integration to occur is a significant change in the Union's budget, one in which financial resources are not only collected by its institutions (with the simple intermediation of national authorities as executive agencies of the EU) but are also decided by the EP and which enables such resources to be mobilised and used in order to enable specific choices about expenditure and, in this manner, the promotion of a policy that provides a specific kind of common good, capital investment in infrastructure. The argument can be divided into three steps: why a European tax is needed, who should pay for it, and why it should cover capital investment in infrastructure.

A. A European Tax

As a first step, the question that arises is whether a European tax is needed. Three arguments, distinct but related, should be considered.

There is, first, the conclusion reached earlier at the end of a retrospective analysis. '*No taxation without representation*' is not simply one of the common constitutional conventions to which Article 6 TEU refers and that are included amongst the general principles of Union law. The association between representation and taxation that is expressed by this maxim lies at the roots of the systems of government that are based on the values common to liberal democracies, especially those that are members of the EU. Some kind of association between representation and taxation should, therefore, characterise the Union itself. A European tax, whatever its object and amount, would strengthen the legitimacy that it receives from the social component of the Union, to which the Court of Justice referred in its landmark decision in *Van Gend en Loos*.[29]

Secondly, I am fully aware that the introduction of a European tax requires a very important and controversial amendment of existing treaties. However, it should not be overlooked that the treaties have already been changed in at least two related aspects, the direct election of the EP and more recently the financial support to countries facing difficulties. They

29 ECJ, Case 26/62, *Van Gend en Loos v Nederlandse Administratie der Belastingen* [1963] ECR 1, § B (holding that 'the preamble to the treaty refers not only to governments but to peoples.... The nationals of the states brought together in the community are called to cooperate ... through the intermediary of the European Parliament').

could, therefore, be changed again, if the necessary political consent is found.

Thirdly, in my view, this change does not necessarily imply a significant quantitative increase of the Union's finances. It implies, rather, a qualitative change in both revenue and expenditure. The implication is that there would not be a further direct commitment to shift financial responsibility for public finance from the national level to the Union level. In other words, neither the traditional philosophy, according to which only a limited EU budget is justified to support specific policy objectives, nor the recent refusal of national policy-makers to increase the size of the budget (in reality, for the first time, it was reduced), would be contradicted.

This argument has a further implication, which is worth mentioning. It concerns a limitation upon European integration which derives from national constitutions and which has been referred to by the German Constitutional Court in its recent rulings. The limitation I am referring to is that national budgets should be limited to an extent that is compatible with the fulfilment of those national policies that are necessary to implement the goals set by the national Constitution.[30] In other and more concise words, national governments need flexibility to deal with their own problems, which are partly different. If the size of the Union's budget does not change, then flexibility is neither eliminated nor undermined.[31] Whether a European levy is intrinsically compatible with national constitutions is another question, and one that some constitutional courts have already resolved, for example, the Italian Constitutional Court in *Frontini.*[32]

B. *Who Should Pay?*

If a European tax is likely to bring about the association between representation and taxation that is lacking in the current system of government of the EU, the question that arises is: who should pay for it?

---

30 See the German Constitutional Court's ruling of 14 January 2014, 2 BvR 2728/13, available (in English) at https://www.bundesverfassungsgericht.de/SharedDocs/Entscheidungen/EN/2014/01/rs20140114_2bvr272813en.html..

31 It might be eliminated or undermined by other measures, such as the Fiscal Compact, but this is another question, which exceeds the scope of this paper.

32 Italian Constitutional Court, Case n. 183/1973, available (in Italian) at http://www.giurcost.org/decisioni/1973/0183s-73.html.

Without going into the details of all the areas of discussion between lawyers and economists, three main points emerge. First, the distinction between direct and indirect taxation is clear in principle but can be less clear in the real world. The traditional administrative distinction between personal taxes and excise taxes, or tariffs, is not necessarily sound from an economic point of view.[33] For our purposes, it suffices to draw a distinction between two typical examples: on the one hand, a direct tax in the form of an income tax (or the equivalent) imposed on individuals and corporations, or a capital gains tax; on the other hand, a sales tax with varying rates for different goods and services. Even with this unsophisticated distinction in mind, it is easy to understand that the proposals made thus far include both kinds of taxation. As a matter of fact, such proposals include, among other things, an EU corporate income tax, excise duties on tobacco and alcohol, a tax on financial transactions, and a climate charge on aviation.

The question that thus arises is: which criterion or set of criteria should be used to make a selection from among these possible EU taxes? In this respect, according to a strand of thought that has gained currency in academic and political circles, the principle of equity should be considered. The principle of equity is deeply embedded in the contributions made by lawyers, political scientists and economists to the study of public finance. In this specific respect, it has a twofold meaning. On the one hand, it implies that EU revenue should be generated from economic activities appropriate to the sector to which they will be redeployed.[34] The line of reasoning proposed here has much in common with this opinion, since it focuses on capital investment for improving the Single Market and enhancing the quality of public utilities throughout the Union's territory. On the other hand, the principle of equity can be regarded as implying that not only individuals should pay for European integration, but also the other subjects who benefit from it, that is to say corporations, especially those which take advantage of the arbitrage between the different national fiscal systems.

Especially after the spread of the recent economic and financial crisis, several observers have called for a European tax on capital gains, seen as a measure that is necessary to make the financial sector pay a 'fair share'

33 See U Hicks, 'The Terminology of Tax Analysis' (1946) 56 *Economic Journal* 38.
34 H Wallace, *Budgetary Politics* (n 21), 55.

and thus to restore the confidence of the public, undermined by the recent excesses of market capitalism. The European Commission elaborated and presented a proposal of this kind in 2012, under which all transactions between financial institutions (banks and hedge funds, of course, but also insurance companies and pension funds) would be affected by an EU tax. Whatever its political expediency, which is still controversial, this proposal is important both symbolically and because of its economic repercussions. But it differs from the measures considered here, for the very simple reason that it has been presented as an enhanced form of co-operation. As a result, it applies only to some countries, not to all. It can, therefore, be regarded as an additional —though substantially very important— element, rather than as an exclusive one in a strategy that attempts to combine representation through the EP with taxation.

C. A Pro-Investment Tax

As a third, and by no means less important, part of my argument, the connection between revenue and expenditure must be considered. In short, the argument is that, if a European tax is introduced, its revenue should be assigned to a specific kind of public expenditure, that which is related to capital investment in physical infrastructures for the delivery of essential public utilities. In other words, as a partial exception to the principle of budgetary unity, specific receipts would be assigned to a specific type of expenditure, which of course requires a definition of the relevant concept of capital investment and the introduction of a specific section in the EU budget.

This part of my argument is based on three elements: i) capital investment in infrastructure is strongly related to the strategy of European integration envisaged by its founding document, the Schuman plan, and is considered —though inadequately— by the current treaties; ii) unlike redistributive policies, this policy is likely to eschew national rulers' objections based exclusively on their 'gains'; iii) last but not least, it has an important dimension in terms of equity between generations.

That the strategy of European integration envisaged by the Schuman plan was based on the use of economic integration in order to achieve political goals —peace and prosperity— and on spill-over mechanism, is too well known to require here more than a brief mention. It ought to be added that such instrumental use of economic integration endorsed the basic principle of the ordo-liberal theory,[35] that is to say a free and competitive economy, where interventionist policies —or *dirigisme*— are justified only in limited cases, such as coal or agriculture. That the same applies to investment in physical infrastructure has been demonstrated by a long tradition of thought, one of the champions of which is Adam Smith of the *Wealth of Nations*.

Though emphasising the virtues of markets, Smith did not neglect the role of the State. He identified three kinds of activities that could be regarded as being inherently public functions, namely, defence and public order, the administration of justice, and public works.[36] Smith focused, in particular, on works such as the construction of bridges and roads. Interestingly, he distinguished between those public works which were necessary either for the defence of society or for the administration of justice, that is to say, the first two categories of public functions, and the other works that were necessary, 'chiefly those for facilitating the commerce of the society, and those for promoting the instruction of the people'.[37] He acknowledged that, as a matter of principle, these works could be, and sometimes in fact were, carried out by private firms. However, he observed that it was, as it still is, often difficult for them to obtain an adequate profit.[38]

The *noyeau dur* of this theory has been contested neither by John Maynard Keynes, who in the 1930's proposed a different theoretical and operational framework for economic policies, nor by his critics who either adhere to the school of public choice or follow Milton Friedman's approach. In contrast with the argument that compulsory taxation is a morally impermissible form of theft, another Nobel prizewinner whose libertarian credentials are beyond any shadow of doubt, Friedrich von Hayek, has convincingly pointed out that when the invisible hand does not provide essential public goods, the State's coercive power to tax may be used to provide them. This is precisely the case with 'public goods' such as network infrastructures.

---

35 See W Ropke, *Against the Tide* (transl. E. Henderson, Chicago, Regnery, 1969).

36 A Smith, An Inqury into the Nature and Causes of the Wealth of Nations (1789, 5th edn), book IV, chapter IX.

37 Ibid, book V, chapter I, third part.

38 For further remarks, see G della Cananea, 'Government Deficits and Investment: A European Framework' (2013) 5 *Italian Journal of Public Law*, 103.

A further demonstration of this can be found in several national constitutions, which —for a variety of reasons— regulate certain kinds of infrastructures, such as ports and railways. It can be found in EU law, too.

Interestingly, the current treaties provide for a European policy of transnational infrastructures. Article 170 TFEU, in particular, makes three main choices. First, it reiterates the traditional philosophy of providing prosperity, by enabling citizens and economic operators to 'derive full benefit from the setting-up of an area without internal frontiers'. Second, it also refers to the Community's traditional favour for 'open and competitive markets' (Article 170, § 2). Thirdly, it specificies that the transnational networks to the establishment of which the 'Union shall contribute' are those in the 'areas of transport, telecommunications and energy infrastructures'. What my argument comes down to is that the EU is already entrusted with the task of promoting such transnational networks, and a determination to use a fully autonomous source of revenue could be used by the EP for this purpose.

This has important consequences for the other two parts of my argument. It is relevant for, unlike redistributive policies such as agriculture, this policy is meant to serve another of the three functions that —after Richard Musgrave— economic theories assign to public finance: that of resource allocation, in order to ensure that resources are used efficiently.[39] The consequence of this can be appreciated from the traditional viewpoint —a further action or policy of the EU is likely to be accepted when all Member States would derive from it sufficient benefit to outweigh the costs.[40] Especially certain transnational networks, such as those for transport, electronic communications and energy, are likely to provide such benefits for all and can thus justify capital investment by the institutions of the EU. This provision of public goods, however, does not prevent each country from individually adding extra expenditure, which may be positively assessed by the institutions of the EU when enforcing the rules of the EMU. These rules treat national deficit differently with regard to the part of the deficit that covers capital investment, on the underlying assumption that, unlike other expenditure, it has the capacity to expand in-

39 R Musgrave, *The Theory of Public Finance* (New York, MacGraw-Hill,1956). His other two branches are that of stabilisation, which aims at ensuring the achievement of high employment and price stability, and the distribution branch, which aims at achieving an equitable distribution of income.

40 H Wallace, *Budgetary Politics* (n 21), 25.

come, not only distributive effects. This runs contrary to the widespread concern that new EU measures would constitute a blow to European competitiveness, which would instead be reinforced.

This brings us to the last part of my argument, that which concerns the effects of capital investment from the point of view of equity between generations. Traditional theories of public finance have convincingly held that, as in business finance, capital investment justifies borrowing, but our concern here is taxation. In this respect, there are good reasons to argue that, if the EU system of government incurs expenses, the benefits of which are spread over a future period (say, ten or fifteen years), it is unfair to ask only the present generation to sustain the whole cost. A European tax of the type suggested here should therefore be regarded as multi-annual or permanent, as distinct from extraordinary measures introduced for a limited time.

Finally, it is important to clarify that my argument is related to, though distinct from, the argument that the European debt crisis has showed that the EMU cannot work without fiscal union. It is related because it argues that a European tax is necessary. It is distinct, however, because my argument is that such tax is long overdue and must be used for the purposes set since Maastricht, particularly for infrastructure, without implying any transfer of either funds or debts from one country to another. Whether a fiscal union requires an EU finance minister, and what kind of democratic oversight is appropriate, is still another question and one that cannot be adequately dealt with here.

Conclusions

This paper set out to examine the likely impact of an 'old' principle of European constitutionalism, that which is expressed by the maxim '*no taxation without representation*', on the current system of government of the EU. It found that such a principle is not merely a vestige of the past but, rather, a common constitutional convention and precisely for this reason it is relevant for EU law.

However, when considering the finances of the Union, it became evident that not only are these still largely derived from the finances of its Member States, but that the decisions about revenue are in the hands of the Member States, not in those of the EP, which is just a spending authority. In this sense and within these limits, there is evidence that the EU is not based on the association of representation with taxation, which we can find in national constitutions. Indeed, there is representation without taxation, which is problematic *per se*. Moreover, it has a negative influence on a culture of rights, as dissociated from (fiscal) duties.

In order to deal with this problem and its negative repercussions, of course, several strategies can be explored and followed. The strategy considered here, whose main task is to ensure a certain degree of association between representation and taxation whilst at the same time using such revenue for delivering 'public goods' to Europeans, consists essentially in introducing a European tax and in assigning its receipts to a specific type of expenditure: capital investment for the physical infrastructure connected with transnational networks. It is helpful to repeat that this is not a proposal, let alone a detailed proposal. It is, rather, one of the possible consequences of the normative line of reasoning developed earlier, the validity of which is not affected by the weaknesses of the inferences enounced here.

4 People and Peoples in EU Law
To Debunk the No-Demos Myth

Tom Eijsbouts

Abstract

This paper debunks popular myths in legal and constitutional doctrine about the impossible relationship between the EU and its Europeans, notably the 'no-*demos'* thesis. And it offers a better reading of the obvious democratic flaws of the EU, a reading in which these flaws are reparable. Notions of 'the people' in (constitutional) law are essentially varied, as they are in common parlance and as 'the people' manifests itself (and manifest *themselves!*) in reality. In law the variety is less wide, but attempts to give a singular The People a last word in search of legitimacy for national politics and/or the Union, will necessarily miss the mark. In referendums, including the one called by the Tsipras government, there is such an attempt to invoke The People's ultimate authority. Legal analysis may help to understand why this fails.

This paper argues for a better understanding of the notions (plural) of 'people', 'peoples' etc. in EU law. Under a close reading, the EU Treaties, like other legal texts, prove to use a variety of notions of 'people'. They distinguish between a) peoples in the *social and historical* or 'traditional' sense, belonging to the *countries* and to *Europe,* and b) peoples in the *constitutional* sense, the citizens, the voters, belonging not to the countries of Europe but to the *Member States* of the EU, viz. to the EU. The *'ever closer union between the peoples of Europe'* typically employs a 'traditional', not a constitutional notion of 'people'. These peoples are not limited to the EU's inhabitants but have included from the start, for example, the Swiss. And these Swiss, one of the 'peoples of Europe', are distinct from the constitutional entity of the citizens of the Swiss Confederation, the state.

As an afterthought, even after an eventual 'Brexit', the ever closer union between the peoples of Europe will continue to include the British peoples (the English, the Welsh, the Scots, the Irish). And, of course, Brexit should be called UKexit. Because it is not Britain that will be exiting Europe but only the UK.

The 'peoples of the Member States', as used formerly in the Treaties, refers to the constitutional people, or 'nation', in each member state. In these Member States themselves, even in the constitutional sense, the notion of 'people' again takes on two distinct meanings: that of the *'original'* people, the founder of the constitution, and that of the *'electoral'* people, which functions inside the constitution, e.g. as the electorate.

There is a painful and almost fateful failure of the *Bundesverfassungsgericht* and its epigonist scholarship to acknowledge the necessary distinction between these different sorts of 'people', even in the federal Basic Law. This amounts to a misleading conflation, playing into the hands of populist thinking.

Introduction

In order to obtain a PhD degree in Law at Leiden University, the young doctor Armin Cuyvers recently defended his thesis that the European Union is an organisation composed not of sovereign Member States but of 'sovereign member *peoples*'. Thus he claimed to solve the problems of the Union's democracy in theory, and to create a perspective for solving them in fact. All on the basis of the EU Member States' popular sovereignties, as recognised from the EU's foundation, as the author sees it:

> As a result, the concept of a 'member people' as used in this thesis refers to those same people [sic] that have been hailed and recognised since the Treaty of Rome, and elevates these entities to the place promised to them by (almost) every treaty since.[1]

---

1 A Cuyvers, *The EU as a Confederal Union of Sovereign Member Peoples* (Leiden, 12 Dec. 2013, PhD). The thesis' point of departure is to be found on p. 44. In note 59 underpinning this passage: 'The preamble of the Rome treaty already spoke of "an ever-closer union among the peoples of Europe". Even more interestingly, the second paragraph of the preamble refers to the Member States as "their countries", i.e. the countries of the member peoples, whereas Art. 137 EEC held that the Assembly would "consist of representatives of the peoples of the States brought together in the Community (…)." The preamble of the Single European Act talks of "the democratic peoples of Europe", and that of the Maastricht Treaty on European Union of deepening "the solidarity between their peoples while respecting their history, their culture and their traditions" as well as repeating the desire to "continue the process of creating an ever closer union among the peoples of Europe." Amsterdam also consistently speaks of the "peoples" in the European Union. Nice does not mention the people at all. Even the Constitutional Treaty, perhaps the most unifying

There is an unmistakeable appeal to this idea. Indeed, if the Member States' *peoples* can be seen to have concluded the Union Treaties and if these peoples formally are also at the base of the Union's government, the problem of democracy all but disappears in theory. And it can be expected to disappear in fact upon the restoration of these Member States' peoples to actual full authority.

At first, I thought this thesis fitted in quite well with an old tradition of daring and original research in the form of a thinking experiment. But subsequent developments made me look at the matter afresh and, together with my appreciation, I felt a dose of suspicion as well.

The first eye-opener was the fact that in the Netherlands alone around the same time two other doctoral theses in law defended roughly the same theory and ideas.[2] And the fact that all three of them acknowledged their debt to the *Lissabon-Urteil* of the *Bundesverfassungsgericht*. So there appeared to be an element of epigonism. Epigonism is the tendency for a pupil to follow a master with a true belief, dropping the latter's reserve and context and topping the master's claim with a disciple's fervour.

The second reason for a better look was a remark by José Torreblanca, a Spanish member of the EU Council on Foreign Relations. Torreblanca had noted that most of the extremist populist political parties across Europe now hold that the Union is really composed of, or belongs to, the Member States' *peoples*. 'What also connects [these populist movements] is the idea of a Europe of the peoples. For them there is no European Union but one which is a confederation of European peoples.'[3]

I am not sure how to account for the fact that these quite similar ideas have sprung up at the same time in both scholarship and political programmes. Do the political parties pick their ideas from scholarship? Do the ideas express a mood change across the continent to which the aca-

in its aims and understanding of the EU (see for instance Art. 1 speaking of "the will of the citizens and States of Europe"), retains its basis in multiple peoples. Its preamble, for instance, still speaks of "the peoples of Europe"'. See for instance Art. I-3 or III-280.

2 J W van Rossem, Soevereiniteit en Pluralisme (Groningen, 2014, PhD thesis); M Duchateau, Het Europees Parlement als transnationale volksvertegenwoordiging (Groningen, 2014, PhD thesis).

3 I take the cue from an article in the Dutch daily *De Volkskrant* (issue of 2 February 2015) in which Torreblanca is quoted. So far I have not received from the author an answer to my request for a personal confirmation of this quote, nor an empirical underpinning. So I can only bank on its plausibility.

demic theories also hearken? As a confirmation of this possibility came the fact that several fellow academics had not only given the *EU of peoples-theory* a favourable reception, but had found them stimulating if not even downright plausible, even upon second and further thought.

My own initial appreciation of the above Leiden PhD thesis was tempered by the idea that we may be dealing with a new source of delusion about the Union and its democratic foundation, and that this might prove even more contagiously deceptive than the old and quite successfully delusive *'no demos'* thesis about the EU. It deserved to be seriously taken to task, and on the basis of EU law. Hence the following exercise.

I. Method

We lawyers are extremely good at dissecting, analysing, dichotomising etcetera, etcetera. We are less good at using or understanding the complementary part of intelligence: its *binding, or synthetic* power. Why is this so? Most simply, because in legal thinking, the law's *binding force, its power of synthesis* is a given. Self-understood, the law's binding is not appreciated, not reflected on, not problematised.[4] We even forget that its plenitude in law is a part of the deal that the full binding force is only aspectual, only legal. Outside of the law, a contract or other obligation has *no* fully compelling force upon the whole relationship of which it is a part.

When we lawyers venture into the *synthetic* or *binding* aspects of full reality, wider than the legal reality, we are easily deceived. This happens when we discuss notions such as '*demos*' or 'people', which claim to denote a force not of *legal* but of *social* and/or *historical* unity. Understanding their binding force to be full and unconditional, as we do the binding force of a legal notion, we may conceptualise and idealise such notions far above their binding capacity and coherence in common sense and reality. There is no legally binding force behind the people and no conceptual singularity flowing from this.

Fortunately, against such essentialising even by lawyers, the very powers of legal analysis itself can be levelled with full force. This is what I

4 'Intelligence, from *legere* (to read, split, distinguish) and *inter-*, denoting *connection, relation*. Most acts of facts of intelligence can be thus understood. In the law, the aspect of *legere* is developed and cultivated much more fully than the aspect of *inter-*.

shall attempt here. Legal distinguishing will be used *against* essentialising notions of the *people*, the *demos* etcetera, to show that there is no singular notion of People or Volk etc. to be found in systems of positive constitutional law, even those proceeding from popular sovereignty, and that doctrinal or theoretical references to such singularity and essentialism ought to be considered with great suspicion.

The present paper is concerned primarily, modestly, with the notions of people, peoples etc. in the EU Treaties, with a side look at the notion of Volk in the Basic Law of the Federal German Republic. It is meant to show that among these notions there is always an essential plurality: that no singular notion can possibly be found in these Treaties as an expression of some normative singularity of national people underlying EU law. And no singular notion of people should be sought in domestic constitutional law.

II. Traditional and Constitutional Peoples; Original and Electoral Ones

In legal texts we usually find two distinct basic concepts of the 'people'. One of these is that of the *'traditional'* people or the people of a *country* or a *land*. A country is *not* a political entity and its people are not a legally consolidated group. It is a non-political community of inhabitants. The other basic concept is that of The People, or the peoples of a state or other public authority, which has constitutional status, both legal and political.

Between these basic concepts there may be overlaps, but there will always be differences, in number as well as nature. Most simply: the Dutch as a people of their *country* will support their football team in the World Cup, under an orange flag. The Dutch as a *People* (capital P) will vote for the national parliament and be represented by this as a whole, under the constitution and under the state banner of red, white and blue.

The *traditional* Dutch people, the football supporters and other versions featuring in cartoons, with wooden clogs etc., have an endless variety. Apart from a type of people clad in wooden clogs, this 'traditional' people may also be portrayed as a people which has conquered lands over the sea, as the tallest people in the world, but also as a people that displayed cowardice in WW II or a mass of hooligans after a football match. The *traditional* people have had an endless variety of manifestations over time, ranging from a quiet and solid community to a teeming rabble, the populace, in times of sedition.

The *political* or *constitutional* Dutch People consist, constitutionally, of the entity of people represented by the Dutch bicameral parliament, the States General, *as a whole*. It has a much greater constancy and sensibility than the *traditional* people, as it is formalised and checked by legal rules.

To conflate the *traditional* people with the *political* people, in order to mobilise the former and its emotional instability directly behind politics, is a mark of fascist totalitarianism, of which Hitler gave clear examples. In a weaker form it is the mark of populism.

Constitutional legal systems in which The People or Das Volk is central as a legal notion, that is to say, constitutions with popular sovereignty, use a *duality*. On the one hand they have the constituent, pre-constitutional People, the founder of the Constitution. Let us call this people the *Original People*. On the other hand, there is the People which votes and is really an institution of the state: the *Electoral People*. These units are not the same. The first is usually represented (in the sense of protected) by the constitutional court; the second by the parliament and government. In the Netherlands, incidentally, there is no such duality, as there is no founding or original People. The constitutional people in the Netherlands has only one persona, that of the electoral People.

III. Peoples, Citizens etc. in the EU Treaties

The above distinctions are useful in helping us to understand references in the EU-Treaties to the notions of people. These Treaties have used these different concepts of people from the start, intending the involvement of not just governments but also people. Let us give the Treaties' provisions a close reading. First of all, the preamble to the 1951 Coal and Steel Treaty read:

> (...) Resolved to substitute for age-old rivalries the merging of their [states'] essential interests; to create, by establishing an economic community, the basis for a broader and deeper community among peoples long divided by bloody conflicts; (...)

What 'peoples' were meant, or what was intended by this reference to 'peoples'? Was *das Deutsche Volk* or *la nation française* among them? In other words, did the treaties refer to the 'Staatsvölker' of the Member States? I do not think so, but it is not fully certain. Fortunately, the preamble to the 1957 EEC Treaty was more articulate about the peoples. It started off by proudly declaring:

> (...) Determined to lay the foundations of an ever closer union among the peoples *of Europe*[5]

and it concluded:

> (...) Resolved by thus pooling their resources to preserve and strengthen peace and liberty, and calling upon the other peoples of Europe who share in their ideal, to join in their efforts.

The 'peoples of Europe' intended here were certainly not the Peoples (*Staatsvölker*) of the Member States. *Europe* itself, as an entity and distinct from the EU, falls in the *country* category, not in that of a public authority. Its *peoples* are not in that of a *state or* other public authority, but are 'traditional' peoples. The peoples of Europe are in the category of the peoples of *countries*, including the Swiss in Switzerland.

The famous phrase *'ever closer union among the peoples of Europe'* is directed not at the voters of the Community Member States, but at the inhabitants of the future and the wider Europe. It *must* have included from the start *the Swiss people or peoples.* And all the others: Romanians, Bulgarians, Greeks, Serbs etc.

The preamble to the 1992 EU Treaty is even more articulate. Its fifth recital reads: '(...) Desiring to deepen the solidarity between their [the heads of states'] peoples, while respecting their history, their culture and their traditions'.

Is this a reference to the Staatsvölker? I do not think so, in view of the 'history, culture and traditions'. The twelfth recital of the Union Treaty amplifies on the old 'ever closer union among the peoples of Europe (...)'. This recurs in Article 1, second paragraph: 'This Treaty marks a new stage in the process of creating an ever closer union among *the peoples of Europe*, (...)'. Note that the words 'union' and 'people' are not officialised, as in 'Union' and 'People', through capitals.

In the third paragraph of this provision, the Union's task 'shall be to organize, in a manner demonstrating consistency and solidarity, relations between the *Member States and their peoples.*' This is different; these peoples are not the *European* social compounds, but the member states' compounds, although it is not certain that these are meant to coincide with the Member State's political Peoples.

5 This preamble prompted the ECJ to digress in *Van Gend & Loos* about the role of nationals, citizens, individuals, etc. in the new legal order. It is an interesting side-window on the subject, which will not be dwelt on here.

One single unmistakeable reference to the Member States' 'Staatsvölker' can be found in Article 10 TEU, where the word 'people', however, does not occur. Paragraph 2 reads:

> Member States are represented in the European Council by their Heads of State or Government and in the Council by their governments, themselves democratically accountable either to their national parliaments, *or to their citizens*.

Accountability 'to their citizens' refers to the members of the Council or European Council who have been directly elected. Through this election, they owe accountability to their electorate or their citizens. So where it is certain that the state-people are involved, the Treaty refers to 'their citizens'.

It is not necessary to be exhaustive in order to form a conclusive, if negative, finding. The terms 'people', 'peoples' and 'citizens', as used in the EU Treaties from the start, do not refer to clear and certainly not to identical coherent entities, legally defined. Quite the opposite: they refer to different things. The *peoples of Europe* include the Swiss and the Norwegians, and are not the same entities as the peoples of the EU Member States. The latter peoples may, again, refer to popular communities or to political communities. Where the Treaties unmistakeably refer to the political communities of the EU Member States that are involved in voting for parliament and government and other forms of political participation, the Treaty in question may use the word [Member States'] *citizens.* The word 'peoples' was used in the constitutional sense in the old Art. 189 EC (post-Maastricht), in which the European Parliament 'shall consist of the representatives of the peoples united in the Community'.

This negative finding can now be flipped onto its positive side. The diversity encountered here is not sloppiness, but legal sophistication in the expression of an essential variety among the inhabitants of the (50 or so) countries of Europe, of the 28 countries whose states are members of the EU, and the voters of the 28 Member States themselves. It amounts, affirmatively, to a normative *refusal* to conflate the different forms of people, and to conflate countries and states.

This distinctive refusal is both conceptually and normatively crucial even outside the EU context. Let me make the following normative claim to underscore it. The Union Treaties do not refer to anything like a singularity or identity in the people-types of the Member States or those brought together in the EU. And this is not a matter exclusive to the EU, it is one that the EU has in common with other civilised forms of political authority, among which, of course, are the EU Member States themselves. After all, these states concluded the Treaties.

In a next step, democracy in the Union need not depend on the presence of a single people or any other popular identity, let alone on a *'demos'*. Which brings us to the 'no-*demos'* thesis.

IV. Debunking the 'No-Demos Thesis'

The 'no-*demos* thesis', coined by law scholars and sanctified by the *Bundesverfassungsgericht*,[6] holds that the EU must fail its claim to democracy because it lacks a basic '*demos*'. This '*demos*' is some authentic 'whole' like the one upon which Athens' ancient democracy is thought to have been based.

In ancient Greece, at least in Athens, whose constitution we know through Aristotle and Thucydides, among others, a common word for the people was indeed *demos*. It was derived from the locality in which people lived together, the village, like the Roman *pagus*. But the term *demos* could have extremely different meanings, ranging from the rabble, the lower classes, the public for whom ceremonies were organised, through to the *pleiones*. According to the authoritative Ostwald:

> Democracy, in [Pericles'] view, does not define those who govern but those to whose welfare the government of the state is geared; the *demos*, in this context, is not the people as a whole, but its largest constituent, the [pleiones], the masses.[7]

And then, in Thucydides' or Pericles' view, democracy did not mean government *by* the people, but *for the benefit of* the many or the masses (*oi pleiones*). '

The term may have tended towards some ideal and singular meaning, that of the 'whole', the ideal meaning (and even criterion!) it is often perceived as having today. But I have found no clear reference to such an original use, not even in Ostwald's impressive book mentioned above. In Athens, in other words, there was a plurality of expressions referring to

6 Lissabon Urteil, marginal no 297.

7 M Ostwald, *From Popular Sovereignty to the Sovereignty of Law. Law, Society, and Politics in Fifth-Century Athens* (Berkeley, University of California Press, 1986), p 183. Those who remember Giscard d'Estaing's Draft of a Constitutional Treaty for Europe may also remember how he got the translation wrong.

popular compounds, similar to our notions. Some of these had a political meaning, while most did not, just as is the case with our use of the terms 'people', 'le peuple', 'das Volk', 'the masses', 'the populace', etcetera, etcetera.

The idea of the People as the essential political bedrock of the sovereign state is a recent invention. First, the idea of the people as a plurality of intelligent beings came in through the Enlightenment, after having been the subject of disdain and fear of uprising before. Then Rousseau turned it back into a singular personality with a singular will (the *volonté générale*). Next, Sieyès turned the third (residual) estate into the supreme entity of *la nation*, to which everyone belongs in principle. And he invented the distinction of the people as *constituant* and *constitué* (the one constituting the state and the other constituted in it), in other words, as I call them, the original people and the electoral one.

A few last words about the 'no *demos*' thesis. It is not entirely wrong to claim that some historical, social and/or cultural unity, or consensus, mostly underpins a democracy. But the democracies of Belgium, Switzerland, India, to name but a few, demonstrate the measure of diversity in language, culture, religion etc. that such a democratic unity may contain.

To reflect this, if you want to use the word '*demos*' reasonably, in a political sense, you might accept the following: whenever and wherever groups of people can live together for a longer time in a single territory and in freedom, without making civil war, there you have a '*demos*'. This is the situation the peoples of Europe are in, seventy years after the end of the last world war.

V. Debunking the Ein Volk

The essential plurality of the notion of 'people' is even part and parcel of constitutions based on popular sovereignty, such as those of the US, France and Germany. The sovereign people is not singular, but appears under two different personae, to be called the *original* and the *electoral* people respectively.

The notion of Volk in the Federal German Constitution is not a singular notion. The Volk figures in two distinct capacities, just like the People in the US Constitution. On the one hand, there is in both the 'original people', the *We the People* of the US and the 'Verfassungsgebende Gewalt' in the

Federal Republic, the founder of the state, whose largely fictitious birth and dormant existence are anxiously secured by their constitutional courts.

On the other hand, there is in both the 'electoral people', which is called upon to act frequently by way of a vote. Between the original and the electoral people in a constitution there are minor overlaps, but these do not make them into a singular entity. Quite the opposite, they are keenly distinct: the one dormant, with the constitutional court as spokesman, the other active with the legislature and the executive as spokesman. Neither of these spokesmen seems always aware that they are serving different masters, as I have analysed in another paper.[8]

Even if these two political people-personae are in reality not always fully separate and even if they overlap sometimes, notably in constitutional amendment when this involves a referendum, the distinction is fundamental and cannot be missed in constitutions of popular sovereignty. The *Bundesverfassungsgericht* seems to miss the distinctions. Allow me to quote from the paper just mentioned, at p. 204:

Breaking down the roles attributed by the court to the people, one obtains at least the following list: a) holder of sovereignty; b) holder of a single majority will; c) source of all state authority; d) body of citizens splitting itself into a majority and a minority; e) ruler by representation; f) original creator of the constitution and the state; g) final dissolver of the constitution and the state. Interestingly, this diversity in the roles of the people seems to be of no concern to the Court. It conceives of the people as one and of its roles as logically flowing from this conceptual unity. The same appears to be the case with the forms of action by the people.

When this distinction between the two *personae* of the state-people is not heeded or is ignored, as in the Lissabon-Urteil, there is a risk of essentialising the state-people in such a way as to absorb not only the two legal (constitutional) personae into a single notion, but also of absorbing and freezing the traditional people, conceptually, into an ideal but illusionary and even perverse notion of a *'demos'*. This is the conceptual conflation breeding scholarly epigonism and even populist illusions like those mentioned at the beginning of the present paper.

8 'Wir Sind Das Volk. Notes About the Notion of "The People" as Occasioned by the Lissabon-Urteil' (2010) 6 *European Constitutional Law Review* 199–222, 2010.

Conclusion: an Answer to Giacinto

To conclude, let me answer the question put to me by my dear colleague Giacinto della Cananea at the Thessaloniki meeting of ECLN at which I presented this paper. 'I agree largely', he said

> with the *pars destruens* of your paper, in which you debunk the idea of the essential unity of the people of a state or of the European Union, whether as a legal fact or a prelegal condition, in the form of a *demos*. That debunking part is effective.
>
> But what about the *pars construens?* There is a real and justified concern beneath the no-*demos* thesis that the European Union is losing touch with the people instead of creating its own comprehensive popular foundation. So one can understand the backlash in favour of the national peoples, even if they often have a populist expression. What is *your* answer to these concerns?

My answer is this: 'I agree that the legal creation of an EU-wide electorate in the form of EU citizenship with voting rights is not catching on as was expected, in terms of political allegiance and unity. The category is in place and requires a lot of development, even if it has a certain relevance already.

'I also agree that it has appeared necessary to base the Union more than maybe was expected on the Member States' constitutions, apart from on its own autonomous political capacity and constitution. The latter capacity and constitution exist, however. And in the main it consists not of the European Commission, the European Parliament and the ECJ, but in the capacity formed by the Member States acting not singly, but together. It is visible most clearly in the way they make Treaties under the driving force of their joint executive, the European Council and its apparatus, including now the Eurosummit, the Commission, the Eurogroup and the other Council formations.

'So where do the *national* voters, the *national electoral people*, come in? In the EC Treaty, Art. 189, they came in as a compound of national peoples or electorates, represented (and compounded) by the European Parliament. In form, this compound has disappeared, as the EP now represents the EU citizens. But underneath this, it is still alive, wherever the European Parliament represents the Member States' (electoral) peoples distinctly, as in its electoral rules of differentiated proportionality.

'By far most importantly, however, the Member States' peoples come in as voting bodies crucial to each of the Member States independently, and become compounded when these Member States act together, in the way of primary legislation (treaties). Each Member State's People, either directly or through its parliament, then has full power of refusal at the approval stage.

'In primary *legislation* (the Treaties) the Peoples come in quite clearly. In EU *executive* action their compound is weaker. But through the responsibility of the members of the EU's main executive body (the European Council) to Member State parliaments or citizens, the Member State Peoples are indirectly alive, even at the EU executive level.

'In no way, however, should we consider them to have a foundational role by themselves.'

Part Two
Economic Measures and European Courts in Times of Crisis

5 Causes of the financial crisis and causes of citizen resentment in Europe: What law has to do with it

Mattias Kumm

Abstract

The structure of financial flows in Europe, organised as inter-state transfers tied to demanding austerity conditions through the ESM mechanism, are in part responsible for resentment and backlash against the European Union by citizens. Such a structure also helps to sustain a misguided narrative about the nature of the crisis, wrongly suggesting that virtuous states are bailing out profligate ones. The central cause for the crisis in Europe is not an undisciplined spending by profligate states, but the asymmetric structural symbiosis between states and banks. Even after the reforms undertaken, states remain lenders of last resort for banks and banks remain lenders of last resort for states. Even though Draghi´s daring policies have contributed significantly to loosening that link, that symbiotic relationship must be further loosened. Banks must be regulated in a way that ensures that the financial sector does not depend on massive tax-payer financed transfers in times of crisis. The reforms undertaken in the past years gesture in the right direction but often remain ineffectual or cosmetic at best. Furthermore, the public costs of bank-bailouts are to a significant extent the result of genuinely European risks, for which it would be appropriate to hold the European Union as a whole accountable. The mechanism through which to organise this European responsibility should not be inter-state transfer mechanisms, such as those foreseen by the ESM. Particularly after the establishment of a Banking Union with the ECB playing a significant supervisory role this money should be paid for by genuinely European funds, raised by European taxes or levies.

Introduction

Even eight years after the beginning of the financial crisis and wide-ranging reforms seeking to address its consequences there is still no consensus on what has caused it and whether the measures taken are adequate to prevent something similar from happening again. The uncertainty over causation is reflected in uncertainty over nomenclature: Was it a Eurocrisis? Was it a sovereign debt crisis? Was it a banking crisis? The choice of nomenclature in describing the crisis is often connected to a basic hypothesis about the primary cause of the crisis. Each of these hypotheses gives a different account of the problem that is at the heart of the crisis, and the constitutional problem it is connected to. And with each diagnosis comes a different approach to therapy. The first part of the paper argues that the primary cause of the crisis is best understood as a banking crisis. At the heart of the crisis lies the asymmetric structural symbiosis between states and banks, in which states are lenders of last resort for banks and banks are lenders of last resort for states. Once it is understood that at the heart of the crisis lies a problem of organising the financial sector in a way that internalises liabilities, the question who should bear the losses and how solidarity should be organised in Europe appears in a new light. In the second part I show why the crisis further strengthens the case for two important reforms: First, the European Union has to be able to raise its own resources, rather than organising European solidarity through interstate transfers (no to a Transfer Union, yes to an Economic Justice Union). Second, the European parliamentary elections need to be turned into a genuine competition for a European government. Not having such reforms is likely to foster further resentment against a European Union in which money is seen to be transferred from virtuous states to profligate ones, with citizens of creditor states feeling resentful against those who appear not to be able to get their act together, while those receiving funds are resentful of the demanding conditions requiring unpopular austerity measures.

I. Three accounts of the crisis

A. A Eurocrisis as a result of faulty constitutional architecture?

For those who refer to the crisis as a *Eurocrisis,* the original sin is believed to be the architecture of the EMU. The EMU was an attempt to create monetary integration without deeper fiscal and political integration. That, however, was a misguided project destined to fail, because the problem of asymmetric shocks can´t be addressed effectively. In the case of a national crisis, like the bursting of a housing bubble in Ireland or Spain created by an influx of speculative capital, capital flows would seize abruptly, creating an economic shock that a state would not be able to effectively respond to. There would be no option to nationally devaluate the currency given a common currency. Thus it would not be possible to increase productivity without having to make politically difficult distributive choices like cutting salaries or public pensions. Nor would there be sufficient labour mobility to ensure that surplus labour moves to areas where there are more jobs. Notwithstanding a legal regime of free movement, the informal cultural barriers to free movement remain considerable. Furthermore, there are no significant federal transfers (for example, in the form of social security payments) to soften the shocks that exist in federal systems, with European structural funds in their current form not playing a major mitigating role.

This is the classic critique of the EMU from right-leaning economists from Werner Sinn to Martin Wolf articulated in the early 90s. It was an analysis that was in part shared by some left-wing analysts who continued to support the EMU, because they believed that, given political resistance to further integration in the form of a political and economic Union at the time, the EMU would create spill-over effects that would in due course create dynamics that would tip the scales in favour of deeper integration.

If this is the correct diagnosis of the crisis, the suggested therapy would be to complement the monetary Union with a fiscal and political Union, or to give up on a common currency (with variations of proposals suggesting a Northern Euro and/or a Southern Euro).

There is clearly something in this analysis that is right. But the analysis is nonetheless too general. Asymmetric shocks are not inevitable. They are the result of aggregate human actions. Law and institutions can be designed in such a way as to make it highly unlikely that they will happen: Asymmetric shocks are not natural phenomena like volcano eruptions or asteroid strikes. If the designers of the EMU believed that the Euro would work, it was because they believed that they had created a legal regime that would make asymmetric shocks improbable. The preparatory period in which the fiscal and economic discipline of each joining state was to be tested, in conjunction with the Maastricht criteria and the Stability and Growth Pact, was to ensure fiscal stability and provide incentive for reform, address the problem of current account imbalances by restructuring the economy and ensuring greater economic symmetry for the long haul. So the question is: What exactly went wrong? Why did the expectations of those who designed the EMU turn out to have been misguided? Why did the legal regime not prevent shocks from happening? What accounts for the specific asymmetric shocks the EU has suffered since 2008? What went wrong?

B. *A sovereign debt crisis as a result of profligate spending of some states?*

One answer to this question is given by those who would refer to the crisis as *a sovereign debt crisis*. The original sin leading to the crisis is not the structure of the constitutional system, but the violation of its constitutional rules. Profligate spending by a number of states, in violation of the Maastricht requirements concerning excessive government deficits under Art. 126 TFEU, as further specified in the Protocol on the Excessive Deficit procedure, is at the heart of the problem. Instead of undertaking structural reforms, macroeconomic imbalances between states were enhanced by weaker states exploiting lowered borrowing costs as a result of Euro-membership, violating their legal obligations under EU Law. The sovereign debt crisis, so the claim goes, is also a rule of law crisis.

Even though this account is ultimately unpersuasive, it does highlight a set of uncontroversial facts. The rules relating to fiscal discipline in the Treaty of Maastricht appear to have been widely violated. On some counts, 23 out of 27 countries are in systematic violation of their fiscal obligations under EU Law. In recent years there were more than 20 states against which excessive deficit procedures were initiated. States chose an easy path to finance debts using the new common currency, which made borrowing cheaper for most, because lenders did not have to hedge against devaluation.[1] Greece was allowed to join the club for political reasons,

---

1 Yet the EMU provided no guarantees against a sovereign default or 'restructuring'. On the contrary, the 'no bailout' clause in Art 123 TFEU made it clear that a default risk remained. Yet the differences in yields between German and PIGS government bonds in the period before 2008 were marginal, suggesting that the market assumed the marginal risk of default to be negligible. There are only two possible explanations of that behaviour. Either markets believed that in a crisis strong states would bail out struggling states, notwithstanding Art 123 TFEU. Or they believed that default was unlikely (but why would they? The European provisions requiring fiscal discipline were widely discarded and the historical record provides no basis for such a belief).

even though it was widely suspected that its budgetary figures were fudged. When Germany and later France violated the rules, the Commission won an excessive deficit procedure case before the ECJ against the negligent Council, which was countered by a revision of the SGP strengthening the discretion of the Council. With France and Germany getting away with impunity, it was clear that they would later lack the authority to insist on other states sticking to the rules.

For those who follow this analysis the therapy consists of a combination of two things. First, to insist that national fiscal discipline is tightened up and that European enforcement mechanisms are strengthened. This is effectively what the Fiscal Pact does. Second, as a last resort, a permanent emergency regime —beyond what the original Art 122 II TFEU offered as a loophole— has to be established, that allows struggling states access to capital provided by other Member States, but only subject to further intrusive conditions relating to structural reforms. This is what the newly introduced Art 136 III TFEU in conjunction with the ESM does.[2] In this way a modicum of solidarity in the form of transfers between states and effective mutualisation of debt balances the common commitment to austerity.[3]

---

2 First this led to the establishment of the EFSF and EFSM as a preliminary remedy. The EFSF and EFSM were based on Art 122 II TFEU, which was argued by some to be in violation of the no-bailout clause of Art 125 TFEU ('a MS shall not be liable or assume commitments of other public authorities…'. This claim is countered by two legal arguments in favour of legality: 1. This falls under the 'external circumstances' exception, which allows temporary measures to be taken to address 'severe difficulties' caused by 'natural disasters or exceptional occurrences beyond its control' (something of a stretch since this was no unfounded speculative attack by financial markets) and 2. This does not constitute EU bailout, but sovereign decisions by nation states to provide support outside the EU mechanism, to which the bailout provision does not apply. The new Art 136 para 3 TFEU, which authorises the establishment of the ESM, solves this problem of a proper legal basis by effectively gutting the no-bailout clause.

3 Those who share this analysis may well debate among themselves how much austerity/budgetary discipline is due (what type of sacrifices can plausibly be demanded of a self-governing Member State?), how much solidarity in the form of transfers between states and mutualisation of debt risks should be incurred (when does the moral hazard issue become too great?) and whether the balance was struck correctly in the ESM and Fiscal Compact. But notwithstanding differences in this regard (social democrats tend to be in favour of more lenience and greater debt mutualisation, conservatives emphasise tough love and pulling yourself up by the bootstraps with aid only as a last resort), the issue is cast as striking a balance between disciplining states not to engage in profligate spending and to bring about reforms increasing

Note how this therapy comes with high costs: First, creditor states are asked to exercise solidarity for what is cast as the failure to act in a responsible and disciplined way by the debtor state. Why should states who did a better job with budgetary discipline and are not plagued by budgetary problems help out? Even within a national community solidarity with those that are worse off is difficult to get political support for, if those that are to receive state aid through transfers can plausibly be cast as slackers who fail to get their act together. Here, too, the tendency in past decades has been to tie aid to demanding conditions. Transfers are resented, whenever the need of the recipient side is easily connected to his/her own failure to make responsible choices. Second, citizens in countries struggling to meet requirements by the Fiscal Pact or the conditions imposed by the ESM in conjunction with access to credits are likely to resent the EU for 'imposing' policies on them, whose effectiveness is highly disputed, but whose effect in imposing pain on the less privileged is clear. This is easily cast as a form of economic imperialism in the name of a neoliberal ideology that draws on anodyne and technocratic-sounding concepts like 'structural adjustment' to hide its political orientation. It is, at any rate, in strong tension with the idea of democratic self-government. Incompatible positions between creditor states, who are reluctant to subsidise what they imagine to be irresponsible behaviour, and debtor states, whose citizens rebel against hardship in part grounded in external impositions, may turn out to be toxic and lead to significant political turmoil. In creditor countries the shift is to a Eurosceptic right, who want to keep their money for themselves and not be forced into a larger community of solidarity. Meanwhile, in debtor countries citizens rebel against public and social services being cut, giving rise to left-wing movements which achieve considerable electoral successes, castigating the EU as a neoliberal and neo-imperial regime in which the rich north exploits and ultimately imposes hardship on the south. Structurally organising solidarity in a way that makes it appear as money flowing from virtuous states to states who fail to do their homework has already fostered resentful nationalism on all sides. It undermines and dos not foster European solidarity.

But the problem is not just that the prescribed therapy fosters resentment on all sides. The problem is that the diagnosis is itself seriously

productivity, thus decreasing the probability of asymmetric shocks in the future, while at the same time providing for a modicum of solidarity between states as a last resort in the form of the ESM.

flawed. The diagnosis starts from a set of relatively uncontested facts, but it draws the wrong conclusion from them. There may be a regrettable lack of fiscal discipline and, perhaps —though less obviously, given substantial 'fudging language' in the SGP and the Fiscal Compact— even a violation of European legal requirements by Member States. But *fiscal discipline turns out to be a remarkably inaccurate variable to predict which state is likely to get into trouble.* The lack of fiscal discipline and noncompliant behaviour with EU norms simply does not explain the crisis: Ireland and Spain were among the most disciplined of the Member States, significantly more disciplined than, say, Germany. Portugal's numbers were largely comparable to France. So what is going on?

C. It's the banks, stupid! On the structural symbiosis between states and banks

The central cause for the crisis in Europe is not undisciplined spending by profligate states, but the asymmetric structural symbiosis between states and banks. Under the original European regime states were lenders of last resort for banks and banks were lenders of last resort for states. That symbiotic relationship must be further loosened. Banks must be regulated in a way that ensures that the financial sector does not depend on massive taxpayer financed transfers. And the ECB in cooperation with the ESM must function as a lender of last resort for states.

1. States as lenders of last resort for banks

Because of serious structural deficiencies in how the financial sector has been regulated, banks can generally depend on being bailed out by states. The scale of the problem is such that the sovereign debt crisis can be, to a large extent, understood as a knock-on effect of a banking crisis. Effectively this means that in the financial sector major risks are socialised, whereas profits remain privatised. This formula should not be dismissed as populist rhetoric. It is a straightforward description of reality. Here it must suffice to invoke one figure and one example to substantiate the strength of the relationship between sovereign debts and bank bailouts. According to Commission statistics, the Commission authorised 4.5 trillion Euros of state aid to the financial sector between October 2008 and October 2011.

That is more than a third of the EU´s GDP and more than six times the original capital stock made available by Member States to the ESM to bail out states. Of course, not all money authorised as state aid was in fact given to banks and not all the money that was given to banks was lost. But the scale of European coordinated state intervention to save the banks was impressive and lies at the heart of the crisis. As a concrete example take Slovenia. In August 2012 the major rating agencies Moody´s and Standard & Poors massively lowered the Slovenian credit ratings and thereby significantly raised their financing costs.[4] Why? Slovenia was regarded as a model country when it joined the EU in 2004 and when it introduced the Euro in 2007. Slovenia´s overall debt remains well under 60% of GDP. The main reason for the negative outlook and significantly higher financing costs are the bad credits of major Slovenian banks. The three largest banks in Slovenia reportedly needed a capital injection to be provided by the state to the tune of 8% of GDP. In conjunction with lower growth prospects and higher lending costs the markets were losing confidence that Slovenia would be able to keep a grip on its financial situation going forward. The stories of Ireland and Spain are similar. Ireland raised its debt/GDP ratio by 25% overnight when the government decided to assume all bank debts in a dramatic decision at the height of the banking crisis. Spain applied for help under the ESM to the tune of 100 billion exclusively to ensure that money was available to bail out its banks (ultimately the required amount was reduced to 59 billion).

2. *Banks as lenders of last resort for states*

The problem is further exacerbated by the fact that it is not within the ECB´s mandate to serve as a lender of last resort for states. Even though its core point —to ensure that states are prevented from simply printing money to cover ever-increasing debts— is well understood and appreciated, there are two consequences connected to this institutional choice.

First, it opens up states to the possibility of successful speculative attacks by financial markets. This very possibility may, in times of high uncertainty and great financial market liquidity, create insecurity and volatil-

4 http://www.moodys.com/research/Moodys-downgrades-Slovenias-government-bond-rating-to-Baa2-from-A2--PR_252281.

ity (a central bank in the background credibly pronouncing that as a last resort it would buy government debt in unlimited amounts makes all speculative attacks futile). This risk, which was believed to exist for Eurozone states, but not the US or Japan, is likely to be priced into bond yields, translating into higher lending costs for states.

Second, given that in the absence of a central bank the capital markets and banks in particular are the lenders of last resort for states, states have an incentive to make it attractive for banks to buy sovereign debt. This is partly done by exempting sovereign debt from capital requirements that generally apply to banks' proprietary trading. In Europe the ECB makes credit available for banks at a very low rate currently approaching zero, which banks may then use to invest in sovereign debt, which in turn is used as security for further credit. Given that rules on capital requirements scandalously continue not to apply to banks as sovereign debt purchasers, banks gain considerable leverage. The downside for banks is that in case of sovereign debt restructuring banks are more likely to face severe problems. The upside is that because of this symbiotic relationship the banks can count on being bailed out by the states. The reason why Greek restructuring presented a serious problem for other countries was that major European banks, French and German banks among them, were significantly exposed to Greek sovereign debt. This would have meant that in the event of a Greek default those banks, too, would have needed to be bailed out by their respective governments. This was a core mechanism through which it was feared that contagion would spread through the European economy. A case in point: The reason why Cyprus was applying for protection under the ESM is directly related to the losses of Cypriot banks incurred as the holders of 22 billion Euros of Greek debt from the Greek restructuring in March 2012. As a result of this restructuring Cypriot banks had to be bailed out by the Cypriot government, ultimately forcing the government to consider protection under the umbrella of the ESM.

3. From diagnosis to therapy

On this diagnosis the basic structure of the therapy appears to be clear, even if a great many issues of detail might remain contested and complicated. The solution would have to have two basic prongs.

a. What a Banking Union must seek to achieve

First, the financial sector and banks in particular have to be regulated in a way that ensures that public to private sector transfers cease to be necessary. Risks should be allocated with the management, shareholders and debtholders of banks, not the public. On the one hand, this can be done by lowering the probabilities of difficulties arising in the first place. This requires stronger capital requirements as in the new Capital Requirement Regulation and Directive, which in its present form is still being criticised as insufficient by the Basel Committee.

Another measure that has been discussed is the legal separation of banks' core financial and commercial activities from its proprietary trading and other risky activities (see High Level Expert Group Report/ Barnier from October 3 2012) but that appears to have gone no-where. Furthermore, the supervision of these rules must be improved, which the new arrangement under which the ECB plays a major supervisory role aims to do, even though the efficacy of such supervision is highly contested. Furthermore, in case difficulties do arise, it is necessary to ensure that banks of any size can be restructured or wound down in a way that limits taxpayer liability (this is what the Bank Recovery and Resolution Directive seeks to achieve). The European insurance scheme that banks are required to maintain is potentially another important piece of the puzzle, even though the scope of the current regime is so limited that it does not go much beyond symbolic politics.

b. The ECB (in cooperation with the ESM) as a lender of last resort

Second, the ECB, in conjunction with the ESM, would have to be able to credibly serve as a lender of last resort. This would ensure emergency funding for states in the absence of functioning markets. To prevent states from abusing this mechanism or inappropriately relying on it instead of making appropriate efforts themselves, a link between debt-purchasing through the ECB and conditionality requirements by the ESM should be established.

There are three ways of doing this, which can only be described and assessed in very basic terms here. The point here is not to provide a comprehensive legal and political analysis, but to gain a deeper understanding of the options available and the types of concerns they would need to address.

Make the ECB the official lender of last resort by changing constitutional prohibitions on the ECB buying state debt directly on the primary market. This is something that would leave an institution like the ECB, which is not independently democratically legitimated and whose independence is protected by strong constitutional rules and not embedded in strong national cultural contexts, too powerful. Given the requirement to amend the Treaty, it is also politically not feasible.

The Draghi solution (presented on Sep. 7 2012): According to this, the ECB could engage in outright monetary transactions (OMTs), purchasing sovereign debt on the secondary market to undercut 'severe distortions' in government bond markets not justified by fundamentals. It would only do so if a state is in cooperation with ESM (and EFSM) supervision. In this way it would thus effectively cut the borrowing costs of debt-burdened Euro-zone members. The ECB would become a fully effective backstop, providing the institutional assurance that the Euro is in fact irreversible and thus discouraging speculation against it. There are two problems with this approach. First, it is a contested question whether these policies are covered by the constitutional mandate of the ECB. The German Constitutional Court has challenged Draghi's policies as *ultra vires*. After the Court made a preliminary reference to the CJEU, the CJEU insisted that the ECB was acting within its powers. At the time of writing it remains an open question whether the German court will accept that judgment or insist that the decision of the CJEU, too, qualifies as an ultra vires act not binding under the German constitution. The court claimed such policies are in violation of the ECB´s mandate to prioritise price stability over other objectives (Art 127 TFEU) and amount to a circumvention of the prohibition to buy sovereign debt directly (Art 123 TFEU). The ECB argues that its policy is driven by concerns to effectively keep interstate rates low and that Art 18 of the ECB statute explicitly authorises the kind of OMTs the ECB expects to engage in. Second, apart from legal issues there are also policy concerns. Because the ECB only buys debt on the secondary market, banks continue to profit as middle-men to the detriment of the public. They take a cut, buying debt from the state and selling it to the ECB at a higher price, thus increasing the cost for the public. Not surprisingly, on the announcement of Draghi´s policy the share prices of the major European banks shot up (Crédit Agricole and Société Générale was up by 8.44 and 7.76% respectively on the day, while Deutsche Bank went up by 7%). n alternative or complementary path would be for the ECB to recognise the ESM as a commercial partner under Art 18 of the ECB Statutes. This would allow the ESM to borrow money from the ECB with which it could buy ailing states' debt on the primary market, which it could then deposit as security with the ECB. The decision to buy government debt would thus be made by the Governing Council. Here, too, there are complicated legal issues that would need to be worked out. On the one hand, the ESM does not need to apply for a bank license (Art 32 para IX ESM). On the other hand, Art 21 of the ECB Statute prohibits lending money to public entities. Yet it is plausible to argue for a narrow interpretation of Art 21 and insist that the ESM does not fall under its scope. Unlike any other public entity that Art 21 appropriately applies to, the ESM is a lending institution, which not only financially but also politically represents all participating Member States, thus ensuring appropriate checks and balances.

This may well be the most attractive solution. It cuts out the middleman (banks) and reduces costs for the public. Like the Draghi plan, the plan requires political endorsement through the ESM mechanism as well as ECB involvement, but it would put the ESM in charge. The ESM, not the ECB, would be the policy agenda-setter. This solution would neither inappropriately empower the ECB, nor does it make it easy for political forces to effectively gain control of the levers of the printing press. On the other hand, the question remains whether markets would trust a stop-gap mechanism that effectively required the potentially strife-torn Governing Council of the ESM to authorise purchases of sovereign debt. But in the end it might not matter whether option 2 or 3 effectively defines European practice. What is far more important is that one or the other is effectively adopted and legally endorsed.

To some extent Draghi´s radical policies of 'quantitative easing' have provided an alternative way to ensure the solvency of the system. The effectiveness in the short term of stimulating economic activity and achieving 2% inflation is in doubt, as ever more radical measures —ranging from negative interest rates to 'helicopter money'— are discussed. Furthermore, the policies' structural pathological effects —from the creation of new asset bubbles to its degressive distributive effects— are worrying. Draghi´s insistence on interpreting the bank´s mandate in such a way that it can effectively serve as a lender of last resort, much like the US Fed or the Japanese central bank, was systemically important, even if legally contested. But without being complemented by a genuine European economic government, the ECB is forced into a central economic governing role that it is not institutionally suited to play, irrespective of interpretative issues concerning its formal legal mandate.

II. Widening the Perspective: Constitutional Reforms?

A. No to a Transfer Union, yes to a Social and Economic Justice Union

1. On legacy loss allocation

The correct analysis of the crisis is not only important for understanding what needs to be done to avoid similar crises in the future. Besides taking measures to ensure that states are adequately supplied with capital in cases of dire need and that in the future the financial sector can no longer count on bail-outs from the taxpayer, the correct analysis also provides the key to the question of how to appropriately allocate losses incurred. So who should be held financially accountable for the mess?

If the crisis were the result of profligate spending on the part of certain states, then it seems logical that these states should first of all bear the burden of their actions before they can count on European support. And it would seem appropriate that any such support would come with further strict conditions attached to counteract free rider concerns. This, in effect, is what the ESM and Fiscal Compact are meant to ensure. But if, as argued above, the sovereign debt crisis is to a large extent the result of a banking crisis, the answer may turn out to be very different.

There is something arbitrary in burdening the states in whose jurisdictions the banks requiring bail-outs happen to have their seat. The banking crisis would not have had the same intensity and structure if it had not been for the European common currency and European freedom of capital guarantees. The EU has exercised its concurrent competencies over the area of banking and financial markets and has now deepened its involvement in the sector by the establishment of a Banking Union. Furthermore, the bank bailouts themselves have considerable cross-border positive externalities. Given the interdependence of the banking sector, the failure of major banks in one state is likely to have had contagion effects across Europe that were difficult to control. It was in the German and French interest that Greece bailed out its banks instead of letting them go bankrupt. Under such circumstances it seems more plausible to allocate financial public sector risks resulting from financial sector failings at the European level. The costs of bank bailouts are to a significant extent the result of genuinely European risks, for which it would be appropriate to hold the European Union as a whole accountable.

2. *From interstate transfers to the EU′s own resources*

But if the European Union as a whole, rather than individual states like Spain, Ireland or Slovenia, is to be held accountable for the costs of the bank bailouts, the mechanism through which this European responsibility should be organised should not be inter-state transfer mechanisms, such as those foreseen by the ESM. *This money should be paid by genuinely European funds, raised by European taxes or levies.* The way money is raised and the channels through which it is spent comes with its own political presumptions and burdens of justification. It should not be understood as a neutral technical device. There is something deeply incongruous and misleading in first having individual states bail out banks and then transferring money from one state to another so that stronger states support weaker states to help them fulfil that task. This mechanism misguidedly creates the impression that stronger states have to bail out weaker ones because they can′t handle their responsibilities, even when the original responsibility should be more properly ascribed to the European Union from the outset. Inter-state transfer mechanisms corrode solidarity in Europe because they give the misleading impression that one state has to ultimately pay for the failures of another.

Note how interstate transfers corrode solidarity even in established federal systems. This is not an issue related to the lack of a European identity. Take the example of Germany′s Länderfinanzausgleich. To simplify somewhat, the rules of fiscal federalism in Germany allocate most federal taxes to the federal government, which spends its money in line with federal policies. Here the question of how much money has flown from one state to another is generally not a high-profile political issue: federal taxes for federal policies help create and sustain a federal political community and its policies. A part of the federal taxes, however, is awarded to the states. Now a small portion of the amount awarded to the states is again redistributed between the states according to certain need-based criteria. As a result, in past years the Bavarians have had to pay roughly 3 billion Euros of the money originally allocated to them in the distributive pot, while the happy-go-lucky 'poor but sexy' city-state of Berlin has received a roughly comparable amount. The nifty Badenwürttembergers have supported the socially generous and undisciplined Bremeners. etc. There is a lot of political theatre and a great deal of animosity that is part of the annual process of re-allocation. This inter-state reallocation creates significant resentment and effectively undermines solidarity. The reason for this is at least in part because Bavarians assume that the money originally allocated to them is what is rightly theirs, and they don't want to have to exercise solidarity for the fact that other states apparently can't get their act together.

Whether or not the Bavarians and Baden-Württembergers have a point is not the issue here. The point here is that the mechanism through which money is distributed comes with assumptions about whose money it is. Once money originally allocated to A flows from A to B, A assumes it is its money and what needs to be justified is why B should have it. If money is distributed to all those living in A and B according to criteria determined in line with a jointly decided policy followed by C, and money is raised by applying general criteria related to the policy benefits bestowed, then the question of how much money flows from A to B becomes moot or at least secondary. Then the question becomes a different one: is this a policy for which C (rather than A and B) should exercise its competencies (assuming they legally have it)? If so, is it a good policy, worth the money that is spent on it? And is the money raised according to appropriate criteria?

Moreover, it is not a good argument to insist that a sufficiently strong identity —an identity that Europeans may be claimed to lack— is a prerequisite for the EU to raise its own resources. Identity may well be relevant for the allocation of competencies and the definition of policies. But once it is decided and accepted that competencies should be allocated and policies defined on a European level with regard to a particular set of issues, then it is unlikely that funding these policies in line with *criteria that are meaningfully connected to the economic benefits bestowed* would be regarded as unacceptable. Genuinely European resources, best raised from taxes or levies that burden actors and transactions that are profiting financially from the internal market (e.g. shareholders, corporations, transactions with strong cross-border dimensions like certain financial transactions), appropriately connect regulatory responsibility with financial accountability. Furthermore, prioritising the taxing of actors and transactions whose tax-burdens have been reduced as a result of competitive pressures to lower tax rates to attract capital and mobile actors to the national jurisdiction (or prevent capital flight) would reflect the promise of the European Union to ensure the fair distribution of burdens in the context of globalisation. The European Union should not become a Transfer Union (this is not about transfers from one state to another); it should become an Economic Justice Union, in which the European Union accepts financial liability for the consequences of its regulatory responsibilities and is able to raise its own resources to do so.

B. *Why the elections to the European Parliament should be turned into a genuine competition for a European government*

However, the inappropriate insistence of Member States on controlling the channels through which resources are funnelled is not limited to the area of finances. Member States, and in particular the executive branches of Member States, have also taken over the European political process and have successfully prevented autonomous European legitimacy resources from being mobilised. Think of the many emergency Council meetings in Brussels in the past few years, where late at night or early in the morning exhausted prime ministers and chancellors have declared agreement on another new mechanism or policy through which the crisis is to be addressed. Think of the ESM in which the Board of Governors, composed of the finance ministers of participating states, calls the shots. Throughout the crisis the European Parliament has not been publically present. Conflicts have been cast as inter-state conflicts, Germany and France against Greece or Spain, donor countries against receiving countries, even though in all of these countries there have been structurally similar divides between left and right, that would have allowed for coalition building and the introduction of a very different kind of debate about the kind of Europe that is desirable. Why did those cross-national debates about alternative futures for Europe not take place? Furthermore, Europe has not only appeared to be deeply divided along state lines but the ultimately agreed-upon solutions have also been cast as inevitable, without alternatives, necessary. If you don´t like these results, you´re inclined to become a Eurosceptic. There is no public representation of an alternative Europe that you could support. Yet it should be clear from the above discussion that there is much that is disputed about how to understand the crisis, what its causes are and what kind of resolution might be desirable. There is also the real danger that the solutions offered might not, in the end, work. Who is going to be held accountable then? How might Europe recover from such a blow?

It is high time to be serious about proposals endorsed, among others, by the current President of the European Parliament Martin Schulz and Wolfgang Schäuble to make the elections for the European Parliament genuine European elections for the choice of the President of the European executive. The last Parliamentary elections provided a good indication of the direction in which this development must go. The different European political groups should present competing 'Spitzenkandidaten' before the election. If the election campaign focused on this, the European Council would, in practice, have to appoint the winning candidate. This dynamic was already in play in the last elections and Juncker was appointed as Commission President on that basis. Once European citizens realise that the European elections will meaningfully influence who the European leadership personnel will be, that is likely to increase their interest in European elections and make them more meaningful. Such a shift is of fundamental importance and the reasons sometimes invoked against it are not persuasive.

It is of fundamental importance because we should not be surprised to see that European citizens disagree about the kind of policy measures that are the best response to the financial crisis and other political issues that the EU rightly addresses through legislation. It is a mistake to insist, as national politicians invariably do when they defend the measures taken at late-night Council meetings under the current regime of executive-dominated intergovermentalism, that there is no alternative to the decision they have made. For many citizens that is the reason why they are turning their back on Europe: They do not like the policy choices generated at the European level, and there is no alternative personnel and menu of policy options present to engage with at the European level, so they associate Europe with those policy choices they deem undesirable. If faced with a genuine choice of personnel, programmes and policies, disgruntled citizens would be able to articulate their dissent not by turning away from Europe and seeking refuge in populist recipes. Instead, they might, as European citizens, vote or mobilise for an alternative Europe, personified in a different President, committed to different policies. Tying the outcome of the European elections to determining the question of who the next Commission President will be will lead not only to a surge of interest in European parliamentary elections and allow the Commission to fulfil the functions assigned to it more effectively, it is also likely to be the best antidote to the spread of nationalist populism and Euroscepticism.

Furthermore, under the Fiscal Treaty and other fiscal crisis-related legislation like the Six-Pack the Commission gains considerable powers to intervene in the budgetary processes of Member States, once they have shown themselves unable to meet the strict budgetary requirements imposed on them. For those powers and the discretion that comes with these powers to be exercised effectively and legitimately, the Commission must be able to rely on the kind of legitimacy that comes with a direct link to the outcome of European elections. Budgetary questions were at the heart of the historical parliamentary struggles for control over a democratically unaccountable executive —they are the inner sanctum of parliamentary prerogatives— and it is unlikely that national Parliaments will give much weight to a Commission that is seen as the instrument of the collective executives of the Member States.

The arguments against such elections are ultimately not persuasive. The current role of the national executives in the European decision-making process is not something that enhances the democratic legitimacy of that process. It is the result of the executive branches having taken over the European decision-making process, with the accountability to national parliaments, even though not without significance, ultimately limited for structural reasons. The claim that small Member States would lose too much influence is also misguided. On the contrary, a stronger Commission President might be a more plausible counterweight to the tendency of two or three large states effectively dominating the decision-making process in Europe.

The claim that European elections can´t be meaningful because statistics relating to electoral participation clearly indicate that European citizens are just not interested in European elections, that there are no genuine European parties and there is no robust European public sphere etc. gets it the wrong way around. The issue is one of sequencing: Only once European elections are appropriately structured to allow citizens to choose between different leadership personnel, programs and policies will the incentives be in place to develop an interest in elections, to restructure parties around European agendas and to have the media focus more strongly on European themes.

Finally, the degressive proportionality of the allocation of parliamentary seats in the EP, does not —contra the German FCC— suggest that it can´t play a central legitimatory role. On the contrary, in conjunction with the weighted voting in the Council such an institutional choice is appropriately sensitive to the nature of the European Union as a Federation of nation states.

Conclusion

There are those that might be wary of a European Union that can raise its own resources through taxes or levies and that establishes genuine electoral politics at the heart of the European political system. Would this not effectively turn the EU into a state? And is that a viable direction in times of rampant Euroscepticism and debates and referenda about exiting the European Union? Of course one could point to all kinds of ways in which the EU would still remain distinguishable from the classic state like France or Britain: its limited competencies across a wide range of core areas of political concern, from social security to defence; its correspondingly relatively low budget in terms of Europe´s GDP, compared to national budgets in terms of their national GDP; the remaining very powerful role of the Council in the European legislative process. This would clearly not be a European superstate (however one might imagine that). Furthermore, pointing to the generally Eurosceptic climate is not much of a counterargument: that climate is at least in part the result of exactly the kind of dysfunctional responsibility fudging political and legal structures that this proposal would hope to overcome.

But it would be a significant shift. For those conceptually wedded to a *sui generis* account of the EU[5], those who insist on making sense of the EU in terms radically different from federal systems, it might come as a shock that there is more conceptual and political continuity between the EU and traditional political forms than they might have thought. But our thinking about how to progressively develop the European Union in order to improve it should not be burdened by ontological pre-commitments

5 Attempts to work out in conceptual and normative terms how to make sense of Europe´s *sui generis* character include a 'conflicts of law' approach (Christian Jörges) or 'demoicracy' (Kalypso Nicolaides), or the idea of 'constitutional tolerance' (Joseph Weiler), or some accounts of 'constitutional pluralism' (Maduro, Kumm, Halberstam). Those approaches and conceptualisations might well remain relevant, but to the extent they do, they would remain so because they describe features that are relevant in federal settings more generally.

concerning its nature. The question is simply whether, given the values Europeans are committed to, a particular reform would enable the European Union to serve its citizens better as a framework for self-government. If a European Union that can raise its own resources through taxes or levies and that establishes genuine electoral politics at the heart of the European political system would make it a better Union, effectively overcoming the crisis and making its recurrence unlikely, while reflecting its basic values, then that is the direction in which it should constitutionally evolve. If it makes the European Union appear more like a federation of nation states, so be it.

6 The Role of Judges and Legislators in the Greek Financial Crisis: A Matter of Competence

George Karavokyris

Abstract

The article examines the relation between legislators and courts in the framework of the recent decisions on the financial crisis. The constitutionality of the austerity measures in Greece and their conventionality in the framework of the European Convention of Human Rights were mainly decided through the test of standards of necessity and proportionality. The standards are words of the ordinary language whose semantic vagueness allows the judge a wide marge of appreciation. They are not pure legal concepts and cannot be signified unless the judge retrieves social, ethical and political considerations. Although the interpretation of standards enforces judicial authority, their flexibility can lead easily on the other hand to judicial self-restraint, like in the most emblematic decisions on the financial crisis. The main argument of this contribution is that this limited —judicial— claim of authority lies on an epistemic and political matter of competence.

Introduction

The inclusion of the financial crisis in the study of one of the most trivial but controversial subjects of constitutional law, the endless dialogue between judges and legislators, is a high intellectual challenge because it implies that unprecedented circumstances may alter the ordinary meanings of words and concepts. The extreme force of economic and political decisions and events may disrupt, directly or indirectly, the constitutional and legal normality and establish a new balance in the complex and dynamic principle of the separation of powers. In fact, the courts-legislators relation captures, in legal terms, the conflict or the consent between liberalism and democracy and thus results in the identification of the legal organ which is actually being granted, within the existing legal and political framework, the most significant role. In other words, the dialogue between the two major actors of contemporary legal systems, the judge and the legislator, should finally be understood as a matter of sovereignty.[1]

In the present study, the relation between legislators and courts will be viewed within the context of the recent decisions on the Greek financial crisis. During the crisis, the impact of the fiscal and economic measures on the Greek legal order has been notably heavy, particularly in the field of individual and social rights, and has evidently enhanced, through the limits of judicial control, the dialogue between the courts and the legislators. Bearing the responsibility for examining the constitutionality of a variety of detailed and technical fiscal and structural measures stemming from the Memoranda agreed between the Greek government, the European Institutions and the IMF, the Greek judge and especially the higher courts, such as the Council of State, have —de jure and de facto— been obliged to essentially give up the comfortable position of any (supposed) neutrality and to become involved in weighing up political and fiscal considerations. The political role of the judge has been emphasised in this development, as the reaction of the Greek Constitution to the financial crisis has been merely a jurisprudential one. Given the fact that the constitutional provisions on state of emergency were textually and substantially inappropriate to respond to the extreme economic circumstances, the legal qualification and appreciation of the Memoranda occurred not in the context of an unprecedented exception but in the context of constitutional normality.[2] Often challenged before the courts, the crisis-legislation led to a series of important judgments, which critically re-defined, through the dynamic interpretation of the Greek Constitution, the limits of the limitations

1 See for the concept of sovereignty O Beaud, *La puissance de l'État*, (Paris, P.U.F., 1994). Also, for the rule of law and the relation between democracy and liberalism see L Heuschling, *État de droit, Rechtsstaat, Rule of Law* (Paris, Dalloz, 2002). On politics and law see L Favoreu, *La politique saisie par le droit* (Paris, Economica, 1988); M Guénaire, 'La Constitution où la fin de la politique' (1991) *Le Débat*, no. 64, pp 149 ff, and in the same volume, S Rials, 'Entre artificialisme et idolâtrie. Sur l'hésitation du constitutionalisme', p 159 ff; D Rousseau, 'La Constitution ou la politique autrement', p 182 ff; L Favoreu, 'De la démocratie à l' Etat de droit', p 158 ff, and M Troper, 'Le droit, la raison, la politique', p 187 ff.

2 See G Karavokyris, *The Constitution and the Crisis*, (Athens, Kritiki, 2014) (in Greek), pp 19 ff and 159 ff and generally on the relation between normality and exception in legal theory M Troper, 'L'état d'exception n'a rien d'exceptionnel' in M Troper, *Le droit et la nécessité* (Paris, P.U.F., 2011) pp 99 ff.

on socio-economic rights and reassessed indirectly the scope of judicial self-restraint or activism.[3] As the intensity of judicial control of the constitutionality of the crisis legislation increases or decreases, the functional range of the legal actors changes, along with the very meaning of the Constitution. The various interpretative shifts and turns during the crisis have amounted to an informal constitutional change, as the text of the Greek Constitution has not been revised or amended. [4]

It is well known that in modern constitutionalism the courts are the authentic interpreters of the law/constitution, i.e. the institutional players who usually have the last word on the exact meaning of legal rules. In a constitutional state, the judicial authority on constitutional matters gives the courts wide scope not only for receiving legislative rules passively, but also, and more essentially, for taking active decisions on their conformity with the Constitution. The courts are being granted authority to disregard or change the rules, when they find them to be in contravention of constitutional precepts.[5] So, with regard to this ample judicial power, we may observe that the courts are not just law-applying organs, with a duty to extend and impose the legislative-general will. They have, in fact, themselves become law-making organs which have the interpretative power to alter the understanding and, most importantly, the legal effect of the legislative and constitutional rules. In the words of Stéphane Rials, the judge is the actual 'priest' of the law.[6]

From a normative point of view, courts and legislators *claim* legal authority and power over legal subjects, which they exercise in the *name* of the law, according to constitutional provisions. Thus, they are both sources

3 See X Contiades and A Fotiadou, 'How Constitutions Reacted to the Financial Crisis' in X Contiades (ed), *Constitutions in the Global Financial Crisis* (London, Ashgate, 2013) pp 9-59.

4 On the concept and the models of constitutional change see X Contiades and A Fotiadou, 'Models of Constitutional Change' in X Contiades (ed), *Engineering Constitutional Change. A Comparative Perspective on Europe, Canada and the USA* (London, Routledge, 2013); M Altwegg-Boussac, *Les changements constitutionnels informels* (Paris, Institut Universitaire Varenne, 2013).

5 See the recent work by D Kyritsis, *Shared Authority. Courts and Legislators in Legal Theory* (Oxford, Hart Publishing, 2014). See also M Troper, 'Justice constitutionnelle et démocratie' (1990) *Revue française de droit constitutionnel*, no. 1, pp 31 ff; JH Ely, *Democracy and Distrust, A Theory of Judicial Review* (Cambridge-Massachusetts, Harvard University Press, 1980).

6 S Rials, 'Entre artificialisme et idolâtrie. Sur l'hésitation du constitutionalisme', pp 159 ff.

of law in sophisticated and pluralistic legal systems and are engaged in the game of the distribution, separation and sharing of powers.

If we adopt the pure/logical positivist approach, the courts solve disputes on the basis of *existing rules*, i.e. norms that have already been created by the legislator and applied by the administration. Taking this for granted, the courts are supposed to further the will of the legislator and assure that he complies with the Constitution. The positivist thesis implies that in the *Constitutional State* the judicial and legislative powers co-exist and interact. More precisely, the first amend the latter, in a sort of *division of labour* between two distinct and connected agents of the legal system. The legal rule definitely emerges at the end of a 'two-step' or 'two-instance' process: its writing by the legislator and its reading/interpretation by the judge.[7] Although normatively exact, this 'shared authority/ sovereignty thesis', which describes the institutional interaction between the judge and the legislator, cannot stand without embracing ex post a certain theory of interpretation. In particular, the real and effective *competence* of the two powers depends upon their state of *discretion* in the law-making process.

Firstly, I shall argue that only a *pragmatological/hermeneutical* theory[8] of interpretation precisely depicts the extreme interpretative power of the judiciary and its relation with the legislature. However, suggesting a theory of interpretation is only a part of understanding the complex way in which the separation of powers is evolving. To put it simply, even if we demonstrate, through a radical freedom of interpretation, that the judiciary can legally claim an unlimited legal authority, this does not necessarily mean that practical authorities do indeed have such authority. On the contrary, *pragmatic* restraints, stemming from the shared authority scheme and the context of the separation of powers, not to mention from entirely non-legal facts and causes (i.e. political and economic necessities), seem to dictate the terms of the dialogue between the authorities. For this reason, an important epistemic and methodological choice is unavoidable before even challenging the relation between the legislator and the courts: the abandonment of pure *normativism* for a critical and realist thesis,

---

7 O Cayla, 'La souveraineté de l'artiste du "second temps"' (1990) *Droits*, no 12, pp 129 ff.

8 See H-G Gadamer, *Vérité et méthode, Les grandes lignes de l'herméneutique contemporaine* (Paris, Seuil, 1996); O Cayla, 'Les juristes à l'épreuve du tournant pragmatique' in D Rousseau (ed), *Le droit dérobé* (Paris, Montchrestien, 2007) pp 37 ff.

which continues to consider the discourse of the legal organs as legally binding speech acts, but at the same time emphasises the extra-legal factors and elements that co-define the meaning of legal rules. In this framework, the realist thesis acquires a particular explanatory force regarding our legal systems (Sec. I).[9]

The jurisprudence of the financial crisis confirms our epistemic hypothesis. The constitutionality of the austerity measures in Greece and their conventionality within the framework of the European Convention of Human Rights have mainly been decided through the test of standards of necessity and proportionality. The standards are words of the ordinary language whose semantic vagueness allows the judge a wide margin of appreciation. They are not pure legal concepts and cannot be signified unless the judge takes into account social, ethical and political considerations.[10] For instance, judging the necessity of the Greek Memorandum with the 'Troika', in other words the constitutionality of an extended programme of structural reforms, also including austerity measures, such as cuts in wages and pensions, implies a political or moral idea about the general interest of the State or the soundness and effectiveness of the financial policy.[11]

Although the interpretation of standards reinforces judicial authority, on the other hand their flexibility can easily lead to judicial self-restraint, as has happened in the most emblematic decisions taken during the financial crisis, or, in contrast, in fewer cases, to judicial activism.[12] The higher courts have mostly hesitated, disregarding the Memorandum laws unless

---

9 See B Leiter, *American Legal Realism*, University of Texas Public Law Research Paper No 42. Available at SSRN: http://ssrn.com/abstract=339562 or http://dx.doi.org/10.2139/ssrn.339562. For other contemporary versions of legal realism, like the Scandinavian and French ones, see J Bjarup, 'The Philosophy of Scandinavian Legal Realism' (2005) *Ratio Juris*, no 18, pp 1-15 and M Troper, 'Une théorie réaliste de l'interprétation' in idem, *La théorie du droit, le droit, l'Etat* (Paris, P.U.F., 2001) pp 68 ff.

10 S. Rials stresses that the standard is not the rule itself but is in the rule. See idem, *Le juge administratif français et la technique juridique du standard* (Paris, L.G.D.J., 1980). See also A Tunc, 'Standards et unification du droit' (1970) *Revue internationale de droit comparé*, vol 22, no 2, pp. 247-61; S Leturcq, *Standards et droits fondamentaux devant le Conseil constitutionnel français et la Cour Européenne des Droits de l'Homme* (Paris, L.G.D.J., 2005).

11 G Karavokyris, *The Constitution and the Crisis* (2014), pp 88 ff.

12 See the recent judgments 2192/2014, 4741/2014 and 2287-90/2015 of the Council of State.

they were obviously contrary to the Constitution. It is indeed true that the way in which the courts perceive their proper competence signifies their auto-*representation* as practical authorities and their status among the State organs.[13] In claiming a restricted amount of authority in adjudicating on the legislation of the financial crisis, the Greek Council of State and the European Court of Human Rights have restated their role —in the contemporary constitutional state— as veto players,[14] with the exception of some recent judgments by the Greek Council of State, particularly during the second phase of the Greek financial crisis (2014 to date). Nevertheless, on the one hand, this tendency towards a jurisprudential turn cannot yet be confirmed as a major informal constitutional change, while, on the other, it rests on a rather precarious appreciation of the real facts of the crisis, leading to an assumption that the intensity of the crisis has been amplified, which is, legally and pragmatically, more than ambivalent (Sec. II).

I shall argue finally that this limited —judicial— claim of authority rests on an epistemic and political matter of competence. The word 'competence' here has a double meaning: the formal competence to decide and the expertise or ability involved in making the decision. These two meanings of the same word are profoundly articulated and both refer to the concept of legitimacy. The courts' trust in the legislator marks the acknowledgement of the latter's epistemic and political excellence at high politics[15] and also an acknowledgement of the ultimate source of the legislator's authority: *elections*. Last but not least, the essential compliance of the judge with the general will of the legislature reminds us that in times of crisis, when the very existence of the State is at stake, the dialogue between the two powers becomes an *interior monologue* of the State (Sec. III).

---

13 M Everson and C Joerges, *Who is the Guardian for Constitutionalism in Europe after the Financial Crisis?*, LSE 'Europe in Question' Discussion Paper Series, No 63/2013, http://www.lse.ac.uk/europeanInstitute/LEQS/LEQSPaper63.pdf.

14 N Alivizatos, 'Judges as Veto Players' in H Doring (ed), *Parliaments and Majority Rule in Western Europe* (Frankfurt, Campus Verlag, 1995), pp 566 ff. and idem, 'Who Decides in Last Resort? Elected Officials and Judges', www.constitutionalism.gr, 10/10/2011.

15 M Tushnet, *Taking the Constitution Away from the Courts* (Princeton, Princeton University Press, 1999).

I. Beyond the Limits of Interpretation

The shared-authority scheme portrays generally or, more precisely, *partially* the institutional dialogue between the parliament and the courts. As we all know, the legislator writes and the judge interprets the rule of law. For the vast majority of constitutionalists, the judge interprets a rule that already exists. Michel Troper has argued that this hypothesis falls inevitably under the epistemic fallacy that consists in confusing the text of law with the law itself.[16] In other words, writing is only one part —the first but not the decisive one— of the lawmaking process. The second one, the act of reading the text, is the crucial phase as the interpreter —and especially the authentic one, if we follow the argument outlined by Kelsen in his Pure Theory of Law— proceeds to an act of volition.[17] If, according to Kelsen, interpretation is indeed an act of will and not of pure reason, it goes without saying that the role of the interpreter becomes more important even than that of the writer of the legal text. However, distinguishing the two moments of the lawmaking process, as a preliminary observation for advancing our argument on the relation between the judge and the legislator, does not necessarily justify or legitimise the absolute power of the latter. Discovering the limits of legal interpretation forms part of a long debate between moral and legal philosophers, constitutionalists and practitioners of the law.

I shall demonstrate that semantic theories of interpretation (logical, analytical positivism),[18] which suggest that the judge is limited by the grammatical structure and the textual meaning of words agreed by the community, in terms of a social linguistic convention, reproduce a *monological* model of interpretation. To put it simply, accepting the semantic argument means that the interpretation of the legal text is a strict logical application of the rule, where the judge examines whether the legislator's will remains confined within the *semiotic* field of the Constitution. In this sense, the

16 M Troper, 'Une théorie réaliste de l'interprétation', (2001) (n 10).

17 H Kelsen, *Théorie Pure du droit*, 2nd edn (Bruxelles-Paris, Bruylant-L.G.D.J., 1996), pp 339-42.

18 A Marmor, Law and Interpretation. Essays in Legal Philosophy (Oxford, Clarendon Press, 1997). See also K Greenawalt, Legal Interpretation: Perspectives From Other Disciplines and Private Texts (Oxford-New York, Oxford University Press, 2010); J Raz, Between Authority and Interpretation: On the Theory of Law and Practical Reason (Oxford, Oxford University Press, 2009).

judge *acts like an automatic machine,* faithfully receiving and retransmitting the message of the legislator, unless there is a logical discordance with the Constitutional text. His judgment on the validity and the constitutionality of the law is devoid of moral or political considerations. It is well known that this positivist theory of jurisprudence, which defends an auto-referential concept of the legal norm, has been severely criticised from an anti-positivist point of view. For instance, the interpretative theory of Ronald Dworkin has convincingly demonstrated the creative role of the judge, especially in the famous 'hard cases', where a textual approach to the Constitution is simply inappropriate for providing us with the best right answer. On the contrary, the latter becomes inevitably a matter of moral and political principle. Thus, Dworkin's latest concept of 'collaborative interpretation' confirms that the dialogue between the authorities or powers is based on political and moral grounds and abstract values, such as democracy, equality, dignity etc.[19] Apart from Dworkin's interpretativism, realist theories of laws stress the gap that exists between the text of the law and the law itself. It is the volitional force of the interpreter that reconstructs the legislator's will and consequently the meaning of the text. On the similar grounds of philosophy of language, the *pragmatic* and *hermeneutical* turn highlighted the historical and contextual relativity of meaning.[20]

From the above epistemic standpoint, searching for logical or grammatical limits of interpretation sounds like sheer vanity or, at worst, a malicious way of imposing as logical and rational assumptions our own moral or political pre-judgments and convictions. On the contrary, the interpretation of a legal text —and of any text— is like an aesthetic and artistic gesture of reading a work of art.[21] If there are restraints, they are pragmatolocigal or hermeneutical which stem from the context of the application of the rule and not the text per se. In other words, the shared authority of the legislator and the judge is less a normative or logical consequence of the separation of powers and more a pragmatological situation in which the interpreter's claim to authority depends upon historical, social, moral,

---

19 R Dworkin, *Taking Rights Seriously* (London, Duckworth, 1978) and idem, *Justice for Hedgehogs* (Cambridge-Massachusetts, Harvard University Press, 2011).

20 O Cayla, 'Langage' in Ph Raynaud and S Rials (eds), *Dictionnaire de philosophie politique* (Paris, P.U.F., 1998), pp 331-38.

21 O Cayla, 'La souveraineté de l'artiste' (1990); G Karavokyris, 'The Art of Law' (2014) *Law and Critique*, vol 25, issue 1, pp 67-85.

political and economic conditions and facts. Therefore, the interpretation should not be reduced to a nihilistic 'anything goes'. It is in reality a 'situated' act, in the continuously changing, in time and space, context of meaning.

A quite instructive example of the non-semantic bounds of interpretation is provided by the famous overrulings of precedent, the radical changes occurring in the meaning of the same text, such as that of the Constitution. In these frequent cases, the text's meaning is significantly altered while the syntax or the grammar of the legal provision remains strictly untouched. As Paul Ricoeur would say, the text is always *oneself as another*.[22] Nevertheless, this evident shift in the meaning of the provision does not imply that the semantically free interpreter has no pragmatic restraints. In a constant dialogue with the legislator, the judge's claim to authority, although superior at a strict normative level, is related to strategic, social and political pressures, ideas and objectives. The judge is not an ahistorical or metaphysical subject. Even in cases of the most radical judicial activism, the judge's interpretative freedom is guided by moral and political principles within a specific context, which has nothing to do with semantics. This methodological assumption underlines the theoretical and practical connection between interpretative freedom and the concept of sovereignty, as the authority that ultimately defines the meaning of the Constitution and therefore changes, formally or informally, its content should be recognised as the legally and politically sovereign organ within the given framework of the separation of powers. Bearing in mind Carl Schmitt's famous definition of a sovereign, according to which the sovereign is he who decides on the state of exception, is fully unable to grasp the concept of sovereignty in periods of constitutional normality and remains essentially outside the legal order, and also that Kelsenian positivism results in a complete neutralisation of the sovereign, who is normatively absorbed by the omnipotence of the legal rule, the noble title of the sovereign is essentially linked to the hermeneutical power.[23] Even if sovereignty depends on a constantly evolving language game between the

22 P Ricoeur, *Oneself as Another* (Chicago, University of Chicago Press, 1995); idem, *De l' interprétation. Essai sur Freud* (Paris, Seuil, 1965).

23 Bodin defines the sovereign as the 'one who gives the law' ('qui donne la loi'). See O Beaud, *La puissance de l'État* (1994). According to an hermeneutical approach, the sovereign is the one that interprets the law authentically, in other words, the legal organ who (re)produces the meaning of the legal texts and —

legal organs, which implies various pragmatic restraints for the interpreter, it should ultimately be understood as the normative power of the one who has the last word on the meaning of the rule. Therefore, sovereignty, just like the act of interpretation, cannot be legally shared or divided, but only exercised by the entitled law implementer, according to his biased (politically, socially, economically, psychologically etc.) volition. The institutional dialogue between the legal and political agents and the shared-authority scheme that describes the context of the interpreter's decision should not be confused with the decision/interpretation itself, which remains, at the same time, normatively sovereign and pragmatically bounded.

In times of crisis, this pragmatically uncertain game of interpretations enters the notably sensitive area of the normative appreciation of so-called 'high politics', where the dialogue between the courts and the legislator restates their proper operational and furthermore constitutional limits.

II. *Judicial Self-Restraint during the Financial Crisis: Legal Techniques and Pragmatological Constraints*

Given that the judge usually has the last word on the constitutionality of a rule in contemporary democracies, we shall accept that even in cases of judicial self-restraint or, the opposite, judicial activism, the choice is attributed to the judge. Put simply, the institutional and normative prevalence of the judge in contemporary legal orders is not to be disputed. On the other hand, the jurisprudence of the financial crisis has highlighted the fact that the judge's claim to authority is not unlimited. Being an historical and moral/political subject, the judge is bounded by his strategic and political considerations.

In particular, judicial restraint rests on sophisticated argumentative and legal techniques. In other words, the courts seem to acknowledge and invoke precise facts and standards, such as 'necessity', 'difficulty', 'public

above all— the meaning of the Constitution. See O Cayla, 'L'obscure théorie du pouvoir constituant originaire ou l'illusion d'une identité souveraine inalterable' in *L'architecture du droit, Mélanges en l'honneur de Michel Troper* (Paris, Economica, 2006), pp 249 ff. The sovereign is defined as the one who formally or informally changes the constitution in the recent work by X Contiades and A Fotiadou, 'Models of Constitutional Change' (2013).

interest' etc. in order to recognise the legislator as the main legal actor who is responsible for dealing with the financial crisis. It is as if the courts were applying without the slightest reserve the famous, in French administrative law, theory of 'exceptional circumstances'.[24] According to the latter, the administrative judge exercises the minimum control over the administrative acts because of the high degree of complexity and difficulty of the litigious situation. For instance, in its famous decision (668/2012) on the first Memorandum, the Greek Council of State stressed that the legislator's task had been notably difficult due to the unprecedented conditions of the economic crisis and the imminent danger of total budgetary derailment. The same language was used by the European Court of Human Rights in its decision on the conventionality of the memorandum in the *Koufaki and Adedy v. Greece* case. [25] The European judge also referred to the extreme economic and financial conditions in Greece, describing the crisis as the worst economic incident of the last decade. Consequently, both courts related the contextual difficulty to the intensity of the judicial control. The fact that Greece was facing an irregular situation attenuated the normative force of the judiciary and widened the margin of appreciation and discretion of the legislature. However, contrary to the 'exceptional circumstances' theory, the judge's interpretation has not been addressed *contra legem* or *contra constitutionem*. The normality of the law has not been interrupted.

In fact, the normative impact of the financial and political context on the extent of judicial control has made itself felt in the proportionality test[26]: in the elastic application of the proportionality principle by the

---

24 See F Saint-Bonnet, *L'État d'exception* (Paris, P.U.F., 2001), p 6 ff; G Camus, *L'État de necessité en démocratie* (Paris, L.G.D.J., 1965).

25 ECtHR 7 May 2013, 57665/12 and 57657/12, *Koufaki and Adedy v. Greece*.

26 For the proportionality principle see X Contiades and A Fotiadou, 'Social Rights in the Age of Proportionality: Global Economic Crisis and Constitutional Litigation' (2012) *International Journal of Constitutional Law*, vol 10, no 3, p 660 ff; S Tsakyrakis, 'Proportionality: An Assault on Human Rights?' (2009) *International Journal of Constitutional Law*, vol 7, issue 3, p 468 ff; G Gerapetritis, *Proportionality in Administrative Law. Judicial Review in France, Greece, England and in the European Community* (Athens, Sakkoulas, 1997); M Cohen-Eliya and I. Porat, *Proportionality and Constitutional Culture*, Cambridge Studies in Constitutional Law (Cambridge, Cambridge University Press, 2013); A Barak, *Proportionality: Constitutional Rights and their Limitations*, Cambridge Studies in Constitutional Law (Cambridge, Cambridge University Press, 2012); M Klatt and M Meister, *The*

Council of State in its 668/2012 decision, as the public interest clause prevailed heavily over the protection of constitutional rights. In other words, the judicial reception and interpretation of non-legal facts, such as the economic and financial conditions, has led to a minimum amount of control being exerted over the Memorandum, via the application of the proportionality principle. The standards have in fact co-defined the constitutionality of the rule (the Memorandum) and incorporated in the legal reasoning the economic and political beliefs of the courts. So, judicial restraint emerges in this case as the sophisticated combination of non-legal elements and the intelligent use of the legal technique of the proportionality test.

The same conclusion could be drawn for the ECtHR's decision in the *Koufaki and Adedy v. Greece* case. The Court underlined that the 'adoption of the impugned measures was justified by the existence of an exceptional crisis without precedent in recent Greek history'. As stressed by the report accompanying Law no. 3833/2010, this was 'the worst crisis in the public finances for decades', which '[had] undermined the country's credibility, thwarted efforts to meet the country's lending needs and pose[d] a serious threat to the national economy'. The report stated that finding a way out of the crisis represented 'a historic responsibility and a national duty' and that Greece had undertaken to 'achieve fiscal consolidation on the basis of precise targets and a precise timetable'. The Court indicated that the legislator had acted in the public interest and with respect for the proportionality principle. Thus, 'the notion of "public interest" is necessarily extensive. As has already been noted, decisions to enact laws to balance State expenditure and revenue will commonly involve consideration of political, economic and social issues, and the margin of appreciation available to the legislature in implementing social and economic policies is a wide one. The Court will thus respect the legislature's judgment as to what is "in the public interest" unless that judgment is manifestly without reasonable foundation. In matters of general policy, on which opinions within a democratic society may reasonably differ widely, the role of the domestic policy-maker should be given special weight.'

In the abovementioned cases, the interpretation of the judge rests on a certain legal qualification of the crisis, on the jurisprudential naming and

---

Constitutional Structure of Proportionality (Oxford, Oxford University Press, 2012).

appreciation of the facts. The severe economic and fiscal conditions that have arisen in the Greek State and the immediate threat of an uncontrolled bankruptcy, in other words a real and not legal or constitutional state of fiscal emergency, are affecting the sovereign act of judicial qualification as pragmatic restraints that the Greek and European judge interpretatively endorse. Hence, before proceeding to a less or more rigorous (proportionality) control of the constitutionality/conventionality of the measures, the judge has already bounded his ruling by a certain interpretation of the 'crisis' which is not legal but extends to various economic or political or even moral considerations regarding what a 'crisis' consists of.[27] Once the judge has agreed with the legislator on the 'real' description of the 'crisis', the scope of the judicial control responds and adapts immediately to the extreme circumstances of the case and results in an emblematic gesture of judicial self-restraint. In contrast, the recent judicial activism of the Greek Council of State in a series of cases concerning the constitutionality of legislation related to the 2nd Memorandum (essentially Law 4093/2012) and, in particular, the further cuts in pensions which have been found to be contrary to Article 22 paragraph 5 of the Greek Constitution (right of social security), depends on a different legal qualification. Specifically, the Council of State (judgments 2287-90/2015) stresses that the financial crisis, as such, should not justify any limitation of the right to social security and therefore should not constitute in this case a well-established and superior reason of public interest in the judicial review. The Greek Court was of the opinion that the urgent phase of the crisis was definitely over and that no threat of immediate bankruptcy existed: as a certain normality within the crisis was being established and, given the fact that a large share of the State's fiscal adjustment measures had already been imposed on the Greek citizens, the usual reference of the legislator to the economic crisis as the justification for the new cuts should be overruled, being obviously disproportionate and inadequate. The Council of State explicitly required a specific, detailed and technically/scientifically articulated study by the legislator of the necessity and efficacy of the new cuts in pensions

---

27 For the notion of legal qualification see O Cayla, 'La qualification ou la vérité du droit', *Droits* (1993) vol 18, p 3 ff; C Vautrot-Schwarz, *La qualification juridique en droit administratif* (Paris, L.G.D.J., 2010), J-J Pardini, 'La jurisprudence constitutionnelle et les "faits"', *Cahiers du Conseil Constitutionnel* (2000) no. 8, http://www.conseil-constitutionnel.fr/conseil-constitutionnel/francais/nouveaux-cahiers-du-conseil/cahier-n-8/la-jurisprudence-constitutionnelle-et-les-faits.52553.htm.

in relation to the sustainability of the social security system and of the concrete effects on the cost of living for pensioners. Put simply, the Court ran a full proportionality test and did not accept that the legislator has supreme discretionary power in the area of fiscal and social security policy. Despite its more than obvious importance concerning the legal appreciation of the crisis, the abovementioned decision by the Council of State should not be considered as a game-changer in the broader scheme of how the principle of the separation of powers is perceived by the courts in times of financial crisis. The crucial distinction of the 2287-90/2015 decisions consists in a new, and rather optimistic, political and economic evaluation of the real facts that, according to the Court, do not match the idea of a 'crisis' that can justify further limitations of socio-economic rights (as in the 668/2012 decision).

Apart from this notable exception, both the Council of State and the ECtHR seem to share the profound conviction that their evident self-restraint is justified not only by the unusual economic circumstances and the extreme difficulty of the legislator's task but also by a general *preconception* about the very competence, in *formal* and *epistemic* terms, of the legislative power in times of financial crisis. The legislator is supposed to be better equipped to deal with the crisis.

III. Authority and Competence

The courts' claim of authority is not an unlimited one. On the contrary, they share their authority with the legislator and, to be more precise, they even grant him priority in dealing legally with the crisis. The reason for this division of labour, which reiterates the meaning of the separation of powers in times of (financial) crisis, is first of all, according to the courts, less a legal and more an epistemic one.[28] The wide discretion of the legislator should not be attributed to his normative superiority. In fact, it is the judge who recognises and validates the cognitive excellence of the legislator, his epistemic competence, in other words, his know-how and his technical and special skills in managing the crisis. Bearing in mind Greece's critical financial situation, the Council of State, in its 668/2012 decision,

28 For the epistemic argument see R Alexy, *A Theory of Constitutional Rights* (Oxford, Oxford University Press, 2002), p 414 ff.

described the Memorandum as a detailed and technical governmental programme, whose rationality and efficiency could not be subjected to strict judicial control. Assuming that he was not entitled or competent enough to thoroughly examine and validate or invalidate the Memorandum, the judge expressed his confidence in the legislator's capacity to formulate financial and economic policy. In such issues, it seems that judicial restraint is dependent upon the content of the disputed law, which, as Mark Tushnet has put it, should belong to 'high politics'. Tushnet's theory on taking important political issues away from the courts, along with the sophisticated theory of 'political questions', explains the wide and legitimate discretion of the legislator in political matters.[29] In the same sense, as already mentioned, the ECtHR underlined the fact that the national legislator is in a much better position than the Court to handle these complicated matters. Even in the recent 2287-90/2015 decisions (see above), the Council of State has not frontally challenged or contested the competence of the legislator but has demanded a thorough justification of measures and further limitations of pensioners' social and economic rights, so as to exercise an effective and complete judicial control.

The word 'competence' has in these cases a double meaning: the formal one, i.e. the legal competence to decide and the substantial or pragmatological one, which concerns the cognitive aspect of the decision. It is obvious that the latter is the criterion guiding judicial restraint. The legislator is supposed to be much more efficient and informed on these matters. Nevertheless, this epistemic assumption fails to entirely explain the reason why the judge's claim of authority in deciding upon the crisis is a rather limited one. Besides, it is well known that in a contemporary constitutional state the judge is awarded the high (normative and intellectual) competence of ensuring the conformity of the legislature's will with the Constitution. So, understanding the redistribution of normative power during the financial crisis and the terms of the dialogue between the legislator and the judge is

29 A Psigas, 'Identifying and Re-signifying the Political Question Doctrine in the Greek Legal Order' (2012) *DtA*, no 47 (in Greek), pp 743-806; A Bickel, *The Least Dangerous Branch. The Supreme Court at the Bar of Politics*, 2nd edn (London and New Haven, Yale University Press, 1986); M Troper, 'Le juge constitutionnel et la volonté générale' in M Troper, *La Théorie du droit, le Droit, l'État* (Paris, P.U.F., 2001), p 215 ff; G Canivet and N Molfessis, *La politique jurisprudentielle, Mélanges en l'honneur de Jacques Boré, la création du droit jurisprudentiel* (Paris, Dalloz, 2007), p 79.

not only a matter of competence, i.e. identifying the legal agent that has the cognitive excellence to deal with the economic and financial issues. This empirical observation remains a *partial* explanation of the way in which the separation of powers generally functions. Deciding which power should deal normatively with the crisis is not only an issue of rational deduction (i.e. the agent who knows best).

Furthermore, judicial self-restraint is based on a political or even moral argument: the legislator's competence is partially acquired from the nature of his decision (a political one) and on the other hand lies essentially in the source of his power, the fact that he has been elected. His cognitive excellence is therefore a side-effect of the democratic argument and is rooted in the modern theory and practice of representation, where the elected representative (the free actor) interprets and signifies the will of the bound author, the people.[30] Thus, the concept of elections has an aristocratic foundation,[31] implying that the individual designated by the people is the one most entitled to express the general will. Therefore, even in the contemporary constitutional state, an elitist conception of governance still has a great impact on the principle of the separation of powers.

Moreover, there is a moral justification for this division of labour between the judge and the legislator, as the representation principle is connected with the value of collective autonomy. When a crisis occurs and urgent dilemmas and choices arise concerning our democratic governance, the elected legislator has to bear the political responsibility of deciding on the people's fate. It is only through this technique that this important decision is attributed to the people, and all of us, as a whole. In times of political and economic crisis, the non-elected judge, despite the fact that his competence is provided by the Constitution, loses in legitimacy because the majority rule prevails when the raison d'être of the State is at stake. Needless to say, the ultimate guardian of *political autonomy* differs from

---

30 B Daugeron, La notion d'élection en droit constitutionnel. Contribution à une théorie juridique de l'élection à partir du droit public français (Paris, Dalloz, 2011).

31 B Manin, *Principes du gouvernement représentatif* (Paris, Calman-Levy, 1995). See also H Pitkin, *The Concept of Representation* (Berkeley, University of California Press, 1967); N Urbinati, *Representative Democracy. Principles and Genealogy* (Chicago, University of Chicago Press, 2006); P Brunet, *Vouloir pour la Nation: le concept de représentation dans la théorie de l'État* (Paris-Rouen-Bruxelles, L.G.D.J. – Bruylant, 2004).

that of *personal freedom*, where the judge is extremely vigilant and suspicious vis-à-vis the majority principle.

This judicial self-restraint in political and financial matters depicts the will of the judge to share not only his authority but also the *political responsibility* for the crisis. Last but not least, it reminds us that the dialogue between the two powers can sometimes be an interior monologue of the State. It is often forgotten that the legislature and the judicial power are in fact the two faces of the same coin. Therefore, when the State is at high risk they both seem to represent the Reason of State (Raison d'Etat), the sovereign necessity to keep the State alive. Ultimately, the core jurisprudence of the financial crisis is a plain proof that the survival instinct of the constitutional state holds a tremendous normative power.

IV. Conclusion: Crisis, Normality and Legitimacy

The relation between the courts and the legislators is not a static one, as its normative status and function essentially depend upon pragmatic or strategic restraints, such as the political, financial and moral circumstances in which the discourse between the legislature and the judiciary evolves and *performs*. The Greek financial crisis seems to be functioning as a distinct and crucial *reason for action* for the legal actors, structuring and dictating their dialogue in terms of judicial self-restraint and the recognition of the legislator's wide discretion. Hence, the financial crisis has restated the operational and axiological scope of the two powers in the contemporary Rule of Law/État de droit: the judge still retains normatively his superior place in the legal system but on the pragmatic and interpretative level the legislator's will is being credited with the benefit and presumption of correctness.[32] The financial crisis has emerged as a new interpretative background, which re-affirms the democratic element of the rule of law and the meaningful weight of political legitimacy when it comes to legal matters of significant political impact, such as the crisis legislation.

The sophisticated dialogue between the courts and the legislator has established a new constitutional normality, as the uneven and unprecedented financial events have been legally absorbed, mainly through the interpreta-

32 See P Blachèr, Contrôle de constitutionnalité et volonté générale (Paris, P.U.F., 2001).

tion of standards (such as 'necessity' and 'public interest'), in compliance with the existing constitutional framework. The legal episode of the financial crisis is not an interval or a constitutional disruption. The constitutional provisions on the state of emergency have not been triggered. The austerity measures and the memoranda agreed with the Troika representatives were adopted *in a normal way*, according to more or less ordinary parliamentary procedures.

However, the so-called 'anti-memorandum' political and legal discourse has severely challenged not only the legality and the constitutionality of the crisis legislation but also its *legitimacy*, claiming that it has in fact been unilaterally *imposed* under the extreme pressure of the Troika and therefore should not be imputed to the Greek authorities and a fortiori to the Greek people.[33] This naturalistic and political discourse fatally ignores the fundamental elements of modern constitutionalism and representative democracy, such as the parliamentary adoption of the austerity measures and their comprehensive judicial review by the highest courts of law. In other words, the extreme *politicisation* of the legal discourse reproduces an absolute confusion of legality and legitimacy, as one's political estimation and disagreement over the law of the crisis results to the most emblematic and radical contempt for the foundations of the legal system and invalidates the reasons of obedience to legal authorities. Nevertheless, in contemporary democracies, the discussion about the legitimacy of the law is essentially connected to its legality, to the condition that all procedural and substantial rules have been thoroughly followed. Otherwise, there is no common democratic ground for the law to be disputed and for the sovereignty of the State to be exercised.

Despite the financial anomaly and the pressure of the European Institutions and the IMF, the crisis legislation has been passed and judged by elected and appointed bodies.[34] In this sense, the respect for the democratic procedures and the constitutional guaranties of the law confirms the very legitimacy of the measures and accredits the interaction between the courts and the legislator, as the entitled representatives of the general will. Taking this into account, the complex way in which the legislator and the

33 See notably G Katrougalos, *The crisis and its way out* (Athens, Livanis, 2012) (in Greek).

34 See G Karavokyris, 'Constitution and necessity in times of crisis: an alternative way of understanding the relation between politics and the law', *European Politeia,* (2015) vol 2, pp 347-65.

judge have communicated and shared their authority during the financial crisis constitutes another chapter in the 'chain novel' of judicial review and its relation to democracy and the Rule of Law.

7 The OMT Case and the Judicial Control of Monetary Policy

Jean-Victor LOUIS[*]

I. Introduction

On June 16 2015 the Court of Justice adopted a judgment[1] which legitimates the Outright Monetary Transactions (OMT) programme of the ECB in a preliminary ruling requested by the Bundesverfassungsgericht (BVerfG). It was the first time that the Constitutional Court had introduced such a request.[2] But this move, far from being made in deference to the Court of Justice, was intended to dictate to it the modalities which would allow the Karlsruhe Court to admit the legality of the OMT programme. The Court of Justice's reply, by recognising the conformity of the OMT to the FEU Treaty, provides a legal framework for the unconventional measures that the crisis has led the ECB to adopt and will perhaps have to decide in the future. Within the regulatory limits fixed by the Treaty (essentially, the respect of monetary policy objectives and the prohibition of monetary financing), the Court recognises that the ECB, within the framework of its Statute, has powers similar to those used by the world's most important central banks. In reporting on the judgment of the Court of Justice, the newspaper *Le Monde* ran the headline: 'A Luxembourg, des juges de plus

*

1 See the judgment of the Court of Justice (Grand Chamber) C-62-14 *Peter Gauweiler et al. v. Deutscher Bundestag* 16 June 2015 EU:C:2015:400. On this decision, see, among others, P Craig and M Markakis, '*Gauweiler* and the Legality of Outright Monetary Transactions', (2016) 41 *Eur.L.Rev.* 1; papers.ssrn/sol3/Papers.cfm?abstract_id=2723459.

2 There is an extensive literature on this decision of the BVerfG of 14 January 2014. See, in particular, the special online issue of the *German Law Journal*, 2014, No 2, and the article by Paul De Grauwe in a blog supported by the LSE's European Institute, 'Why the European Court of Justice Should Reject the German Constitutional Court's Ruling on Outright Monetary Transactions', available at blogs.lse.uk/europpblog/2014/03/04, followed by a great number of comments. See also the references in J.-V. Louis, 'La Cour constitutionnelle allemande et la politique monétaire', éditorial, (2014) *Cahiers de droit européen* 268-81.

en plus puissants'.[3] As a matter of fact, it is the ECB which received confirmation of its remarkable importance in the EMU governance. Above all, the judgment of the Court of Justice, with some conditions, legitimates non-conventional measures of monetary policy. A legitimacy denied by those who were of the view that monetary policy had in some way become a kind of 'outlaw' area. Different logics were confronted and in the end a realistic and conciliatory way was adopted.

After some general thoughts on the constitutional position of the ECB and the legal control of its activities, we will comment on some aspects of the order of the BVerfG, analyse the conclusions of the Advocate General Cruz Villalón and the Court's judgment before drawing some conclusions, while bearing in mind that the last word will be for the BverfG.[4]

II. The ECB and the Court of Justice

The draft Protocol on the Statute of the ESCB and the ECB, as proposed by the Committee of Governors of the Central Banks of the EEC to the intergovernmental conference in 1991, included a provision which has become Art 35 on 'Judicial Control and Related Matters', which states in its first paragraph: 'The acts or omissions of the ECB shall be open to review or interpretation by the Court of Justice in the cases and under the conditions laid down in this Treaty. The ECB may institute proceedings in the cases and in the conditions laid down by the Treaty.'

This formulation, which may be considered as an affirmation of general principles without going into specifics, was justified by the fact that the committee of Central Bank lawyers who drafted this provision considered that it was the task of the intergovernmental conference that would negotiate the future Maastricht Treaty to specify 'the cases and conditions' referred to in Art 35, which indeed was done by the IGC through relevant amendments to the Treaty.

---

3 *Le Monde*, Économie section, 16 June 2015.

4 Meanwhile see: final judgment of the GFCC of 21 June 2016, 2 BvR 2728/13 et al. – OMT, not yet published, English press release 34/2016 of 21 June 2016: „Constitutional Complaints and Organstreit Proceedings Against the OMT Programme of the European Central Bank Unsuccessful", available at http://www.bundesverfassungsgericht.de/SharedDocs/Pressemitteilungen/EN/2016/bvg16-034.html.

Until the Lisbon Treaty, the ECB was not an 'institution' like the other classic EU institutions (including the Court of Auditors since the Maastricht Treaty), but as far as its *jus standi* before the Court of Justice was concerned, its assimilation with the institutions was complete for appeals for annulment, as well as appeals for failure to act and for preliminary rulings of the Court of Justice with two exceptions: its active legitimation in annulment cases was limited (the ECB, like the Court of Auditors, could only act for annulment in order to safeguard its prerogatives) and actions for failure to act were only open to the ECB in areas falling within its competences and in actions and proceedings brought against the ECB.

When the ECB became an institution under Art 13 of the TEU, as amended by the Lisbon Treaty, nothing changed for the *jus standi* of the ECB before the Court of Justice except for the introduction of its complete assimilation with the other institutions as far as actions for failure to act were concerned (Art 265 TFEU). The limitation concerning the active legitimation to act for annulment was maintained.

The judicial status prescribed for the ECB had four complementary justifications for the authors of the Statute of the ESCB and the ECB: to ensure respect for the commitments which had been subscribed[5], to preserve legal certainty, to include without restriction the ESCB and the ECB in the EU legal order and to contribute to their legitimacy.

The judicial status of the ECB was also a contribution to its independence by centralising its legal control. Of course, direct appeals have to answer to the conditions of admissibility laid down by the Treaty.

The object of this contribution finds a justification in a paper by Prof. Herwig Hofmann which underlines the contribution of the Court's OMT (*Gauweiler*) judgment to the judicial control of the actions of central banks:

With the possibilities of judicial review of the actions of central banks, *Gauweiler* marks a big step towards developing accountability in legal terms while respecting technical expertise and the discretion which was conferred on the ECB in order to back that up.[6]

---

5 See *Vers un système européen de banques centrales*. Projet de dispositions organiques, rapport du groupe présidé par Jean-Victor Louis (Éditions de l'Université de Bruxelles, 1989) 24; see also projet d'article 16.

6 See H Hofmann, 'Gauweiler and OMT: Lessons for EU Public Law and the European Economic and Monetary Union' Working Paper, in the version of 19 June 2015, 21, available at ssrn.com/abstract=2621933.

III. The Limits of Judicial Control on Monetary Policy, the Policy of Communication and the OMT Decision

If it is clear that ways exist for the Court of Justice to exercise legal control over the acts of the ECB, the next question relates to the nature and limits of this control. In the interwar period, Ralph George Hawtrey, who was a director at the British Treasury, wrote a famous book entitled *The Art of Central Banking.*[7] This celebrated author developed ideas about the role of central banks, which were based on their dynamic role in promoting or restricting credit by discretionary measures.

We underscore the use of the word 'discretionary' to qualify the policies of a central bank. In his conclusions on the OMT case, Advocate General Cruz Villalón points to the large margin of discretion that the ECB is to be allowed in its conception and implementation of EU monetary policy. For him:

> The Courts, when reviewing the ECB's activity, must … avoid the risk of supplanting the Bank, by venturing into a highly technical terrain in which it is necessary to have an expertise and experience which, according to the Treaties, devolves solely upon the ECB. Therefore, the intensity of judicial review of the ECB's activity, its mandatory nature aside, must be characterised by a considerable degree of caution.[8]

In its judgment of 16 June 2015, the Court also refers to the 'choices of a technical nature and to…forecasts and complex assessments' in preparing and implementing the OMT programme, which justify the ECB being 'allowed, in that context, a broad discretion'. Nevertheless, the Court adds, 'where an EU institution enjoys broad discretion, a review of compliance with certain procedural guarantees is of fundamental importance'.[9]

---

7 RG Hawtrey, *The Art of Central Banking* (Abingdon Oxon, Frank Cass & Co, 1932), 3rd and last edn 1970. Before this, he had also written a book entitled *Currency and Credit*, 1st ed (London, Longmans, Green & Co, 1919). See L Brillant, 'Ralph George Hawtrey, Charles Rist and the French Translation of *Currency and Credit*' (1935)', available at eet.pixel-online.org/files/research_papers/FR/BrillantLucy_EuropeanContract_%20Pixel_Rist&Hawtrey_July2014.pdf.

8 Conclusions, point 111. It should be noted that the Advocate General – who, in note 59, quotes some authors in support of his affirmation – refers to the 'Courts' in the plural, meaning the Court of Justice but also the BVerfG, which does not observe this kind of auto limitation.

9 See Judgment of 16 June 2015, aff. C-62/14, paras 68 and 69.

The difference between the situation described by Hawtrey and the present one is the increased volatility of the economic situation due in large part to globalisation and the uncertainty that derives from it. The decisions of the Federal Reserve and the evolution of the economy in the US or in China and other emerging markets have, more than ever before, an impact on the markets in Europe. Although there are many contacts and also measures of assistance (such as swap agreements in times when the markets are in need of liquidity) between the G7 and G20 central banks, one cannot speak of coordination among them. Nevertheless, their dependence on each other is, to different degrees, real. This global volatility is, to be sure, one of the reasons for the attitude of the ECB at its beginning: when its president was asked about the future evolution of the interest rates, the answer given by President Trichet was: 'we never predict (or precommit)'. This attitude was also the manifestation of a specific conception of central banking. The Central Bank had to surprise. The limited communication policy was conceived as a way of guaranteeing the efficacy of its monetary policy measures. This mentality was bound to evolve.[10] As early as in 2004, the then Governor (not yet chairman) of the Federal Reserve, Ben S. Bernanke, in a talk with the significant title 'Central Bank Talk and Monetary Policy', referred to the 'increased prominence of FOMC's post-meeting statements',[11] for which there were three reasons: to provide the public with as many explanations about [its] decisions as possible, to lead to better policy decisions, 'because engagement with an informed public provides central bankers with useful feedback…' and because 'open and clear communication by the policy committee… makes monetary policy more effective in at least three distinct ways': the near-term predictability of FOMC rate decisions, which reduces risk and volatility in financial markets, communicating the central bank's objectives and policy strategies, can help to anchor the public's long-term ex-

10 See the suggestive analysis of the different kinds of transparency and of the evolution of central banks, NN Dincer and B Eichengreen, 'Central Bank Transparency and Independence: Updates and New Measures', *Bank of Korea Working Paper* No 2013-21, 4 September 2013, 52 pages.

11 A practice which started in 1994, as observed by Chairman Bernanke in a speech at 'The First 100 Years of the Federal Reserve: The Policy Record, Lessons Learned, and Prospects for the Future', a conference sponsored by the National Bureau of Economic Research, Cambridge, Mass., July 10 2013 (p 5 of the transcript of the speech). Before, Federal Reserve officials 'believed … that the ability to take markets by surprise was important for influencing financial conditions'.

pectations, and in particular, its expectations on inflation. Clear and open communication enhances the effectiveness of monetary policy by helping 'to align financial market participants' expectations about the future course of monetary policy more closely with the FOMC's own plans and projections'.[12] 'Forward guidance', as used by the world's more important central banks, is a development of this philosophy. Mario Draghi has introduced this element into the arsenal of the ECB's monetary policy.[13] Providing forward guidance 'has implied communicating not only how the ECB's Governing Council assesses current economic conditions and the risk to price stability over the medium term, but also what this assessment implies for its future monetary policy orientation.[14] This strategy is related to the ECB aims of ensuring the medium-term stability of the rates applied by the Bank on its main operations, which are kept low so that the ECB can restore a rate of inflation which is less than but close to 2 per cent, in conformity with the definition of its monetary policy confirmed in 2003. The decisions announced in this respect are based on non-binding macroeconomic forecasts established by the ECB's staff and on a policy debate at the level of the Governing Council introduced by a report presented by the member of the Board of Directors in charge of the economic department.[15] Advocate General Cruz Villalón, in his conclusions in case C-62/14, un-

---

12 See the Remarks by Governor Ben S. Bernanke at the Japan Society Corporate Luncheon, New York, October 7 2004, 'Central Bank Talk and Monetary Policy'. Later on, in a speech at the Institute for Monetary and Economic Studies International Conference, Bank of Japan, Tokyo, on May 25 2010, Chairman Bernanke united the three concepts 'Central Bank independence, transparency, and accountability'. On transparency, see the article by I Begg, 'Contested Meanings of Transparency in Central Banking' (April 2007) Vol. 5 *Comparative European Politics* 36-52, and the quoted literature.

13 On forward guidance see P Praet, 'Current Issues and Challenges for Central Bank Communication', speech delivered at the conference entitled 'The ECB and its Watchers XV', Frankfurt am Main, March 12 2014, and 'The ECB's Forward Guidance' *ECB. Monthly Bulletin*, April 2014, 65-73.

14 'The ECB's Forward Guidance' (n 12) 65.

15 It should be noted that recently central banks have made unexpected moves, such as the National Bank of Switzerland, when on January 15 2015 it announced the floor price of 1.20 francs to one euro and considerably cut the (negative) interest rate, or the Bank of Canada, when on January 21 2015 it cut the core interest rate in response to the lowering of the oil price etc: see M Charrel, 'Les banques centrales font des surprises', *Le Monde*, 3-4 May 2015. For some, the merits of forward guidance should not be overestimated. Governor Stephen S. Poloz of the Bank of Canada explained in a speech at the Canada-United Kingdom Chamber of

derlines the role of public communication in contemporary policy.[16] As we will comment on later, the Court and its Advocate General require the ECB to provide explanations for the motives behind its actions. The ECB has given an extensive explanation of its motives for establishing the OMT in its press release of 6 September 2012, press conferences, conferences, articles in the *ECB Monthly Bulletin*, 'monetary dialogue' with the European Parliament and speeches by members of the Executive Board. We will see that most of the Court's analysis has been based on the press release, to which some elements drawn from draft legal implementation documents were added. It is actually a well-known fact that the mere adoption of the OMT programme, which has not been implemented up to now, has been sufficient in order to achieve the objectives of the ECB's action: to re-establish the canals of transmission of monetary policy.

It is also well known that the decision to rely on OMT was taken as a follow-up to a declaration made by President Draghi in a lecture in London, announcing, at a very critical moment for the single currency, that 'Within our mandate, the ECB is ready to do whatever it takes to preserve the euro'.[17] It was very clear that the ECB would take radical measures in order to fight the fragmentation of financial markets, which called for re-establishing the transmission of monetary policy. At his press conference of 2 August 2012, President Draghi revealed that investors were retreating into their national markets and that the Interbank market wasn't working between Member States. Extraordinary premiums were being asked from some States for their loans. Those premiums were due for covering not on-

---

Commerce, London, March 26 2015, that if 'forward guidance is a valuable part of the central bank tool kit (…) statements to explicitly guide market expectations about the future path of interest rates are best reserved for extraordinary times, such as when policy rates are at the effective lower bound, or during periods of market stress' (p. 4 of transcript of speech.).

16 See Conclusions, points 73 and 89. It is a well-known fact that the ECB has decided to publish an 'account' (without indication of the votes cast) of the monetary policy meetings of the Governing Council in order to increase the transparency of its decisions. The first account which concerns the meeting of 21-22 January 2015 was published on 19 February 2015. See E Mourlon-Druol, 'Excitement and Frustration: the Publication of the First ECB "minutes"', 19 February 2015, available at www.e-mourlon-druol.com/excitement-and-frustration-the-publication-of-the-first-ecb-minutes/.

17 Speech at the Global Investment Conference, London, 26 July 2012. The verbatim of the speech is available at www.ecb.eu/press/key/date/2012/html/sp120726.en.html.

ly liquidity and solvability risks but also the risk of convertibility. In the words of the President of the ECB: '*Risk premia that are related to fears of the reversibility of the euro are unacceptable, and they need to be addressed in fundamental manner.*' In the words of someone at the heart of the action, the situation was such that the single monetary policy had shifted from 'one size fits all' to 'one size fits none'.[18]

In one[19] of the many (critical) comments on the OMT decision by the Bundesverfassungsgericht of 14 January 2014,[20] authors remark that '*a sovereign can be in a situation when the inducing effect of an interest rate increase is always outweighed by an increased probability of default that it triggers.*' So, the default probability is higher than the interest rate promise can justify. The objective of the measures to be taken is not, for these authors, to 'neutralise' the differences between the rates —in other words, to harmonise them— but to put a 'brake' on the expectations leading to a bad equilibrium.[21]

IV. The OMT and the Order by the BVerfG for a Preliminary Ruling of the Court of Justice

The OMT, as specified in the 'decision' of 6 September 2012, were qualified as open market operations (by definition on the secondary market), based on Art 18, para 1 of the ESCB and ECB Statute, linked to a request for intervention made by the Member State concerned to the EFS/ESM, which includes the conditionality linked to such intervention. This conditionality, intended to fight moral hazard, is in line with the spirit of the Court's decision in the *Pringle* judgment on the ESM.[22] Among other features, sovereign obligations purchased by the ECB would have a maturity of between one and three years. For the complainants who had introduced constitutional requests and the applicant (the parliamentary group Die Linke) which had introduced an 'Organstreitverfahren' before the BVerfG

18 Speech by B Coeuré, 'Outright Monetary Transactions, One Year On', 2 September 2013.

19 See C Gerner-Breuerle, E Kusük and E Schuster, 'Law Meets Economics in the German Federal Constitutional Court: Outright Monetary Transactions on Trial' (2014) 2 *German Law Journal* 281-320, especially 293.

20 2 BvR 2728/3.

21 See Gerner-Breuerle, 'Outright Monetary Transactions' (n 19) 300.

22 See C-370/12 *Pringle* 27 November 2012, EU:C:2012:756, para 136.

for having allowed the OMT programme, the measure was an *ultra vires* act in the meaning of the case-law of the Constitutional Court. It violated the prohibition of monetary financing (Art 123 TFEU). It was not an act of monetary policy but of economic policy. Making this mechanism contingent on the assistance mechanisms (EFSF/ESM), including the conditionality inherent in them, was contrary to the independence of the ECB, which also had no mandate to defend the euro by any means. Among other arguments, the complainants alleged that the OMT decision could create a liability and payment risk for the federal budget.[23]

The Bundesbank set out before the Court a position contrary to the views of the ECB. It questioned the assumption of a disruption to the monetary policy transmission mechanism invoked by the ECB to justify the OMT decision. It rejected the views of the specialised literature that interest spreads on government bonds could be split into either justified or irrational components. The Bundesbank also stressed, using arguments that could be applied to any kind of so-called 'quantitative easing', that the purchase of government bonds on the secondary market disconnect the benefiting state's financing terms from the financial market. The large-scale purchase of government bonds carries considerable risk and can lead to an ever-increasing amount of Member State's debts being assumed by the Eurosystem. Furthermore, every loss it incurs burdens the German federal budget without parliamentary monitoring.[24]

These arguments developed by the Bundesbank are quoted here because they were largely followed by the Constitutional Court, an attitude which justified the title of an article about the BVerfG's order: 'In the ECB We Do Not Trust'.[25] The Constitutional Court relied categorically on the expertise of the German Central Bank against the arguments of the ECB. The title of section 3 of Part II of its decision may be mentioned in this regard: 'Irrelevance of a Reference to a Disruption to the Monetary Transmission Mechanism'. The BVerfG relies especially on the 'efficient markets theory' to which the Bundesbank oddly enough[26] still seems to ad-

23 Order, para 5.

24 Paras 13-15.

25 T Beukers, 'The Bundesverfassungsgericht Preliminary Reference on the OMT Program: "In the ECB We Do Not Trust. What About You?"' (2014) *German Law Journal* 343-68.

26 See P De Grauwe, 'Economic Theories that Influenced the Judges of Karlsruhe', *VOX*, 13 March 2014.

here: 'Spreads always only result from the market participants' expectations and are, regardless of their rationality, essential for market-based pricing' (point 98). The debate between the ECB and a central bank of the Eurosystem before a national court, whatever its prestige, is precisely what should have been avoided, considering the necessary authority of the central bank. This appeal could appear paradoxical in a country so attached to the principle of central bank independence, at the national as well as at the supranational level.

We will confine ourselves to making three remarks on the BVerfG's order.

The *first remark* concerns the decision by the Constitutional Court to declare as admissible the requests made by the complainants and the applicant against the decision of the Governing Council to adopt a decision on OMT, the Bundestag's refusal to exercise its overall budgetary responsibility and the Federal Government's failure to bring an action against the ECB before the Court of Justice on account of this decision. Our remark is by no means original. Judge Lübbe-Wolff, in her dissenting opinion, has based all her argumentation on this point and many commentators have made concurring observations. The Constitutional Court has pushed to the extreme the argument based on Art 38, section 1 of the Grundgesetz on the right to vote. Quoting a former decision,[27] the Court recalls that, in its view, this provision 'does not merely guarantee that a citizen has the right to elect the German Bundestag and that the constitutional principles of electoral law will be complied with in the election'. There is also a 'fundamental democratic content of this right': 'the subjective right to partake in the election…and to thereby *contribute to the legitimation of state authority by the people at the federal level and to influence the exercise of authority*'.[28] In other words, if we apply this doctrine to the present case, the citizen is legitimated, through his/her appeal, to assist in correcting the attitude of the Bundestag if this institution has, by its negligence, not reacted against an *ultra vires* policy of the ECB and by doing so, violated the 'integration programme' that the Court has given itself the mission to preserve.

The admissibility of a request introduced by a private person, as justified by the Constitutional Court, appears to be extremely close to the *actio*

---

27 BVerfGE 89, 155 <171> and <172>.

28 The italics are ours.

popularis and has no equivalent in other Member States with a constitutional court or a supreme court in charge of protecting the constitution of the state. As stressed by Judge Gerhardt in his dissenting opinion[29]: 'By admitting… an *ultra vires* review that is based on the allegation of a violation of Art 38 sec 1 GG, the door is opened to a general right to have the laws enforced (allgemeiner Gesetzvollziehungsanspruch), which the Basic Law does not contain' (cf. BVerfGE 132, 195<235> with further references).

As observed by Judge Lübbe-Wolff, 'at any rate, what the plaintiffs, insofar as they turn against federal inaction with respect to the OMT decision, petition the Federal Constitutional Court to order goes, in my view, beyond the limits of judicial competence under the principles of democracy and separation of powers'.

The *second remark* relates to the way the BVerfG conceives its relations with the Court of Justice with regard to the procedure of requesting a preliminary ruling. It is very difficult to recognise in this request the Constitutional Court's will to conform itself without reservation to the ruling of the Court of Justice, whatever its substance. It has been rightly observed[30] that the Constitutional Court accepts the authority of the Court's decision only 'in principle'. It is indeed remarkable that the BVerfG, after having characterised the OMT as a 'manifest and structurally significant *ultra vires* act',[31] as it announced in its decision of 6 September 2012 and developed in the order, listed the conditions under which it could lift the objections against it. It is not the first time that a Court asking for a preliminary ruling has set out its views on the possible answers to the questions it has raised, although it is, to say the least, unusual that, as a condition for accepting its ruling, it stipulated that the Court of Justice should adopt its own interpretation of the issues at stake. Some Member States have observed before the Court that a request for a preliminary ruling in validity was not a mechanism conceived in order to make it easy for national jurisdictions to control the validity of the Union's actions to which they themselves proceed, as in the present case, but to guarantee that this control should be exercised before the jurisdictional organ which was exclusively

29 Dissenting opinion, para 6.

30 See M Wendel, 'Exceeding Judicial Competence in the Name of Democracy', (2014) 2 *European Constitutional Law Review* 263-307.

31 On this concept, see 2 BvR 2661/06, 6 July 2010 (*Honeywell*), point 61.

competent, i.e. the Court of Justice.[32] For the Advocate General, who devotes a number of remarks on this problem, it was a 'functional' difficulty of this preliminary request.

Our *third remark* is that the Constitutional Court expressly evokes the possibility that the OMT may constitute a violation of the 'constitutional identity' of Germany. The Court, among the 'relevant legal provisions and jurisprudence', refers to its case-law in this field. Three elements are of prime importance in this context. First, if an action by an institution or other agency has consequences which affect the constitutional identity protected by Art 79, sec 3 GG, it is, from the outset, inapplicable in Germany. Second, it is up to the Constitutional Court to determine the inviolable core content of the constitutional identity and to review whether the action (according to the interpretation given by the Court of Justice in a preliminary ruling) interferes with this core.[33] Third, constitutional identity is not to be confused with national identity, as protected by Art 4 para 2 TUE, because, for the Constitutional Court, the review of constitutional identity 'is not to be assessed according to Union law but exclusively to German constitutional law'.[34]

With regard to the Constitutional Court's pretension to invoke the constitutional identity of Germany if it is not satisfied by the Court of Justice's response to its order, we have sympathy with the view expressed in his conclusions by Advocate General Pedro Cruz Villalón:

> The first is that it seems to me an all but impossible task to preserve *this* Union, as we know it today, if it is to be made subject to an absolute reservation, ill-defined and virtually at the discretion of each of the Member States, which takes the form of a category described as 'constitutional identity'. That is particularly the case if that 'constitutional identity' is stated to be different from the 'national identity' referred to in Article 4(2) TEU.
>
> Such a 'reservation of identity', independently formed and interpreted by the competent — often judicial — bodies of the Member States (of which, it need hardly be recalled, there are currently 28) would very probably leave the EU legal order in a subordinate position, at least in qualitative terms. Without going into details, and without seeking to pass judgment, I think that the characteristics of the case before us may provide a good illustration of the scenario I have just outlined.[35]

---

32 Conclusions of the Advocate General, para 35.

33 Order, point 27.

34 Point 103.

35 Conclusions, 14 January 2015, points 59 and 60.

Constitutional identity is an element of national identity and we know that, contrary to the wishes of some authors,[36] the Court of Justice has applied a proportionality test in its famous *Omega*[37] and *Sayn-Wittgenstein* decisions which both related to general principles of Community/Union law and national constitutional law, respectively, the principles of human dignity and the principle of equality, both pertaining to the common values as described by Art 2 TEU (in its Lisbon version).

The reference to constitutional identity is particularly odd in this case because it bears on a possible (remote) violation of the overall budgetary responsibility of the Bundestag: the BVerfG feared the risk of huge losses that could be assumed by the ECB due to its OMT, with the consequence that these losses might eventually be transferred to the State budget. It is a constant concern in the case-law of the Constitutional Court in relation to European integration, and especially since the mechanisms of assistance (EFSF/ESM) were established, to insist on the prerogatives of the Bundestag. Budgetary autonomy is a central preoccupation of the Court. It was listed in the *Lisbon* decision among the policy sectors pertaining to the core of prerogatives protected by the 'eternal' clause of Art 79 sec 3 GG. In the present context, authors have mentioned that it is in the nature of a central bank to support losses,[38] sometimes very important, especially in respect of their exchange reserves, and that there are, in the Statute of the ESCB and the ECB, provisions regarding the procedure to be followed in the event of losses (Art 33).[39] Authors have also mentioned the fact that there is no obligation to compensate in one exercise for the accumulated debts, which can anyway be absorbed by gains in later exercises. One should remember the fluctuations of TARGET outstanding balances and

---

36 See, in particular, LFM Besselink, 'Respecting Constitutional Identity in the EU', Observations on Case C-208/09, *Ilonka Sayn-Wittgenstein*, 22 December 2010 (2012) 49 *CML Rev* 671-93.

37 C-36/02 *Omega* judgment of 14 October 2004 EU:C:2004:614.

38 'Losses have indeed been recorded by the ECB in carrying out conventional monetary policy operations in the past (1999, 2003 and 2004)', see Vergote et al., 'Main Drivers of the ECB Financial Accounts and ECB Financial Strength over the First 11 years', *ECB Occasional Paper* No 111, May 2010, 28-29, quoted by AL Riso, 'An Analysis of the OMT Case from an EU Law Perspective' in H Sickmann, V Vig and V Wieland (eds), *The ECB's Outright Monetary Transaction in the Courts*, Institute for Monetary and Financial Stability, 1/2015, 27, fn 50.

39 This argument will be used by the Court of Justice, see its judgment, para. 125 and below, p. 117 (around fn. 67-68 – pagination to be verified in the proof).

the volatility of foreign currencies, which constitute the exchange reserves of the ECB and the NCBs. As we will see, the Court of Justice observed that the OMT includes inherent limitations to the risk of losses.[40]

V. The Conclusions of the Advocate General

Despite what he called the 'functional' problems created by the request for a preliminary ruling in this case, the Advocate General suggested that the Court should consider giving an answer on the substance of the matter to the Constitutional Court. He motivated his opinion on the intention affirmed in *Honeywell*,[41] namely, that of keeping the dialogue among jurisdictions open. The simple fact that this request for a preliminary ruling was made would indicate the fair aspiration that the interpretation given by the Court could serve as the basis for building an answer to the questions raised in the main procedure.[42] The Advocate General refers to the principle of loyal cooperation which is also applicable to jurisdictions, and 'as far as the Court of Justice is concerned, that principle, in the circumstances of this case, entails a two-fold obligation':

> In the first place, substantively, that principle requires the Court of Justice to respond in the greatest spirit of cooperation possible to a question which has itself been referred to it in the same spirit... In particular, if the national court, in explaining the extent to which the act in question causes it to have serious doubts as to validity or interpretation, has been particularly plain-spoken, that will have to be interpreted as an expression of its level of concern in that regard. I understand that that is the sense of the German Government's appeal for 'constructive' treatment of the present case.
>
> In the second place, and this is above all what is in issue now, the principle of sincere cooperation requires a particular effort on the part of the Court of Justice to provide an answer on the substance to the questions referred, notwithstanding all the difficulties to which ample reference has been made here. That would require the Court of Justice to proceed on the basis of a particular assumption regarding the ultimate fate of its answer.[43]

In the same spirit, the Advocate General suggested that the Court should consider as admissible the request introduced by the Constitutional Court,

40 See judgment, paras 123 et seq.

41 BVerfG, 2 BvR 2661/06, 6 July 2010.

42 Conclusions, point 63.

43 *Ibid.* points 65 and 66.

against the views of governments which have defended before the Court the provisional feature of the ECB's 'decision' of 6 September 2012, which included the main features of the OMT as well as draft guidelines on the OMT. He saw in these acts a general action programme capable of having a decisive impact on the legal situation of third parties, which justified a non-formalistic approach.[44]

We will observe that the Court arrived at the same conclusion as far as the admissibility of the request was concerned, but resolved the question by referring to its case-law on other matters and avoided giving an opinion on the so-called 'functional difficulty' invoked by the Advocate General. In these differences we may see the specific nature of the role and responsibility of these two actors in a case before the Court.

On the substance, and looking at the first question on the difference between economic and monetary policy (Art 119 TFEU), the objectives assigned to the ECB by Art 127 paras 1 and 2, and the limits of monetary policy, the Advocate General first refuted the argument that the OMT were to be listed as economic policy measures and not monetary policy measures. He supported the view that monetary policy is part of general economic policy and the mere fact that it has indirect effects on the economic policy of the Union and the Member States could not transform a monetary policy measure into an economic one. In order to qualify as a monetary policy in a functional conception of its role, a measure has to be implemented through monetary policy instruments.[45]

The Advocate General also mentioned as an objective of monetary policy the maintenance of financial stability,[46] a superior objective, as recognised by the Court in its decision in *Pringle.* He also referred to the punctual support of the economic policy within the Union, as a secondary objective of the ECB. But was the ECB's role not ambiguous? This was the view presented by some plaintiffs in their observations before the Court, a view that was decisively if implicitly rejected by it.

---

44 *Ibid.* point 76.

45 *Ibid.* points 129 and 130.

46 Point 131. An objective remaining implicit in the ESCB and ECB Statute. In this context, see 'Navigating Monetary Policy in the New Normal' speech by Christine Lagarde at the ECB Forum on Central Banking, *Monetary Policy in a Changing Financial Landscape,* May 25, 2014: 'The crisis has also made clear that financial stability is an essential policy objective, and one that is here to stay. But should that job be given to monetary policy?', available at www.imf.org/external/np/speeches/2014/052514.htm.

The Die Linke parliamentary group, an applicant in the 'Organstreit proceedings' before the BVerfG, and other applicants

have stressed that the ECB is not referring simply to compliance with an assistance programme from which it is wholly detached. On the contrary, the ECB actively takes part in those financial assistance programmes. Those applicants submit that the ECB's argument is seriously undermined by its 'dual role', as (i) holder of a claim the basis for which is a government bond issued by a State and (ii) supervisor and negotiator of a financial assistance programme applied to the same State, with macroeconomic conditionality included.[47]

The Advocate General agreed in substance with this approach. He pointed out that 'the rules of the ESM, but also the experience of financial assistance programmes which have been implemented or which are still ongoing, amply demonstrates that the ECB's role in the design, adoption and regular monitoring of those programmes is significant, not to say decisive'.[48] He asked that 'a functional distance' should be kept between the two programmes: the assistance through the ESM/EFSF and the OMT. The ECB should refrain from 'any direct intervention' in the programmes decided within the framework of the ESM/EFSF.[49] With this appraisal, the Advocate General went a long way towards the approach followed by the European Parliament in a famous 'resolution on the enquiry on the role and operations of the Troika (ECB, Commission, IMF) with regard to the euro area programme countries'.[50] For the Advocate General,

> the conclusion reached above does not prevent the ECB from regularly participating in financial assistance programmes as they are provided for in the

47 Point 142.

48 Point 143.

49 Point 150. On this problem see the report of the European Parliament of 28 February 2014 on the enquiry on the role and operations of the Troika (ECB, Commission and IMF) with regard to the euro area programme countries, A7-0149/2014 and T Beukers, 'The New ECB and its Relationship with the Eurozone Member States: Between Central Bank Independence and Central Bank Intervention' (2013) 50 *CML Rev* 1579-1620, especially 1588 et seq, cited in n 73 of the Advocate General's conclusions.

50 EP A7-0149/2014, para 55 in which the EP notes that the mandate of the ECB is 'circumscribed by the Treaty to the areas of monetary policy and financial stability and that involvement of the ECB in the decision-making process related to budgetary, fiscal and structural policies is not foreseen by the Treaties'. On the ECB's standpoint on the matter, see 'Exchange of Views of Benoît Coeuré with ECON on Troika Matters', 13 February 2014.

> ESM Treaty. The fact that such a programme is adopted in no way predetermines the future existence of the necessary conditions for the ECB to activate the OMT programme.[51]

As we will see, the Court chose to avoid this problem and proposed a reasoning which, in its view, clearly distinguished between the roles of the ECB and the ESM in the OMT.

After having rapidly dealt with the arguments about selectivity (the OMT concerned only countries with problems)[52] and circumvention (the ECB's conditionality would be less strict than the ESM's), the Advocate General looked at the conformity of the OMT programme with rules of primary law. First, he dealt with the statement of reasons that is essential for an OMT decision, before going on to examine the three components of proportionality: suitability, necessity and proportionality *stricto sensu*.[53] The requirements relating to the statement of reasons have to be scrupulously respected for reasons of transparency and judicial control. The Advocate General lists very specific elements that are, in his view, necessary in this perspective: In that respect, the ECB will, in the first place, have to provide precise information showing there to be a significant change in market conditions giving rise to external disruption affecting the monetary policy transmission channels. Likewise, the ECB has to show to what extent its transmission channels have been blocked, it not being sufficient merely to make a statement to that effect. The ECB must put forward matters which show that such a blockage exists. Finally, it is necessary to make those reasons publicly known, ensuring that the aspects which are strictly necessary and whose disclosure might jeopardise the effectiveness of the programme remain confidential, but starting from the basis that, as a general rule, the reasoning will be fully transparent.[54]

Nevertheless, the Advocate General was satisfied by the 'ample additional information' that supplemented the details contained in the press release of 6 September 2012 given by the ECB within the framework of the

---

51 Point 149.

52 On the selectivity point see A Thiele, 'Friendly or Unfriendly Act. The "Historic" Referral of the Constitutional Court to the ECB's OMT Program' (2014) 2 *German Law Journal* 241-64, especially 257. Selectivity can be required in order to preserve the singleness of monetary policy. This is also the opinion of the Court of Justice.

53 Point 169.

54 Point 167.

proceedings. In the event of the programme being implemented, and only then, 'both the legal act which gives it form, and its implementation, must satisfy the requirements relating to the statement of reasons, as they have been described in points 166 and 167 of the Opinion'. The reasoning adopted by the Court, as we will see, might appear somewhat different from that of the Advocate General.

On the suitability of the measure, the judgment of the Advocate General was favourable. There was a coherence between the means of the policy and its objectives. It was also favourable on the necessity test. The Advocate General began by observing that 'although the measure under consideration here may pass the suitability test, the means used may none the less be excessive if compared with the other options that would have been available to the ECB'.[55] He also noted that 'The OMT programme is not a measure for intervening generally and in every circumstance in the secondary government bond market'.[56] He announced his intention to proceed by examining 'whether the ECB has adopted a measure that was strictly necessary'. OMT were necessarily to be limited in time because they were… short term in nature. On the alternative conditions proposed by the BVerfG, the Advocate General stated that an *ex ante* limitation of the volume of the operations would 'seriously undermine' their efficacy. He was also of the opinion that to confer a privileged position on the ECB and not a *pari passu* regime 'would call into question the position of other creditors and, indirectly, the final impact on the value of the bonds on the secondary market'.[57]

On the proportionality issue *sensu stricto*, the Advocate General recognised that a large margin of manoeuvre should be given to the ECB. The institution had emphasised that its interventions in the security market would be subject to quantitative limits but these limits would be neither decided beforehand, nor legally predetermined for the success of the operations.

For the Advocate General, risks were inherent in the interventions of central banks in the market. There was no reason to believe that risks would be excessive and that ECB solvency would be called into question, with repercussions on Member States' budgets. The immediate objective of the OMT was to repair the transmission of monetary policy by reducing

55 Point 177, referring to the case-law of the Court.
56 Point 178.
57 Point 183.

the interest rates up to the point where they would recover to levels considered to be coherent with the market and the macroeconomic situation of the State concerned.[58]

In conclusion on this point, the Advocate General requested, in case of the possible use of OMT, a confirmation of the 'strict proportionality' of the programme and an effective respect for this limitation.

The *second preliminary question* related to the compatibility of the OMT with the prohibition of monetary financing under Article 123 para 1 TFEU. This provision prohibits the direct purchase by the ECB and national central banks of the instruments of their public debt. Article 18 para 1 of the Protocol on the Statute of the ESCB and the ECB expressly allows the ECB to buy these instruments on the markets. Only the circumvention of the prohibition of Article 123 para 1 TFEU is prohibited.[59]

The Advocate General considered, one by one, the 'technical features' of the OMT —some of which had been included in the ECB's press release of 6 September 2012 and some of which had not— which the BVerfG believed might violate the prohibition of monetary financing: the partial or total renunciation of rights (no privileged status for the ECB —*pari passu* clause—, the possible obligation to renounce rights in case of debt restructuration), the exposure to an excessive risk of default, holding bonds until maturity (which was not within the ECB's proclaimed intentions), time of purchase, and encouragement to purchase newly issued bonds. Of all the BVerfG's arguments to which the Advocate General replied, he singled out the necessity for the ECB to allow a market price to be formed for the bonds:

> any implementation of the OMT programme must, if the substance of Article 123(1) TFEU is to be complied with, ensure that there is a real opportunity, even in the special circumstances in issue here, for a market price to form in respect of the government bonds concerned, in such a way that there continues to be a real difference between a purchase of bonds on the primary market and their purchase on the secondary market.[60]

Hence, in conclusion (point 263), the Advocate General proposed that the Court should reply:

> (1) The Outright Monetary Transactions (OMT) programme of the European Central Bank, announced on 6 September 2012, is compatible with Article

58 Point 198.

59 See Regulation No 3603/93, recital 7.

60 Conclusions, point 252.

> 119 TFEU and Article 127(1) and (2) TFEU, provided that, in the event of that programme being implemented, the ECB refrains from any direct involvement in the financial assistance programmes to which the OMT programme is linked, and complies strictly with the obligation to state reasons and with the requirements deriving from the principle of proportionality. (**2**) The OMT programme is compatible with Article 123(1) TFEU, provided that, in the event of the programme being implemented, the timing of its implementation is such as to permit the actual formation of a market price in respect of the government bonds.

VI. The Court's Decision

In contrast with the conclusions of its Advocate General, the Court was to deal with the question of considering the questions referred to for a preliminary ruling and the admissibility of the reference without relying on arguments proper to the monetary policy nature of the OMT decision. It preferred, in a more detached way, to invoke its general case-law which could provide guidance for a solution by distinguishing from the present case those cases in which it declared that it had no jurisdiction. In particular, the judgment mentions a) that Art 267 of the FEU Treaty establishes a procedure for direct collaboration between the Court and the courts of the Member States, b) that the request before it directly concerns the interpretation and application of EU law, c) that there was a need for a preliminary ruling in order to enable the national court to deliver a judgment, and d) that the assessment of the facts is a matter for the national court and that the Court has to give its interpretation only on the basis of the facts which the national court has placed before it.[61] And, with great sobriety, the Court adds in paragraph 16:

> It must also be borne in mind that it is settled case-law of the Court that a judgment in which the latter gives a preliminary ruling is binding on the national court, as regards the interpretation or the validity of the acts of the EU institutions in question, for the purposes of the decision to be given in the main proceedings (see, inter alia, judgments in *Fazenda Pública,* C-446/98, EU:C:2000:691, paragraph 49, and *Elchinov*, C-173/09, EU:C:2010:581, paragraph 29).

This general affirmation of the binding character of a preliminary ruling – which is essential for the functioning of the system – evidently excludes a

61 See para 15 and the case-law quoted.

reasoning on the basis of *ultra vires* by the BVerfG when the Court of Justice has declared that the decision *sub judice* was legal. Does it also exclude a condemnation of the OMT on the basis of a possible violation of the constitutional identity of the Federal Republic? The Court apparently hopes that the BVerfG will draw its own conclusions on this topic but its affirmation is made in general terms.

After having considered the questions referred for a preliminary ruling, the Court takes a position on the admissibility of the request for the ruling. It replies to the multiple arguments advanced by a number of governments and the institutions (EP, Commission and ECB) against the admissibility. The arguments were numerous: the ECB's 'decision' had been included in a press release, the act was 'preparatory', the dispute 'contrived and artificial', and the 'decision' was to be completed by legal acts. The Court responds to these objections by referring to what it has established in its earlier comments: it is up to the national court to determine the need for an interpretation or an appreciation of validity. It is not up to the Court to make this assessment. Furthermore, under German law preventive legal protection might be granted if some conditions were met. The Court also refers to cases submitted by British courts where it has decided

> that the opportunity open to individuals to plead the invalidity of an EU act of general application before national courts is not conditional upon that act actually having been the subject of implementing measures adopted pursuant to national law.

The Court considers it sufficient 'if the national court is seised of a genuine dispute in which the question of validity of such an act is raised on indirect grounds'.[62]

Thereafter, the Court enters into the *substance* of the request.

---

62 The Court quotes the judgments in C-491/01 *British American Tobacco (Investments) and Imperial Tobacco* EU:C:2002:741 paras 36 and 40 and C-308/06 *Intertanko and Others* EU:2008:C:312 paras 33 and 34. On the arguments of the Court in this part of the judgment, see HCH Hofmann, '*Gauweiler* and OMT' (n 5), especially 'Section C. Reviewing an Announcement of a Possible Future Policy Programme'. This author sees in this judgment a confirmation of the importance of regulating information and a confirmation that the criteria for review are 'an important clarification'. But he also mentions that the Court only acknowledges this approach in the context of a preliminary ruling. A direct action for annulment would not have been admissible. For Hofmann, the review of a general programme is justified by the Advocate General on the basis that this programme 'is capable of having a very direct impact on the future legal situation of individuals'.

The Court analyses 'whether a programme for the purchase of government bonds on secondary markets, such as the programme announced in the press release, can be covered by the powers of the ESCB' (paragraph 33). Two remarks on this formulation: first, the Court intends to limit its interpretation to the OMT as defined in the press release of 6 September 2012, but the question is: could its judgment be recognised as having a wider scope? We will attempt to answer this question in our conclusions. The second remark relates to the fact that the Court always refers in its judgment either to the ECB or to the ESCB. It almost completely ignores the Eurosystem,[63] which is a configuration of the ESCB, as far as its main competences are concerned, and will coexist with the latter for as long as some of the EU Member States remain outside of the euro area. Up until the time that all Member States have joined the euro area, the ESCB will remain largely an empty shell. The Court chooses to ignore that. Is this perhaps to give a perennial value to its judgment?

Under the title 'Powers of the ESCB', in paragraphs 34 to 45, the Court recalls what might be called 'the basics of monetary policy'. This includes the definitions given by the Treaty of monetary union and of monetary policy (Art 119(2) TFEU), as an exclusive competence (Art 3(1) (c) TFEU concerning the respective roles of the ECB, and its organs, and of the NCBs (Art 282(1) TFEU, 127-33 TFEU, 129(1) TFEU).

Paragraph 40 of the Court's judgment relates to Art 130 TFEU on the independence of the ESCB. The Court sets out that this article 'is intended to shield the ESCB and its decision-making bodies from external influences which would be likely to interfere with the performance of [their] tasks…' And the Court concludes, quoting its former case-law: 'Article 130 TFEU is, in essence, intended to shield the ESCB from all political pressure, in order to enable it effectively to pursue the objectives attributed to its tasks…, as the Court said in its judgment on *Commission v ECB*, C-11/00, EU:C:2003:395, paragraph 134'. Perhaps, in this regard, we should add that, in the meantime, since the entry into force of the Lisbon Treaty, the ECB has become an 'institution', called under Art 13 TEU to engage in a 'loyal cooperation' with the other institutions. Engaged as it is in a quasi-permanent dialogue with the competent EU institutions and

---

The Court will not enter into this debate simply because the details given in the press release appear to be sufficiently precise.

63 It mentions once (in para 36) Art 282 para 1 TFEU, which introduces the concept of Eurosystem in the Treaty (see also Art 1 of the ESCB and ECB Statute).

bodies, a dialogue initiated well before the change in the EU 'constitution', the ECB is far from being the 'ivory tower' which some believed it had to remain in order to preserve its independence. It has become part of the 'government' of the EU, in the US conception of the term. In this context, the ECB is naturally subject to influences and its accountability has developed. What is essential for the ECB, in our view, is that it should preserve its capacity to make its own judgments and to resist possible attempts by others to give it instructions.

Under the title: 'the delimitation of monetary policy', the Court essentially applies to 'a programme such as that at issue in the main proceedings' (paragraph 47) the doctrine set out on the subject in its *Pringle* judgment (C-370/12, EU:C:2012:756). First, it considers the objectives of the programme and second, its means.

On the *objectives*, the Court remarks that they aim at safeguarding the singleness and 'an appropriate transmission' of monetary policy. As in the *Pringle* judgment, the Court remarks that the contribution of a monetary policy to the stability of the euro area does not mean that a monetary police measure can be assimilated to an economic policy measure.

On the *means*, the Court observes that Art 18.1 of the ESCB and ECB Statute allows the ECB and the NCBs to 'operate in the financial markets by buying and selling outright marketable instruments in euro', as stated in the press release of September 2012. In this context, the Court answers the argument presented by the applicants on the selectivity nature of the programme. This feature is intended to remedy the 'disruption to the monetary policy transmission mechanism caused by the specific situation of government bonds issued by certain Member States'. It does not *per se* disqualify the measures as relating to monetary policy. On the other hand, no provision of EU law 'requires the ESCB to operate in the financial markets by means of general measures'.

More comments are devoted to the delicate question of any OMT programme's being conditional upon full compliance with EFSF or ESM macroeconomic adjustment programmes. This part of the decision is particularly interesting in comparison with the position adopted by the Advocate General in his conclusions. In line with its view that monetary policy measures may have an effect on the economic situation without becoming economic policy measures, the Court holds that such 'indirect effects do not mean that such a programme must be treated as equivalent to economic policy measures' since the ECB, under the Treaty, 'without prejudice to the objective of price stability, is to support the general economic policies' in the Union (paragraph 59). The Court insists on the fact that, in doing this, the ECB should act 'in a wholly independent manner'. In this way it ensures that 'the monetary policy measures it has adopted will not work against the effectiveness of the economic policies followed by the Member States' (paragraph 60). The Court adds that, 'since the ESCB is obliged, under Article 127(1) TFEU, read in conjunction with Article 119(3) TFEU, to comply with the guiding principle that public finance must be sound', the conditions included in the programme preventing it 'from acting as an incentive to Member States to allow their financial situation to deteriorate, cannot be regarded as taking the programme beyond the confines of the monetary policy framework laid down by primary law' (paragraph 61).

The Court specifies that full compliance of the Member States with conditions stated by the adjustment programme is not sufficient to trigger the intervention of the ESCB in an OMT programme: the intervention is 'strictly conditional to disruptions of the monetary policy transmission mechanisms or the singleness of monetary policy' (paragraph 62). Hence, the purchase of government bonds on the secondary market subject to the condition of compliance with a macroeconomic programme 'could be considered as falling within economic policy when the purchase is undertaken by the ESM' — here the Court refers to its *Pringle* decision (paragraph 60) — although this 'does not mean that this should equally be the case when that instrument is used by the ESCB in the framework of a programme such as that announced in the press release' (paragraph 63).

The difference between the objectives of the ESM and those of the ESCB is 'decisive': for the ESCB it is price stability, while the ESM's intervention is intended 'to safeguard the stability of the euro area' (paragraph 64, with a reference to the *Pringle* judgment, paragraph 56). In paragraph 65, the Court extends its analysis of the difference between the two interventions: the OMT may not serve to 'circumvent' the conditions proper to the ESM's activity on the secondary market. It must 'be implemented independently on the basis of the objectives particular to monetary policy' (paragraph 65).

This subtle analysis by the Court aims to answer those among the applicants, and the BVerfG, who have argued on the basis of the *Pringle* decision in order to contest the legal position of the ECB. It also serves as a response to the view expressed by the Advocate General which, as we have mentioned, introduced a kind of caveat to the intervention of the

ECB in the management of adjustment programmes. We will return to this point in the conclusions.

The second part of the judgment is set out under the title 'Proportionality'. This principle, 'according to the settled case-law of the Court', requires that the acts in question 'be appropriate for attaining the legitimate objectives pursued by the legislation at issue and do not go beyond what is necessary in order to achieve these objectives' (paragraph 67). The 'broad discretion' which is allowed in the implementation of a programme includes 'the necessity to make choices of a technical nature and to undertake forecast and complex assessments' (paragraph 68).[64] Nevertheless, in a way that conforms with its earlier case-law, in paragraph 69, the Court states that

> where an EU institution enjoys broad discretion, a review of compliance with certain procedural guarantees is of fundamental importance. Those guarantees include the obligation for the ESCB to examine carefully and impartially all the relevant elements of the situation in question and to give an adequate statement of the reasons for its decisions.

The next two paragraphs (70 and 71) deal with the 'statement of reasons', a requirement laid down by Art 296(2) TFEU. The Court refers on this point to 'what it has consistently held, as summed up in the judgment in *Commission v. Council* C-63/12, EU:C:2013:752, paragraphs 98 and 99 and the case-law cited'.

In paragraph 70 the Court recalls that

> although the statement of reasons for an EU measure… must show clearly and unequivocally the reasoning of the author of the measure in question, so as to enable the persons concerned to ascertain the reasons for the measure and to enable the Court to exercise its power of review, it is not required to go to every relevant point of fact and law.

In addition, this obligation 'must be assessed with reference not only to the wording of the measure but also to its context and the whole body of legal rules governing the matter in question'.

After having observed that 'an examination of whether the obligation to provide a statement of reasons has been satisfied may be undertaken only

64 The Court refers to its judgment in C-59/11 *Association Kokopelli* EU:C:2012:447 para 38 and the case-law cited. Professor Hofmann, in his already quoted paper (n 5), mentions the looser nature of this criterion compared with the one proposed by the Advocate General in point 177 of his conclusions. We will return to this point.

on the basis of a decision that has been formally adopted' (paragraph 71), the Court declares that

> in this case, the press release, together with the draft legal acts considered during the meeting of the Governing Council at which the press release was approved, make known the essential elements of a programme such as that announced in the press release and are such as to enable the Court to exercise its power of review.

The way to approach the question of the statement of motives seems to differ – we will return to this point – from that adopted by the Advocate General in his conclusions, although the result, as far as the 'decision' of the ECB is concerned, concurs.

On the appropriateness of the OMT, the Court begins by expressing a position directly opposite to that adopted by the BVerfG and the Bundesbank.[65] It remarks that the 'high volatility and extreme spreads' observed in some countries were not just motivated by 'macroeconomic differences between the States concerned' but 'were caused, in part, by the demand for excessive risk premia… such premia being intended to guard against the risk of a break-up of the euro area' (paragraph 72). Hence, for the ECB, the severe undermining of the monetary policy transmission mechanism gave rise to fragmentation in terms of bank refinancing conditions and credit costs, with the consequence of greatly limiting 'the effects of the impulses transmitted by the ESCB to the economy in a significant part of the euro area' (paragraph 73). And, in the next paragraph, the Court underlines, in a general way, its findings by concluding that 'it does not appear that that analysis of the economic situation of the euro area at the date of the announcement of the programme in question is vitiated by a manifest error of appreciation' (paragraph 74).

The Court also responds to the BVerfG by observing (in paragraph 75) that the contestation of the ECB's analysis does not, in itself, suffice to call that conclusion into question, given that questions of monetary policy are usually of a controversial nature and in view of the ESCB's broad discretion, nothing more can be required of the ESCB apart from that it use

---

65 See BVerfG, 2 BvR 2728/13, 14 January 2014, paras 13 and 98. According to the Bundesbank, 'interest spreads on government bonds cannot be split into … justified or irrational components' (para 13) and for the BVerfG 'Spreads always only result from the market participants' expectations and are, regardless of their rationality, essential for market-based pricing'.

its economic expertise and the necessary technical means at its disposal to carry out that analysis with all care and accuracy.

This passage of the judgment offers a remarkably favourable appraisal of the action of the ECB, in strong contrast with the harsh criticism expressed by the BVerfG.[66]

On the basis of this analysis, the Court concludes that the ESCB could legitimately take the view that the OMT programme was justified (paragraph 80).

The Court goes on to decide that 'such a programme does not go manifestly beyond what was necessary to achieve the objectives of the ESCB' (paragraphs 81-90). The implementation of the programme is by no means automatic: the announcement made in the press release of September 2012 is to be followed, if necessary, by a second phase, namely the implementation of the programme, which will be dependent upon an in-depth assessment of the requirements of monetary policy; furthermore, it should be noted that more than three years after the announcement of the programme, it has still not been implemented. On the other hand, 'the potential scale of the programme is limited in a number of ways' (paragraph 85). In this regard, the Court quotes the fact that the ESCB may only buy bonds of Member States 'undergoing a macroeconomic adjustment programme and which have access to the bond market again' and that the programme will be limited to 'bonds with a maturity of up to three years, the ESCB reserving the right to sell at any time the bonds it purchased' (paragraph 86). A programme with such a restricted volume could legitimately be adopted by the ESCB without a limit being set prior to its implementation —a question asked by the BVerfG in its order (paragraph 100)—, which would be likely to reduce its effectiveness (paragraph 88). One question that arises on this point is: should the adoption of a programme of purchasing government bonds be only permitted if the government whose bonds are purchased is subject to an ESM adjustment programme? We will return to this point in our conclusions.

The Court also justifies the selectivity of the programme which the BVerfG had criticised in its judgment (paragraph 73). For the Court of Justice, the OMT programme intends to 'rectify the disruption of monetary policy which arose as a result of the particular situation of government bonds issued by certain Member States'. Selective measures are necessary

66 See T Beukers, 'In the ECB We Don't Trust.' (n 24).

in order to prevent the scale of the OMT programme being needlessly increased (paragraph 89). A final remark by the Court in this section: a weighing-up of the various interests at play will 'prevent disadvantages from arising, when the programme is implemented, which are manifestly disproportionate to the programme's objectives' (paragraph 91).

The next issue dealt with by the Court is that of the compatibility of the programme with the prohibition of monetary financing included in Art 123(1) TFEU, an issue raised by the referring Court (paragraphs 93-121). It is not possible here to enter into all the details of the reasoning of the Court on this point. It owes much for its structure and motivation to the *Pringle* judgment that is repeatedly quoted by the Court. From the combination of Art 123(1) TFEU and Art 18(1) ESCB and ECB Statute, it emerges that the direct purchase of government bonds by the ESCB is prohibited, while the acquisition of such bonds on the secondary market is allowed. Nevertheless, the purchase of bonds on secondary markets under conditions which would, in practice, have 'an effect equivalent to that of a direct purchase' is also prohibited. 'In addition', the Court refers to the need to take account of the objective of Art 123(1) TFEU in order to determine which forms of purchases of government bonds are compatible with this disposition. As in the *Pringle* decision, with regard to Art 125 TFEU, the Court refers to the preparatory work of the provision, which, with Art 124 TFEU (prohibition of privileged access of the public sector to the credit institutions) and Art 125 TFEU (prohibition of bailing out), forms a kind of code of budgetary discipline. The Court mentions that the aim of Art 123 TFEU is 'to encourage the Member States to follow a sound budgetary policy'. It also refers to the prohibition on circumventing the prohibition of direct purchase by making purchases in the secondary market, a prohibition laid down in the seventh recital of the preamble to Regulation No 3603/93 of 13 December 1993 specifying definitions for the application of the prohibitions referred to in Art 123 and 125(1) TFEU (OJ 1993 L332, p.1).

Hence the necessity of sufficient safeguards in order to ensure that direct purchase is avoided. The limits and safeguards are listed by the Court: purchases are to take place only on the secondary markets, although, in practice (paragraph 104), such purchases could have an equivalent effect to direct purchase

> if the potential purchasers of government bonds on the primary market know for certain that the ESCB was going to purchase bonds within a certain period and under conditions allowing those market operators to act, de facto, as in-

> termediaries for the ESCB for the direct purchase of those bonds from the public authorities and bodies of the Member State concerned.

The Court refers to the draft decision and draft guideline produced by the ECB which express the conditions of these operations. It mentions that 'the ECB has also made clear before the Court that the ESCB intends [,,,] to ensure that a minimum period is observed between the issue of a security on the primary market and its purchase on the secondary market' (paragraph 106). This necessity of a 'time gap' between the issue and the purchase of government bonds was one of the points mentioned by the BVerfG in its order.

The Court appears to be satisfied that the ECB will institute the necessary guarantees in order to prevent the implementation of the programme from having the same effect as the direct purchase of government bonds (paragraph 107). To be sure, as the Court observes in paragraph 108, referring to the conclusions of the Advocate General, the BVerfG is right in pointing out that the ESCB's interventions have had some influence on both the primary and the secondary markets but this is an inherent feature of purchases on the secondary market which are allowed by the TFEU.

The Court also raises the question of whether the programme could circumvent the objective of Art 123(1) TFEU if it lessened 'the impetus of the Member States concerned to follow a sound budgetary policy' (paragraph 109). Here also, the Court finds that guarantees built into the programme would prevent this risk from occurring.

At the end of its judgment, the Court briefly looks at the arguments raised against the programme by the referring court which it has not previously examined. It mentions that even if 'that programme could expose the ECB to a significant risk of losses, that would in no way weaken the guarantees which are built in the programme in order to ensure that the Member States' impetus to follow a sound budgetary policy is not lessened' (paragraph 123). Those guarantees are also likely to reduce the losses. On the other hand (paragraph 125),

> a central bank, such as the ECB, is obliged to take decisions which, like open market operations, inevitably expose it to the risk of losses and Article 33 ESCB and ECB statute duly provides for the way in which the losses of the ECB must be allocated, without specifically delimiting the risks which the Bank may take in order to achieve the objectives of monetary policy.

At the end of its judgment, the Court refers to the lack of privileged creditor status for the ECB, which exposes it 'to the risk of a debt cut decided upon by the other creditors of the Member State concerned', a question which seems to be very important for the BVerfG.[67] The Court observes that 'such a risk is inherent in a purchase of bonds on the secondary markets, an operation which was authorised by the authors of the Treaties, without being conditional upon the ECB having privileged creditor status' (paragraph 126).

After all, monetary policy is a question of risk management.[68]

The Court concludes by ruling that Articles 119 TFEU, 123(1) TFEU and 127(1) and (2) TFEU and Articles 17 to 24 of the Protocol on the Statute of the ESCB and the ECB must be interpreted as permitting the ESCB to adopt a programme for the purchase of government bonds on secondary markets, such as the [OMT] programme…

In its judgment of 21 June 2016, the BVerfG allows the *Bundesbank* to participate in the implementation of the OMT programme only if, and to the extent that, the preconditions defined by the Court of Justice are met; i.e. if:

- purchases are not announced;
- the volume of the purchases is limited from the outset;
- there is a minimum period between the issue of the government bonds and their purchase by the ESCB that is defined from the outset and prevents the issuing conditions being distorted;
- the ESCB purchases only government bonds of Member States that have bond market access enabling the funding of such bonds;
- purchases are only in exceptional cases held until maturity;
- purchases are restricted or ceased and purchased bonds are remarketed should the intervention become unnecessary.[69]

For the BVerfG, the respect of these limits was the *conditio sine qua non* in order to admit the compatibility of the ECB's OMT decision with the

67 BVerfG order, point 88.

68 See SS Poloz, Governor of the Bank of Canada, 'Monetary Policy as Risk Management', 12 December 2013. Gregory Claeys observes in his paper: 'The Treaty gives a mandate to the ECB to maintain price stability, not to protect its balance sheet' (n 80) 18.

69 Our quotation follows the translation of para. 206 of the BVerfG's judgment of 21 June 2016, as reproduced in Press release No.34/2016 of 21 June 2016, quoted in note 4 above. It should be noted that there is some misunderstanding between the BVerfG and the ECJ on the *ex ante* requirement for the ECB to limit the volume of the bond purchases. For the ECB, this limit is only a *de facto* one: see para.116 of the ECJ judgment of 16 June 2015.

Constitution.[70] They correspond to the proper limits announced or accepted by the ECB in the use of this new instrument of monetary policy. They also answer a number of concerns expressed by the BVerfG in its order of 2014.

VII. Conclusions

The great merit of the Court of Justice's judgment is the confirmation of the fact that OMT, as described in the press release of 6 September 2012, and in the light of the draft decision and guidelines adopted by the Governing Council, are compatible with the Treaties. This recognises that the ECB should be able to make recourse to instruments of monetary policy comparable to those used by the world's main central banks. A comment on a blog by Professor Paul De Grauwe[71] responded to the criticism of the BVerfG order by this renowned economist by stating that: 'courts are not required to understand central banking. Courts are required to understand things like the statutes of the ECB, EU law and, in this case, German law. If its statutes do not allow the ECB to fully act like a central bank…[t]hen those statutes should be changed'. It will not be necessary for EU law to be adjusted on this particular point. The Court has laid down a legal basis for the future actions required by the Eurosystem.

It is noteworthy that, in some important respects, there are differences between the approach adopted by the Advocate General and the Court's method of reasoning in its judgment. In this regard, we may observe that the Court avoids some forms of reasoning that might antagonise the BVerfG. This is particularly clear if we compare the Advocate General's allusion to the 'functional problems' created by this request (points 46-48) with the way in which the Court limits itself to a discreet but nevertheless firm affirmation of the binding nature of such a ruling (paragraph 16). The Advocate General bases his reasoning on questions like the admissibility

70 On the case law of the BVerfG concerning the control of constitutionality of EU law, see C D Classen, 'Confiance mutuelle et identité constitutionnelle nationale – quel avenir dans l'espace juridique européen? A propos de la décision de la Cour constitutionnelle allemande sur le mandat d'arrêt européen du 15.12.2015' 52 *CDE*, (2016), 667-86.

71 P De Grauwe, 'Why the European Court of Justice Should Reject the German Constitutional Court's Ruling' (n 2). Comment by Klaus Kastner.

of the request by referring to the specificity of the subject. He gives a very clear opinion on the delicate question of constitutional identity. He characterises the OMT as pertaining to unconventional measures of monetary policy applicable in extraordinary times, as they certainly are. This explains, in his view, the strict requirements he would like to impose on the ECB with regard to its motives for implementing an OMT programme (points 176 and 167), while effectively admitting that so long as the programme was not implemented, the motives given by the ECB could be considered as sufficient. The Advocate General pleaded for the ECB's role in managing ESM adjustment programmes to be limited.

The ECJ, for its part, does not rely on the specificity of central bank communication in order to decide on admissibility. It resorts to its settled case-law concerning very different economic sectors in order to find the answers to this question, just as it does in order to establish the requirements of motivation of the decision. It manifestly relies on the precedents in order to consolidate the conclusion it reaches[72] and it tries to avoid an excessive intrusion into a very complex and technical policy. This does not prevent it from referring to the ECB's position when it looks at the appropriateness of the OMT programme.[73] Furthermore, in agreement with the Advocate General, its approach is unequivocal on questions raised by the parties before the BVerfG and by the Constitutional Court itself, such as the absence of privileged status for the ECB, especially in the case of restructuration of a government debt, or the absence of the imposition of a maximum limit on the outright operations and on the risk of losses, which it minimises and justifies. No privileged status for the ECB, no *ex ante* maximum limit for the volume of the operations and clarification of the question of losses and risk: these were capital questions raised in its order by the BVerfG.

As we have seen, the Court and the Advocate General referred to different case-laws to judge the proportionality of the measures. The test proposed by the Advocate General seems to be more rigorous than that adopted by the Court. Professor Hofmann, in the analysis already quoted, underlines the central importance of this instrument for 'ensuring legality

---

72 See D Simon and A Rigaux, 'Le 'précédent' dans la jurisprudence du juge de l'Union', in *Europe(s), Droits(s) européen(s). Une passion d'universitaire.* Liber Amicorum en l'honneur du professeur Vlad Constantinesco, (Brussels, Bruylant, 2015) 546-78, especially 569.

73 See paras 72 and 73.

and accountability of acts' and 'protecting discretionary powers'.[74] He is of the opinion that if 'the Court has taken the right steps to submit ECB action to the proportionality test (…) much needs to be done to better develop the criteria' of this test.

The Advocate General had linked the compatibility of the OMT programme with the Treaty provisions on monetary policy to the requirement for the ECB to refrain 'from any direct involvement in the financial assistance programmes to which the OMT programme is linked'.[75] In its judgment the Court has ignored this view of the Advocate General. It believes that the differences between the objectives of the ESM and those of the ECB prevent any inclusion of the OMT in economic policy.[76] It is, indeed, true that the ECB's objective is to restore monetary stability and that its advisory competence provided for by Art 282 para 5 TFEU and Art 4(b) of the ESCB and ECB Statute allows it to give its opinion to the 'institutions, organs and organisms of the EU and to national authorities'. However, one cannot neglect the *political* argument, as it was raised in the procedure, which relates to a question of accountability more than of competence.

The insistence with which the Court —especially in the pronouncement of its verdict— repeatedly refers to 'a programme such as that announced in the press release'[77] does not mean that the doctrine laid down in this decision could not be valid for other operations that include the purchase of government debt. Any future programme, adopted like the OMT in 'exceptional and extraordinary circumstances',[78] like a number of monetary policy measures adopted since 2009 by the ECB,[79] will be judged on its own merits. It will have to pass the tests established by the OMT judg-

---

74 H Hofmann (n 5) 21. Professor Hofmann refers to the judgment in C-343/09 *Afton Chemical* 8 July 2010, EU:C:2010:419, para 45 where the Court, referring to its case-law, has used the formula: 'when there is a choice between several appropriate measures recourse must be made to the least onerous', which is very close to the criterion mentioned by the Advocate General in point 177 quoted above.

75 See conclusions, points 143 et seq and point 263 (1).

76 See the judgment, para 64.

77 See, for example, paras 112 and 128.

78 See conclusions, point 166.

79 See P Cour-Thimann and B Winkler, 'The ECB's Non-Standard Monetary Policy Measures. The Role of Institutional Factors and Financial Structure', ECB Working Paper Series No 1528/April 2013; G Claeys, 'The (Not So) Unconventional Monetary Policy of the European Central Bank since 2008', In-Depth Analysis

ment. An analysis of the economic situation which makes the programme necessary and of the programme's conformity to EU primary law, as well as an examination of the proportionality of the intended measures, will be necessary. The Court will be helped in this task by the criteria provided by the *Gauweiler* judgment, which it could possibly further refine.[80]

European Parliament June 2014 IP/A/ECON/2014-02, PE 518.781; 'ECB Announces Expanded Asset Purchase Programme' Press Release 22 January 2015, available at www.ecb.europa.eu/press/pr/date/2015/html/pr150122_1.en.html. The ECB Working Paper mentioned in this note describes the 'non-standard measures' adopted by the ECB as 'a *complement* to its interest instrument, not as a *substitute* as it is the case for the bulk of unconventional policies of other major central banks'. (p 20). Gregory Claeys underlines in the document requested by the European Parliament that measures adopted by the ECB 'were mainly directed at ensuring the provision of liquidity and repairing the bank-lending channel, through changes to its usual framework for the implementation of monetary policy'. The problem is now how to address weak inflation in the euro area. This is the purpose of the 'expanded asset purchase programme' adopted by the ECB on 15 January 2015, in which it was intended that such purchases should be carried out until at least September 2016. This programme is, in the current language, called 'Quantitative Easing' (QE) by analogy with the programme pursued by the Fed and the Bank of England. See G Claeys, A Landro and A Mandra, 'European Central Bank Quantitative Easing: The Detailed Manual', *Bruegel Policy Contribution* (2) March 2015. The authors note that since the press conference of March 2015, the programme seems to have changed names and they call it the 'Public Sector Purchase Programme' (PSPP), which seems to correspond more closely to its nature.

80 See on this subject, J-V Louis, 'The EMU after the *Gauweiler* judgment and the Juncker report', 2016, 23, *Maastricht Journal of European and Comparative Law*, 1 Special Issue: The European Court of Justice, the European Central Bank, and the Supremacy of EU Law, 55-78 (61-66).

8 The material core of the constitution: A nationalidentity-based limitation of European integration or a focus of shared European values?

Jiří Zemánek

Abstract

Even a constitution with provisions interpreted as a limit to European integration that can never be exceeded, could be changed, in some countries by a constitutional amendment, in some others by the *pouvoir constituant*, i. e. in a way of constitutional uprising. However, any such a constitutional change has to respect some basic limits - a common core of all European national constitutions. Such a „common core" is a denominator shared by the constitutional provisions at both levels, national as well as European. Therefore, it is a proper linkage for multi-level constitutionalism, putting together constitutional foundations of Member States with fundamental values and principles governing the European Union itself.

I. A Matter of Equivalence

Since the European Union is not simply an association of states, but a venture of constitutional quality, it is a substantive issue of immediate relevance to safeguard the liberal democratic values and fundamental rights which are currently questioned, even more so after the executive settlement of the public debt crisis, the recent terrorist incidents in Paris and elsewhere, the erosion of asylum policy in the course of the sudden influx of refugees, developments in Hungary and Poland, Brexit, etc. We need an efficient protection of 'a union of shared values' against any undermining of the very core of the European integration project, regardless of its source. In fact, we need citizens and resident legal persons — who enjoy benefits from the access to cross-border movements — to assure themselves of the legitimacy of the decisions they are exposed to. Political changes that do not respect liberal values, even if achieved through a democratic process, cannot be perceived as legitimate.

A mutual stabilisation of values within the multilevel Europe requires consensus on substantive and procedural guarantees among the Member States and Union institutions. Judicial review by the Court of Justice of the enforcement of obligations under the Treaties at national level (proceedings on the infringement of Union law, on its interpretation by way of preliminary ruling and the early warning and sanction mechanism for wrongful conduct of a Member State under Article 7 TEU) is to be governed by equivalent criteria of reference, governing the control of validity of supranational acts (the action for annulment) or omissions (the action for failure to act), as well as remedies used for contesting the constitutionality of the impact at national level of directly applicable Union acts or implementation measures of national law (ultra vires doctrines, material core and eternity clauses). Otherwise, a potential conflict between jurisdictions, leading to their self-assurance rather than to a productive communication, with destructive effects on their legitimacy, will be unavoidable.

II. National and European Perspectives of the Common Constitutional Values

Does a common constitutional core, which should accompany the advancement of any autonomous branch of the multilevel system without suppressing specific features of its authenticity, really work? Do some requirements exist — over those of a liberal democratic state, ensuing from the sovereign people and social contract — which any constitution must meet, so that it may be called the constitution of a Member State of the European Union? On the other hand, are some essentials of national constitutions — the 'material core' or 'eternity provision'— referred to by the case-law of several constitutional courts, conditioning or limiting the progress of European integration, internalised (enough) by the Court of Justice and in the decision-making practice of other Union institutions?

Concerning the *democratic pillar of legitimacy*, a differentiated picture emerges. The famous British political scientist Colin Crouch has said that in the era of global capitalism liberal democracy has become a mere chimera. He understands this system as 'post-democracy', where representation of the whole ('common interest') is superseded by lobbying and transnational corporations, which take over a large part of the role of states in economic governance.

Another political scientist, the Czech philosopher Václav Bělohradský, stresses — with a critical reference to Václav Havel — that the most significant consequence of globalisation is the retreat of competition between the political actors, i. e., the disappearance of clashes over the justification of power as a material source of legitimacy for political decision-making. Power is becoming a mere matter of fact, lacking any formal consensus expressed by citizens in a public election. The political consensus has been substituted in an informal way — by the behaviour of citizens as market consumers ('voting by purse'), etc. The classic, 'old democratic' political parties have lost their dominant position in the political life of their societies. Their former appeal has been largely eroded by the fragmentation of the space for public discourse, which is susceptible to networking by new media like the internet, facebook etc.

Following this view, politics allegedly need not care about its legitimacy. It can concentrate on the technology of the execution of public power, privatised by transnational corporations, and on the effectiveness of the enforcement of the decisions they adopt. However, whereas the breakdown of democracy may be reconciled at the national level, this path does not seem to be plausible at the supranational level: the European Union has always been criticised for its 'unacceptable structural democratic deficit', a critique that was perpetuated, in particular, in the case-law of the German Federal Constitutional Court.[1] As is well known, this Court reinforced its ultra vires doctrine by combining the substantive content of the fundamental right to vote guaranteed in Article 38 GG and the 'eternity clause' of Article 79 para 3 GG.[2]

What can we, the lawyers, who are used to thinking in terms of formal institutions, do with such an interpretation of the principle of democracy? If no real competition over public power exists, an effective survey of its performance becomes unrealistic. The uneasy functioning system of democratic decision-making is locked into the national state, while the number of issues calling urgently for a supranational solution is growing. When a national state loses its competitiveness in the global financial mar-

1 German Federal Constitutional Court 2BvE 2/08 *Vertrag von Lissabon*, para 264.

2 See the rejection of this assessment expressed by D Thym, 'In the Name of Sovereign Statehood: A Critical Introduction to the Lisbon Judgment of the German Constitutional Court' (2009) 49 *Common Market Law Review*, pp 1795-1822.

kets and the EU, at a supranational level, is not empowered to effectively remedy the situation, distrust of citizens regarding the capacity of the European Union to gain control over crises will grow and the calls for a re-nationalisation of a number of European policies will become stronger.

The process of European supranational democracy should go hand-in-hand with the enhanced empowerment of the EU authorities. It should enable to the citizens a real political choice between different options, which could increase their interest in the European parliamentary elections, which in recent years have faced low attendance of electorate. It means a more politicised, an ever greater integration of citizens than that achieved until now. Instead of waiting for a 'European demos' as a would-be basis of citizens' representation at the supranational level, forms of transnational participatory democracy, focusing on the individual, could be developed, in an attempt to replace post-democratic paths of 'executive federalism',[3] practised by Euro-summit diplomacy and intergovernmental bargaining. The multilevel system of the Union cannot be satisfied by state-like paradigms of accountability and legitimacy of political actors.

III. Breakdown of National Democracies in the Assertion of their Autonomies

The recent crises have primarily been not technical and national in character, but of a political and transnational nature. There are two reasons for this, which refer to the real causes of the crises: a) different democratic malfunctions that the Member States and the European Union have not properly eliminated, and b) the Union's delayed reaction as a symptom of the disturbance of the process of European integration and its authority.

The level of cooperation reached in the Union is such that it can be effectively and legitimately governed only with the participation of its citizens. The justification of Union policies cannot be constructed as a challenge to national democratic legitimacy, but it has to entail Union-based opportunities for meeting citizens' aspirations on security and social justice, which Member States taken individually cannot offer to them. It is indispensable that democracy should go hand in hand with the principle of

3 J Habermas, *Zur Verfassung Europas. Ein Essay* (Berlin, Suhrkamp Verlag, 2011), p 81.

social justice, so that citizens can understand not only the benefits of European integration, but also why these benefits are subject to some duties towards others. Rights must be accompanied by the effective reinforcement of the civic solidarity within the Union as a legitimate basis for responsible and accountable economic and political governance.[4]

The crises have originated in the democratic failures of some Member States of the Eurozone and the Schengen area, which have been unable to 'internalise the externalities' they imposed on other Member States when breaking their respective obligations (to control excessive cross-border capital flows, to check people migrating from non-member countries eligible for asylum status and to protect — with the support of the Union — the external border of the Schengen area against those who are not eligible to enter). Such 'spill-overs' of autonomous, inefficient national measures, placing a burden of troubled understanding on the other Member States, are incompatible with the idea of democracy.[5] The incapacity of the Union to balance such pressures threatening the general stability of the whole is attributable to the dispersed nature of its political existence and its dependence on national politics. The real democratic deficit of the Union is the lack of European politics.

IV. More European Democracy

There are queries that instruments of financial solidarity and debt dispersion (eurobonds), ensuing from the European Stability Mechanism Treaty and affecting each other's state debt, will work, since national democracies will be exposed to a confrontation: some states will perceive themselves as suffering from the moral hazards of others, whereas these others will feel themselves to be instructed by the former. However, the financial solidarity of the Union must be distinguished from transfers between States and merely follow the profit generated by the performance of Euro-

4 G Davies, Social Legitimacy and Purposive Power: The End, the Means and the Consent of the People, in D Kochenov, G de Búrca, A Williams (eds), *Europe's Justice Deficit?* (Oxford, Hart Publishing, 2015), p. 259-74.

5 M P Maduro, A New Governance for the European Union and the Euro: Democracy and Justice, in European Parliament, Directorate-General for Internal Policies, *Challenges of Multi-Tier Governance in the European Union. Effectiveness, Efficiency and Legitimacy* (Brussels, European Parliament 2013), p. 31.

pean integration, since responsibility of States becomes illusive. On the other hand,_this applies to the redistribution of the financial burden connected with the flow of migrants into the Schengen area. Both can be accomplished under the rules in force and Union values.

The alternative model requires providing the Union with adequate financial and technical means of intervention, which will supplement, and also partially substitute national ones, though requiring an extension of the existing, or the conferral of new, competencies in sensitive areas of national sovereignty – budgetary policy and territorial integrity.

Union policies should be changed so as to improve communication with citizens and increase the Union's capacity to induce real systemic reforms at national level as convincing solutions, allowing the Union to complement the increased discipline and responsibility it can impose on the Member States. There is an important constitutional momentum in this: any legitimate supranational political decision can be made only by an accountable Union body and with the involvement of the European Parliament, even when it implies a very complex and time-consuming debate. However, it is the only way of gaining the people's support for unpopular measures.

New administrative capacities in the reinforced European monetary union and Schengen area, entrusted with supervisory powers over the Member States, will have to be subjected to the rules generated by the Community method of decision-making. The Court of Justice, when reviewing the instruments (ESM, Fiscal Compact) that had been adopted for the sustainability of national budgetary policies under the supplemented Article 136 TFEU, did not identify any inconsistencies with the existing scope of the Union‘s values and provisions of law.[6] In a short-term perspective, the European Parliament should participate in the assessment of annual analyses of economic growth made by the European Commission under the 'European Semester', a more binding settlement of the respective national policies. So far the Treaty has not needed to be changed. Nevertheless, if violations of Member States' obligations on the avoidance of excessive public debt are to be legally prosecuted, the reduction or elimination of the ban on the Court of Justice's power of control would require a Treaty amendment,[7] with approval given in accordance with the

6 Case C-370/12 *Pringle* [2012].

7 I.e. the deletion of para 10 from Article 126 TFEU, excluding the action for infringement of Union law by a Member State.

respective Member States' democratic constitutional requirements. In a long-term perspective, a new institutional reform of the Union, based on a democratic Europe-wide debate about the (non-)finality of the integration process and transnational democracy, seems to be reasonable.

At the present time, the European public debt and Schengen area crises have only a European democratic solution, which cannot be replaced by a couple of sophisticated but isolated decisions taken by national parliaments only.

V. The Notion of a 'Common Constitutional Core'

Article 2 TEU lists the basic values and principles of the EU, which are common to both the European Union and the Member States. The list does not exceed the requirements of a liberal democratic state governed by rule of law, except in respect of the principle of tolerance, specifying the human dignity of the individual and his/her equal participation in ruling and administering public affairs. In its famous *Omega* case[8], the Court of Justice accepted the arguments presented by the German Supreme Administrative Court not only because of the position of human dignity as a specific feature of the German constitutional identity, but because there was a broad consensus among Member States concerning this shared value articulated in Article 1 of the Charter of Fundamental Rights of the European Union, which is to be respected also by the Court of Justice.

The same conception of shared values was also a starting-point for the Czech Constitutional Court in its judgment on *The Treaty of Lisbon I*:

> *At the core of European civilisation there are values common to all cultures, which form foundations of any human being's self-determination. The functional forms of social co-habitation are founded on an individual's conscious self-restriction and acceptance of order. The same principles lead to higher forms of effective human organisation, whether municipality, state or integration of states.*[9]

A minimum level of tolerance of differences, mutual recognition and trust among the participating members is necessary, if the multilevel system of the European Union and its Member States is to function effectively. Recent efforts by the European Commission to reinforce the mechanism of

---

8 Case C-36/02 *Omega* [2004] ECR I-09609.

9 Pl. ÚS 19/08, available at: www.usoud.cz/nalus.

value stabilisation under Article 7 TEU, called by Armin von Bogdandy 'the reverse Solange'[10], have allowed Member States to act autonomously in protecting fundamental rights and the rule of law only so long as the Member State can guarantee the substance of these constitutional values in a way consistent with the European Union's standards. If a Member State fails to do this, an individual may start proceedings against it on the basis of the common European core of national constitutions.

My thesis is that even a constitution with provisions that are interpreted as imposing a limit on European integration and that can never be exceeded, could be changed, in some countries by a double constitutional amendment and in any country by *pouvoir constituant*, i. e. by a form of constitutional uprising. However, any new constitutional change should respect some basic limits — a common core of all European national constitutions. Such a 'common core' is a shared denominator of all constitutional systems at both levels — national and EU. Therefore, it is a suitable linkage for multilevel constitutionalism, putting together the constitutions of the Member States with the constitutional foundations of the Union itself.

VI. Does Sovereignty Matter?

If this thesis is developed further, we can distinguish between 'eternal provisions' (like *Ewigkeitsklausel* of Article 79 para 3 GG) and 'material cores' (like *Struktursicherungsklausel* of Article 23 para 1 GG). While the former often reflect the unique past experience of a country, differentiating it from another, cannot simply be removed from the constitution and must be respected[11], the latter demonstrate existing similarities and analogies,

10 See A v Bogdandy, M Kottmann, C Antpöhler, J Dischen, S Hentrei, M Smrkolj, 'Ein Rettungsschirm für europäische Grundrechte. Grundlagen einer unionsrechtlichen Solange-Doktrin gegenüber Mitgliedstaaten' (2012) *Zeitschrift für ausländisches öffentliches Recht und Völkerrecht* 72, pp 45-78; for the related project: *Reverse Solange – Protecting the Essence of Fundamental Rights against EU Member States*, the website at http://www.mpil.de/en/pub/research/areas/law-european-union/reverse-solange.cfm.

11 Following examples of such differences may be provided: the system of representation in the French Senate, reflected in the right to vote of EU citizens in municipal elections, the Czech reaction to the European Arrest Warrant (prohibition 'to force a citizen to leave his/her homeland'), a relic of the former totalitarian, non-democratic political regime in the Czech Republic, the strong religious tradition in

since they 'codify' —as a rule, in general terms only— the foundations of liberal democracy shared by all Member States as well as by the European Union itself. Both are interrelated, since specific features of a national constitution can be comprehended by others only towards the background of values they have in common. National identity should not be understood as an instrument of resistance of the national constitution against deprivation of its unique qualities, but as a source of general principles that have traditionally been institutionalised in the nation state and then have to be adjusted for a supranational environment.[12] This can happen only within the communication between the European legal order and national constitutional systems, represented by their respective law-making and judicial authorities.[13] The foundations of liberal democracy could be revised, if the development of the system as a whole it necessitated, though not on the basis of a unilateral action, which would threaten the dynamic stability of constitutional 'statics' of the European integration project and its participating actors.

Could these 'eternal provisions' or 'material cores' become a real barrier to European integration, if the European Union — for once — would be moving towards a federation-like structure in a political union? The Czech Constitutional Court has in this respect been aware of the question, whether sovereignty forms a part of the 'eternal provision' or 'material core', identifying both concepts with the clause of Article 9 para 2 of the Constitution: *Any changes in the essential requirements for a democratic state governed by the rule of law are impermissible".*

Sovereignty in its traditional perception as an independent and exclusive (*ultima ratio*) power at the top of the politico-legal hierarchy no longer forms an essential part of the 'eternal provisions' or 'material core' of the state. A non-sovereign state-member of a federation guarantees rule of law, if the federal state itself — as a sovereign — protects this principle, regardless of understanding the rule of law in terms of formal and procedural legality or in terms of material values.

The same may be true in the case of democracy, since legitimacy in post-national societies is based on citizens sharing values and political as-

---

Poland, leading to the adoption of Protocol no. 30 concerning the application of the Charter of Fundamental Rights of the European Union, etc.

12 T Wischmeyer, 'Nationale Identität und Verfassungsidentität. Schutzgehalte, Instrumente, Perspektiven', 140 *Archiv des öffentlichen Rechts* (2015), p 460.

13 Loc. cit.

pirations rather than on ethnicity or language. The answers of the German and the Czech constitutional courts, as presented in their 'Lisbon' decisions, did not diverge in their statements about a need to compensate for the transfer of powers from national to supranational level by introducing measures that would lead to a new quality of integration and strengthening of the democratic legitimacy of the execution of new supranational powers through an adequate representation of citizens. However, they differed in their assessment of the democratic potential of the European Union to guarantee such representation. Using the vocabulary of the American Revolution, the German Federal Constitutional Court held that the *representation* of citizens at the European level was not in balance with the amount of *taxation*, which was therefore a responsibility of the *Bundestag* as a sovereign (*Integrationsverantwortung*). The Czech Constitutional Court considered the democratic capacity of the European Union to be strong enough to legitimise the conferral of certain new powers, so that the concept of sovereignty could be relaxed. In the Czech Constitutional Court's view, the sovereignty of the *state* no longer forms part of the 'eternal provisions' of the Czech Constitution, but the sovereignty of *the people* does.

The normative effects of the 'material core' of the Czech Constitution on the requirements of Union law have been overestimated, since the Union Treaties has been incorporated into the Czech legal order with the direct approval of the people as the *pouvoir constituant*, a power obtained in the referendum on the ratification of the Treaty of Accession, based on the special constitutional act. The Constitution was adopted by the Czech National Council at the end of 1992, i. e. through the approval given still by the parliamentary authority (*pouvoir constitué*) of the ending Czechoslovakia, not of the would-be new state Czech Republic.

If European Union is to advance beyond its present *status quo*, the people's sovereignty could be limited by a decision made within the existing constitution. If it is to survive this change, however, the risk of its destabilisation will have to be reduced through a gradual adaptation or process of constitutional change. In countries where sovereign independence is stipulated expressly in 'eternal provisions', the adoption of a new constitution would be necessary. The example of Austria demonstrates, that the constitution can de facto be taken as a 'rest-constitution', so that two parallel constitutions — the national one and the supranational one – could co-exist in a complementary way (*Doppelverfassung*) .

State sovereignty as a precondition of democracy can be substituted by other guarantees of 'governance of the people and by the people'. The internal cohesion of the constitution is to be protected through a step-by-step interpretation, making European integration one of the basic characteristics of the 'material core'. The redefinition of the term *'We, the people'* in the U.S. Constitution during its over-two-centuries-long history or the reunification of Germany under Grundgesetz without enforcing Article 146 clearly show that even such a fundamental change can take place without any self-destructive effects.

However, European integration introduces new elements of cohesion for national constitutions, too. The national constitutional identities of Member States have their European dimension, whether expressed in an explicit provision of the constitution or in an interpretative sentence of the constitutional court. This —more or less intensive— attachment is a footing for the opening of the nation state towards the European Union, but also for its co-responsibility for the mutual value stabilisation within the multilevel constitutional system.[14] The concept of multilevel constitutionalism, facing some reservations,[15] has been criticised from the *Kelsenian* ′Grundnorm′ perspective[16] as well as from the pluralist perspective, excluding a unity of the two legal orders, each of them claiming autonomy.[17] This 'constitutional compound' is to be understood —primarily— as a creature not of states, but of the citizens acting through, and represented by, their national governments in the name and on behalf of the citizens, who are also 'masters of the treaties', just as they are the masters of their national constitutions: "the constitution of a supranational Union … is based upon, and complementary to, the national constitutions".[18]

---

14 I Pernice, 'Der Schutz nationaler Identität in der Europäischen Union', 136 *Archiv des öffentichen Rechts* (2011), pp 203-204.

15 For an overview of the reception of this concept see I Pernice, 'The Treaty of Lisbon. Multilevel Constitutionalism in Action', 15 *Columbia Journal of European Law* (2009), pp 352-353.

16 M Jestaedt, 'Der Europäische Verfassungsverbund – Verfassungstheoretischer Charme und rechtstheoretische Unsuffizienz einer Unschärferrelation', in R Krause et al. (eds), *Gedächtnisschrift für W. Blomeyer* (Duncker und Humblot 2004), p 638.

17 R Barents, 'The Fallacy of European Multilevel Constitutionalism', in M Avbejl and J Komárek (eds), *Constitutional Pluralism in the European Union and Beyond* (Hart 2012), p 153.

18 I Pernice, 'Multilevel Constitutionalism and the Crisis of Democracy in Europe', in 11 *European Constitutional Law Review* (2015), p 544.

I can imagine — in the future — a case in which a constitutional change is not admitted not because it undermines state sovereignty for 'a benefit' of the European Union, but because it would limit some of the requirements of the common identity of the Member States, based on mutual respect rather than on their exclusivities.

VII. Conclusion

While the case law of some constitutional courts evokes the impression that European integration could reach its finality in 'eternal provisions' or 'material core', as the basic characteristics of a national constitution, in the future the fact of 'being integrated' could become an internal limitation on constitutional changes, not necessarily in a formal way ('an eternal membership of the European Union'), but as a material limit required for preserving the consistency of the constitution (observance of the fundamental values of membership) and one of its key functions, forming part of national identity. If the process of European integration is to advance, 'material core' need not remain a concept guaranteeing 'a secure distance' between the Member States and the unpredictable behaviour of the Union institutions, but rather an instrument bringing the Member States and the European Union closer together through communication on the constitutional essentials they have in common.

Article 4 para 2 TEU on the observance of the equality and national identity of the Member States by the European Union is not necessarily only a barrier against an excessive execution of the Union's powers, but it also challenges the Court of Justice to interpret Union law as a legal order *permeable* to influences originating in national constitutional systems.[19] This perspective could supersede the imperatives of state sovereignty, since it announces a move from a mere interaction between various constitutional actors underlining their unique features, towards the construction of a common space of European constitutionality.

Article 4 para 2 TEU should not serve as a means of ostracising the doctrine of absolute primacy of Union law by a unilateral action at national level. It is a supranational concept, the explanation of which is a task of

19 For the concept see also M Wendel, Permeabilität im europäischen Verfassungsrecht. Verfassungsre; chtliche Integrationsnormen auf Staats- und Unionsebene im Vergleich (Mohr Siebeck, Tübingen, 2011).

the Court of Justice, acting in cooperation with national judiciaries. It is up to the Court of Justice to release — as the case may be — a Member State from its Treaty obligation on the grounds of national identity, if these grounds do not undermine the cohesion of Union law. The reference to national identities in Article 4 para 2 TEU should support the effect of Union law in the Member States just by reflecting the fundamentals of the political and constitutional system of one of these States, which have their equivalent expression in others.

The interpretation of Article 4 para 2 TEU is to be governed by the notion of 'unity in diversity': Union law respects national identity not as a mere case of individual self-assessment or historical patrimony, but as a plurality of constitutional analogies, insofar as they incorporate 'an implicit European dimension'. This interpretation should reflect the specific constitutional requirements of the other level, mutual awareness of exceeding the competences assigned to each level and the readiness of both levels to support each other in protecting shared basic values and principles. It is to be implemented through strategies of conflict prevention, including self-restriction and a timely dialogue.

This development of the Court of Justice's case law could contribute to the multilevel system of European integration and to the convergence of the 'material cores' of the Member States' constitutions based on shared values, amounting to a European constitutional identity.

9 The impressive resilience of the Greek Constitution in the current financial crisis in Europe.

Antonis Manitakis

Abstract:

The most remarkable and, indeed, the most curious thing in Greece's case, as far as the impact of the 'crisis' on its Constitution is concerned, is that, in spite of the terrible, unprecedented and unending fiscal crisis that the country is undergoing, the Greek Constitution has displayed *a striking resilience.* Unlike the tattered and discredited *political regime*, the *constitutional regime-politevma*, together with the aura of constitutional legitimacy that surrounds it, is still *bearing up* and *holding firm*, while at the same time *adapting itself*, in a consistently *gentle* though steady manner, to the constantly changing, fluid and extraordinary economic conditions. The resilience of the *Greek constitutional order* to the shock waves of the 'crisis' coincides with, and is manifested in, the equally striking *ability* of this constitutional order to *adapt* to both the multiple demands of the *European integration process* and the 'real' coercive forces of the globalised market economy. The radical changes that have been observed in the economy or in social matters during the crisis cannot be described as exceptions to constitutional normality, nor do they overturn established jurisprudence. *They form part of the existing constitutional normality, as 'momentary breaks' in the continuity of a long constitutional tradition.*

I. The paradox: a resilient constitutional regime in spite of a collapsing political system.

The most remarkable and, in fact, the most curious thing in Greece's case, as far as the impact of the 'crisis' on its Constitution is concerned —and also the opposite, the impact of the Constitution on the 'crisis'— is that, in spite of the terrible, unprecedented and unending fiscal crisis that is ravaging the country, the Greek Constitution has displayed *an impressive resilience.*[1]

In other words, what can be observed during the seven-year-long recession (2009-2016) and the implementation of a brutal EU programme of fiscal adjustment and harsh austerity, is that the *government of the country* has, by and large, been conducted *with respect for the constitutional rules of the democratic and parliamentary regime.* It is characteristic that, during this period, three general elections have been held (in 2009, 2012 and 2015 —twice in the latter year, in January and September, together with a referendum), a smooth transfer of power has taken place from a centre-right to a left-wing government and there have been five changes of government and four prime ministers, all in conditions of democratic and constitutional normality. And all this has occurred in spite of the political polarisation, the social tensions and the shocks to the economy. The democratic regime and the parliamentary system of government *have, during the crisis, functioned normally, displaying respect for their fundamental principles,* without the legitimacy of the Constitution being seriously called into question, without the smooth operation of democratic parliamentary government being upset or its very continuance being threatened, and, above all, without there being any question of suspending personal or collective liberties and imposing an emergency regime (Article 48 of the Constitution).[2]

---

1 On the concept and theory of resilience of the constitution in the financial crisis, our contribution is based on the recent study by X Contiades and A Fotiadou entitled 'On Resilience of Constitutions. What Makes Constitutions Resilient to The External Shocks?', *International Constitutional Law Journal*, 1/ 2015, pp 3-26. On the reaction of the constitutions to the financial crisis see X Contiades (ed), *Constitutions in the Global Financial Crisis. A Comparative Analysis* (Farnham, Ashgate 2013), in particular the synthetic study by X Contiades and A Fotiadou, 'How Constitutions Reacted to the Financial Crisis', ibid., pp 9-59. With regard to the impact of the crisis on the Greek Constitution, see the study by X Contiades and I Tassopoulos, 'The Impact of the Financial Crisis on the Greek Constitution', ibid, pp 195-217.

2 For this reason we believe that, from a constitutional point of view, the views of some constitutional theorists are constitutionally unfounded when they argue that the country is in a 'state of emergency' (état d'exception) and that the courts, when they invoke the vague concept of 'the general social, economic or public interest' or when they assess the legitimacy or illegitimacy of violations of individual and social rights on the criterion of the principle of proportionality or its necessity, in effect they are acting as if they were invoking the 'law of necessity'. In acting in this

The Greek people have endured and continue to endure with admirable fortitude an 'extremely critical' economic situation, without losing their faith in the democratic regime or their confidence in the pluralistic parliamentary system of government. And all this despite the fact that the political forces and the politicians have lost their credibility, the old party system has completely collapsed and the political system has crumbled under the weight of cases of corruption, party clientelism and depravity and, above all, the inability of different governments to handle the crisis.

Unlike the tattered and discredited *political regime*, the *constitutional regime* (i.e. that established by the Constitution), together with the constitutional legitimacy that envelops it, is still *bearing up* and *holding firm*, while at the same time *adapting itself, gently* but steadily, to the constantly changing, fluid and extraordinary economic conditions.[3]

This peculiar situation, in which the Constitution is displaying resilience while the political system is collapsing, has another, positive side

---

way the courts give constitutional legitimacy to exceptional circumstances, thereby endowing them with a permanent character and bringing them into the realm of constitutional normativity. For the opposite standpoint, see I Kamtsidou, 'Un état d'exception nullement exceptionnel. La crise souveraine et le crépuscule de la Constitution. Un aperçu historique' (2015), www.constitutionalism.gr, and for the concept of a constitutional/legal normality through the legal interpretation of standards, such as necessity, in the Greek legal order, G Karavokyris, 'Constitution and necessity in times of crisis', *European Politeia*, 2/2015, pp 347-65. See also for the concept of 'state of emergency' ML Basilien-Gainche, *État de droit et états d'exception. Une conception de l'État* (Paris, P.U.F., Fondements de la politique, 2013) and F Saint-Bonnet, *L'état d'exception*, (Paris, P.U.F., Léviathan, 2001). .

3 On the consequences of the debt crisis in Europe, with a focus on Greece, see the astute observations by Y Drossos in 'Love's Labour's Lost: fighting austerity and crisis with obiter dicta. A gloss on the expediency of constitutional justice in times of crisis' (2013) https://www.academia.edu/5265793/; L Papadopoulou, 'Can constitutional rules, even if "Golden", tame the Greek public debt?', in: M Adams, F Fabbrini, P Larouche (eds), *The Constitutionalization of European Budgetary Constraints* (Oxford, Hart Publishing, 2014), pp 223-49. See also, in a comparative context, X Contiades, *Constitutions in the global financial crisis* (n 1); S Fabbrini, *Which European Union? Europe after the Euro Crisis* (Cambridge, Cambridge University Press, 2015); C Schweiger and J Magone, *The effects of the Eurozone Sovereign Debt crisis: differentiated integration between the EU* (London and New York, Routledge, 2015); Kaarlo Tuori and Klaus Tuori, *The Eurozone crisis. A constitutional analysis* (Cambridge, Cambridge University Press, 2014); A Metaxas and I Pernice, *Europe in crisis: between law and politics* (Sideris-Friedrich Ebert Stiftung, 2015); A Hinarejos, *The Euro area crisis in constitutional perspective* (Oxford, Oxford University Press, 2015).

for the constitutional institutions: *throughout this period, there has been no crisis of power or governability*. Governments have been formed without undue delays and have formulated and carried out government policies within the framework of the programme of fiscal adjustment, implementing the provisions of the memoranda of understanding. They have governed, while their parliamentary power has rested on the government majorities imposed by the Constitution, and they have passed measures in accordance with the relevant constitutional and parliamentary procedures.

The above findings —if taken no further— support a clear and simple, though ultimately, as we shall see later, simplistic, assertion: that the *existing constitutional order is perfect, displays no weaknesses and therefore does not need to be changed!* Nothing could be further from the truth.

It is true that the Constitution is, for the time being, performing *its legitimising function* perfectly. The dire economic and political crisis has not, it seems, had a negative impact on the validity and application of the Constitution and especially on the institutions of the rule of law. It has not, *in any event, caused a legitimation crisis* with regard to the authority of the Constitution. The citizens' respect for the Constitution has remained unshaken. Besides, the ruling bodies have taken care to observe the basic letter of the Constitution, and the political institutions have generally operated within the framework of constitutional legality.

This idyllic picture of the Greek constitutional reality is, however, too good to be true. It is a wonderful picture only if we ignore its one-sidedness and disregard the well-noted —though few, it is true— violations of the Constitution by the ruling power, as well as the serious 'material' damage or losses that have been inflicted on social rights and the social acquis.[4]

II. The reaction of the Constitution to the handling of the crisis in the course of its practical implementation

The foregoing findings conceal, through their one-sidedness, invisible facets of the constitutional and political reality, which are just as important

4 C Kilpatrick and B De Witte (eds), *Social Rights in Time of Crisis in the Eurozone: The role of fundamental rights challenges*", EUI Department of Law, Research Papers, http://cadmus.eui.eu/bitstream/handle/1814/31247/LAW%20WP%202014%2005%20Social%20Rights%20final%202242014.pdf.

as the visible ones. Above all, they conceal the interactive relationship between the Constitution and the crisis and particularly the Constitution's influence on the handling of the crisis. And, of course, they do not explain the paradox that we noted at the beginning: how is it that, at a time when the country has been experiencing dire economic and social problems, its system of government has functioned smoothly, in a context of constitutional legality and normality?

An answer to the above question can be provided by investigating the way in which this same reality is influenced by the implementation and interpretation of the Constitution by the legislators and judges respectively.

The advantage of adopting this perspective lies in the fact that, from this point of view, the constitutional reality will be examined through a multifocal analysis of the way in which the Constitution is implemented in practice. This impels the researcher to focus his research on the two most basic functions of the constitutional state: that of enacting laws and that of (constitutional) justice. The investigation of these functions also leads to a comparison being drawn between the work of the legislator and that of the judge: Zeus is drawn up against the demigod Hermes. In the shadow of the confrontation between these two another confrontation takes place: that between Law and Politics.[5]

Concerning the examination of jurisprudence relating to the 'crisis', combined with the European programme of fiscal adjustment into the Greek legal order —at the same time that the Greek legislator was adopting a massive and chaotic amount of legislation—, the following findings may be observed:

5 M Everson- and C Joerges, 'Who is the guardian for constitutionalism in Europe?' in: LSE 'Europe in Question' Discussion Paper Series, 63/2013, www.lse.ac.uk. For the relation between politics and law see indicatively M Tushnet, *Taking the constitutions away from the courts* (Princeton, Princeton University Press, 1999); M Troper, *Le constitutionnalisme entre droit et politique* (Paris, CURAPP, Droit et Politique, PUF, 1991), p 68.

A. *Resilience through adaptation: compliance with the country's international obligations; constitutional changes through informal amendments to the Constitution.*[6]

The resilience of the Greek constitutional order in the face of the shocks dealt by the 'crisis' is not merely a sign of a transitory endurance or a temporary resistance to the pressures being placed upon it but also coincides with, and is manifested in —and this is in fact the reason for its impressive endurance— an equally impressive *capacity to adapt* (or *adaptability*) to both the multiple demands of the *European integration process* and the 'real' coercive forces of the globalised market economy.

This adaptability has been achieved by virtue of the flexible *constitutional mechanisms for incorporating the international and European legal orders* into the national one. It has been based entirely on the special constitutional provisions catering for Greece's participation in the European integration processes that were put in place by the legislator who drew up the Constitution of 1975. These are, namely, the highly functional and, as things have proved, *far-sighted* provisions of Article 28 paras. 2 and 3 of the Constitution, which *establish an informal procedure for amending the Constitution through the ratification of international treaties*, in contrast to the formal and inflexible procedure for constitutional reform. The ratification by the Greek parliament of European treaties that provide for or entail the transfer of sovereign powers to the EU, or restrictions on national sovereignty —as has happened in the case of the European mechanisms for preserving fiscal stability— has brought about *imperceptible amendments to the regulatory content of the Constitution and the exercise of national sovereignty, with the blessings of the Constitution itself.*

The constitutional provisions mentioned above have created *a broad and welcoming gateway for the incorporation of European and international law* into the Greek legal order, and at the same time have equipped the latter with all those mechanisms that are necessary for it to adapt easily

6 On constitutional change and the adaptation of the constitutions see X Contiades (ed), *Engineering Constitutional Change. A Comparative Perspective on Europe, Canada and the USA*, (London and New York, Routledge, 2013) and M Altwegg-Boussac, *Les changements constitutionnels informels*, (Paris, L.G.D.J.- Institut Universitaire Varenne, 2013); D Oliver and C Fusaro, *How Constitutions change: A comparative study* (Oxford, Hart Publishing, 2011).

and comfortably to the demands of the current international situation and the changes occurring in international society.

The provisions have thus endowed the Greek constitutional order with a great degree of flexibility in respect of its constitutional procedures. They have enabled it to participate, directly and actively, in the European integration processes and, through simple decisions by Parliament, to *automatically adapt itself* to every decision or act of the EU bodies, even those of intergovernmental character, such as the acts and decisions of the European Council of Heads of State and Government. And all this has been achieved without engaging in the arduous and time-consuming process of reforming a rigid Constitution.

In this way the Constitution has gradually been changing in texture, and, in terms of its relations with the international and European legal order, has become less rigid and more flexible.

The flexibility of the Constitution has a bearing on sensitive and key areas of the state as it concerns the international relations of the Greek state as well as its ongoing participation in the European integration process. It therefore has a direct bearing on national and state sovereignty, which in turn is changing, shedding its *egocentric, undivided and indivisible* character in favour of a *collective, shared and joint* type of sovereignty.[7]

The Greek state's recent painful experience of implementing the European Stability Mechanism of fiscal adjustment has shown that Greece does indeed possess all the necessary constitutional mechanisms to enable it to participate in the European project in a smooth and orderly way, without legal obstacles, both in times of crisis and in periods of normality. Neither the exceptional and urgent circumstances of the excessive public debt nor the threat of bankruptcy or even Grexit have necessitated recourse to emergency procedures or the suspension of constitutional legality.[8]

These crises have been dealt with by implementing the relevant constitutional procedures for enacting emergency laws and taking the fiscal and economic measures imposed by the EU in order to combat the debt crisis,

---

7 For the impact of EU integration on state sovereignty see C Beaudoin, *La démocratie à l'épreuve de l'intégration européenne* (Paris, L.G.D.J., 2014), p 108.

8 For the judicial consideration of the exceptional and urgent circumstances see P Pikrammenos, 'Public Law in extraordinary circumstances from the viewpoint of the procedure of judicial review' in: *Studies on the Memorandum* (in Greek), (Athens, Athens Bar Association, 2013), pp 11-21.

provided that these measures are justified, and not merely occasioned, by clear grounds of public interest.[9]

The extraordinary legislative measures that have been taken to deal with the economic crisis and secure a permanent and steady fiscal balance have been based on established constitutional provisions and procedures and have been carried out within the framework of the *existing constitutional legality and normality*, which they have confirmed without there being any need for it to be suspended. These measures, therefore, have not been of a temporary or transitional character, nor of course have they lain somewhere between '*droit*' and '*non-droit*', as some Greek legal theorists have claimed.[10] They have been enacted in order to last, they have come to stay, they have been carried out within the framework of the existing constitutional legality and now form part of a 'normal' constitutionality.[11]

Even when the extraordinary legislative procedure provided for by Article 44 (1) of the Constitution has been activated ('Under extraordinary circumstances of an urgent and unforeseeable need, the President of the Republic may, upon the proposal of the Cabinet, issue acts of legislative content') —and it is true that this has happened quite often, so often in fact that on some occasions it has unfortunately come to appear normal[12]—

---

9 For the concept of public interest see V Kapsali, 'Public interest and judicial review on the ground of economic freedom', *Revue Hellénique des Droits de l'Homme*, 38/2008, p 511 (in Greek); C Yannakopoulos, 'The public interest from the scope of the financial crisis', *Journal of Administrative Law*, 1/2012, p 100 (in Greek); I Mathioudakis, 'Transformations of the cash public interest in periods of severe economic crisis', *Journal of Administrative Law*, 4/2011, p 478 ff. (in Greek).

10 The opposite view is held by C Yannakopoulos, 'Un État Devant la Faillite: entre Droit et Non-Droit' (2013), http://docplayer.fr/4507630-Un-etat-devant-la-faillite-entre-droit-et-non-droit.html..

11 See G Karavokyris, *The Constitution and the Crisis* (Athens, Kritiki, 2014), p 38 (in Greek). This view is also held by E Venizelos, 'State Transformation and the European Integration Project: Lessons from the financial crisis and the Greek paradigm' www.ceps.eu/system/files/SR%20No%20130%20State%20Transformation%20and%20European%20Integration.pdf.

12 G Gerapetritis, 'Economic Crisis as element of deregulation of the hierarchy of sources of law: Inevitability or alibi?' in: *Studies on the Memorandum* (in Greek) (Athens, Athens Bar Association, 2013), pp 230-43. For other legal orders affected by the financial crisis see also A Ruiz Robledo, 'The Spanish constitution in the turmoil of the global financial crisis' in: X Contiades (ed), *Constitutions in the Global Financial Crisis* (n) p 145; C Piccardi, 'The economic crisis and the na-

even in this case, the 'enactment of extraordinary laws' has taken place within the framework of the existing constitutional legality.

B. *Resilience through an informal change in the Constitution via jurisprudence: the privileged judicial techniques of resorting to the vague concept of 'the public interest' and the criterion of 'proportionality'.*

However, it is not merely the *procedural flexibility* that it has gained in the speedy enactment of laws and the incorporation of international agreements into the Greek legal order that has helped to give the Constitution its resilience and adaptability. It is also the informal change that has occurred in its regulatory function *through the way it has been interpreted by the constitutional justice system.* The latter, through its interpretations of the Constitution in the course of trying cases that have questioned the constitutionality of laws implementing '*crucial*' fiscal, tax and insurance policies, has fashioned, refashioned and shaped *constitutional arguments and jurisprudential constants or criteria* of a kind that enable and prompt the legislator and the government to deal in a balanced and measured way with violations of constitutional rights, *particularly those of a social nature*, when public interest aims defined by the government are *truly* served.

Having as a guide and justification for the rights violation that may have been caused, the *serving of public interest aims*, and with the *principle of proportionality as a balancing criterion*, the judge of constitutionality has measured and weighed up in the cases placed before him —always on the basis of their specific legal and factual circumstances— the magnitude of the rights violation in the light of the public interest aim or public policy that was being served. And this is clear in all the jurisprudence that has been produced during the crisis.

The *protective, and therefore regulatory, content or the meaning of constitutional rights is neither certain nor unvarying.* Their 'real meaning' is neither discovered nor revealed by the judge as something fixed and un-

tional parliaments: the Italian experience', http://www.parlamento.it/documenti/repository/affariinternazionali/ecprd2012/4_Piccardi_EN.pdf; X Contiades and A Fotiadou, 'How constitutions reacted to the financial crisis' in X. Contiades (ed), *Constitutions in the Global Financial Crisis* (n), p 16.

changing. He shapes and fashions it, not in a general or abstract way, nor in an arbitrary fashion or out of nothing, but basing his interpretation on the previous relevant jurisprudence, which he supplements or amends, following well-established and tested methods and constraints and always providing a detailed statement of reasons for his decision.

More specifically, when the judge is called upon to assess a legislative measure that implements a public policy in the light of the public interest aim that is being served and the possible violation of a right, he proceeds to balance things up and make legal assessments or characterisations and appraisals of the constitutionality of public policies. He *judges* and *assesses* public policies from a constitutional perspective, with reasoning and arguments centred around two related and close syllogisms: *the means-end syllogism (examination of the rationality of the measure)* and the '*balancing' syllogism,* when he finds that there is a conflict of constitutional goods or interests.

In the last few years the jurisprudence of the Council of State, which in practice performs the function of a Constitutional Court, has consistently judged the legitimacy or illegitimacy, the constitutional justifiability or unjustifiability of violations or restrictions of individual or social rights on the criteria of 'proportionality' and 'the public interest'.[13] This judicial practice is an indication of an advanced form of judicial constitutional review. Although formally this form of review is advanced in comparison to the review of formal constitutionality, since the judge reviews the aim of the law, in the cases that have been tried during the period of the crisis, judges have *restricted themselves* to carrying out a legal evaluation and assessment of the 'factual circumstances' that came under the concept of the public interest and they have confined themselves to ascertaining whether public interest grounds have played an 'actual' role or not in each case,

13 For the role of proportionality in the Greek jurisprudence produced during the crisis see especially the study by X Contiades and A Fotiadou, 'Social Rights in the Age of Proportionality: Global Economic Crisis and Constitutional Litigation', *International Journal of Constitutional Law*, 3/2012, pp 660-86. For the proportionality principle see also M Cohen-Eliya and I Porat, 'Proportionality and Constitutional Culture', Cambridge Studies in Constitutional Law (Cambridge, Cambridge University Press, 2013); A Barak, 'Proportionality: Constitutional Rights and their Limitations', Cambridge Studies in Constitutional Law (Cambridge, Cambridge University Press, 2012); and for a critical point of view S Tsakyrakis, 'Proportionality: An assault on human rights?', *International Journal of Constitutional Law* (2009), pp 468-93.

without assessing or weighing up further the suitability, the expediency, or the proportionality and balance between the violation of a right and the pursued aim. They have believed that such a substantive assessment should exclusively be made by the governing majority, and they have restricted themselves to attempting to ascertain the necessity of each measure.[14]

III. Towards a malleable or flexible constitutional normality. The 'crisis' as a momentary yet decisive 'discontinuity' in a long constitutional continuity.

The practice of Greek judges of making very frequent recourse to reviewing the constitutionality of the concepts of 'the public interest' and 'proportionality' is not, however, a jurisprudential practice that has appeared during the recent crisis. *It does not constitute an 'exceptional' and 'irregular' judicial outlet for jurisprudence that has arisen as a result of the country's exceptional economic circumstances*. It is the same, well-established form of jurisprudence that has been followed for years, both in periods of normality and in times of paradigm change like the present one. The economic crisis has not led to a change in judicial methods, nor to the invention or application of new ones. *In Greece no crisis jurisprudence exists or has developed.* The judicial constitutional review of laws basically still is and has remained, since the time it was established, an investigation of limits, a review of unconstitutionality and not of constitutionality.

Moreover, the judge who reviews the constitutionality of laws in Greece, even when he makes an advanced and thorough review of the constitutionality of a law, takes care to place judicial restrictions on himself, imposing, of his own accord, limits and self-restrictions on the judicial review that he is undertaking. What is more, he has long recognised the fact that *the political power has a broad freedom to freely determine public*

14 See E Venizelos (n 11), p 22, and the contribution by G Karavokyris, 'The role of judges and legislators in the Greek financial crisis. A matter of competence' in the present volume; M Perakis, 'The passive form of Judicial Activism: Judicial self-restraint while balancing fundamental rights and public interest in the age of economic crisis', and T Ziamou, 'Controlling the legislator's intent in the "crisis jurisprudence" of the Greek Council of State', *European Politeia*, 2/2015, pp 289-321 and 429-49.

policy, on the basis of the government policy that has been approved by Parliament. This is acceptable so long as this public policy, as expressed in the law, does not exceed the limits of the Constitution and does not infringe upon constitutional freedoms (negative articulation).

And this is precisely what the judge of constitutionality did both in the era of state interventionism and the era of privatisations. And this is just what he is doing today, in this period of crisis. The individual criticisms that jurisprudential commentators have made of individual judicial decisions, noting contradictions, tergiversations, lacunas or excesses, even when the decisions have been justified, do not disprove the general findings stated above, nor do they refute the general long-standing tendency in our constitutional jurisprudence.

Therefore, the radical developments that may be observed in Greek jurisprudence during the period of crisis cannot be regarded as an exception to normality, nor as a refutation —and of an exceptional kind at that— of established jurisprudence. *They form part of the existing constitutional normality, as a momentary 'discontinuity' in the country's constitutional continuity, in a long constitutional parliamentary tradition that stretches back over two centuries.*

Nevertheless, in a gradual, informal and inconspicuous manner, they have been shaping *a new normality*. A constitutional normality that, compared with the past, is characterised by a more pronounced regulatory (or semantic) 'plasticity or flexibility', thanks mainly to the malleable use of judicial tools like proportionality and the public interest.[15]

A constitutional normality which, in any case, appears to be abandoning its one-sided and monolithic rule-of-law orientation, the orientation that has characterised the 1990's and 2010's, that is to say, the unilateral insistence on the part of the judge of constitutionality to protect, at all costs and above all else, the rights and freedoms of litigants, individuals and groups. In this period of crisis, judges appear to be becoming increasingly aware of the need to protect not only the constitutional legality of rights but also the legality that promotes and guarantees public policies that do indeed serve the aims of the general public, social and economic interest.

---

15 See note 11 above and for the concept of normality and its relation with standards in particular see also S Rials, *Le juge administratif et la technique du standard (Essai sur le traitement juridictionnel de l'idée de normalité)* (Paris, L.G.D.J., 1980).

This change of perspective is evident not only in jurisprudential practices but also in legislative and administrative practices. It appears that there is a desperate search for *a balanced and measured form of protection* —one that varies with the prevailing conditions and circumstances— *for the rights of individuals and groups which, however, is combined with the simultaneous protection of public interest aims and goods* in the implementation of public policies.

IV. Conclusion

In conclusion, in this paper I have sought to show simply, through the examples of jurisprudence and legislation, that, on the one hand, Greece is indeed going through a terrible structural crisis of adjustment to the new economic reality, which looks as if it is not going to be a passing phenomenon but a long and drawn-out one. And this is because its structures are rusty and antiquated, as are its administrative practices and political culture, which dates from the last century.

On the other hand, beyond the crisis, and in spite of the crisis and the gloomy economic and political outlook that has taken shape, our constitutional reality is —unlike the political and economic realities— displaying signs of an *impressive resilience and adaptation to the new European and globalised reality*.

Part Three
Citizens, Rights and New Techniques for Enhancing Legitimacy

10 Opinion 2/13 of the European Court of Justice in the Context of Multilevel Protection of Fundamental Rights and Multilevel Constitutionalism revisited

Ana Maria Guerra Martins

Abstract

In Opinion 2/13 on the draft agreement on the European Union's accession to the European Convention on Human Rights (ECHR), the Court of Justice of the European Union (CJEU) held that the draft agreement was not compatible with European Union law (EU law), that is to say, with Article 6(2) of the Treaty on European Union (TEU) or with Protocol No 8 relating to Article 6(2) TEU. This is without doubt one of the most significant rulings in the history of the European integration process, due to its legal and political consequences. In this study, however, we will not elaborate on the future of the EU accession to the ECHR after Opinion 2/13. We will focus instead on the question of whether the conclusions of the Court could have been different if it had taken into account the multilevel protection of fundamental rights and multilevel constitutionalism, which is a theory that tries to explain how the legitimacy of public authority is rooted in individuals, as citizens of Member States and citizens of the Union.

I. Introduction

A. The background of Opinion 2/13

On 18 December 2014, the CJEU delivered Opinion 2/13[1] on whether the draft agreement on the European Union's accession to the ECHR was compatible with EU law. It concluded that it was not compatible with Article 6(2) of the Treaty on European Union (TEU) nor with Protocol No 8 relating to Article 6(2) TEU.

---

1 ECLI:EU:C:2014:2454.

For the second time in the history of its case law,[2] the Court has blocked the Union's accession to the ECHR, in spite of the explicit competence conferred on the Union by the TEU after Lisbon.[3] According to the Court, the draft agreement providing for accession was, *grosso modo*, contrary to the specific characteristics of EU law[4] and its legal autonomy.[5]

---

2 See Opinion 2/94 of 28 March 1996, ECLI:EU:C:1996:140.

3 Cf. Article 6 (2) TEU. On the EU's accession to the ECHR in the Treaty of Lisbon compare T Lock, 'Accession of the EU to the ECHR – Who Would be Responsible in Strasbourg?' in D Ashiagbor et al (eds), *The European Union after the Treaty of Lisbon* (Cambridge, Cambridge University Press, 2012) 109 et seq; G Gaja, 'Accession to the ECHR' in A Biondi et al (eds), *EU Law after Lisbon* (Oxford, Oxford University Press, 2012) 180 et seq; MJR de Mesquita, *A União Europeia após o Tratado de Lisboa* (Coimbra, Almedina, 2010) 83 et seq; E Bribosia, 'Le traité de Lisbonne: un pas supplémentaire dans le processus de constitutionnalisation des droits fondamentaux' in P Magnette and A Weyembergh (eds), *L'Union européenne: la fin d'une crise?* (L'Université de Bruxelles, Brussels 2008) 195 et seq; FB Rohmer, 'Valeurs et droits fondamentaux' in E Brosset et al (eds), *Le Traité de Lisbonne – Reconfiguration ou déconstitutionnalisation de l'Union européenne?* (Émile Bruylant, Brussels, 2009) 158 et seq.

4 According to the Court, 'these characteristics include those relating to the constitutional structure of the EU, which is seen in the principle of conferral of powers referred to in Articles 4(1) TEU and 5(1) and (2) TEU, and in the institutional framework established in Articles 13 TEU to 19 TEU' and 'EU law is characterised by the fact that it stems from an independent source of law, the Treaties, by its primacy over the laws of the Member States.' See, to that effect, the judgments in C-6/64 Costa EU:C:1964:66, 594 and C-11/70 Internationale Handelsgesellschaft EU:C:1970:114 para 3; Opinions 1/91 EU:C:1991:490 para 21 and 1/09 EU:C:2011:123 para 65; and the judgment in C-399/11 Melloni EU:C:2013:107 para 59, and the direct effect of a whole series of provisions which are applicable to their nationals and to the Member States themselves (the judgment in C-26/62 van Gend & Loos, EU:C:1963:1, 12 and Opinion 1/09 EU:C:2011:123 para 65).' See paras 165-166 of Opinion 2/13.

5 On the autonomy of EU law see, among others, I Pernice, 'The Autonomy of the EU Legal Order – Fifty Years After *Van Gend*' in A Tizzano et al (eds), *50ème Anniversaire de l'arrêt Van Gend en Loos 1963-2003* (Luxemburg, Office des publications de l'Union européenne, 2013) 55 et seq; P Gragl, *The Accession of the European Union to the European Convention on Human Rights* (Oxford, Hart Publishing, 2013) *maxime* 19-49; P Craig, 'EU Accession to the ECHR: Competence, Procedure and Substance' (2013) 36 (1) *Fordham International Law Journal* 1142 et seq; JP Terhechte, 'Autonomie und Kohärenz – Die Eigenständigkeit der Unionsgrundrechte im Zuge des EMRK-Beitritts der Europäischen Union', in J Iliopoulos-Strangas et al (eds), *Der Beitritt der Europäischen Union zur EMRK* (Baden-Baden, Nomos, 2013) 34 et seq; T Lock, 'Walking on a Tightrope: The Draft ECHR Accession Agreement and the Autonomy of the EU Legal Order' (2011) 48 (4) *CML Rev*

To be perfectly honest, this was not completely surprising, taking into account that a number of previous rulings[6] had been in a similar direction. Even so, most people would have expected that the Court would not apply its case law on human rights matters and would weigh up the advantages of EU accession to the ECHR, which have been noted by scholars[7] and some European institutions, such as the Commission,[8] for decades. Among these advantages should be included a greater adherence to the multilevel protection of fundamental rights, which would surely increase the legitimacy of the EU, since it would effectively have to abide by the same international catalogue of fundamental human rights – the ECHR – and come under the same international jurisdiction – the ECtHR – as its Member States. Furthermore, possible gaps in either the EU or national fundamental rights systems could be filled in by the ECHR. Finally, individuals would be able to hold the EU itself and not only the Member States responsible in Strasbourg, which would contribute to a better protection of their fundamental rights and to an increase in the legal certainty of the system.[9]

1028 et seq; T Schilling, 'The Autonomy of the Community Legal Order: An Analysis of Possible Foundations' (1996) 37 (2) *Harvard International Law Journal* 380 et seq; JHH Weiler, 'The Autonomy of the Community Legal Order – Through the Looking Glass' (1996) 37 (2) *Harvard International Law Journal* 411 et seq; FE Dowrick, 'A Model of the European Communities Legal System' (1983) *Yearbook of European Law* 169 et seq.

6 See Opinion 1/91 of 14 December 1991, ECLI:EU:C:1991:490; and Opinion 1/09 of 8 March 2011, ECLI:EU:C:2011:123.

7 See, among others, G Cohen-Jonathan, 'Le problème de l'adhésion des Communautés européennes à la Convention européeenne des droits de l'homme', in *Mélanges offerts à Pierre-Henri Teitgen* (Paris, Pedone, 1984) 82 et seq; JP Jacqué, 'The Convention and the European Communities' in RSt Macdonald et al (eds), *The European System for the Protection of Human Rights* (Dordrecht, Nijhof, 1993) 889 et seq.

8 See the Memorandum on the Accession of the European Communities to the Convention for the Protection of Human Rights and Fundamental Freedoms COM (79) 200 final, 2 May 1979, in *Bulletin of the European Communities*, Supplement 2/79.

9 On the reasons for accession, see, among others, M Claes and Š Imamovic, 'National Courts in the New European Fundamental Rights Architecture' in V Kosta et al (eds), *The EU Accession to the ECHR* (Oxford, Hart Publishing, 2014) 164; E Steiner and I Rătescu, 'The Long Way to Strasbourg – The Impact of CJEU's Opinion on EU's Accession to the ECHR' (2015) *European Yearbook on Human Rights* 53-55.

In this context, the legal and political significance of Opinion 2/13 is unquestionable. It is '*without a shadow of doubt one of the most important rulings of the Court of Justice*'[10] and few rulings of the CJEU have aroused so much immediate criticism as Opinion 2/13.

B. Scholars' Reactions

Apart from the blogosphere,[11] one of the most prestigious EU law reviews – the Common Market Law Review – published an editorial comment claiming '[t]he Opinion of the Court, (…), appears to reflect a somewhat formalistic and sometimes uncooperative attitude in defence of its own powers vis-à-vis the European Human Rights Court (ECtHR)'.[12] Steve Peers characterises the Court's Opinion as 'a clear and present danger to human rights protection'[13] and Sionaidh Douglas-Scott agrees with him, adding that 'Opinion 2/13 does not take rights seriously'.[14] Piet Eeckhout claims that 'the CJEU's objections to the Accession Agreement do not persuade, and are not in accordance with the limited conditions imposed

---

10 A Łazowski and RA Wessel, 'When Caveats Turn into Locks: Opinion 2/13 on Accession of the European Union to the ECHR' (2015) 16 (1) *German Law Journal* 179-212, at 210. Also available at www.utwente.nl/bms/pa/research/wessel/wessel108.pdf.

11 The blogosphere reacted immediately. See S Peers, 'The CJEU and the EU's Accession to the ECHR: a Clear and Present Danger to Human Rights Protection', www.eulawanalysis.blogspot.pt/2014/12/the-cjeu-and-eus-accession-to-echr.html; M Wendel, 'Mehr Offenheit wagen! Eine Kritische Annäherung an das Gutachten des EuGH zum EMRK-Beitritt', *VerfBlog*, 2014/12/21, www.verfassungblog.de/mehr-offenheit-wagen-eine-kritische-annäherung-das-gutachten-des-eugh-zum-emrk-beitritt/; LFM Besselink, 'Acceding to the ECHR Notwithstanding the Court of Justice Opinion 2/13', *VerfBlog,* 2014/12/23, www.verfassungsblog.de/acceding-echr-notwithstanding-court-justice-opinion-213/.

12 'Editorial Comments: The EU's Accession to the ECHR – A "NO" from the ECJ!' (2015) 52 (1), *CML Rev* 1.

13 S Peers, 'The EU's Accession to the ECHR: the Dream Becomes a Nightmare' (2015) 16 (1) *German Law Journal* 219 et seq.

14 S Douglas-Scott, 'Opinion 2/13 on EU Accession to the ECHR: a Christmas Bombshell from the European Court of Justice', p. 5, UK Constitutional Law Blog, 2014/12/24 www.ukconstitutionallaw.org, available also at www.verfassungsblog.de/author/sionaidh-douglas-scott.

by Art 6(2) TEU and by Protocol 8'.[15] For the same author, 'Opinion 2/13 is based on a concept of autonomy which borders on autarky'.[16] Paul Gragl – who is an expert on the subject of the EU's accession to the ECHR – wrote that 'Opinion 2/13 leaves a bitter taste and a fair share of pessimism among all those who are interested in human rights and their effective protection and enforcement'.[17] Even Finisk Korenica – who recently wrote a PhD thesis on EU Accession to the ECHR, in which he often agrees with the Court – believes that 'the opinion confirms (…) the very allergic tendency of the Luxembourg Court to recognize external control from an international court. Such aversion, as shown in this Opinion, goes far beyond the likely situations that may emerge in practice'.[18]

In fact, few scholars have entirely supported Opinion 2/13.[19]

C. *Purpose of the Present Study*

It is not our intention here to join our voice to this chorus of protests.[20] The main purpose of this study is neither to criticise the Court's views in

15 P Eeckhout, 'Opinion 2/13 on EU Accession to the ECHR and Judicial Dialogue – Autonomy or Autarky?', *Jean Monnet Working Paper* 01/15, 39, available at www.jeanmonnetprogram.org/papers/15/documents/JMWP01Eeckhout.pdf.

16 Ibid.

17 P Gragl, 'The Reasonableness of Jealousy: Opinion 2/13 and EU Accession to the ECHR', 2015 *European Yearbook on Human Rights* 47.

18 F Korenica, The EU Accession to the ECHR – Between Luxembourg's Search for Autonomy and Strasbourg's Credibility on Human Rights Protection (Heidelberg, Springer, 2015) 408.

19 See D Halberstam, '"It's the Autonomy, Stupid!" A Modest Defense of Opinion 2/13 on EU Accession to the ECHR, and the Way Forward', *University of Michigan Law School, Public Law and Legal Theory Research Paper Series*, No 432, February 2015, available at papers.ssrn.com/sol3/papers.cfm?abstract_id=2567591; D Halberstam, 'A Constitutional Defense of CJEU Opinion 2/13 on EU Accession to the ECHR (and the Way Forward)', *VerfBlog,* 2015/3/12, www.verfassungsblog.de/a-constitutional-defense-of-cjeu-opinion-213-on-eu-accession-to-the-echr-and-the-way-forward/#.VgbS528g9dg; C Krenn, 'Autonomy and Effectiveness as a Common Concern: A Path to ECHR Accession After Opinion 2/13' (2015) 16 (1) *German Law Journal* 147 et seq.

20 See also J Nergelius, *The Accession of the EU to the European Convention on Human Rights – A Critical View of the Opinion of the Court of Justice*, SIEPS, 2015:3, 27 et seq, available at www.sieps.se;_E Dubout, 'Une question de confi-

general nor to seek solutions[21] in order to solve the legal and political problems that Opinion 2/13 has created either for the EU or for the ECHR. On the contrary, bearing in mind two statements made by the Court – the Union is not a State[22] but it has a '*constitutional structure*'[23] – we think that it makes perfect sense to assess whether the final decision of the Court is consistent with these two starting points. In other words, we intend to assess whether an adequate constitutional theory, which includes the multilevel protection of fundamental rights in Europe, as one factor of legitimacy, among others, could have led the Court to other conclusions.

Before continuing, we would like to stress that, independently of the political consequences of Opinion 2/13, which are somewhat catastrophic for the EU's accession to the ECHR —since, according to Article 218 (11) TFEU, the agreement may not enter into force unless it is amended or the Treaties are revised, which will be a somewhat difficult task—, the decision of the Court must be respected. That is to say, we cannot accept the idea that Opinion 2/13 does not prevent the accession.[24] In our view, it does. In a political entity such as the EU, which has to submit itself to the

---

ance: nature juridique de l'Union européenne et adhésion à la Convention européenne des droits de l'homme' (2015) 51 *Cahiers de droit européen* 73 et seq.

21 Some articles have already been published with this aim in mind. See I Pernice, 'L'adhésion de l'Union européenne à la Convention européenne des droits de l'homme est suspendue – Remarques à propos d'un avis surprenant de la Cour de Justice de l'Union européenne du 18 décembre 2014' (2015) 51 *Cahiers de droit européen* 47 et seq; JP Jacqué, 'Pride and /or Prejudice? Les lectures possibles de l'avis 2/13 de la Cour de Justice' (2015) 51 *Cahiers de droit européen* 19 et seq; T Lock, 'The Future of the EU Accession to the ECHR after Opinion 2/13: Is it Still Possible and is it Still Desirable?', *University of Edinburgh School of Law Research Paper* No 2015/18 (*Europa Working Paper* No 2015/02), available at ssrn.com.abstract=2616175.

22 See para 156 of the Opinion – 'the EU is, under international law, precluded by its very nature from being considered a State.'.

23 See para 165 of the Opinion – '(…) these characteristics include those relating to the constitutional structure of the EU.'.

24 Besselink proposed solving the accession with a 'Notwithstanding Protocol' that should read: *'The Union shall accede to the European Convention for the Protection of Human Rights and Fundamental Freedoms, notwithstanding Article 6(2) Treaty on European Union, Protocol (No 8) relating to Article 6(2) of the Treaty on European Union and Opinion 2/13 of the Court of Justice of 18 December 2014.'* In Besselink, 'Acceding to the ECHR Notwithstanding the Court of Justice Opinion 2/13' (n 11).

rule of law, the decisions of the courts must be respected regardless of whether we find their content pleasing or not.

In the following sections we will begin by providing a brief description of the multilevel protection of fundamental rights in Europe in the context of multilevel constitutionalism. Then we will go on to give a brief summary of the seven issues in the draft agreement that the Court's Opinion considers contrary to the Treaties. Finally, we will set out the reasons why we believe that the Court would have reached different conclusions if it had taken multilevel constitutionalism into account.

II. Multilevel Protection of Fundamental Rights in the Context of Multilevel Constitutionalism

A. Multilevel Protection of Fundamental Rights and EU Accession to the ECHR

Before analysing Opinion 2/13, we briefly need to clarify what is meant by the multilevel protection of fundamental rights and multilevel constitutionalism in this study, since legal theory uses these expressions in different senses.

The multilevel protection of fundamental rights seeks to express the idea that fundamental rights protection in the legal space of Europe is currently based on '*three layers of norms and institutions which overlap and intertwine to ensure an advanced degree of protection of fundamental rights*'.[25] In fact, fundamental rights are protected and enforced by national, EU and international (in this study only the ECHR will be taken into account) norms and institutions, each layer having a substantive catalogue of fundamental rights and institutional remedies (with special emphasis on judicial review by courts).

The multilevel protection of fundamental rights is supposed to bring many benefits to individuals. First of all, it may 'prevent gaps occurring in legal protection that may arise from the increasing complexity of societal life. (…). Secondly, the plurality of jurisdictions brings with it many ad-

25 F Fabbrini, Fundamental Rights in Europe – Challenges and Transformations in Comparative Perspective (Oxford, Oxford University Press, 2014) 4.

vantages. Additional courts can give innovation impetus to a deadlocked jurisprudence and break new ground.'[26]

The relationship between national (*maxime* constitutional), EU and ECHR law has never been simple and it is not expected to become easier with the accession.[27]

As the Advocate General Kokott pointed out in her opinion:

> [T]he proposed accession of the EU to the ECHR will create a special, possibly even unique, constellation in which an international, supranational organisation – the EU – submits to the control of another international organisation – the Council of Europe – as regards compliance with basic standards of fundamental rights. As a result, in areas governed by EU law, not only national courts and tribunals and the EU Courts, but also the European Court of Human Rights (ECtHR) will be called upon to oversee the observance of fundamental rights.[28]

The EU's accession to the ECHR would certainly have permitted a better multilevel protection of fundamental rights in Europe. As Adam Łazowski and Ramses A. Wessel claim, in examining the way the political power of the EU might affect the fundamental rights of human beings (EU citizens and foreigners), these rights '*will be better guaranteed when the acts of the EU institutions are subjected to the same scrutiny as the acts of Member States' organs. (...) the current state of constitutional development of the EU legal order not only allows, but perhaps even demands, external scrutiny*'.[29]

B. Multilevel Constitutionalism

European multilevel protection of fundamental rights is anything but an element of the *constitutionalism beyond the state* theory. Some scholars have long tried to integrate the European Communities and their respec-

---

26 A Voßkuhle, 'Protection of Human Rights in the European Union. Multilevel Cooperation on Human Rights between the European Constitutional Courts' 3-4, see *Our Common Future,* Hannover/Essen, 2-6 November 2010, available at www.ourcommonfuture.de.

27 In this direction: M Claes and Š Imamovic, 'National Courts in the New European Fundamental Rights Architecture' (n 9) 159.

28 View of the Advocate General Kokott relating to Opinion 2/13, ECLI:EU:C:2014:2475, para 25.

29 Łazowski and Wessel, 'When Caveats Turn into Locks' (n 10) 212.

tive treaties into a broader constitutional theory that could not be solely anchored in the state. New concepts, like transnational constitutionalism,[30] constitutional pluralism,[31] multilevel constitutionalism,[32] or, more recently, global constitutionalism,[33] have emerged and have rapidly circulated in the post-Westphalian world, not without being criticised by those who still remain faithful to state constitutionalism[34] and by those who draw special attention to the limits of these theories.[35]

---

30 See M Neves, Transconstitucionalismo (São Paulo, WMF Martins Fonseca, 2009) 83 et seq; AMG Martins, A natureza jurídica da revisão do Tratado da União Europeia (Lisboa, Lex, 2000) 303 et seq; idem, Curso de Direito Constitucional da União Europeia (Coimbra, Almedina, 2004) 119 et seq; idem, A igualdade e a não discriminação dos nacionais de Estados terceiros legalmente residentes na União Europeia – Da origem na integração económica ao fundamento na dignidade do ser humano (Coimbra, Almedina, 2010) 22-23; idem, Manual de Direito da União Europeia (2nd ed., Lisbon, Almedina, 2017) 37 et seq.

31 For further reading on constitutional pluralism, see M Avbelj and J Komárek (eds), *Constitutional Pluralism in the European Union and Beyond* (Oxford, Hart Publishing, 2012); JHH Weiler, 'Prologue: Global and Pluralist Constitutionalism – Some Doubts', in G de Búrca and JHH Weiler (eds), *The Worlds of European Constitutionalism* (Cambridge, Cambridge University Press, 2012) 8 et seq; D Halberstam, 'Local, Global and Plural Constitutionalism: Europe Meets the World', in de Búrca and Weiler, *The Worlds of European Constitutionalism* 150 et seq; N Krisch, 'The Case for Pluralism in Postnational Law', in de Búrca and Weiler, *The Worlds of European Constitutionalism* 203 et seq; MP Maduro, *A Constituição Plural – Constitucionalismo e União Europeia* (Cascais, Principia, 2006) 15 et seq.

32 On multilevel constitutionalism see, above all, I Pernice, 'Multilevel Constitutionalism and the Crisis of Democracy in Europe' (2015) 11 *European Constitutional Law Review* 541 et seq; idem, 'The Treaty of Lisbon: Multilevel Constitutionalism in Action' (2009) 15 (3) *The Columbia Journal of European Law* 349-407; idem, 'Multilevel Constitutionalism in the European Union' (2002) 27 (5), *EL Rev* 511-29; idem, 'Multilevel Constitutionalism and the Treaty of Amsterdam: European Constitution-Making Revisited?' (1999) 36 (4) *CML Rev* 707 et seq.

33 On global constitutionalism see, above all, N Walker, 'Constitutionalism and Pluralism in Global Context', in Avbelj and Komárek (n 31) 17 et seq.

34 See R Barents, 'The Fallacy of Multilevel Constitutionalism', in Avbelj and Komárek (n 31) 153 et seq.

35 Compare R Harmsen, 'The (Geo-) Politics of the EU Accession to the ECHR: Democracy and Distrust in the Wider Europe', in Kosta et al (n 9) 199 et seq; L Lixinski, 'Taming the Fragmentation Monster through Human Rights? International Constitutionalism, "Pluralism Lite" and the Common Territory of the Two European Legal Orders', in Kosta et al (n 9) 219 et seq.

Although this study is naturally not the appropriate place to elaborate on these issues, we would like to state that our own position is quite close to Ingolf Pernice's multilevel constitutionalism theory. However, in our opinion, the latter should also integrate the ECHR.

Delving further into multilevel constitutionalism theory, we would say that constitutionalism in Europe also includes the EU and, in our view, with regard to the field of fundamental rights, it is also and, at least partially, anchored in the Council of Europe, particularly in the ECHR. As Christian Tomuschat argues, the ECHR '*is not a treaty like another bilateral treaty that the EU concludes with other subjects of international law, especially third States (...) it is a parallel or "neighbor" constitution'*.[36][37]

The concept of multilevel constitutionalism was '*suggested by Ingolf Pernice in 1995 in order to describe and explain the specific constitutional nature of European integration*'.[38] However, Ingolf Pernice's original concept did not emphasise the protection of fundamental rights as it focused mainly on the existence of a European Constitution outside the state,[39] which '*arises from both national and European constitutional levels*',[40] forming two levels of a unitary system – a composed constitutional system (*Verfassungsverbund,*[41] *constitution composée*[42]) – in terms of substance, function and institutions. Multilevel constitutionalism is a process that affects national and European law simultaneously. '*Both constitution-*

36 C Tomuschat, 'Der Streit um die Auslegungshoheit: Die Autonomie der EU als Heiliger Gral' (2015) 42 (5-8) *Europäische Grundrechte-Zeitschrift* 136.

37 In the original: 'ist kein Vertrag wie jeder sonstige bilaterale Vertrag, den die EU mit anderen Völkerrechtssubjekten, insbesondere dritten Staaten, abschließt (...) "Parallel- oder Nebenverfassung"'.

38 FC Mayer and M Wendel, 'Multilevel Constitutionalism and Constitutional Pluralism – Querelle Allemande or Querelle d'Allemand?' in Avbelj and Komárek (n 31) 127.

39 Pernice, 'Multilevel Constitutionalism in the European Union' (n 32) 511-29; idem, 'Multilevel Constitutionalism and the Treaty of Amsterdam' (n 32) 707 et seq.

40 Mayer and Wendel, 'Multilevel Constitutionalism and Constitutional Pluralism' (n 38) 130.

41 I Pernice, 'Europäisches und nationales Verfassungsrecht', in *Veröffentlichungen der Vereinigung der Deutscher Staatsrechtslehrer* 60/2000 (Berlin, Walter de Gruyter, 2001) 163 et seq.

42 I Pernice and FC Mayer, 'De la Constitution composée de l'Europe' (2000) 36 (4) *Revue Trimestrielle de Droit Européen* 623-48.

al levels are in permanent interdependency'.[43] The European constitutional process encompasses both national and primary EU law as '*two interdependent, interwoven, and reciprocally influential parts of one unit*'.[44]

In his most recent essays,[45] Ingolf Pernice apparently shifts the focus '*on the correlation of national and European law from the perspective of both states and citizens*'.[46] This means that EU integration has an impact both on the states and their citizens.[47] '*The EU is an instrument of the states and their peoples for meeting new challenges and for achieving certain common political goals*'.[48] Following this line of reasoning, Ingolf Pernice stresses that '*multilevel constitutionalism thus encourages conceptualizing the European Union from the perspective of its citizens*'.[49] This element strengthens '*the need to ensure an effective protection of the rights of the individuals*',[50] which, according to Giancito della Cananea, suggests a very important shift of paradigm.[51]

Nevertheless, as far as we can understand, Ingolf Pernice's definition of multilevel constitutionalism only comprises two layers of normativity and institutions – national law (*rectius*, constitutional law) and EU law.

In our opinion, taking into account the role that individuals currently play in the legitimation of political power, the multilevel protection and enforcement of fundamental rights should be envisaged as anything but a central element of multilevel constitutional theory. Once this premise is accepted, it will be easier to accept that ECHR law is without doubt a relevant source of fundamental rights in Europe. Consequently, multilevel

43 Pernice, 'The Treaty of Lisbon: Multilevel Constitutionalism in Action' (n 32) 373.

44 Ibid. 374.

45 See Pernice, 'Multilevel Constitutionalism and the Crisis of Democracy in Europe' (n 32) 544 et seq.

46 Pernice, 'The Treaty of Lisbon: Multilevel Constitutionalism in Action' (n 32) 372.

47 In our PhD thesis, more than fifteen years ago, we characterised the EU as a union of states and people. See Martins, *A natureza jurídica da revisão do Tratado da União Europeia* (n 30) 303 et seq.

48 Pernice, 'The Treaty of Lisbon: Multilevel Constitutionalism in Action' (n 32) 376.

49 Ibid.

50 G della Cananea, 'Is European Constitutionalism Really "Multilevel"?' (2010) 70 (2), *Zeitschrift für ausländisches öffentliches Recht und Völkerrecht* 300.

51 Ibid.

constitutionalism should also integrate that level of normativity and institutional tools.

In other words, in the fundamental rights arena, ECHR law and ECHR institutions – that is to say a third level – would cooperate, collaborate, intervene in and interact with the European constitutional process. Exactly how they would intervene and interact is difficult to say as there is no historical experience of this.[52]

Continuing with the attempt to define multilevel constitutionalism, according to Ingolf Pernice, it includes a vertical relationship between the EU and its Member States and a horizontal cooperation and mutual recognition between the Member States.[53] As it does not presuppose any hierarchical relationship between the national and European levels of law,[54] this relationship is pluralistic and cooperative.[55]

In our opinion, this pluralistic and cooperative relationship should be extended to ECHR law. This means, in terms of fundamental rights, that multilevel constitutionalism presupposes a cooperative and mutual recognition not only within two layers but within three layers of protection and enforcement – national law, EU law and ECHR law.

Considering the fact that the functioning of the system is not based on a hierarchical relationship, but depends on mutual trust between the institutions of each layer, with special emphasis on the courts, every highest court is the guardian of fundamental rights within the layer to which it belongs. As a consequence, multilevel constitutionalism in Europe presupposes the existence of several guardians of fundamental rights that could have different views of the same problem and all aspire to pronounce the last word, which could lead to divergent decisions. So far no definitive solution has been proposed for this problem, but one of the means to prevent the proliferation of conflicts is judicial dialogue, although this is not the appropriate place to expand upon this issue.[56]

---

52 Wendel, 'Mehr Offenheit wagen!' (n 11).

53 Pernice, 'The Treaty of Lisbon: Multilevel Constitutionalism in Action' (n 32) 379-83.

54 Ibid 383.

55 Ibid.

56 For further developments see M Cartabia, 'Fundamental Rights and the Relationship among the Court of Justice, the National Supreme Courts and the Strasbourg Court' in A Tizzano et al (eds), *50ème Anniversaire de l'arrêt Van Gend en Loos* 155 et seq; AMG Martins and MP Roque, 'Judicial Dialogue in a Multilevel Constitutional Network – the Role of the Portuguese Constitutional Court' in M Ande-

Much more could be said about the protection and enforcement of fundamental rights in the context of multilevel constitutionalism. However, discussion of this issue lies outside the scope of the present study. Now we must turn to Opinion 2/13 itself, starting with a brief summary.

III. Summary of CJEU Opinion 2/13

First of all, we would like to point out that the task of the Court in this case was relatively clear: it had to determine whether the draft agreement was in accordance with Article 6(2) TEU and Protocol 8, which previewed the specific conditions of EU accession to the ECHR.[57]

Secondly, however, it is important to draw attention to the fact that Article 6(2) TEU does not only state that the EU has the power to accede to the ECHR; it also imposes EU accession as a requirement. To put it in other terms, the EU has no choice whether to accede or not.[58] In our opinion, the Court should have paid greater consideration to this duty.

After a rather brief consideration of the issues, the CJEU concluded that:

> [I]t must be held that the agreement envisaged is not compatible with Article 6(2) TEU or with Protocol No 8 EU in that:
>
> it is liable adversely to affect the specific characteristics and the autonomy of EU law in so far it does not ensure coordination between Article 53 of the ECHR and Article 53 of the Charter, does not avert the risk that the principle of Member States' mutual trust under EU law may be undermined, and makes no provision in respect of the relationship between the mechanism established by Protocol No 16 and the preliminary ruling procedure provided for in Article 267 TFEU;
>
> it is liable to affect Article 344 TFEU in so far as it does not preclude the possibility of disputes between Member States or between Member States and

---

nas and D Fairgrieve (eds), *Courts and Comparative Law* (Oxford, Oxford University Press, 2015) 300-28.

57 These conditions were: i) the accession shall not affect the Union's competences as defined in the Treaties; ii) the accession shall not affect the powers of the institutions; iii) the accession agreement shall make provision for preserving the special characteristics of the Union and Union Law.

58 For an exposition of the reasons why the Union should accede to the ECHR, *cf.* 'Editorial Comments' (n 12) 4.

the EU concerning the application of the ECHR within the scope ratione materiae of EU law being brought before the ECtHR;

it does not lay down arrangements for the operation of the co-respondent mechanism and the procedure for the prior involvement of the Court of Justice that enable the specific characteristics of the EU and EU law to be preserved; and

it fails to have regard to the specific characteristics of EU law with regard to the judicial review of acts, actions or omissions on the part of the EU in CFSP matters in that it entrusts the judicial review of some of those acts, actions or omissions exclusively to a non-EU body.[59]

By contrast, the view of Advocate General Kokott seems to be much more constructive, concluding that:

[T]he draft revised agreement on the accession of the European Union to the European Convention for the Protection of Human Rights and Fundamental Freedoms presented in Strasbourg on 10 June 2013 is compatible with the Treaties, provided it is ensured, in such a way as to be binding under international law, that:

having regard to the possibility that they may request to participate in proceedings as co-respondents pursuant to Article 3(5) of the draft agreement, the European Union and its Member States are systematically and without exception informed of all applications pending before the ECtHR, in so far and as soon as these have been served on the relevant respondent;

requests by the European Union and its Member States pursuant to Article 3(5) of the draft agreement for leave to become co-respondents are not subjected to any form of plausibility assessment by the ECtHR;

the prior involvement of the Court of Justice of the European Union pursuant to Article 3(6) of the draft agreement extends to all legal issues relating to the interpretation, in conformity with the ECHR, of EU primary law and EU secondary law;

the conduct of a prior involvement procedure pursuant to Article 3(6) of the draft agreement may be dispensed with only when it is obvious that the Court of Justice of the European Union has already dealt with the specific legal issue raised by the application pending before the ECtHR;

the principle of joint responsibility of respondent and co-respondent under Article 3(7) of the draft agreement does not affect any reservations made by contracting parties within the meaning of Article 57 ECHR; and

the ECtHR may not otherwise, under any circumstances, derogate from the principle, as laid down in Article 3(7) of the draft agreement, of the joint re-

59 Opinion 2/13, para 258.

sponsibility of respondent and co-respondent for violations of the ECHR found by the ECtHR.[60]

In this study we will concentrate on analysing the Court's Opinion. The view of Advocate General Kokott will also be referred to where appropriate.[61]

A closer look at the Court's Opinion permits us to identify three groups of objections. The first group concerns the possibility that EU accession to the ECHR may generally violate the integrity and autonomy of EU law; the second one concerns the institutional innovations, and the last one concerns the jurisdiction of the CJEU over Common Foreign and Security Policy (CFSP).

60 View of Advocate General in Opinion 2/13, para 280.

61 For an overview of the position of the Advocate General and Opinion 2/13 of the CJEU, see, among many others, Nergelius (n 20) 17 et seq; M Berger and C Rauchegger, 'Opinion 2/13: Multiple Obstacles to the Accession of the EU to the ECHR' (2015) *European Yearbook on Human Rights* 61-73; 'Editorial Comments' (n 12) 7-11; Peers, 'The EU's Accession to the ECHR: the Dream Becomes a Nightmare' (n 13) 215-17; J Odermatt, 'Working Paper: A Giant Step Backwards? *Opinion 2/13* on the EU's Accession to the European Convention on Human Rights' 5-10, available at www.fp7-frame.eu/wp-content/materiale/w-papers/WP150-Odermatt.pdf; E Spaventa, 'A Very Fearful Court? The Protection of Human Rights in the European Union after Opinion 2/13' 12-21, available at www.corteappello.milano.it/allegato_corsi.aspx?File_id_allegato=1862; P Gragl, 'The Reasonableness of Jealousy' (n 17) 31-36; S Douglas-Scott, 'Opinion 2/13 on EU Accession to the ECHR' (n 14).

To be honest, we have to admit that throughout the negotiations[62] over the draft agreement[63], scholarship[64] and some European institutions[65] had

---

62 On the negotiations over the draft agreement see Korenica, *The EU Accession to the ECHR* (n 18) 106 et seq; A Drzemczewski, 'EU Accession to the ECHR: The Negotiation Process', in Kosta et al (n 9) 17 et seq; O De Schutter, 'L'adhésion de l'Union européenne à la Convention européenne des droits de l'homme: feuille de route de la négotiation' (2010) 21 (83) *Revue trimestrielle des droits de l'homme* 540 et seq; SS Caballero, 'Crónica de una adhesión anunciada: algunas notas sobre la negociación de la adhesión de la Unión Europea al Convénio Europeo de Derechos Humanos' (2011) 15 (38) *Revista de Derecho Comunitario Europeo* 99-128.

63 On the draft agreement itself see Korenica (n 18) 108 et seq; P Gragl, 'A Giant Leap for European Union Human Rights? The Final Agreement on the European Union's Accession to the European Convention on Human Rights', available at www.academia.edu (2014/12/29) 1 et seq; T Lock, 'Walking on a Tightrope' (n 5) 1025 et seq.

64 See, among many others, P Gragl, 'A Giant Leap for European Union Human Rights?' (n 63) 3 et seq; P Craig, 'EU Accession to the ECHR' (n 5) 1115 et seq; JMP de Nanclares, 'The Accession of the European Union to the ECHR: More than Just a Legal Issue', *Working Papers on European Law and Regional Integration* No 15/2013, 1 et seq; Terhechte, 'Autonomie und Kohärenz' in J Iliopoulos-Strangas et al (n 5) 37 et seq; AMG Martins, 'A Portuguese Perspective of the Accession to the European Union to the European Convention of Human Rights' in J Iliopoulos-Strangas et al (n 5) 205 et seq; MJR de Mesquita, 'Remarques sur la "valeur ajoutée" de l'adhésion de l'Union européenne à la Convention européenne de Droits de l'Homme pour la protection des droits fondamentaux des particuliers en Europe' in J Iliopoulos-Strangas et al (n 5) 277 et seq; W Obwexer, 'Der Beitritt der EU zur EMRK: Rechtsgrundlage, Rechtsfragen und Rechtsfolgen' (2012) 47 (2) *Europarecht* 119 et seq; P Gragl, *The Accession of the European Union to the European Convention on Human Rights* (n 5) *maxime,* 87 et seq; JP Jacqué, 'The Accession of the European Union to the European Convention on Human Rights and Fundamental Freedoms' 2011 48 (4) *CML Rev* 1012 et seq; B Bertrand, 'Cohérence normative et contentieux – à propos de l'adhésion de l'Union européenne à la Convention européenne des droits de l'Homme' (2012) 128 (1) *Revue du Droit Public* 190 et seq; T Lock, 'Walking on a Tightrope' (n 5) 1025 et seq; N O'Meara, 'A More Secure Europe of Rights? The European Court of Human Rights, the Court of Justice of the European Union and EU Accession to the ECHR' (2011) *German Law Journal* 1818 et seq; De Schutter, 'L'adhésion de l'Union européenne à la Convention européenne des droits de l'homme' (n 62) 547 et seq; C Ladenburger, 'Vers l'adhésion de l'Union européenne à la Convention européenne des droits de l'homme' (2011) 47 (1) *Revue trimestrielle de droit européen* 21 et seq; T Lock, 'EU Accession to the ECHR: Implications for Judicial Review in Strasbourg' (2010) *EL Rev* 777 et seq.

65 Cf. *Discussion document of the Court of Justice of the European Union on certain aspects of the accession of the European Union to the European Convention for the Protection of Human Rights and Fundamental Freedoms* of 5 May 2010, avail-

frequently pointed out several difficulties and potential incompatibilities between that draft agreement and EU primary law. In this study we will not return to this subject.[66] We will concentrate on the objections of the CJEU.

A. Violation of the integrity and autonomy of EU Law

The first concern of the CJEU relates to Article 53 ECHR, which gives authorisation for Member States to have higher rights than the Charter on Fundamental Rights of the EU (CFREU), once the law has been fully harmonised by the EU. According to the Court, Article 53 ECHR should be coordinated with Article 53 of the Charter, as interpreted by the Court in *Melloni.*[67] This means that where the EU legal act calls for national implementing measures, national authorities and courts remain free to apply national standards of protection of fundamental rights, provided that the level of protection provided by the Charter, as interpreted by the Court, and the primacy, unity and effectiveness of EU law are not thereby compromised. The Court considered that EU Member States could use Article 53 ECHR to adopt higher standards of fundamental rights in matters covered by harmonised Union law. For the Court, it was necessary to ensure coordination between Article 53 CFREU and Article 53 ECHR, as long as the autonomy of EU law was not affected.[68]

---

able at curia.europa.eu.jcms/jcms/P_64268 and *Joint communication from Presidents Costa and Skouris* of 24 January 2011, available at www.echr.coe.int/Documents/UE_Communication_Costa_Skouris_ENG.pdf. See also the European Parliament Resolution of 19 May 2010 on the institutional aspects of the accession of the European Union to the European Convention for the Protection of Human Rights and Fundamental Freedoms (OJEU C 2011/C 161 E/12). On the position of the European Parliament see R Passos, 'The Protection of Fundamental Rights in Europe Before and After the Accession of the European Convention on Human Rights: A View from the European Parliament' in J Iliopoulos-Strangas et al (n 5) 125 et seq.

66 We have already written on this subject: AMG Martins, 'O Parecer n.º 2/13 do Tribunal de Justiça relativo à compatibilidade do projeto de acordo de adesão da União Europeia à Convenção Europeia dos Direitos do Homem', in Marcelo Rebelo de Sousa / Eduardo Vera-Cruz Pinto (coordenadores), *Liber Amicorum Fausto de Quadros*, vol. I, Coimbra, Almedina, 2016, p. 97-129.

67 C-399/11 *Melloni* Judgment of 26 February 2013, ECLI:EU:C:2013:107, para 60.

68 See Opinion 2/13, paras 187-89.

The second objection of the Court concerns the principle of 'mutual trust' between EU Member States in the Area of Freedom, Security and Justice (AFSJ), which obliges the Member States to presume that all other Member States are in compliance with EU law and particularly with the fundamental rights recognised by EU law, except in exceptional circumstances, as interpreted by the CJEU.[69] EU accession to the ECHR, according to the Court, would require a Member State to check that another Member State had observed fundamental rights, which would undermine the autonomy of EU law.[70]

The Court's third concern relates to Protocol 16, which was opened to signature in 2013 and has not yet entered into force. This protocol gives the highest national courts of High Contracting Parties the power to submit queries to the ECtHR concerning interpretation of the ECHR. The CJEU was particularly concerned about the impact that this procedure might have on the autonomy and effectiveness of the preliminary ruling procedure.[71]

The fourth concern of the CJEU was that Article 33 ECHR allows for inter-state disputes between ECHR High Contracting Parties regarding alleged breaches of the Convention. The Court found that this possibility violated Article 344 TFUE, which prohibits the EU Member States to submit a dispute concerning the interpretation or application of the Treaties to any method of settlement other than those provided for in the EU Treaties. This possibility could undermine the autonomy of EU law. Only the express exclusion of the possibility of EU Member States bringing disputes connected with EU Law before the ECtHR would be compatible with Article 344 TFUE.[72]

B. *Institutional Innovations*

Concerning institutional innovations, the Court was particularly concerned about the co-respondent mechanism that created a new procedure whereby the EU and a Member State could be parties to an ECtHR case. The Court

69 See CJEU, Joined cases C-411/10 and C-493/10 *N.S. and M.E.* Judgment of 21 December 2011, ECLI:EU:C:2011:865, paras 78-80.

70 See Opinion 2/13, paras 190-95.

71 See Opinion 2/13, paras 196-200.

72 See Opinion 2/13, paras 201-14.

found this procedure incompatible with EU law for several reasons. First, it would give the ECtHR the power to interpret EU law when assessing the admissibility of requests to apply this procedure, and consequently, the ECtHR would be able to assess rules of EU law concerning the division of powers between the EU and the Member States; secondly, a ruling by the ECtHR on the joint responsibility of the EU and its Member States could impinge on Member State reservations to the Convention, and the ECtHR should not have the power to allocate responsibility for breach of the ECHR between EU and Member States, since only the CJEU can rule on EU law.[73]

The other institutional innovation that disturbed the Court was the prior involvement procedure that was included in the draft agreement to take into account the concerns of the Presidents of both Courts in their Joint Communication. The Court found the form of this procedure would violate EU law if it did not reserve to the EU the power to rule on whether the CJEU had already dealt with an issue or not. Alternatively, the ECtHR would be called on to decide whether the CJEU had already ruled on the same question of law. In addition, this procedure would permit the ECtHR to rule on the interpretation of the EU Treaties and the case law of the CJEU[74].

C. CJEU Jurisdiction over Common Foreign and Security Policy

The last point of the draft agreement that the Court considered incompatible with EU primary law – and this was perhaps the most complex issue faced by the Court – was the potential jurisdiction of the ECtHR over some CFSP acts.

As a matter of fact, the Court of Justice does not have jurisdiction in CFSP matters except in certain narrow and strictly-defined cases provided for in Article 275 TFEU. Otherwise, the draft agreement would have created a situation whereby the ECtHR would have jurisdiction over certain acts that are not reviewable by the CJEU.

According to the Court, this possibility would violate EU law as a non-EU court could not be given the power of judicial review over EU acts,

73 See Opinion 2/13, paras 215-35.

74 See Opinion 2/13, paras 236-48.

even though the CJEU had no jurisdiction itself regarding the majority of CFSP issues.[75]

After this brief overview, we will now look at Opinion 2/13 from the perspective of multilevel constitutionalism.

IV. Opinion 2/13 from the perspective of multilevel constitutionalism

A. General Framework

Recalling that, in its Opinion, the Court drew attention to the constitutional structure of the EU,[76] accepting

> the fact that the EU has a new kind of legal order, the nature of which is peculiar to the EU, its own constitutional framework and founding principles, a particularly sophisticated institutional structure and a full set of legal rules to ensure its operation, has consequences as regards the procedure for and conditions of accession to the ECHR[77]

and also recalling the fact that some scholars have even suggested that the Court's reasoning might be justified by an attempt to defend the constitutional nature of the Union[78], we will begin by clarifying what, in our opinion, the consequences of multilevel constitutionalism are within the scope of the protection and enforcement of fundamental rights.

Only then will we be able to assess, firstly, whether the CJEU had actually any kind of constitutionalism in mind and, secondly, whether it took into consideration multilevel constitutionalism theory.

---

75 See Opinion 2/13, paras 249-57.

76 See para 157 of the Opinion – 'As the Court of Justice has repeatedly held, the founding treaties of the EU, unlike ordinary international treaties, established a new legal order, possessing its own institutions, for the benefit of which the Member States thereof have limited their sovereign rights, in ever wider fields, and the subjects of which comprise not only those States but also their nationals' (see, in particular, the judgments in C-26/62 van Gend&Loos EU:C:1963:1, 12, C-6/64 Costa EU:C:1964:66, 593 and Opinion 1/09 EU:C:2011:123 para 65).

77 Para 158 of the Opinion.

78 E Dubout, 'Une question de confiance: nature juridique de l'Union européenne et adhésion à la Convention européenne des droits de l'homme' 75; H Labayle and F Sudre, 'L'avis 2/13 de la Cour de Justice sur l'adhésion de l'Union européenne à la Convention des droits de l'homme: pavane pour une adhésion défunte?' (2015) 31 (1) *Revue française de droit administratif* 4-9, 15.

In our point of view – which does not intend to be indisputable[79] – the protection and enforcement of the fundamental rights of individuals should currently be the *noyau dur* of every constitution. Even within the state, the political decisions of a parliamentary majority should respect the fundamental rights. That means the fundamental rights could be seen as trumps against the majority.[80] Taking this into account, the EU and the ECHR can only be understood and accepted by individuals, as long as they add something to the effectiveness of the protection of fundamental rights, and, from there, draw legitimacy. As a matter of fact, the states are not always able and prepared to respect fundamental rights, to preserve peace and to face the common challenges posed by globalisation. If the multilevel constitutional system, both, the EU and the ECHR, would have the effect of placing less and not more importance on fundamental rights, it would be very hard to convince individuals to adhere to and to legitimate a constitutional network that undermined their rights.[81] We cannot accept that these new instruments have been established with the opposite effect, i.e., a lower standard of protection. Therefore, in our opinion, a multilevel constitutional system should achieve a higher standard of protection and enforcement of fundamental rights than that achieved by any single constitutional layer on its own.

As a result, each constitutional layer should respect the fundamental rights protected and enforced by other constitutional layers. That is to say, EU law and the CJEU should respect the fundamental rights protected and enforced by national constitutional layers and ECHR law, and vice versa. This is actually the meaning of Article 53 CFREU and of Article 53 ECHR. We will return to this argument later.

In conclusion, since the protection of fundamental rights in Europe is currently based on national law, EU law and (to a lesser extent) ECHR law, a comprehensive multilevel constitutional theory should be able to

---

79 Contra, see among many others, R Medeiros, *A Constituição Portuguesa num Contexto Global* (Lisbon, UCP, 2015) 91 et seq.

80 R Dworkin, *Taking Rights Seriously* (London, Duckworth, 1977) xi.

81 In a similar direction, but without mentioning multilevel constitutionalism, see C Franzius, 'Strategien der Grundrechtsoptimierung in Europa' (2015) 42 (5-8) *Europäische Grundrechte Zeitschrift* 152.

guarantee a better enforcement and effectiveness of fundamental rights and a higher standard of fundamental rights' protection.[82]

It would be possible to achieve this goal in multilevel constitutionalism if national law, EU law and ECHR law were all founded on common values and principles. In fact, in Europe the values of respect for human dignity, freedom, democracy, equality, the rule of law and respect for human rights are shared by the EU and its Member States, as can be clearly seen in Article 2 TEU[83], and also by the Council of Europe, as is clear in the following excerpt from the preamble to the ECHR:

> [*R*]*eaffirming their profound belief in those fundamental freedoms which are the foundation of justice and peace in the world and are best maintained on the one hand by an effective political democracy and on the other by a common understanding and observance of the human rights upon which they depend*; (…) *the governments of European countries which are like-minded and have a common heritage of political traditions, ideals, freedom and the rule of law (...).*

That is to say, national law, EU law and ECHR law are all based on similar values, which favours a mutual interpenetration, interdependence, interaction and reciprocal influence between the three bodies of law and a progressive convergence of fundamental rights. Otherwise, conflicts would arise so often that they would become the norm rather than the exception and they would destroy the constitutional order in a relatively short time. This does not mean that there are no punctual divergences, but such divergences are not the rule.

Actually, the mutual interpenetration, interdependence, interaction and reciprocal influence between the different levels of normativity and judiciary should be envisaged as another characteristic of multilevel constitutionalism in the field of fundamental rights. This means that the participation either of a state or the EU in the international human rights law sys-

82 In the same vein: H Labayle and F Sudre, 'L'avis 2/13 de la Cour de Justice sur l'adhésion de l'Union européenne à la Convention des droits de l'homme: pavane pour une adhesion défunte?' (n 78) 20.

83 Article 2 TEU reads: 'The Union is founded on the values of respect for human dignity, freedom, democracy, equality, the rule of law and respect for human rights, including the rights of persons belonging to minorities. These values are common to the Member States in a society in which pluralism, non-discrimination, tolerance, justice, solidarity and equality between women and men prevail.'.

tem necessarily implies an interference of this system in the domestic affairs of that state and a fortiori in the affairs of the EU.[84]

To put it in other words, if the EU accedes to the ECHR, no-one can seriously expect that EU law will remain untouched as long as the treaties on human rights continue to aim at filling the gaps in the level of protection provided by individual states. '*There is no doubt that being bound by the ECHR under international law will impose restrictions on the exercise of its existing competences*'.[85] The accession of the EU to the ECHR, one consequence of which would be the EU's submission to the jurisdiction of the ECtHR, would naturally affect the autonomy of the EU legal order, as it affects the autonomy of the domestic legal order of every single Member State.[86]

In addition, the accession to a human rights treaty by a state always implies interference in the domestic affairs of that state. That is to say, the international law principle of non-interference in internal affairs does not apply to human rights matters. Otherwise, the states could prevent the enforcement of international laws on human rights.[87] If the EU accedes to the ECHR, it will be subject to the same rules as individual states.

In the case of the European Union, this interference would not be so deep as in other cases because, according to the case law of the CJEU, fundamental rights, as guaranteed by the ECHR (and as they result from the constitutional traditions common to the Member States) 'shall constitute general principles of the Union's law' (Article 6(3) TEU).[88]

---

84 According to Johan Callewaert, 'Beim Beitritt der EU geht es also darum, dass auch die EU es akzepetiert, sich von Zeit zu Zeit etwas "stören" bzw. Ihre Handlungen und Konzepte hinterfragen lassen' (EU accession to the ECHR means that from time to time the EU should let the ECtHR 'trouble' her, that is to say their actions and concepts may be questioned by the ECtHR): J Callewaert 'Der Beitritt der EU zur EMRK: Eine Schicksalsfrage für den europäischen Grundrechtsschutz' (2014) 8 Strafverteidiger 505.

85 View of the Advocate General Kokott relating to Opinion 2/13, EU:C:2014, para 40.

86 Christoph Krenn considers that it is not only the EU which is concerned about this but domestic systems are also autonomous and care about their autonomy: see C Krenn, 'Autonomy and Effectiveness as a Common Concern: A Path to ECHR Accession After Opinion 2/13' 162.

87 See O De Schutter, *International Human Rights Law: Cases, Materials, Commentary*, 2nd edn (Cambridge, Cambridge University Press, 2015) 113 et seq.

88 Before the Treaty of Lisbon, the CJEU had already built up a firm and consistent case law in this direction. See, among many others, CJEU, C-4/73 *Nold* judgment

As a consequence, the EU would currently have to apply (albeit only substantially) the fundamental rights contained in the ECHR and in its protocols and, in addition, under the terms of Article 52 (3) CFREU, in so far as the Charter contains rights guaranteed by the ECHR, the meaning and scope of those rights would be the same as those laid down by the ECHR, admitting, however, that Union law provides more extensive protection.

In other words, the material scope of the draft agreement is much more restrictive – the EU would accede solely to the ECHR, the Protocol, and Protocol No 6, that is to say, to the two protocols to which all Member States are already parties. Consequently, the impact of the ECHR on the EU would be less significant than if the EU had never established any relationship with the ECHR.

Furthermore, the *jus cogens*-[89] nature of some human rights provisions, such as the prohibition of torture[90] (Article 3 ECHR) or the prohibition of slavery (Article 4 [1] ECHR), bind either the states or the EU. This means that, independently of the EU's accession to the ECHR, the EU is already bound by these provisions.[91]

Finally, the real binding effect of international human rights law depends on the submission of states, in the fields regulated by the human rights treaties, to an international jurisdiction, with each state relinquishing the monopoly of its own jurisdiction.[92] In other words, if this applies to individual states, it cannot be different in the case of the EU.

---

of 14 May 1974 ECLI:EU:C:1974:51; C-36/75 *Rutili* judgment of 28 October 1975 ECLI:EU:C:1975:137; C-44/79 *Hauer* judgment of 13 December 1979 ECLI:EU:C:1979:290; C-222/84 *Johnston* judgment of 15 June 1986 ECLI:EU:C:1986:206; C-299/95 *Kremzow* judgment of 29 May 1997 ECLI:EU:C:1997:254.

89 According to Article 53 of the Vienna Convention on the Law of Treaties (1969) and Article 53 of the Vienna Convention on the Law of Treaties between States and International Organizations or between International Organizations (1986), a jus cogens norm is a peremptory norm of general international law accepted and recognised by the international community of States as a whole as a norm from which no derogation is permitted and which can be modified only by a subsequent norm of general international law having the same character.

90 De Schutter, *International Human Rights Law* (n 85) 299 et seq.

91 It is debatable whether a regional *jus cogens* does actually exist. This is not the right place to discuss this issue.

92 For further developments, see AMG Martins and MP Roque, 'Chapter 18 – Universality and Binding Effect of Human Rights from a Portuguese Perspective' in R

Nevertheless, multilevel constitutionalism does not imply either a hierarchy of legal orders that participate therein or a hierarchy of judiciaries. Consequently, there are several courts that control the enforcement of fundamental rights and none of them can be considered as having the last word. Andreas Voβkuhle has introduced a legal concept, inspired by the multilevel constitutionalism theory, in order to explain this reality. This is the concept of '*europäische Verfassungsgerichtverbund*'[93] ('multilevel cooperation of the European constitutional courts'), which 'refers to the cooperative, non-hierarchical handling of multilevel constitutional issues by several constitutional courts, i.e., a composite multilevel structure of constitutional jurisdictions which entertain complementary and comparative relationships'.[94]

Taking this situation into account, the cooperative judicial dialogue between the highest national courts (especially the constitutional courts), the CJEU and the ECtHR assumes a huge importance in respect of the prevention of conflicts between the different highest courts.[95] In fact, the principle of cooperative judicial dialogue between constitutional courts, the CJEU and the ECtHR has already been applied for a long time[96] and the CJEU has always contributed to and benefited from this dialogue. How-

Arnold (ed), *The Universalism of Human Rights*, Jus Gentium: Comparative Perspectives on Law and Justice 16, (Dordrecht, Springer, 2013) 310 et seq.

93 This expression has recently been used by the *Bundesverfassungsgericht* in a Decision of the Second Senate of 21 June 2016 (para. 140), known as the Decision OMT, para. 140).

94 A Voβkuhle, 'Multilevel Cooperation of the European Constitutional Courts – *Der Europäische Verfassungsgerichtsverbund*', (2010) 6 (1) *European Constitutional Law Review* 184.

95 Stressing the role of judicial dialogue in the fundamental rights context, cf. C Grabenwarter, 'The Cooperation of Constitutional Courts in Europe – Current Situation and Perspectives', in *XVIe Congrès de la Conférence des Cours Constitutionnelles européennes – La coopération entre les Cours Constitutionnelles en Europe – Situation actuelle et perspectives*, vol. I, (Vienna, Verlag Österreich, 2014) 35 et seq; A Popov, 'L'avis 2/13 de la CJUE complique l'adhésion de l'Union européenne à la CEDH' (2015) *Revue des Droits de l'Homme* 8, available at http://revdh.revues.org/1065; A Voβkuhle, 'Multilevel Cooperation of the European Constitutional Courts – *Der Europäische Verfassungsgerichtsverbund*', (2010) 6 (1) *European Constitutional Law Review* 175 et seq; M Cartabia, 'Europe and Rights: Taking Dialogue Seriously' (2009) 5 (1) *European Constitutional Law Review* 21 et seq.

96 On judicial dialogue see our study: Martins and Roque, 'Judicial Dialogue in a Multilevel Constitutional Network' (n 56) 300-328.

ever, this dialogue will only be fruitful if the Courts trust each other. That is to say, cooperative judicial dialogue implies a mutual judicial trust between the highest courts. Moreover, multilevel constitutionalism presupposes a sincere cooperation between all the players, and not only between the EU and its Member States.

Having said this, it needs to be emphasised that the obligations of the EU Member States founded on EU law will not change as a result of EU accession to the ECHR. In other words, EU Member States – as Contracting Parties of the ECHR – will not be authorised by EU accession to violate EU law. As a consequence, the EU Member States' obligations towards the EU will remain unaffected, unless EU law rules otherwise.

To conclude, in the field of the protection and enforcement of fundamental rights, in our view, multilevel constitutionalism implies respect for the following principles:

a) the principle of a higher protection of fundamental rights;
b) the principle of common values between the Member States, the EU and the Council of Europe and its Member States;
c) the principle of cooperative judicial dialogue;
d) the principle of sincere cooperation and mutual trust.

In the next few sections, we will examine Opinion 2/13 on the basis of these principles.

1. Principle of a Higher Protection of Fundamental Rights

Starting with the principle of a higher protection of fundamental rights, in our view, the Court does not follow this constitutional perspective in Opinion 2/13 and this is quite clear in several parts of the Opinion. The Court seems to be stuck in a more traditional constitutional view that does not establish sufficient, if any, bridges between the three levels of norms and institutions that interact with each other in the field of fundamental rights in Europe.

In other words, the Court seems to adhere to an 'exclusivist' constitutionalism that envisages the EU as a rather formal entity which is almost isolated in the legal world and not a multilevel constitutionalism that views the EU legal order as part of a wider and multi-layered constitutional order.

As Henri Labayle and Frédéric Sudre have argued, '*since the hierarchical path is closed, the Court of Justice reasons in terms of exclusivity*'.[97] In fact, Opinion 2/13 is anchored in a rather formalistic, restrictive and exclusivist constitutional vision of the EU, which will be hardly acceptable to other players such as the ECtHR and the constitutional courts, which seem to be the privileged interlocutors of the CJEU.

In our opinion, this perspective explains why the Court is so concerned with its own interpretation of the CFREU, the primacy and autonomy of EU law and apparently less engaged in the protection and enforcement of fundamental rights.[98] To quote Piet Eeckhout, 'the CJEU hardly mentions that objective of strengthening the fundamental rights protection of real human beings'.[99]

We are not arguing that the Court does not care about the enforcement of fundamental rights, as some have claimed since the beginning of European integration. The point we would like to make is another one: the multilevel constitutionalism principle of a higher level of protection of fundamental rights would, in principle, have permitted an interpretation of the draft agreement in conformity with EU law in the following cases:

a) Coordination between Article 53 of the Charter and Article 53 ECHR

As for the coordination between Article 53 of the Charter and Article 53 ECHR, the CJEU considered that the EU Member States could use Article 53 ECHR to adopt higher standards of fundamental rights in matters covered by harmonised Union law, which runs counter to the primacy of EU Law. Therefore, Article 53 ECHR, which permits the Contracting Parties to have a higher level of protection of fundamental rights than that provid-

---

97 '*La voie hiérarchique étant fermée, la Cour de Justice raisonne en termes d'exclusivité*', H Labayle and F Sudre, 'L'avis 2/13 de la Cour de Justice sur l'adhésion de l'Union européenne à la Convention des droits de l'homme: pavane pour une adhésion défunte?' (n 78) 15.

98 Adam Łazowski and Ramses A. Wessel counter-argue that the Court took fundamental rights seriously, but it needed more time to explore the Charter and its potential. According to these authors, '*it seized the opportunity to start building a wall of case law based on the Charter before the European Union accedes to the ECHR. Looked at from this perspective, Opinion 2/13 is undoubtedly an important element in this jigsaw puzzle*', Łazowski and Wessel (n 10) 209.

99 Eeckhout, 'Opinion 2/13 on EU Accession to the ECHR' (n 15) 7.

ed by the ECHR, could be in conflict with Article 53 of the Charter, as interpreted by the Court in *Melloni.*

First of all, it should be emphasised that the factual and legal situation in the *Melloni* case was of a rather particular nature, since it concerned the interpretation and, if necessary, the validity of Article 4a(1) of Council Framework Decision 2002/584/JHA of 13 June 2002 on the European arrest warrant and the surrender procedures between Member States,[100] as amended by Council Framework Decision 2009/299/JHA of 26 February 2009 ('Framework Decision 2002/584').[101] It also concerned, if necessary, an examination of the issue of whether a Member State may refuse to execute a European arrest warrant on the basis of Article 53 of the CFREU, on the grounds that such an action would infringe the fundamental rights —rights guaranteed by the national constitution— of the person concerned.

Apart from the fact that the interpretation of Article 53 of the Charter in *Melloni* is far from being peaceful,[102] the truth is that, according to the Court:

> [T]his interpretation of Articles 47 and 48(2) of the Charter is in keeping with the scope that has been recognised for the rights guaranteed by Article 6(1) and (3) of the ECHR by the case-law of the European Court of Human Rights (see, inter alia, ECtHR, Medenica v. Switzerland, no. 20491/92, § 56 to 59, ECHR 2001-VI; Sejdovic v. Italy [GC], no. 56581/00, § 84, 86 and 98, ECHR 2006-II; and Haralampiev v. Bulgaria, no. 29648/03, § 32 and 33, 24 April 2012).[103]

This means that it is unreasonable to allege that the Court did not take into account the multilevel protection of fundamental rights in Europe. However, in our opinion, the Court adopted a rather rigid position concerning the relationship between fundamental rights and the primacy of EU law that is understandable in the context of the European arrest warrant and the surrender procedures between Member States, but this rigid stance should not have been extended to other areas. The principle of a higher protection of fundamental rights should be viewed as an existential requirement, like the principle of primacy.

---

100 OJ 2002 L 190, 1.

101 OJ 2009 L 81, 24.

102 For a rather critical view see Nergelius (n 20) 28 et seq.

103 C-399/11 *Melloni* Judgment of 26 February 2013, ECLI:EU:C:2013:107 para 50.

In fact, Article 53 of the CFREU clearly states that 'nothing in this Charter shall be interpreted as restricting or adversely affecting human rights and fundamental freedoms, as recognised (…), including the European Convention for the Protection of Human Rights and Fundamental Freedoms, and by the Member States' constitutions'. In our opinion, the Court could have interpreted Article 53 of the Charter differently, as long as it was ready to accept higher standards of fundamental rights emanating from the ECHR and the constitutions of Member States.[104]

To be honest, this is not the first time that the Court has sacrificed fundamental rights in favour of the primacy of EU law.[105] In fact, this question focuses on an old and well-known dispute between the constitutional courts of the Member States and the Court of Justice that has not yet been resolved. This dispute concerns who should be regarded as the final arbiter of fundamental rights in Europe,[106] an issue which lies outside the scope of this study.

This position of the Court may trigger new adverse reactions from the constitutional courts of the Member States and may open a 'Pandora's box', which everyone has reason to fear, including the Court of Justice itself.

As has already been stated in an editorial comment:

> [T]he somewhat inflexible defence of its judicial powers at the expense of an accession of the EU to the ECHR may, unfortunately, lead to an (unexpected) backlash in the relationship between the ECJ and the constitutional courts of the Member States, who may, paradoxically, draw some inspiration from the ECJ's attitude. Constitutional Courts may be willing to defend their judicial powers (with regard to fundamental rights) vis-à-vis the ECJ in a fashion parallel to the ECJ vis-à-vis the ECtHR.[107]

---

104 In the same vein: Popov (n 91) 5.

105 At the very beginning of the European integration process, the Court of Justice refused to accept that fundamental rights were part of EC law (see C-1/58 *Stork*), although this would soon change (see C-26/69 *Stauder*, C-11/70 *Internationale Handelsgesellschaft*).

106 For further developments: M Kumm, 'The Jurisprudence of Constitutional Conflict: Constitutional Supremacy in Europe Before and After the Constitutional Treaty' (2005) 11 (3) *European Law Journal* 262 et seq; idem, 'Who is the Final Arbiter of Constitutionality in Europe?' (1999) 36 (2) *CML Rev* 351 et seq.

107 'Editorial Comments' (n 12) 15. In a similar vein: Łazowski and Wessel (n 10) 212; Nergelius (n 20) 48.

b) Area of Freedom, Security and Justice

Another objection of the Court that, in our opinion, could have been avoided if the Court had used the tools of multilevel constitutionalism, concerns the AFSJ. In fact, in a field that is rather conducive to the violation of fundamental rights, extreme situations, such as those involving individuals who fear being repatriated or sent to countries they do not wish to go to because they are likely to be arrested or detained, require the highest level of protection of fundamental rights.[108]

However, in Opinion 2/13 the Court maintained its traditional 'exclusivist' constitutional view, appearing to be more preoccupied with the autonomy of EU law and with the preservation of its own interpretation of EU law than with the protection of fundamental rights.

The Court's emphasis on the principle of 'mutual trust' between EU Member States in the AFSJ, founded on the Dublin rules on asylum responsibility, led the Court to reaffirm its own jurisprudence and to fear interaction with a more protective system of fundamental rights for asylum-seekers than the Dublin system, such as the recent case law of the ECtHR.[109]

If the Court had taken the principle of a higher protection of fundamental rights into account, instead of rigidly adhering to its own jurisprudence and to the principle of autonomy of EU law, the fact that a Member State could check that another Member State had observed fundamental rights, would not constitute an insurmountable problem.[110]

In our view, the scope of the principle of 'mutual trust' (or mutual recognition) is not so narrow that it applies only between EU Member States. As we will see below, it should apply in all directions and between every single constitutional player.

---

108 In the same vein: E Spaventa, 'A Very Fearful Court?' (n 61) 19.

109 See *Tarakhel v. Switzerland* App. no 29217 Judgment of 4 November 2014, available at www.hudoc.echr.coe.int/.

110 Cf. E Dubout, 'Une question de confiance: nature juridique de l'Union européenne et adhésion à la Convention européenne des droits de l'homme' 95 et seq.

c) Jurisdiction over Common Foreign and Security Policy

Finally, although the lack of jurisdiction over the CFSP was perhaps the most difficult question that the Court had to consider, the Court could have benefited from the input of multilevel constitutionalism and the principle of a higher protection of fundamental rights.[111] To a certain extent, this was the position of the Advocate General Kokott.[112]

The Court is right when it said that, in order to preserve the specific characteristics of the EU, a non-EU court could not be given the power of judicial review over EU acts, even though the CJEU has no jurisdiction itself in most CFSP issues.

However, in our opinion, this is only a partial view of the problem. In fact, the monopoly of the CJEU's jurisdiction over EU acts is not the most unique feature of EU law. On the contrary, respect for human dignity and respect for fundamental rights in general also constitute specific characteristics of the EU. The Court could have anchored its reasoning in these two points, and it could have accepted this part of the draft agreement. Theoretically, the CFSP could have been the field in which individuals could actually have gained more protection of their fundamental rights with the EU's accession to the ECHR, because this is a field in which the EU has no real jurisdiction. In practice, the direct violation of an individual's rights by an act of the Union that is excluded from the Court's jurisdiction is somewhat rare.

Not wishing to jeopardise the specific characteristics of the EU, the CJEU rejected the conformity of the draft agreement on this matter.

2. *Principle of Common Values between the EU Member States, the EU, the Council of Europe and its Member States*

Another significant element of multilevel constitutionalism that the Court apparently did not consider concerns the existence of common values within the Member States, the EU, the Council of Europe and its Member States. In fact, the Court of Justice referred only to the common values between the Member States and the EU (Article 2 TEU).[113] This reference is

111 In the same vein: Popov (n 91) 7.

112 See paras 82-103 of the Advocate General's View.

113 Para 168 of the Opinion.

fully understandable, so long as these common values are so relevant that respect for them constitutes a condition for accession to the Union (Article 49 TEU) and the persistent violation of them by a Member State might lead to the suspension of certain rights of that Member State (Article 7 TEU).[114]

However, as mentioned above, the EU and its Member States also share some values (and principles) with the Council of Europe and its Member States.

The Court could have looked at these common values and could have highlighted the influence that each has had on the other in the past, which has progressively led to a convergence in fundamental rights matters, instead of creating the possibility of future divergences.

This approach would have been of greater benefit to EU law than the 'exclusivist' view of the Court. For example, in the field of CFSP, EU accession to the ECHR could have filled the gaps in human rights protection that exist in this area and the same could be said for the field of AFSJ. Furthermore, the objections of the Court concerning Article 53 ECHR in connection with Article 53 CFREU did not take into due consideration the fact that the common values justify the input of many provisions from the ECHR into the CFREU.

114 On the common values between the Member States and the EU see AMG Martins, 'Os valores da União na Constituição Europeia' (2005) 84 *Colóquio ibérico: Constituição europeia, Boletim da Faculdade de Direito da Universidade de Coimbra, Studia Jurídica* 497 et seq; V Constantinesco, 'Valeurs et contenu de la Constitution européenne' in *Uma Constituição para a Europa*, (Coimbra, Almedina, 2004) 161 et seq; F Sorrentino, 'Brevi reflessione sui valori e sui fini dell'Unione Europea nel progetto di costituzione europea' (2003) 9 *Diritto Pubblico* 810-11; R Bieber, 'Ingérence ou manifestation d'une responsabilité commune? – La protection des valeurs de l'Union européenne à l'égard des Etats-membres', in Institut Suisse de Droit Comparé (ed), *L'intégration européenne: historique et perspectives* (Zurich, Schulthess Verlag 2002) 95 et seq; AMG Martins, 'Les valeurs communes et la place de la Charte en Europe' (2002) 14 (1) *European Review of Public Law* 130 et seq; F Schorkopf, *Homogenität in der Europäischen Union – Ausgestaltung und Gewährleistung durch Art. 6 abs. 1 und Art. 7 EUV* (Berlin, Dunker & Humblot, 2000) 36 et seq.

3. Principle of Cooperative Judicial Dialogue

Turning to the principle of cooperative judicial dialogue, in our view, this was not taken into due consideration by the CJEU in its formulation of Opinion 2/13. On the contrary, it seems to have been overly influenced by a principle of distrust.

As Eleanor Spaventa has pointed out, Opinion 2/13 'is also disappointing because it shows a Court's profound distrust of both national courts (and their compliance with the principle of loyal cooperation) and of the European Court of Human Rights'.[115]

Many of the Court's objections could have been avoided if the Court had considered a proper cooperative judicial dialogue.

Above all, the tension between Article 53 of the ECHR and 53 of the Charter, as interpreted by the Court of Justice, presupposes that the ECtHR would force an EU Member State to apply a national standard of human rights protection which is higher than the Convention standard. On the other hand, a higher national standard of protection would be imposed not by the ECtHR, but by the Convention itself.[116] The CJEU seems to have feared that the ECtHR would exceed its jurisdiction and start to control national standards of protection and, in an indirect way, the uniform standard imposed by the Charter. However, nothing in the former jurisprudence of the ECtHR indicates that it would be likely to do this.

Another position of the CJEU that reveals an enormous distrust of all other courts concerns Protocol 16, which would enable the highest courts and tribunals of the Member States to request advisory opinions.[117] As we have already mentioned, the EU would not become a signatory to this protocol as a result of its accession to the ECHR and, anyway, the Protocol has not yet entered into force. Otherwise, such a problem may arise with or without EU accession, whenever all or some EU Member States ratify the Protocol.[118]

Nevertheless, if by chance the highest court of a Member State used the Protocol in a way that violated EU law, this is a problem that would have to be solved by EU law and its remedial mechanisms.

115 E Spaventa, 'A Very Fearful Court?' (n 61) 12.

116 For developing this topic, see Eeckhout (n 15) 10-14.

117 For an elaboration of this topic, see ibid 17-18.

118 In the same vein: Korenica (n 18) 416-18.

The position of the Court in this case seems to presuppose that 'Member State highest courts cannot be trusted to respect EU law. That is not a position that is conducive to genuine judicial dialogue'.[119] The same Court that interprets the principle of mutual trust between the EU Member States, which does not clearly result from the Treaties, in a rather rigid manner, also fails to take into due consideration the principle of sincere cooperation between the Member States and the Union provided for in Article 4(3) of the TEU.[120]

The Court's objection relating to Article 33 of the ECHR,[121] which permits inter-state disputes, presupposes a climate of suspicion between the CJEU and the ECtHR that is barely credible in a multilevel constitutional system. For the CJEU:

> [O]nly the express exclusion of the ECtHR's jurisdiction under Article 33 of the ECHR over disputes between Member States or between Member States and the EU in relation to the application of the ECHR within the scope ratione materiae of EU law would be compatible with Article 344 TFEU.[122]

Actually, this is a step backwards in the judicial dialogue between these two Courts. Even prior to accession, EU primary law has been reviewed in the context of individual applications. In the *Matthews* case,[123] for example, the ECtHR decided that the citizens of Gibraltar should be able to vote in European Parliamentary elections.

Furthermore, 'the purpose of the accession is to enable individuals to complain to the ECtHR about the Convention violations by the EU'.[124]

---

119 See Eeckhout (n 15) 18.

120 Article 4 (3) TEU reads: 'Pursuant to the principle of sincere cooperation, the Union and the Member States shall, in full mutual respect, assist each other in carrying out tasks which flow from the Treaties.
The Member States shall take any appropriate measure, general or particular, to ensure fulfilment of the obligations arising out of the Treaties or resulting from the acts of the institutions of the Union.
The Member States shall facilitate the achievement of the Union's tasks and refrain from any measure which could jeopardise the attainment of the Union's objectives.'.

121 Especially on this issue see SO Johansen, 'The Reinterpretation of TFEU Article 344 in Opinion 2/13 and its Potential Consequences' (2015) 16 *German Law Journal* 169 et seq.

122 Para 213.

123 *Matthews v UK* Application no. 24833/94 Judgment of 18 February 1999, available at www.hudoc.echr.coe.int/eng.

124 See Eeckhout (n 15) 24.

Even in issues like the co-respondent mechanism and the prior involvement procedure, where the Court and the Advocate General took a similar position and, in our opinion, were right, there is no sign, in the Opinion of the Court, that these obstacles could be better overcome through a permanent, mutual and profound dialogue between the two Courts. Bearing in mind that the ECtHR has mostly respected the competence of the CJEU,[125] the Court could have acknowledged this fact. However, it seemed to be too fearful of the ECtHR's interference in its competence, striving to prevent such a situation.

Finally, several statements made by the CJEU concerning the exclusion of ECtHR jurisdiction over the EU in certain cases, such as in the fields of the CFSP and AFSJ, are hardly compatible with a proper judicial dialogue.

The CJEU could have used the ECtHR's jurisdiction in CFSP matters as an argument to extend its own jurisdiction in this field or to interpret the provisions of the EU treaties in a wider sense. In contrast, it preferred to argue the exclusivity of its own jurisdiction, which is somewhat disputable in this context.

4. *Principle of Sincere Cooperation and Mutual Trust*

As has just been pointed out, multilevel constitutionalism presupposes a sincere cooperation between all the players, and not only between the EU and its Member States. This sincere cooperation is based on the existence of mutual trust between all the players.

Taking this into consideration, at least two of the CJEU's fears appear to be unfounded.

The first fear relates to Protocol 16. Apart from the fact that this protocol is not included in the draft agreement, it has not yet entered into force

125 See, for instance, *Bosphorus* application 45036/98 Judgment of 30 June 2005, available at http://hudoc.echr.coe.int/eng, which is an example of a case in which '*the ECtHR and the ECJ are singing in harmony*', J Klabbers, *Treaty Conflict and European Union* (Cambridge, Cambridge University Press 2009) 172. On the future of the Bosphorus case see O De Schutter, 'Bosphorus Post-Accession: Redefining the Relationships between the European Court of Human Rights and the Parties of the Convention', in Kosta et al (n 9) 177 et seq; P Gragl, *The Accession of the European Union to the European Convention on Human Rights* (n 5) 69-75.

and no-one can predict what its future will be. Furthermore, it does not compete with the preliminary ruling based on Article 267 of the TFEU. '*The Protocol no. 16 advisory opinion is different in nature, as it will be limited to the highest national court, it is never obligatory and the opinion itself is not binding*'.[126]

Anyway, if the Court had taken the principle of sincere cooperation into account and had trusted the EU Member States, it could have omitted the reference to Protocol 16. If in future any Member State used the procedure provided for in that protocol, violating its duties under the preliminary reference procedure, EU law has various mechanisms at its disposal, including judicial ones, enabling it to punish the Member State.[127]

The same can be said of Article 33 of the ECHR, which allows for inter-state disputes between ECHR Contracting Parties over alleged breaches of the Convention. If EU Member States decided to submit a dispute concerning the interpretation or application of the EU Treaties to the ECtHR, it could constitute a violation of EU law, including a violation of Article 344 of the TFEU itself, and the EU Member States are fully aware of this.

V. Concluding Remarks

From the aforegoing discussion a number of conclusions may be drawn.

Although the Treaty of Lisbon had imposed on the Union an obligation to accede to the ECHR (Article 6 (2) TEU), the Court of Justice, for the second time in the history of its case law, rejected, in Opinion 2/13, EU accession to the ECHR. In the view of the Court, a number of issues in the draft agreement were not compatible with Article 6(2) of the Treaty on European Union nor with Protocol No 8 relating to Article 6(2) TEU.

These issues concerned the coordination of Article 53 ECHR with Article 53 CFREU, as is interpreted by the Court; the principle of mutual trust in the field of AFSJ, which obliges the Member States to presume that all

126 Á Mohay, 'Back to the Drawing Board? Opinion 2/13 of the Court of Justice on the Accession of the EU to the ECHR – Case note' (2015) 1 *Pécs Journal of International and European Law* 35.

127 Apart from the political mechanism foreseen in Article 7 TEU, EU law has judicial remedies against the Member States, such as the infringement procedure (Articles 258-60).

other Member States are in compliance with EU law and particularly with the fundamental rights recognised by EU law, except for exceptional circumstances as interpreted by the CJEU; Protocol 16, which enables the highest national courts of High Contracting Parties to address queries to the ECtHR on matters concerning the interpretation of the ECHR; Article 33 of the ECHR relating to inter-state disputes; the co-respondent mechanism that would create a new procedure whereby the EU and a Member State could become parties to an ECtHR case, the procedure for prior involvement of the CJEU and the judicial review in CFSP matters.

According to the Court, the principle of autonomy and the specific characteristics of EU law, including the Court's monopoly on the interpretation of EU law, were violated by the draft agreement.

Bearing in mind that the issue of the EU's accession to the ECHR has been on the EU's agenda for decades, Opinion 2/13 has had an enormous legal and political impact. In such a sensitive matter, one would have expected the Court to display a more cooperative attitude with the Member States, with the EU institutions that had conducted what were particularly tough negotiations and, last but not least, with other Courts that also form part of the European multilevel system of fundamental rights, such as the highest national courts, including the constitutional courts, and the ECtHR.

In spite of drawing attention to the constitutional structure of the EU, the Court seems to have rejected the multilevel constitutionalism theory, anchoring its position in an 'exclusivist' constitutionalism, in which the EU as a constitutional entity must preserve its own legal autonomy and specific characteristics at any cost.

In our view, the Court could have decided otherwise if it had considered the draft agreement in the context of multilevel constitutionalism, in which the different components – EU law, national laws and ECHR law – need to work together towards a major objective, namely a higher level of protection of fundamental rights. This would have permitted an interpretation of the draft agreement in conformity with EU law in at least three areas – the coordination of Article 53 ECHR with Article 53 CFREU, the principle of mutual trust between EU Member States in the AFSJ, and the jurisdiction over CFSP.

Another constitutive element of multilevel constitutionalism that the Court apparently overlooked was the existence of common values within the Member States, the EU, the Council of Europe and its High Contracting Parties, which could contribute to the convergence of fundamental rights. The Court referred only to the common values of the Member States and the EU.

Furthermore, in Opinion 2/13, the Court seems to be stuck in a view of the EU constitutional system that is more closely related to a hierarchical judicial order than to a cooperative judicial dialogue. In our opinion, the objections concerning Article 53 ECHR, Protocol 16 and Article 33 ECHR are based on a distrust of both national courts and the ECtHR. In other words, without the acceptance of the principle of cooperative judicial dialogue and the principle of sincere cooperation and mutual trust between all players, it is impossible to avoid jurisdictional conflicts, which would not help to reinforce the protection and enforcement of fundamental rights in Europe.

In Opinion 2/13, it is evident that the Court does not trust anyone, except itself. For the Court, the EU Member States, national courts, and the ECtHR can endanger the autonomy of EU law, the specific characteristics of the EU and the monopoly of its jurisdiction.

This position of the Court may be rather problematic, since it may open a 'Pandora's box' of adverse reactions from all the other players, which everyone has reasons to fear, including the Court of Justice itself.

11 Towards a right to care in EU Law: Issues of legitimacy, gender and citizenship

Anna-Maria Konsta

Abstract

In a number of cases, the Court of Justice of the EU (CJEU) has recognised a right of residence and extended citizenship rights for a third-country national who is a family member of an EU citizen, by holding that the person concerned is the EU citizen's 'primary carer'. In other cases, however, the CJEU has limited these same citizenship rights. Questions of legitimacy arise in relation to the limits of its competence to create new law and new concepts which may go as far as to create new rights or limit existing ones.

It can also be observed, that a form of gender bias has developed in the CJEU case-law, while a broader interpretation of the concept of 'care' in accordance with the notion of social family, which is connected with bonds of affection among its members regardless of their gender, could remedy the bias and finally lead to the proper institutionalisation of an autonomous right to care. Again, the question is whether it is for the CJEU or for the legislator —within the limits of EU competence— to develop the right to care based on the right to residence of primary carers.

From a gender theory perspective, the legal recognition of the concept of 'care' allows for the reconciliation of the public and private divide, and marks a new era in reconceiving family relations and law, which is now more than ever an imperative need in an era of economic and financial crisis for the Member States.

I. The Legislative Framework

In the European Union (EU) context, different kinds of citizenship rights apply: regular EU nationals' citizenship rights, rights for third-country nationals married to an EU citizen, and rights for non-EU nationals. EU workers have benefited from the freedom to work in another Member

State since the 1960s. This freedom was enshrined in the EU Treaties from the very beginning of the European project in 1957, and is now laid down in Article 45 of the Treaty on the Functioning of the European Union (TFEU). Moreover, secondary legislation has been adopted on the matter. For example, Regulation (EU) 492/2011 details workers' rights to free movement and defines specific areas where discrimination on grounds of nationality is prohibited.[1]

Tackling discrimination against workers from other Member States and raising awareness of EU nationals' right to work in other EU countries are the main objectives of Directive 2014/54/EU of the European Parliament and of the Council on measures facilitating the exercise of rights conferred on workers in the context of freedom of movement for workers.[2]

Immigration laws in the Member States are largely adaptations to the requirements of two EU directives, one regarding family reunification of nationals of non-Member States (2003/86/EC)[3] and the other on long-term residents in the EU (2003/109/EC)[4]. Thanks to the social objectives of the Treaty of Rome, envisaged from the very beginning (Articles 117 ff.), it was possible to recognise the right to family reunification, involving spouses, the children of each spouse and their parents 'whatever their nationality' —forming part of the 'bonds of affection' which are recognised by European social law.[5]

More than twenty years ago, with the Treaty of Maastricht, one of the most important rights for EU citizens was recognised, i.e. the right to move and reside freely within the territory of the Member States (Articles 20 (2) and 21 TFEU). This right was recognised for all EU citizens, irrespective of whether they are economically active or not (21 TFEU).

---

1 Regulation (EU) 492/2011 of 5 April 2011 on freedom of movement for workers within the Union, codifying Regulation (EEC) 1612/68 and its successive modifications (Council Regulations 312/76 and 2434/92, and Article 38(1) of Directive 2004/38/EC), OJ L141/1, 27 May 2011.

2 Directive 2014/54/EU of the European Parliament and the Council of 16 April 2014 on measures facilitating the exercise of rights conferred on workers in the context of freedom of movement for workers, OJ L 128/8, 30 April 14.

3 Council Directive 2003/86/EC of 22 September 2003 on the right of family reunification, L 251/12, 3 October 2003.

4 Council Directive 2003/109/EC of 25 November 2003 concerning the status of third-country nationals who are long-term residents, *OJ L 016, 23 January 2004.*

5 Y Kravaritou, 'Liens affectifs et droit social européen' in *Liber amicorum Jean-Victor Louis* (Bruxelles, Bruylant, 2002).

The specific rules and conditions applying to free movement and residence are set out in a Directive agreed by Member States in 2004 (Directive 2004/38/EC).[6]

II. Extension of Citizenship Rights

In exercising the right of free movement and residence, EU citizens may be accompanied by their close family members, such as their spouse, partner, children or parents (Art 2(2) of Directive 2004/38/EC). However, this right is subject to certain conditions. First, it cannot be invoked by an EU citizen residing in a Member State unless his/her situation has a sufficient link with EU law (e.g. the citizen has in the past resided in another Member State). Second, the EU citizen must be economically active or self-sufficient and be able to sustain his/her family members and have a comprehensive social insurance cover (Art 7(1) of the Directive). Moreover, ascendants (parents) of the EU citizen are required to be financially dependent on the EU citizen (Art 2(2) of Directive 2004/38/EC).

In the following cases, however, the Court of the EU (CJEU) has recognised a right of residence for a family member of an EU citizen, despite the fact that one or more of the conditions described above were not satisfied. The Court justified its judgments in these cases by holding that the person concerned was the 'primary carer' of children having a right of residence under EU law.[7]

Even if initially EU citizenship rights were designed to involve only market-based rights, the ECJ expanded citizenship by also including social rights for EU citizens, such as in the case of Martinez Sala (C-85/96),[8] where a Spanish mother who resided in Germany for many years, but had

---

6 Directive 2004/38 of the European Parliament and of the Council of 29 April 2004 on the right of citizens of the Union and their family members to move and reside freely within the territory of the Member States, amending Regulation (EEC) No 1612/68 and repealing Directives 64/221/EEC, 68/360/EEC, 72/194/EEC, 73/148/EEC, 75/34/EEC, 75/35/EEC, 90/364/EEC, 90/365/EEC and 93/96/EEC, OJ L 158/77, 30 April 2004.

7 N Cambien, 'EU Citizenship and the ECJ: Why Care about Primary Carers?', paper presented at the EUSA Conference 2013, available at www.euce.org/eusa/2013/papers/4j_cambien.pdf (accessed on 30 November 2015) 1-2.

8 Case C-85/96, *Martinez Sala* [1998] ECR I-2691.

never worked there due to her childcare responsibilities, could claim welfare benefits in Germany.

In the Carpenter case (C-60/00),[9] the Court recognised for the first time residence rights for the primary carers of young children. Mary Carpenter was a third-country national who had lived for several years in the UK with her husband and his children by a previous marriage when a deportation order was made against her. The difficulty in this case was that she invoked a right to reside in the UK with a UK national, so the cross-border element could not be established for the EU law provisions on free movement to apply. However, the Court held that a refusal of a right of residence to Ms Carpenter would deter Mr Carpenter from exercising his right to provide services in another Member State, because it would be difficult for him to move to other Member States since he would need to look after his children. The Court in its justification used the concept of the 'effet utile' of EU law in the sense that the refusal to grant residence rights to the primary carer of Mr Carpenter's children would take away the useful effect of the latter's freedom to provide services. Moreover, the CJEU concluded that the decision to deport Ms Carpenter constituted an infringement of Article 8 of the European Convention on Human Rights (ECHR), which enshrines the right to family life, and that deportation was not proportionate to the objective pursued.

The Court went further in decoupling citizenship from market rules by granting direct effect to provisions on citizenship, namely Article 18(1) TEC (now Art 21 (1) TFEU) protecting the right of all EU citizens to reside within the territory of the Member States, in the joint cases Baumbast and R (C-413/99).[10] In the Baumbast case, the children of an EU citizen were allowed to remain in the UK in order to complete their education even after their father, a German national, had ceased to work there. Consequently, for the children to be allowed to remain in the UK in order to continue their education, a corresponding right to reside had to be granted to the primary carer of those children, who was Mr Baumbast's Colombian wife, even if in this case the primary carer had no other right to reside under EU law. Even if the CJEU derived the right to education for children solely from Article 12 of Regulation (EEC) 1612/68, it held that this article had to be interpreted in line with Article 8 ECHR (right to family life).

9 Case C-60/00 *Carpenter* [2002] ECR I-6279.

10 Case C-413/99 *Baumbast and R* [2002] ECR I-7091.

In both these cases the Court recognised implicitly the role of women in care work by taking into account the fact that a refusal to renew the residence permit of a male EU citizen's wife would leave their children without their primary carer.[11]

In the Zhu and Chen case (C-200/02),[12] Ms Chen, a Chinese national, travelled to Belfast in order to give birth to her daughter on the island of Ireland (i.e. in Northern Ireland). The child was immediately registered as an Irish citizen, as provided for under the Irish Constitution as it then stood. The family wished to reside in the UK, but was refused permission to do so by the UK's Home Office. To the Chinese government the child was an Irish national. As a foreigner she could apply to stay in the country of her parents, i.e. China, for not more than thirty days at a time and then only with the permission of the authorities. The expulsion of Ms Chen from the UK would, therefore, have led to the separation of mother and daughter.

The CJEU in the Chen case decided that the right of residence of a child that is an EU citizen would lose any useful effect if the primary carer of the child who is a non-EU citizen were deprived of the right to reside in the host Member State. Though secondary EU law, namely Directive 2004/38/EC, held that a mother could not derive a right of residence from her child's citizenship since the former was not the dependant of the latter, the Court reinterpreted the meaning of dependency in this case as a two-way reversible phenomenon. It should be noted that in the Chen case, the primary carer had more than sufficient financial means to support the child. The Court in this case again implicitly recognised the predominant

---

11 In two more recent cases, *Ibrahim* and *Teixeira*, with facts similar to those in *Baumbast*, the Court confirmed its previous holding (Case C-310/08 *Ibrahim* [2010] ECR I-1065 and Case C-480/08 *Teixeira* [2010] ECR I-1107). The primary carer of a school-going child of a former migrant worker who does not live in the Member State anymore can invoke a right of residence in this Member State even after the child reaches the age of majority, for as long as the child continues to need the presence of the primary carer, in order to complete his or her education. In Czop and Punakova (Joined Cases C-147/11 and C-148/11 *Czop and Punakova* [2012] nyr), the Court confirmed this case-law, but it specified that it only applied with regard to children of former or actual migrant workers and not with regard to children of former or actual self-employed persons. See also S Currie, 'EU Migrant Children, their Primary Carers and the European Court of Justice: Access to Education as a Precursor to Residence under Community Law' (2009) 16(2) *Journal of Social Security Law* 76-105.

12 Case C-200/02 *Zhu and Chen* [2004] ECR I-9925.

role of women as primary carers and enriched European social citizenship by performing a sort of judicial gender mainstreaming,[13] and by considering 'bonds of affection' as contributing to the full enjoyment of fundamental rights.

The Court confirmed this reasoning in the Zambrano case (C-34/09).[14] It held that the Colombian parents of two Belgian children —born and raised in Belgium and who had never exercised free movement rights— could not be denied residence and work permits where it would have the effect of 'depriving the Union citizens of the genuine enjoyment of the substance of the rights' conferred by their status as EU citizens. The Zambrano case effectively redefined the scope of application of EU law, extending its reach to an otherwise 'purely internal situation' by dispensing with the cross-border element usually required to trigger EU law. Although not explicitly covered by the Court, the Zambrano parents were not able to be self-sufficient in another Member State to enable a Chen-type scenario.

In the Zambrano case the Court seemed to have made a definite choice to expand EU citizenship rights, such as the right to move and reside freely within the territory of the Member States (Articles 20 (2) and 21 TFEU), which is normally reserved to EU citizens, to other categories of people such as third-country nationals who are considered to be the primary carers of an EU citizen. In all of the cases discussed above, the mother or the wife of the EU citizen-father of the children was always involved as the primary carer. In this way, migrant women that are mothers of EU citizens enjoy more social citizenship rights than migrant women who are not mothers of EU citizens, or not mothers at all. Connecting social citizenship rights for migrant women with motherhood perpetuates from a gender theory perspective the public/private sphere divide.[15] Motherhood either enables or constrains autonomy. The caregiving that mothers provide to their children enables them to become autonomous persons, but at the

---

13 S Millns, 'Gender Equality, Citizenship, and the EU's Constitutional Future' (2007) 13(2) *European Law Journal* 233ff.

14 Case C-34/09 *Gerardo Ruiz Zambrano v Office national de l'emploi (ONEm)* [2011] ECR I-1177. For a detailed discussion of the case see K Hailbronner and D Thym, 'Case Note on *Ruiz Zambrano*' (2011) 48(4) *Common Market Law Review* 1253–70.

15 See eg M Fineman and I Karpin (eds), *Mothers in Law: Feminist Theory and the Legal Regulation of Motherhood* (New York, Columbia University Press, 1995).

same time this caregiving constrains maternal autonomy and exerts pressure on working women who are forced to balance their lives on a tightrope between the private and the public sphere. The ideology of motherhood is still born out of a still powerful public/private divide which holds women responsible for the family (i.e. the private sphere) and turns them into a separate category from men who still dominate the public sphere.[16] In none of the above-discussed cases has the Court connected caregiving with fatherhood, or with any other form of caregiving which is independent from parenthood.

It has been argued that the CJEU in the cases where it extended citizenship rights and went beyond the scope of existing EU secondary legislation, has engaged in a sort of judicial activism or judicialisation of the decision-making process, which has undermined the role of the EU's democratically elected legislator, namely the European Parliament, and has thus contributed to the EU's democratic deficit.[17] However, the Court cannot be accused of contributing to the democratic deficit when it expands existing rights and thus protection to people living and working in the EU. It has done so in the past with its case-law on gender equality and the Defrenne cases in the 1970s.[18] The Court granted direct effect to Article 119 EEC Treaty (now 157 TFEU) on equality of pay for men and women and recognised that the principle of equality forms an integral part of the general principles of Community law; it so contributed to a legislative reform

16 See eg SB Boyd, DE Chunn, F Kelly, W Wiegers, *Autonomous Motherhood?: A Socio-Legal Study of Choice and Constraint* (Toronto, Bufallo, London, University of Toronto Press, 2015).

17 See eg AJ Menéndez, 'European Citizenship after Martinez Sala and Baumbast. Has European Law Become More Human but Less Social?' (2009) 11 *ARENA Working Paper* 2.

18 In Case 43/75 *Gabrielle Defrenne v Société anonyme belge de navigation aérienne Sabena (Defrenne II)* [1976] ECR 455, the EEC Court established that the principle of equal pay for men and women for the same job done, as laid down by Article 119 of the Treaty of Rome, is one of the foundations of the Community and, when submitting claims in Member States' national courts, individuals can invoke Article 119 of the Treaty of Rome if remuneration is not in accordance with the principle of equal pay in the same establishment or service, whether private or public (recognition of both vertical and horizontal direct effect of a treaty provision). In the subsequent Defrenne III case (Case 149/77 *Gabrielle Defrenne v Société anonyme belge de navigation aérienne Sabena (Defrenne III)* [1978] ECR 1365, the Court recognised that the principle of equality forms an integral part of the general principles of Community law.

on gender equality through the adoption of gender equality Directives. In this respect the Court seemed to follow the path of the Warren Court of the USA which through its historically significant decisions in the 1950's and 1960's contributed to the expansion of civil rights in the USA and, as a consequence, to the gradual elimination of race segregation and to the strengthening of the civil rights movement.[19]

However, judicial activism is problematic and may add to the EU's legitimacy problems in cases where the Court limits rights which have already been enshrined in the EU 'constitutional' texts, as it did in the following cases, regardless of its previous case-law.

III. Limitation of Citizenship Rights

In the McCarthy case (C-434/09),[20] the CJEU held that the refusal to grant a UK residence permit to the Jamaican husband of a woman with dual Irish/UK nationality who was neither economically active nor self-sufficient and relied on state benefits, did not deprive her of the substance of her citizenship rights. The EU Court held more specifically that the national measure had neither the effect of depriving her of the genuine enjoyment of the substance of her rights as a Union citizen (Art 20 TFEU) nor the effect of impeding the exercise of her right to reside and move freely within the territory of the EU (Art 21 TFEU).

After McCarthy, one may argue that for a national measure to fall within the scope of EU law, the latter must produce either a 'deprivation effect' or an 'impeding effect'. The 'deprivation effect' derives from Article 20

---

19 The Warren Court refers to the Federal Supreme Court of the USA during the period when Earl Warren served as Chief Justice from 1953 until his retirement in 1969. Justice Warren with his liberal views is thought to have contributed to the adoption of historically significant decisions that brought an end to racial segregation in the US. One landmark decision of the Warren Court was *Brown v. Board of Education of Topeka*, 347 U.S. 483 (1954), in which the Court declared state laws establishing separate public schools for black and white students to be unconstitutional. The decision overturned the *Plessy v. Ferguson* decision of 1896, which allowed state-sponsored segregation, insofar as it applied to public education through the doctrine 'seperate but equal'. For more information on the Warren Court see eg M. Tushnet (ed.) *The Warren Court in Historical and Political Perspective* (University of Virginia Press, 1993).

20 Case C-434/09 Shirley McCarthy v Secretary of State for the Home Department [2011] ECR I-3375.

TFEU and does not require a cross-border link but a de facto loss of one of the rights attached to the status of the EU citizen. In contrast, the 'impeding effect' is linked to Article 21 TFEU and falls under the traditional line of case-law according to which the application of the Treaty provisions requires the existence of a cross-border link. The 'deprivation' and 'impeding' effect may be subject to different requirements, but are not necessarily mutually exclusive. A national measure that applies in a cross-border context may produce both types of effects.[21] In the case-law that follows, the EU Court opted for a strict interpretation of those cases in which a national measure is capable of producing a 'deprivation effect'.

The Dereci case (C-265/11)[22] concerned applications made by Mr Dereci and four other non-EU nationals for residence permits to entitle them to live and work in Austria. Each applicant had family members living in Austria. In Mr Dereci's case, his Austrian wife was an EU national so the Family Reunification Directive could not apply; only the case law on the Zambrano case could possibly apply. However, the CJEU held that denial of the 'genuine enjoyment of the substance of rights' referred to situations in which the Union citizen has to leave not only his or her own Member State but the territory of the Union as a whole. This applied only to exceptional situations, where the effectiveness of Union citizenship would otherwise be undermined. Crucially, the Court held that the fact that it might be desirable, for economic or family reasons, to keep the family together was not sufficient in itself to support the view that the Union citizen would be forced to leave.

It is questionable if the outcome of this case would have been the same if the roles were reversed and the EU citizen was the father, while the mother was asking for a residence permit. Would it not be easier to grant the mother the role of the primary carer and allow her to stay in the EU? It is obvious that the Court in the Dereci case engages in a sort of profiling with regard to the kind of person that can be accepted in EU territory. A male, third-country immigrant who is economically dependent on his EU-citizen wife is not welcome in EU territory. Economic considerations here prevail over the right to family life or the rights of the children.

21 K Lenaerts, 'EU Citizenship and the European Court of Justice's 'Stone-by-Stone' Approach' (2015) 1 *International Comparative Jurisprudence* 1, 4.

22 Case C-256/11 Murat Dereci and Others v Bundesministerium für Inneres [2011] ECR I-11315.

In the Iida case (C-40/11),[23] the EU Court held that the Japanese father of a German child who lived in Austria with her mother could not invoke a right of residence in Germany —where he worked and resided— on the grounds that he was the father of an EU citizen, since it would not deprive the daughter of the genuine enjoyment of her rights nor would it impede her from moving freely within the EU.

In both the Dereci and Iida cases fathers were denied a right to residence. Apparently, it is more difficult to recognise fathers as the primary carer of a child, possibly due to a dominant gender-specific stereotyping.

Male spouses were also excluded under the same line of argument in the Joined Cases O, S & L (C-356/11, and C-357/11).[24] These cases concerned women who were third-country nationals, lived in a Member State and had children from a first marriage who were EU citizens. Later, they remarried, taking as husbands men who were third-country nationals and had another child with them. Subsequently, their husbands' applications for residence permits were refused on grounds of insufficient means of subsistence.

According to the EU Court, the children were not 'legally, financially or emotionally dependent' on their step-fathers. Moreover, their mothers already had permanent residency and thus the failure to grant residence permits to the step-fathers would not have compelled the Union citizens to leave. However, in this case, the Court recognised the right to family life and applied the Family Reunification Directive (Directive 2003/86/EC), and recognised the mothers as 'sponsors' within the meaning of Article 2(c) of the Directive. The Directive applies only to family members of third-country nationals who are residents, a fact which precluded the applicants in the Dereci case from relying on it.

The Alokpa case (C-86/12)[25] concerned a Tongolese mother of two children who were French nationals but were born and resided with their mother in Luxembourg. The authorities of Luxembourg refused to grant the mother a right of residence and issued an order for her to leave the country. Unlike the mother in the Chen case, who possessed sufficient resources of her own, even though she had no job, to sustain her children,

---

23 Case C-40/11 *Yoshikazu Iida v Stadt Ulm* [2012] nyr.

24 Joined Cases C-356/11 and C-357/11 O. and S. v Maahanmuuttovirasto and Maahanmuuttovirasto v L. [2012] nyr.

25 Case C-86/12 Adzo Domenyo Alokpa and Others v Ministre du Travail, de l'Emploi et de l'Immigration [2013] nyr.

Ms Alokpa had no means of subsistence and she and her children were reliant on the social welfare system of Luxembourg. But although Ms Alokpa had been offered a job in Luxembourg, she could not take it due to her lack of a residence and work permit.

The Advocate General Mengozzi held in his Opinion of the case[26] that 'sufficient resources' for the purpose of Article 7(1)(b) of Directive 2004/38/EC were satisfied by the definite prospect of future financial resources being gained through the job offer and its subsequent acceptance by Ms Alokpa. The CJEU, however, did not consider that the promise of future earnings meant that the requirement of Article 7(1)(b) of the Directive was met, and left this as a question of fact to the referring court.

In the Alokp case the Court further concluded that being forced to leave Luxembourg would not result in an obligation to leave the whole territory of the EU. As the children were French nationals, Ms Alokpa had a right to reside in France as the primary carer of her children, and as a result the refusal of the authorities of Luxembourg to grant her a residence permit did not constitute a deprivation of the genuine enjoyment of the children's EU citizenship rights.

In this case the Court negates the very essence of supranational EU citizenship. It implies that if the family moved to France, the children would then be in exactly the same situation as the Zambrano siblings living in the country of their nationality and they could be protected by their right to EU citizenship under Article 20 TFEU: a right which, according to the judgment in this case, does not exist while they reside in Luxembourg. By trying to limit the effect of the Zambrano case-law in the future, the CJEU implies that EU citizenship is no longer additional to national citizenship, i.e. does not provide EU citizens with extra rights alongside their national ones but is hierarchically inferior to national citizenship. Thus, the Court limits EU citizenship by suggesting that national citizenship is superior to the federal concept of EU citizenship, and in this way it implicitly negates the very idea of primacy of EU law over national law. Moreover, it seems that the poor third-country-national mother in the Alokpa case, in contrast to the rich third-country-national mother in the Chen case, derives fewer rights from the EU's legal framework on citizenship.

---

26 Opinion of the Advocate General Mengozzi for Case C-86/12, delivered on 21 March 2013, ECLI:EU:C:2013:197.

In a way the Alokpa case further limits the results of both the Ruiz Zambrano and Zhu and Chen cases. After Alokpa, the rationale underpinning the Ruiz Zambrano case concerns the Member States of which the child-EU citizen is a national, whilst the line of case-law stemming from the Zhu and Chen case is directed towards the host Member State. Furthermore, unlike a residence permit granted under Article 21 TFEU, a residence permit granted under Article 20 TFEU is not subject to the conditions laid down by Article 7(1)(b) of the 2004/38/EC Directive.[27]

The CJEU in the Alokpa case makes absolutely no reference to fundamental rights, namely the rights in Articles 7 and 24 of the Charter of Fundamental Rights of the EU which enshrine the right to family life and children's rights respectively. In the Ruiz Zambrano case the Court's holding was implicitly based on considerations relating to the need to respect fundamental rights, the right to family life in particular.[28] Also, in the Zhu and Chen case, the EU Court paid special attention to the position of younger children by recognising the impossibility of them residing in a Member State independently and by recognising more extensive rights for their family members than those enjoyed by family members of other Union citizens.[29]

27 K Lenaerts, 'EU Citizenship and the European Court of Justice's "Stone-by-Stone" Approach' (n 21). In this article, in order to justify the limitation of citizenship rights after Ruiz Zambrano, the President of the EU Court argues that this new approach to the Ruiz Zambrano case has been built up progressively in an incremental manner by the consequent case-law in Dereci, Iida, Ymeraga and Alopka. He claims that one has to view the EU Court in the way a common law court operates and he even mentions the statement made by the US Federal Supreme Court Justice Oliver Wendell Holmes Jr. (1841-1935): 'The life of the law has not been logic, it has been experience'. In other words, Justice Lenaerts implicitly accepts that the EU Court deviates from its previous case-law by following the art of 'distinguishing' followed by common law courts, which is quite interesting from a comparative law perspective.

28 N Cambien, 'Union Citizenship and Immigration: Rethinking the Classics' (2010) 5(1) *European Journal of Legal Studies* 10, 23. For a discussion on the emergence of EU family law see C Deliyanni-Dimitrakou and C Akrivopoulou, *Fundamental Rights and Private Relations in Greek and European Law* (Athens-Thessaloniki, Sakkoulas, 2015) 219-39.

29 See eg the McCarthy case (C-434/09) and the Ymeraga case (C-87/12) where there were no children involved.

IV. Concluding Remarks on the Right to Care

The term 'primary carer' is a relatively new concept in EU law, and did not appear in EU legislation or EU case-law until the Baumbast judgment. However, if we examine the concept from a comparative law perspective, it is a well-known notion in a number of common law judicial systems around the world. The term 'primary carer' is quite commonly used in the UK, and is also an important and well-defined legal concept in other English-speaking countries like Australia and the United States. In almost all of the cases discussed above in which the CJEU expressly mentioned in its judgment the term 'primary carer', the referring court was an English court. By contrast, the concept is alien to other, continental European, legal systems.[30] The primary carer is that person who effectivelytakes care of the child.

On the basis of the EU legislative framework and case-law discussed above, it should be clear that it is mainly three categories of persons who are privileged to invoke a right of residence in their capacity as primary carers, namely, the ascendants of an EU citizen, the spouse of the parent of an EU citizen and the registered partner of the parent of an EU citizen. However, the category of ascendant-primary carers could be interpreted broadly so as to cover non-biological ascendants like a step-parent or an adoptive parent.

It can be argued that other family members than those just mentioned should also be entitled to residence under Article 8 ECHR if they are the primary carer of a child. In order to be faithful to the actual meaning of the term 'primary carer', the category of ascendants should be given a wide

30 This explains the difficulty of translating 'primary carer' in other languages, as is illustrated by the different language versions of the *Baumbast and R* judgment. For instance, in the official French version of the judgment, 'primary carer' is translated by the rather descriptive expressions 'le parent qui a effectivement la garde de ces enfants', 'la personne assurant effectivement sa garde', or 'le parent qui garde effectivement l'enfant'. The translations just quoted indicate that the essence of the notion of primary carer is that the person it refers to 'effectively cares for the child' or 'is the person who mainly takes care of the child'. This is confirmed when we look at the definition of the concept in other legal systems in which it has traditionally existed. For instance, the 'Family Assistance Guide' of the Australian government explains that, for the purposes of the Family Assistance Act, a primary carer is the 'member of a couple identified as having greater responsibility for the children'. See Cambien (n 7) 9-11.

interpretation and should also cover, for instance, siblings, aunts and uncles, foster parents, legal guardians and, possibly, the unmarried and non-registered partner of one of the parents regardless of their sex or sexual orientation. Also, both parents or partners could be recognised as the primary carer of their child, and the multiple primary carers could be recognised by law, in order to ensure the respect of family life of Article 8 ECHR and Article 7 CFREU. Article 2 of Directive 2004/38/EC could be amended and a new category of privileged family members could be added, namely the primary carer or carers. The important thing is who actually takes care of the child and what is the best interest of the child in all these cases. This broader interpretation is also in accordance with the extended notion of social family, which is connected with 'bonds of love' in contrast to the notion of the biological family.[31] From a gender theory perspective, the legal recognition of the concept of 'care' marks a new era in our understanding of family relations and law and allows us to reconcile the public and the private divide.

The decision to use the term 'primary carer' and not 'custodian of the child' is quite bold and constitutes the basis for the formation of a new two-faceted EU right: the right to care and to be cared for. This is a right which is not expressly mentioned in the EU Charter of Fundamental Rights, but could be assumed by the combined interpretation of Article 7 (respect for private and family life) in conjunction with Article 24 (protecting the rights of the child) and, more specifically, paragraphs 2 and 3, which provide for 'the child's best interest as a primary consideration' and the right of the child to maintain on a regular basis a personal relationship and direct contact with both the parents. Also the right to care and to be cared for may derive from Article 7 in conjunction with Article 25, which provides for the rights of the elderly to lead a life of dignity and independence and to participate in social and cultural life.

---

31 In the case *Marinis v Greece* (application No 3004/10, judgment of 9 October 2014) of the European Court of Human Rights, the biological father was not recognised as a part of the child's life and family due to the fact that the child had not had contact with him for years and had not developed bonds of affection with him. The Court accepted that there was no actual family relation nor any manifestation of affection or love between the biological father and the child, so article 8 of the ECHR could not apply. For the notion of 'social family', see eg R Edwards, V Gillies, JR McCarthy 'Biological parents and social families: legal discourses and everyday understandings of the position of step-parents' (1999) 13(1) *International Journal of Law, Policy and the Family* 78-105.

Is it for the EU Court to develop such an extended right to care, or is it for the EU legislator? The Court paved the way with the Zambrano case when it extended citizenship rights of residence to the primary carer third-country national of an EU citizen. There was, of course a drawback after the decision on the Dereci case. Was it the fear of blunt judicial activism that triggered this setback, or was it the fear that EU citizenship was interpreted in such a broad manner that it exceeded the scope of Article 20 TFEU by transforming EU citizenship into a federal concept, i.e. hierarchically superior to national citizenship? It is true that the Court in all the above-discussed cases had to make a difficult choice in order to balance the rights stemming from national citizenship with those deriving from EU citizenship, and, in the process, it first expanded and then limited citizenship rights. But again, what role EU citizenship is about to play in the future is a political choice, and it is definitely connected to the dilemma between supranationalism and intergovernmentalism, which today more than ever before, with the rise of nationalism and extremism in Europe, tends to be substituted by the predicament between integration or disintegration.

Nevertheless, the relevant primary legislative framework is already enshrined in the EU Charter of Fundamental Rights. The Court, however, cannot substitute the EU legislator who is the only one responsible for amending Article 2 of Directive 2004/38/EC in order to include new categories of privileged family members that could eventually be considered as primary carers by the CJEU. In this respect, new secondary EU legislation should be adopted that would refine the concept of primary carer while taking into account the new forms of family that have emerged. This new secondary legislation should, of course, ensure both the dignity of the person who is to be cared for, and the dignity of the carer(s),[32] Its adoption may possibly then open the way for a broader interpretation of EU citizenship by the CJEU that could be inclusive of the right to care.

32 As provided in the preamble of the Charter of the FREU, which states: 'Conscious of its spiritual and moral heritage, the Union is founded on the indivisible, universal values of human dignity, freedom, equality and solidarity (…)'. Also, Chapter 1 of the Charter is dedicated to dignity. Article 1 of the Charter states: 'Human dignity is inviolable. It must be respected and protected.' Human dignity in the Charter is not only a fundamental right but also constitutes the basis of all fundamental rights. There are some other articles in the Charter, such as the rights of the elderly and those connected to fair and just working conditions, which expressly mention dignity in their text (Articles 25 and 31 CFREU).

In an era of economic and financial crisis during which the social welfare state has practically collapsed, and many EU countries, such as Greece, are facing a severe humanitarian crisis, the minimum amount of protection for the young and the elderly must be ensured. The right to have time for caring and the right to be cared for, accompanied of course by a living wage, are integral parts of a European social citizenship model[33] expressing the 'bonds of affection'[34] in European Union law.

33 A-M Konsta, 'Gender and Plastic Citizenship in European Social Law' in M-A Moreau (ed), *Before and After the Economic Crisis: What Implications for the European Social Model?* (Cheltenham, Edward Edgar Publishing, 2011) 129, 138.

34 Y Kravaritou, 'Liens affectifs et droit social européen' (n 5).

12 E-Government and E-Democracy: Overcoming Legitimacy Deficits in a Digital Europe?

Ingolf Pernice

Abstract

Many political initiatives of the European Union are focusing on the development and application of new information and communication technologies (ICT) with regard to the Single Market and, in particular, with regard to administrative processes at the Union level and among the Member States. While considerable progress has already been made, and the notion of e-government has played a role in these developments, the discussion on the key constitutional issue of the democratic legitimacy of the European Union seems to have remained rather untouched by, and insulated from, the world of the internet. Yet, ICT and, in particular, the internet and e-democracy seem to offer considerable opportunities for enhancing transparency, citizens' information and participation in the decision-making processes, and control of the policies made at Union level. Using the theoretical distinction, borrowed from Vivien A. Schmidt, of input-, output- and through-put legitimacy, it seems to be possible not only to depict the tools of e-government and e-democracy as bridges spanning the gap between the citizens and their political institutions in the EU, but also to explore the potential for further development with a view to overcoming the legitimacy deficits in the 'digital Europe'.

Introduction

Euroscepticism is spreading around the 28 Member States. People seem to be more and more disappointed with the European Union. The financial crisis, the difficulties of dealing with the Ukraine problem and, more recently, the failure to find an adequate European response to the refugee-crisis have created the feeling that the EU is unable to meet the citizens' aspirations for peace, freedom and prosperity. There is an increasing gap between the institutions and the individual, and people seem to be abandoning their hope that European integration would be the solution for many of their problems; indeed, more and more people see the EU itself as the problem, not the solution.

On the other hand, European institutions have been making great efforts to design new policies, not only to cope with the crisis, but also to prepare the Union for the future and enable it to meet new challenges. One of these challenges is the digital revolution. Although the opportunities it offers in terms of economic efficiency and new patterns of social interaction and political discourse are many, the use of information technologies poses new threats to privacy and security, such as mass surveillance, cyber-crime and cyber-attacks.

The present chapter focuses on the activities of the EU related to the internet and strives to identify and further develop aspects that may have a positive impact on the relationship between the citizen of the Union and the institutions. Though it is clear that there is no general and explicit strategy of using the information technologies for enhancing democratic legitimacy in the Union, many measures in different areas seem to —directly or indirectly— contribute to, or offer new opportunities for bringing individuals closer to the institutions, offering more transparency, access to information, direct participation and, to some extent, tools for enhancing political accountability and, thus, democratic control at the Union level. E-government and e-democracy seem to be the key words for describing elements of a possible strategy for bridging the gap between the EU and its citizens, and regaining their support for the EU so as to overcome existing legitimacy deficits.

In May 2015 the European Commission published a communication on the 'Digital Single Market Strategy for Europe',[1] an agenda aiming at boosting the growth and competitiveness of our industries. But the strategy is not about business only. It also includes the public sector and society:

> A digital economy can also make society more inclusive. Citizens and businesses are not currently getting the full benefits from digital services (from e-

1 Communication from the Commission to the European Parliament, the Council, the European Economic and Social Committee and the Committee of the Regions COM(2015) 192 final of 6 May 2015, A Digital Single Market Strategy for Europe [2015].

government, e-health, e-energy to e-transport) that should be available seamlessly across the EU.[2]

Chapter 4.3.2. of the Strategy deals with e-government and describes what is meant by this. It states that online public services need to be promoted to 'modernise public administration, achieve cross-border interoperability and facilitate easy interaction with citizens'. In this respect, online public services are considered 'crucial to increasing cost-efficiency and quality of the services provided to citizens and companies'. The communication proposes to introduce the 'Once Only' principle ensuring that 'public administrations reuse information about citizens or companies that is already in their possession without asking again'.[3]

One of the existing services is the range of websites of the European institutions providing broad overviews and explanations of their activities, the policies of the Union, EU legislation and the case-law of the European Court of Justice (ECJ). In diverse policy fields, EU legislation already provides for electronic communication in order to facilitate use of the freedom to provide services and the freedom of establishment,[4] to facilitate free trade and the application of the regime on public procurement.[5] The General Regulation on Data Protection[6] and other legislative initiatives like the Network and Information Security (NIS) Directive[7], as part of the

2 Ibid, para 4 (p 14).

3 Ibid, para 4.3.2 (p 16).

4 Directive 2006/123/EC of the European Parliament and of the Council of 12 December 2006 on services in the internal market [2006] OJ 2006 L 376, pp 36–68, recitals 46, 52-54, 96, 112 and Articles 7 (3), 8, 21 (1), 22 (1), 22 (2) (c) and (3) (d), 28 (6), 34 (1), 36. 37(2).

5 See Directive 2014/24/EU of the European Parliament and of the Council of 26 February 2014 on public procurement and repealing Directive 2004/18/EC [2014] OJ L94/65 and Directive 2014/25/EU of the European Parliament and of the Council of 26 February 2014 on procurement by entities operating in the water, energy, transport and postal services sectors and repealing Directive 2004/17/EC [2014] OJ L94/243.

6 Regulation (EU) 2016/679 of the European Parliament and of the Council of 27 April 2016 on the protection of natural persons with regard to the processing of personal data and on the free movement of such data, and repealing Directive 95/46/EC (General Data Protection Regulation) OJ L 119/1.

7 Meanwhile adopted as Directive (EU) 2016/1148 of the European Parliament and of the Council of 6 July 2016 concerning measures for a high common level of security of network and information systems across the Union, OJ L 194, p.1-30.

European Cybersecurity Strategy,[8] tend to promote trust in the internet and online services, so that people do not hesitate to use the new technology for their own benefit.

With the 'Malmö-Declaration' of 2009[9] and the 'eGovernment Action Plan 2011-2015', decided in 2010,[10] important initiatives have been taken by the EU on e-governance. The e-SENS (*Electronic Simple European Networked Services*) project, co-financed by the EU, was started in 2013 with a view to consolidating, improving, and extending technical solutions in order to foster electronic interaction with public administrations across the EU. A key issue is the interoperability of the national ICT-solutions, which have so far concentrated on:

making it easier for companies to set up business electronically

enabling electronic procurement procedures for businesses

creating seamless access to EU legal systems

making it easier to use healthcare services abroad in cases of emergency[11]

---

8 European Commission, Network and Information Security (NIS), available at www.ec.europa.eu/digital-agenda/en/news/network-and-information-security-nis-di
rective. Joint Communication to the European Parliament, the Council, the European Economic and Social Committee and the Committee of the Regions, Cybersecurity Strategy of the European Union: An Open, Safe and Secure Cyberspace JOIN(2013) 1 final [2013]. For an overview on the proposed measures see EU Cybersecurity plan to protect open internet and online freedom and opportunity – Cyber Security strategy and Proposal for a Directive, available at www.ec.europa.eu/digital-agenda/en/news/eu-cybersecurity-plan-protect-open-internet-and-online-freedom-and-opportunity-cyber-security.

9 Ministerial Declaration on eGovernment approved unanimously in Malmö, Sweden, on 18 November 2009 available at www.ec.europa.eu/digital-agenda/sites/digital-agenda/files/ministerial-declaration-on-egovernment-malmo.pdf.

10 See Communication from the Commission to the European Parliament, the Council, the European Economic and Social Committee and the Committee of the Regions. The European eGovernment Action Plan 2011-2015: Harnessing ICT to promote smart, sustainable & innovative Government COM(2010) 743 final [2010].

11 See the website of the project e-SENS (*Electronic Simple European Networked Services*): www.esens.eu/home/.

So far, however, not much has been proposed on e-democracy,[12] and there is no systematic agenda for this issue.[13] Yet, in a similar way to e-government, which is believed to allow better delivery of government services to the people, the internet should be used more strategically as a tool to allow better communication of the citizens' will to the government and, thus, as a tool for improving democratic ownership and direct participation in EU governance. Its potential for strengthening the relationship between the citizens and their political institutions and leaders —be it at local, regional, national or European level— has yet to be explored. At the EU level, in particular, it is important to tackle the problems of the institutions' geographical and political remoteness from the citizens and the complexity and sometimes obscurity of the decision-making processes. Therefore, the specific tools offered by the internet to facilitate both e-government and e-democracy could be instruments for overcoming legitimacy deficits in the EU.

Surprisingly, the internet and the use of digital technologies are not mentioned in any of the proposals and discussion papers regarding democratic legitimacy in the debate and the official papers on the reform of the EU. Yet, what I have described, at the ECLN-Conference of 2012 in New York, as the 'principle of open democracy', one of the basic characteristics

12 As there are plenty of ideas about, and attempts at conceptualising, e-democracy, at this stage it may suffice to say that it means application of ICT with a view to empowering the citizen as a participant in the political process. For what it could ultimately imply, see M Behrouzi, *Democracy as the Political Empowerment of the Citizen: Direct-Deliberative e-Democracy* (Lanham, Lexington Books, 2006) 1-3, and with an emphasis on the close relationship of the idea to e-government ibid, pp 100-104. For a general study on e-democracy see:'OECD, Promise and Problems of E-Democracy: Challenges of Online Citizen Engagement', available at www.oecd.org/gov/public-innovation/35176328.pdf. A more sceptical approach is adopted by G Smith, *Democratic Innovations. Designing Institutions for Citizen Participation* (New York, Cambridge University Press, 2009) 142-61: 'The promise of e-democracy has yet to be fulfilled' (ibid, p 160). For a more optimistic view on the potential of e-democracy see J Freeman and S Quirke, 'Understanding E-Democracy. Government-Led Initiatives for Democratic Reform' (2013) 5 *Journal of eDemocracy and Open Government* 141. See also E Magrani, *Democracia Conectada – A Internet como Ferramenta de Engajamento Político-Democrático* (Rio de Janeiro, FGV Dereito Rio, 2014).

13 For an important inititiative of the European Parliament most recently: Ramón Jáuregui Atondo, Report on e-democracy in the European Union: potential and challenges (2016/2008 (INI)), of 16 February 2017.

of the European Union,[14] seems to be open for development through e-government and e-democracy as two instruments to be used for enhancing the legitimacy of the European system of governance, a system that is based upon the citizens who are, ultimately, the authors as well as the subjects of the Union's public authority.[15] Or, to put it as a question: has a digital Europe the potential to be more democratic —democracy being understood as a form of government ensuring the maximum degree of self-determination for the subjects of public authority?[16] Can we strengthen the democratic legitimacy of the EU through developing instruments that belong to what we understand as e-government and e-democracy?

First of all, it seems to be necessary to explain what is meant by e-democracy, particularly in regard to the European Union. One might think initially of the citizens' initiative provided for in Article 11 § 4 TEU. If it is true that the regulation on the citizen's initiative[17] provides for an electronic collection of signatures, this does not in itself, however, turn the citizens' initiative into a tool of e-democracy. I resist giving a definition of

14 See I Pernice, 'The EU – A Citizens' Joint Venture. Multilevel Constitutionalism and Open Democracy in Europe' in JM Magone (ed), *Routledge Handbook of European Politics* (Abingdon, Routledge, 2015) p 184 (192-95).

15 For more details of this concept on the basis of 'multilevel constitutionalism' see ibid, p 186. The theoretical foundations, with the sovereignty of the citizen at the centre of the concept, are developed in I Pernice, 'Europäisches und nationales Verfassungsrecht, Bericht' in J Ipsen (ed), *Veröffentlichungen der Vereinigung der Deutschen Staatsrechtslehrer 60* (Berlin, De Gruyter, 2001), p 148, 160-3, 165-8: sovereignty today means self-determination of the individual as a matter of human dignity. Similarly focusing on the individual, see Behrouzi, *Democracy as the Political Empowerment* (n 11), where the author talks about 'the sovereign powers of the individual citizen' and distinguishes between 'the macro principle of the political sovereignty of the individual' and 'the micro principle of the "social autonomy" of the individual' (p 3). See also ibid, pp 13-17: 'Democracy as the Political Sovereignty and Social Autonomy of the Citizen'.

16 In this sense, with a reference to the German Constitutional Court and others, see G Lübbe-Wolff, 'Europäisches und nationales Verfassungsrecht, 3. Bericht' in J Ipsen (ed) *Veröffentlichungen der Vereinigung der Deutschen Staatsrechtslehrer 60* (Berlin, De Gruyter, 2001) p 246, at 252.

17 Regulation 211/2011 of the European Parliament and of the Council of 16 February 2011 on the citizens' initiative [2011], OJ 2011 L65/1; see in particular the Commission Implementing Regulation (EU) 1179/2011 of 17 November 2011 laying down technical specifications for online collection systems pursuant to Regulation (EU) No 211/2011 of the European Parliament and of the Council on the citizens' initiative [2011] OJ 2011 L301/3.

e-democracy from the outset. In 2009 the UK Parliament's Office of Science and Technology explained some aspects of e-democracy and its possible developments in future, and referred to websites, such as those for the streaming of all Parliament proceedings (parliamentlive.tv), the electronic communication of citizens with their elected representatives (writetothem.com), online-consultations (forums.parliament) and e-petitions to the Prime Minister (petitions.number10.gov). Also blogs and social networks were mentioned.[18] These examples shed some light on what e-democracy is about. E-democracy, though, is not a settled term, but a programme of creativity, inviting the development of innovative uses of the internet with a view to facilitating, promoting and enhancing the inclusion and active participation of citizens in the political processes at all levels.

E-government[19] and e-democracy are distinct aspects of the same thing; they relate to different applications of the internet, while with regard to the relationship between citizens and the public authorities they go hand in hand. If well understood and implemented, both terms describe instruments for tightening this relationship, giving it real life and so enhancing the legitimacy of the European Union and its policies. In this context Article 1 (2) TEU seems to play a particularly important role. It reads as follows:

> This Treaty marks a new stage in the process of creating an ever closer union among the peoples of Europe, in which decisions are taken as openly as possible and as closely as possible to the citizen.

The principles referred to in this fundamental provision of the Treaty, and, in particular, the openness of the decision-making processes and their closeness and proximity to the citizen, can greatly benefit from the internet. In order to explore the potential of the internet for serving the principles of openness and proximity, the key notions relating to the internet and legitimisation in the European Union, which will be considered later in this paper, are:

---

18 Parliamentary Office of Science and Technology, postnote 2009 no. 321, E-Democracy, www.parliament.uk/documents/post/postpn321.pdf.

19 For the concept and its legal implications in Germany see the comprehensive study by M Eifert, *Electronic Government. Das Recht der elektronischen Verwaltung* (Baden-Baden, Nomos, 2006), with a brief survey of the European dimension (ibid, pp 425-50).

- e-government: better delivery of public services to the citizen
- open government, or better access to information and transparency
- participatory deliberative democracy and better inclusion of the citizen[20]
- the European digital public sphere and political accountability

These four aspects seem to be essential for the citizens of the Member States, enabling them to take ownership of the European Union and helping to strengthen the legitimacy of the Union and its policies. Legitimacy is understood in a broader democratic sense as a general acceptance by those concerned of —or the identification of the citizens with— the constitutional setting, its procedures and the decisions (outcome) so produced, as their own method of self-government, regardless of whether or not each individual likes each particular decision taken by the competent authorities regarding his or her case, views or interests. Borrowing from the terms developed by Fritz Scharpf and expanded by Vivien A. Schmidt, legitimacy means *output* legitimacy with regard to the acceptance of the decisions taken as being effective and useful (government *for* the people). It is based upon *input* legitimacy in the sense of the people's will finding an expression in the policies decided by the competent institutions following the procedures applicable in each case (governance *by* the people). And it is conditioned by *throughput* legitimacy, focusing on the internal processes and practices of EU governance and, in particular, the interest mediation *with* the people. Thus, as Schmidt puts it, throughput legitimacy concerns 'the quality of the governance process, not just the effectiveness of the outcomes or the participation and representation of the citizenry'.[21]

20 For the complementary function of public deliberation and citizens' participation for the legitimacy of EU policies see GFCC, Judgment of 30 September 2009, 2 BvE 2/08 and 5/08, and 2 BvR 1010/08, 1022/08, 1259/08, 182/09 – *Lisbon Treaty*), para. 272: It is true that the merely deliberative participation of the citizens and of their societal organisations in the political rule – their direct involvement in the deliberations of the institutions with the power to take binding political decisions – cannot replace the legitimising connection based on elections and other votes. Such elements of participative democracy can, however, complement the legitimation of European public authority.' For a thorough study of deliberative democracy see George Gerapetritis, 'Deliberative Democracy within and beyond the State', in this volume.

21 VA Schmidt, 'Democracy in Europe' in JM Magone (ed), *Routledge Handbook of European Politics* (Abingdon, Routledge, 2015) pp 280, 282.

These conceptual distinctions do not present sharply separable categories that can be easily applied to the diverse forms of citizens' information, participation and obedience in a political system. The specific ways in which the relationship between citizens and their political institutions is formed and functions somewhat overlap and are mutually supportive. Nevertheless, it seems worthwhile to ask to what extent certain relevant aspects of e-government can be related and possibly contribute to *output* legitimacy by ensuring better delivery of public services to citizens (I. below). Also, diverse aspects of e-democracy should rather be discussed as concerning either *input* legitimacy, as far as the election and control of decision-makers are concerned (II. below) or the *throughput* legitimation of Union policies regarding the internal decision-making processes, the inclusion of, and the interest mediation *with* the people on each particular issue (III. below).

I. E-government: better delivery of public services to the citizen as a case of output-legitimacy

If e-government is about the better delivery of public services to the citizen, it can be dealt with as a question of *output* legitimacy both at the national and the European level. As Brussels is remote for most of the citizens of the Union who live geographically far away from the European institutions, whatever services the EU is offering or delivering to the citizen, it is thanks to the internet that for many these services can be delivered in a timely and effective manner. Any assessment of the attempts to promote e-government within the EU must be based upon the understanding that, given the primary responsibility of the Member States for the administrative implementation of Union law, only part of the output of EU action is directly provided by European services. Most of it will be provided by national, regional or local administrations. It is vital, then, to understand e-government as a shared responsibility, a responsibility that is borne by the public authorities at all levels. Member States have the responsibility to ensure that their internal administrations establish and offer adequate electronic services. European e-government would not be effective if there were no proper technical infrastructure in place and no system interoperability or close cooperation throughout the Union.

A. EU-strategies for e-government

E-government is progressively gaining ground within the Member States, such as through the German E-Government Act of 2013,[22] but also at the EU level. In the 'Malmö-Declaration', the competent ministers of all the Member States agreed upon their 'Joint Vision on Policy Priorities for 2015', as follows:

> We aspire to a vision whereby European governments are recognised for being open, flexible and collaborative in their relations with citizens and businesses. They use eGovernment to increase their efficiency and effectiveness and to constantly improve public services in a way that caters for users' different needs and maximises public value, thus supporting the transition of Europe to a leading knowledge-based economy.[23]

It is on the basis of this Declaration that the Commission has adopted an 'eGovernment Action Plan 2011-2015',[24] in which it defines four political priorities for e-government, as follows:

- Empower citizens and businesses
- Reinforce mobility in the Single Market
- Enable efficiency and effectiveness
- Create the necessary key enablers and pre-conditions to make things happen

---

22 Available at www.gesetze-im-internet.de/englisch_egovg/englisch_egovg.html. For the situation in France see the 'Feuille de Route du Gouvernement sur le numérique', www.eurocloud.fr/doc/feuille-route-gouvernement-numerique-fevrier-2013.pdf, and the internet platform www.service-public.fr/. For an overview of the situation in the other Member States see the factsheets published by the European Commission presenting inter alia the E-Government strategy and legal framework for each of the 28 Member States and six additional countries: www.joinup.ec.europa.eu/community/nifo/og_page/egovernment-factsheets.

23 Ministerial Declaration on eGovernment approved unanimously in Malmö, Sweden, on 18 November 2009, available at: www.ec.europa.eu/digital-agenda/sites/digital-agenda/files/ministerial-declaration-on-egovernment-malmo.pdf.

24 See Communication COM(2010) 743 final, The European eGovernment Action Plan 2011-2015 [2010].

An update for the strategy is promised for 2016.[25] But already much earlier EU action provides us with important examples of the implementation of these goals.[26]

B. E-government by legislation: The Services-Directive

A leading example is Directive 2006/123 on Services in the Internal Market.[27] Also, the Commission's Quick Guide to the application of EU directives deserves to be mentioned, where the Commission explains what the Directive on services is about so as to facilitate the establishment of businesses and the provision of services across borders within the EU.[28] In order to simplify the free establishment of businesses, the Directive also provides for 'points of single contact' in each of the Member States, accessible through the internet. Article 8 of the Directive, in particular, concerns 'Procedures by electronic means' and states:

> 1. Member States shall ensure that all procedures and formalities relating to access to a service activity and to the exercise thereof may be easily completed, at a distance and by electronic means, through the relevant point of single contact and with the relevant competent authorities.
>
> 2. Paragraph 1 shall not apply to the inspection of premises on which the service is provided or of equipment used by the provider or to physical examination of the capability or of the personal integrity of the provider or of his responsible staff.

---

25 See Communication COM(2010) 743 final, The European eGovernment Action Plan 2011-2015 [2010]. Here the Commission states: 'Our goal is to optimise the conditions for the development of cross-border eGovernment services provided to citizens and businesses regardless of their country of origin. This includes the development of an environment which promotes interoperability of systems and key enablers such as eSignatures and eIdentification'. Meanwhile see: Communication from the Commission to the European Parliament, the Council, the European Economic and Social Committee and the Committee of the Regions: EU eGovernment Action Plan 2016-2020 Accelerating the digital transformation of government (COM(2016) 179 final).

26 For an overview see the fact sheet on 'eGovernment in the European Union', regularly updated www.joinup.ec.europa.eu/sites/default/files/ckeditor_files/files/eGov EuropeanUnionMay2015.pdf.

27 Directive 2006/123 on services in the internal market [2006] OJ L376/36; see also above n 4.

28 European Commission, Quick Guide, available at www.ec.europa.eu/internal_mar ket/eu-go/index_en.htm.

> 3. The Commission shall, in accordance with the procedure referred to in Article 40(2), adopt detailed rules for the implementation of paragraph 1 of this Article with a view to facilitating the interoperability of information systems and use of procedures by electronic means between Member States, taking into account common standards developed at Community level.

The internet is used here to allow citizens an easier use of the freedoms granted in the Treaties by ensuring that the Member States take the appropriate measures. In this vein, recital 52 of the Directive explains:

> The setting up, in the reasonably near future, of electronic means of completing procedures and formalities will be vital for administrative simplification in the field of service activities, for the benefit of providers, recipients and competent authorities...

The Directive also compels the Member States to assist market operators in taking full advantage of their freedoms in practice: Article 21 § 1 subpara 2 of the Directive states:

> Where appropriate, advice from the competent authorities shall include a simple step-by-step guide. Information and assistance shall be provided in a clear and unambiguous manner, shall be easily accessible at a distance, including by electronic means, and shall be kept up to date.

Providers of services shall, under Article 22 of the Directive, be compelled to make available to the recipients of their services their name, legal status and form, geographical address etc. 'by electronic means', so that they can be easily informed. Cooperation among the Member States and mutual information exchange are other ways in which the Directive strives to make the system efficient. Recital no. 112 states:

> Cooperation between Member States requires a well-functioning electronic information system in order to allow competent authorities easily to identify their relevant interlocutors in other Member States and to communicate in an efficient way.

Accordingly, Article 28 § 6 requires an information exchange between Member States 'by electronic means', and Article 34 § 1 of the Directive provides that:

> The Commission, in cooperation with Member States, shall establish an electronic system for the exchange of information between Member States, taking into account existing information systems.

The Directive shows how the EU is striving to make e-government beneficial to individuals and the internal market more effective. The Commission now envisages going a step further and providing common rules on the points of single contact with a view to creating a 'single digital gateway for Europe'.[29] In order to make this possible and, more generally, to ensure the availability of high-speed broadband internet and access to Europe-wide digital service infrastructures, the Commission has already proposed (in 2013) the establishment of the 'Connecting Europe Facility', which is a part of the Europe Infrastructure Package providing for funding to facilitate 'an efficient flow of private and public investments to stimulate the deployment and modernisation of broadband networks'.[30]

C. Encouragement: Taking the citizen Seriously

Another more general, primarily online tool for helping citizens and businesses solve their problems with European institutions regarding the benefits of the internal market is SOLVIT, a website which promises 'solutions to problems with your EU rights'.[31] As the 'Internal Market Scoreboard' of the Commission explains in the 2013 report, 'there is a SOLVIT centre in each Member State, established as a part of the national administration. To resolve problems, SOLVIT centres cooperate directly with each other via an online database'.[32] As the internal market exists for the citizen, providing assistance to the citizen in order to help them find their way through the provisions governing the internal market is of great importance.

Other measures by the EU have contributed to establishing the rather technical conditions for a broader use and application of e-government. Two examples are the eSignature Directive 1999/93,[33] and Regulation

---

29 Communication COM(2015) 192 final, para 4.3.2. See already the call for a 'Conference on Points of Single Contact: Working Towards a Single Digital Gateway for Europe', 17 December 2014, www.ec.europa.eu/enterprise/newsroom/cf/itemdetail.cfm?item_id=7998&lang=en&title=Conference-on-Points-of-Single-Contact%3A-working-towards-a-single-digital-gateway-for-Europe.

30 European Commission, Connecting Europe Facility, available at: www.ec.europa.eu/digital-agenda/en/connecting-europe-facility#Article.

31 European Commission, SOLVIT, available at: www.ec.europa.eu/solvit/.

32 European Commission, Single Market Scoreboard, SOLVIT reporting period 01/2013 – 12/2013.

33 Directive 1999/93 of the European Parliament and of the Council of 13 December 1999 on a Community framework for electronic signature [1999] OJ L13/12, amended by Regulation 1137/2008 of the European Parliament and of the Council of 22 October 2008 adapting a number of instruments subject to the procedure laid

910/2014 on electronic identification and trust services for electronic transactions in the internal market, establishing rules for trustworthy authentification and electronic signatures applicable to all participating trans-border transactions and procedures in the area of e-government.[34] With the application of these instruments throughout the EU, the 2014 public procurement reform package foreseeing a transition to full e-procurement by October 2018[35] has a better chance of coming into effect.

While none of these measures expressly refers to democracy or legitimacy of the Union, they nevertheless serve the citizens' interest in providing for efficient and participative public services, taking the individual seriously as an active partner in a dialogue with the authorities. Accordingly, the eGovernment Action Plan of 2010 gives special emphasis to 'user empowerment', as follows:

> Empowerment means increasing the capacity of citizens, businesses and other organisations to be pro-active in society through the use of new technological tools. Public services can gain in efficiency and users in satisfaction by meeting the expectations of users better and being designed around their needs and in collaboration with them whenever possible. Empowerment also means that governments should provide easy access to public information, improve transparency and allow effective involvement of citizens and businesses in the policy-making process.[36]

More concretely, the Commission states that 'increasing effective eGovernment means that services are designed around users' needs and provide flexible and personalised ways of interacting and performing transactions with public administrations'.[37] It adds:

> Social networking and collaborative tools (e.g. Web 2.0 technologies) enable users to play an active role in the design and production of public services. Though still small, there are a growing number of services targeted at the needs of citizens, often developed by civil society organisations which are

---

down in Article 251 of the Treaty to Council Decision 1999/468/EC, with regard to the regulatory procedure with scrutiny [2008] OJ L311/1.

34 Regulation 910/2014 of the European Parliament and of the Council of 23 July 2014 on electronic identification and trust services for electronic transactions in the internal market and repealing Directive 1999/93/EC [2014] OJ L257/73.

35 See Communication COM(2015) 192 final, para 4.3.2 with references to Dir 2014/24 and Dir 2014/25.

36 eGovernment action plan (n 22), para 2.1.

37 Ibid, para 2.1.1.

> based on the effective collaboration between the private and the public sector.[38]

Other issues addressed in the action plan concern transparency[39] and, more broadly, the involvement of citizens and businesses in policy-making processes:

> The envisaged actions will improve the ability of people to have their voice heard and make suggestions for policy actions in the Member States and the European Union as a whole. These actions will build on projects on eParticipation already launched under the Competitiveness and Innovation Framework Programme (CIP), e.g. by using e-Petitioning ICT tools to support 'citizens initiatives', or on new calls for proposals to be opened under the seventh EU Framework Programme (FP7).[40]

All these statements show a new approach regarding the status of the citizen in the Union. Citizens are not treated merely as a subject of the crown or of another authority, but as citizens who are recognised as active partners in the system. Nor is the state presented to the individual as a 'black box'. Through e-government he or she is taken seriously as a relevant actor and a constituent part of a comprehensive system of governance including the administrations of the Member States and the European Union. The result is a better output, more efficiency and an easier acceptance of public authorities' actions and is thus beneficial to the legitimacy of the Union and its policies.

II. E-democracy: Enhancing citizen's participation in framing EU Politics as a case of input-legitimacy

Input legitimacy is usually considered in terms of the elections of the legislative and executive powers in a political community. It concerns the way in which the people's representatives are chosen and mandated for implementing their political programmes and acting in the public interest. To be meaningful for democratic legitimacy, elections must be based upon a certain level of transparency in the political institutions and decision-making processes. Democratic elections presuppose people taking responsibility and ownership, and the right conditions for a free discourse in a

38 Ibid, para 2.1.2.
39 Ibid, para 2.1.4.
40 Ibid, para 2.1.5.

public sphere. E-voting, however, has not yet been practiced at EU level, and only limited experience with e-voting has been gained —in Estonia.[41]

While elections can be understood as the principal instrument available for ensuring *input* legitimacy, referenda, citizens' initiatives, petitions and even polls and the underlying forms and processes of deliberative democracy[42] can also be associated with *input* legitimacy.[43] In contrast to e-voting, e-petitions are already a common practice around the Union, and the first steps towards direct democracy through the European citizens' initiative (Article 11 § 4 TEU), with the internet as an enabling tool, have been taken at EU level.

There are doubts, however, about the concept of *input* legitimacy being applicable at EU level for the conditions for it are not given in this case (A. below). As the discussion on this point does not take into account the internet, it may be asked whether the internet offers solutions to the problem (B. below). The Constitutional Convention's publication of its texts and proceedings on a special website seems to be a first step towards a more inclusive political process (C. below).

A. Questioning input-legitimacy in the EU

No small number of authors contest the claim that *input* legitimacy plays a relevant role in the EU. One of the arguments put forward is that there is no government which could be voted in and out by the people.[44] Powerful Member States with the greatest bargaining power have 'an undemocratic

41 See the fact sheet on Estonia (March 2015): 'eGovernment in Estonia', available at: www.joinup.ec.europa.eu/sites/default/files/ckeditor_files/files/eGov%20in%20Estonia%20-%20January%202015%20-%20v_17_Final.pdf, which states that in the 2015 general elections as many as 176,491 voters cast their vote electronically. For a short comment see: J Merkert, 'Wahl in Estland: Ein Fünftel gibt Stimme per I-Voting ab' in *Heise online* 27 February 2015, www.heise.de/newsticker/meldung/Wahl-in-Estland-Ein-Fuenftel-gibt-Stimme-per-I-Voting-ab-2561003.html.

42 See for details Gerapetritis (n 20).

43 See R Hrbek, 'Die Europäische Bürgerinitiative: Möglichkeiten und Grenzen eines neuen Elements im EU-Entscheidungssystems' (2012) 1 *integration* 35, 44; The Netherlands Scientific Council for Government Policy (WRR), *Rediscovering Europe in the Netherlands* (Amsterdam, Amsterdam University Press, 2007) 111.

44 See Schmidt, 'Democracy in Europe' (2015) 285; see also JHH Weiler, 'To be a European Citizen – Eros and Civilization' in G Bousquet et al (eds), *Working Paper Series in European Studies*, special edn (Madison, Spring, 1998) pp 8 and 40:

advantage in the closed-door negotiating sessions of the Council'. Others observe a 'thinness of the communicative processes that articulate citizen ideas and concerns in the European public sphere', and a 'lack of a common European language, of real European media or of a European public opinion' is blamed for a 'fragmentation of discourse'. It is more common for political actors to speak to their national publics in their national languages.[45]

Is there a 'European public sphere'?[46] What are the conditions for the evolution of a European public sphere and what could be the role of the internet in creating such a sphere? In regard to what other conditions of democratic legitimacy is the internet about to make a difference?

B. *What does the internet offer?*

The internet gives people, businesses and public authorities access to borderless information, communication, interaction and networking. Notwithstanding the increased risks and challenges with regard to privacy and security, and in spite of still unsolved problems relating to the limited access to the internet, net neutrality or what is called the digital divide, the potential of the internet as a tool for facilitating political processes, participation and control at all levels of the Union's political system is considerable. The empowerment of the citizen brought about by the internet is due to its capacity to enhance transparency (i), to enable the evolution of a European public sphere (ii), to facilitate elections, political dialogue and accountability (iii) and also to improve citizens' participation in the political decision-making processes (iv).

'the basic condition of Representative Democracy is, indeed, that at election time the citizens (…) can throw the scoundrels out -- that is, replace the Government'.

45 Ibid, pp 285-86, with references to Grimm, Habermas, Weiler.

46 Based upon a broad concept of 'public sphere', though without reference to the internet, see P Häberle, *Gibt es eine Europäische Öffentlichkeit?* (Berlin, Walter de Gruyter, 2000), and id., *Europäische Verfassungslehre* 7th edn (Baden-Baden, Nomos, 2011) 168-84, with an emphasis on cultural aspects and a partially positive answer, though criticising a lack of transparency in the decision-making in Brussels (see also ibid, pp 182, 214-16, 500-02).

1. Transparency

There is no political accountability and no effective democratic control without transparency and access to information. Transparency is a basic condition for democracy.[47] Through websites and interactive tools for all institutions, parties and political leaders, the internet allows for more transparency in the political processes: Since the Treaty of Lisbon, negotiating sessions of the Council have been public, at least when it deliberates and votes on a draft legislative act (Article 16 § 8 TEU), as they can be observed in real-time streams.[48] Debates of the European Parliament can be followed through the internet, thanks to a public stream on the website of the European Parliament.[49] A website of the Commission also gives access to an overview on the diverse steps and the actual status of the legislative process for each legislative proposal (pre-lex),[50] allowing the public to react, where deemed appropriate, directly through the diverse channels offered by the internet.

These are but a few examples of transparency in European politics that would not be possible without ICT. Other modes of transparency clearly exist, thanks to the internet, such as well-known leaks from public —and secret— services. This raises the question of 'leaks and legitimacy'; for example, the question of whether the new possibilities offered by the internet for communicating leaks to the public add to the legitimacy of political decision-making,[51] a question that will be left open here. At least, the easier possibility of leaks may have a chilling effect upon public —and also private— authorities regarding the proper exercise of their powers. Trust and transparency, then, are closely linked. Already the mere existence of

47 See Lübbe-Wolff, 'Europäisches und nationales Verfassungsrecht' (2001) 276-78. For a theoretical and practical account see C Sobotta, *Transparenz in den Rechtsetzungverfahren der Europäischen Union. Stand und Perspektiven des Gemeinschaftsrechts unter besonderer Berücksichtigung des Grundrechtes auf Zugang zu Informationen* (Baden-Baden, Nomos, 2001) 36-49, 87-277.

48 See the website of the European Council: Live streaming, videos and photos, available at: www.consilium.europa.eu/en/press/audiovisual/.

49 See European Parliament EUROParlTV, available at: www.europarltv.europa.eu/en/about-europarltv/about-us.aspx.

50 European Commission, EuR-Lex Access to European Union law, Search in legislative procedures, available at: www.eur-lex.europa.eu/collection/legislative-procedures.html?locale=en.

51 I owe this question to Jeanette Hofmann. Not much has been written on it.

the internet and its applications, like instruments for free access to information in general, can exert a positive impact on the behaviour of authorities.[52]

2. An Evolving European Public Sphere

Where issues of greater political importance are dealt with at the European level, a European public sphere is already evolving, with even, in certain cases, a European public opinion. Let me name but a few examples of this phenomenon, such as the reform of the Treaties prepared by the Constitutional Convention, following the principles of the Laeken-Declaration of 2001,[53] and the current debate on the financial crisis, Greece and the stabilisation of the Euro. More recently, the refugees from Iraq and Syria have reached the headlines of the media Europe-wide, as an issue that cannot be resolved by individual Member States but requires a European solution.

Legislative proposals like the Directive on Services or, more recently, the new Directive of 2013 on Audiovisual Media Services (AVMSD)[54]

---

52 In this vein, access to environmental information for the public was considered as an effective tool for ensuring better implementation of European environmental law within the Member States: see Directive 2003/4/EC of the European Parliament and of the Council of 28 January 2003 on public access to environmental information and repealing Council Directive 90/313/EEC, OJ L41/26. See also Pillar One of the Aarhus-Convention; for an overview see the Commission's website www.ec.europa.eu/environment/aarhus/legislation.htm. For a more general treatment see: I Pernice, 'Verfassungs- und europarechtliche Aspekte der Transparenz staatlichen Handelns, 2. IFG-Tagung Berlin am 6./7. September 2012' in A Dix et al (eds) *Informationsfreiheit und Informationsrecht. Jahrbuch 2013* (Berlin, Lexxion, 2014) 17-34.

53 See Annex I in the Annexes to the Presidency Conclusions – Laeken, 14 and 15 December 2001 (SN 300/1/01 REV 1), where, in the final paragraphs, it is stated that: 'In order for the debate to be broadly based and involve all citizens, a Forum will be opened for organisations representing civil society (the social partners, the business world, non-governmental organisations, academia, etc.)'. See also the press release of 18 February 2003, IP/03/244, www.europa.eu/rapid/press-release_IP-03-244_de.htm, and below II.3.

54 See: European Commission, Online Public Consultation on Directive 2010/13/EU on Audiovisual Media Services (AVMSD), www.ec.europa.eu/digital-agenda/en/news/public-consultation-directive-201013eu-audiovisual-media-services-avmsd-media-framework-21st.

have become widely known to the European public, and the debate on the Commission's proposal of a general regulation on data protection[55] shows how much European policies figure in the news headlines throughout Europe. Other examples are the rejection of the Anti-Counterfeiting Trade Agreement (ACTA) as a consequence of a Europe-wide internet campaign,[56] or the present discussion on the Transatlantic Trade and Investment Partnership (TTIP) and investor-state dispute settlement arrangements at large.[57] The discussion on TTIP has at least prompted the Commission to make public the draft of a parallel agreement with Canada, to provide an idea of what the relevant provisions look like,[58] and to develop a transparency strategy for the TTIP negotiations.[59] Online information and documentation, with the possibility of feedback from the general public, are a first step towards encouraging an informed discussion of the common issues across the European Union and beyond.

New instruments stimulating the development of a European public sphere include public video streams of the debates in the European Parliament[60] and of public lectures and discussions like the 'Humboldt-Reden zu Europa'.[61]

As in multilingual federal states, language problems do not prevent the formation of a public sphere. Automatic translation, progressively available as a particular application of ICT, may facilitate, in future, the emer-

---

55 Above, note 6. See also European Commission, Online consultation on the legal framework for the fundamental right to protection of personal data, www.ec.europa.eu/justice/newsroom/data-protection/opinion/090709_en.htm.

56 See eg: www.secure.avaaz.org/en/stop_acta/.

57 European Commission. Online public consultation on investment protection and investor-to-state dispute settlement (ISDS) in the Transatlantic Trade and Investment Partnership Agreement (TTIP), www.trade.ec.europa.eu/consultations/index.cfm?consul_id=179; specialised forums have emerged for the critical assessment of current issues, such as: *VoteWatch Europe*, www.votewatch.eu; *attac,* www.attac.de/startseite/; a promising discussion platform has been developed by academics: *publixphere,* www.publixphere.net/i/publixphere-de/instance/publixphere-de; see also *Dublin European Institute* Blog, www.europedebate.ie/about-3/.

58 See the Commission's website on CETA, inviting the public for comments: www.ec.europa.eu/trade/policy/in-focus/ceta/. For TTIP see: www.ec.europa.eu/trade/policy/in-focus/ttip/index_en.htm.

59 See the Commission's website: www.ec.europa.eu/trade/policy/in-focus/ttip/index_en.htm.

60 See above, nn 44 and 45.

61 See, for some examples (Barroso, Renzi, Voßkuhle et al.): www.youtube.com/results?search_query=Humboldt-Reden+zu+Europa.

gence of a European public sphere across borders. Now, already, blogging activities and discussion platforms[62] and social networks on the internet are taking the place, at least in part, of traditional media and allow easy borderless public communication among those who are interested. If there is a lack of direct accountability among political leaders in the Commission or the Council to the European Parliament or the national parliaments respectively, the diverse internet-based instruments have a fair chance of developing into forums where politicians can be held directly accountable to civil society and the citizens, as implied by Article 10 § 2 subpara 2 TEU.

3. E-voting, Political Dialogue and Accountability

General elections and referenda are a field in which the internet has not yet been successfully applied, and it is questionable if e-voting is a desirable alternative at all to the existing procedures in which people gather in person at the polling stations, discuss the elections and lend their support to the person or party of their choice.[63] As soon as the risks of manipulated counting and secrecy of the votes are technically eliminated and problems of security and data protection are solved[64] —blockchain technology could be the way forward[65]— however, both ways of voting may be of interest to citizens, particularly those who have no easy access to the

62 With the interesting proposal to create Massive Open Online Deliberation Platforms (MOOD's) see: Dirk Helbing/Stefan Klauser, ,How to make democracy work in the digital age', The Huffington Post of 8 April 2016, at: http://www.huffingtonpost.com/entry/how-to-make-democracy-work-in-the-digital-age_us_57a2f488e4b0456cb7e17e0f.

63 For the Estonian experience see above n 38.

64 For some criteria see the interdisciplinary study by K Bräunlich et al, *Sichere Internetwahlen. Ein rechtswissenschaftlich-informatorisches Modell* (Baden-Baden, Nomos, 2013).

65 See Matthew Daniel, 'Blockchain Technology: The Key to Secure Online Voting' (*Bitcoin Magazine*, 27 June 2015) https://bitcoinmagazine.com/articles/blockchain-technology-key-secure-online-voting-1435443899 accessed 31 May 2016. See also Nick Abouzeid, 'Ukraine Governemnt Plans to Trieal Ethereum Blockchain-Based Election Platform' (*Bitcoin Magazine*, 25 February 2016) http://www.nasdaq.com/article/ukraine-government-plans-to-trial-ethereum-blockchain-based-election-platform-cm585001 accessed 31 May 2016.

polling stations.[66] So far the internet has at least offered plenty of opportunities for individuals to be informed about and become familiar with the political programmes, the personalities of the candidates and the political situation relating to the elections. It also provides easy access to information on the candidates' pasts and the positions of the parties, their ambitions and policies in the preceding periods and thus enhances transparency as a basis for more rational choices.

E-democracy involves an ongoing discussion between the representatives and their electorate or constituency. Personal websites of the political actors, social networks, blogs, even e-mail and twitter allow for more intensive communication, in particular where direct personal contact is made difficult by the EU system of national lists and the absence of defined constituencies.

4. Participation: 'Speaking with Your Government'

'Speaking with your government' means getting involved, and this is greatly facilitated by the internet: Article 11 § 1 and § 2 TEU expressly state that 'the institutions shall maintain an open, transparent and regular dialogue with representative associations and civil society'. And Article 2 of Protocol (2) to the Treaty of Lisbon, on the application of the principles of subsidiarity and proportionality, compels the Commission to 'consult widely' before proposing legislative acts. This 'discursive participation' in the framing of political decisions plays an increasing role where patterns of representative democracy suffer from the complexity of European politics and an increasing lack of democratic transmission of the political will through classic elections.[67] Both of the latter are simplified and accelerated by the internet, so that the active participation of individuals, stakeholders and experts in the decision-making processes can more easily take place in order to produce an appropriate and satisfying outcome. Accordingly, the Commission's official website 'Your Voice in Europe' gives direct online access for all open consultations and offers the relevant consul-

66 See already U Karpen, 'E-Voting as an Instrument of E-Democracy' in S Flogiatis et al (eds), *E-Government and E-Democracy. E-Gouvernement et E-Démocratie* (London, Esperia Publications, 2006) 149-69, pleading for 'pilot experiments' with non-political elections as a first step.

67 For more details see Lübbe-Wolff (n 14) 280-85.

tation document.[68] It also provides access to the contributions made by stakeholders and individual citizens under this procedure,[69] inviting users to provide feedback, as in the case of the consultation open between 26 March and 30 June 2015 on the issue 'Towards a new European Neighbourhood Policy'.[70]

As a matter of fact, citizens' participation in EU matters has not yet reached significant dimensions, and the question may be raised of whether the institutions, parties and political actors would be prepared —technically and in terms of mind, manpower and time— to respond adequately if citizens really made use of the instruments made available to them.[71] ICT solutions, like big data analysis and machine learning, also exist and are further developed for the screening of comments, suggestions and critiques, and the use of the new opportunities may develop over time depending on the increasing digital competence of people, and the need and willingness to participate and to make a difference. They are already in place for the online participation of interested people in conferences and forums, such as the Internet Governance Forum (IGF), where open discussions are organised on issues relating to the proper regulation of the internet.[72]

C. *An open constitutional process: The example of the Constitutional Convention*

An important example of an early application of the internet in a constitutional process was the establishment in 2001 of the 'futurum' website,

68 Website available at: www.ec.europa.eu/yourvoice/consultations/index_en.htm.

69 European Commission, Your voice in Europe, Closed consultations, available at: www.ec.europa.eu/yourvoice/consultations/2015/index_en.htm.

70 European Commission: Consultation 'Towards a new European Neighbourhood Policy', available at: www.ec.europa.eu/enlargement/neighbourhood/consultation/index_en.htm.

71 See the critical comments by C Schulzki-Haddouti, 'EU-Kommission gewährt Informationszugang nach Gutsherrenart', in *Heise online* of 17 August 2015, www.m.heise.de/newsticker/meldung/EU-Kommission-gewaehrt-Informationszugang-nach-Gutsherrenart-2781506.html.

72 See the website of the IGF: www.intgovforum.org/cms/; see also I Pernice, 'Global Constitutionalism and The Internet. Taking People Seriously' in R Hofmann (ed), *The Pasts and Futures of Law beyond the State* (Frankfurt, Campus, 2015), forthcoming (also as HIIG Discussion Paper Series No. 2015-01), fns 62-69.

which was set up by the Constitutional Convention in preparation for the reform of the Treaties.[73] Not only were all documents relevant to the work of the Convention available there, but the Convention also invited the public at large to comment and contribute with written proposals. Even if the process may not have triggered the anticipated level of participation, and in spite of other shortcomings in this attempt to organise an inclusive, Europe-wide discourse based upon the internet, this first experience of an open, transparent and participative process, including all the lessons learned from it, should be used by any future Convention as a model for the negotiations of amendments to the Treaties under Article 48 TEU.

III. Throughput Legitimacy in a digital Europe

If the effectiveness of the outcomes is a matter of *output* legitimacy, and elections, representation or the direct participation of the citizenry concerns *input* legitimacy, *throughput* legitimacy, as mentioned above, is about the quality of governance processes and concerns the internal decision-making processes, the inclusion of, and the interest mediation *with* the people. E-government and e-democracy in a number of issues favour the effectiveness of the outcomes and also the representation and participation of the citizenry in political or administrative processes, and it cannot be denied that the two overlap each other to a certain extent. What is more, it is possible to say that e-government and e-democracy, as described, encompass devices that enhance the inclusion of, and the interest mediation *with* the people in many cases and thus add to *throughput* legitimacy.

73 For a critical account of this 'Forum' see: M Bayer, Der Konvent zur Zukunft Europas. Deliberativ-demokratische Verfassunggebung für die Europäische Union – Zugleich ein Beitrag zum Begriff der Verfassunggebung (Baden-Baden, Nomos, 2007) in particular pp 405-12. The 'futurum'-website is closed, but the archive is available at: www.european-convention.europa.eu/EN/bienvenue/bienvenue2352.html?lang=EN. For the inauguration of the website see: www.europa.eu/rapid/press-release_IP-01-328_en.htm. For comments see: J Scott, 'The Culture of Constitution-Making? "Listening" at the Convention on the Future of Europe' (2002) 3 German Law Journal; A Frisch, 'Das Potential deliberativer Demokratietheorie für die Konzeptualisierung von Demokratie in der Europäischen Union' (2007) 3 Journal of Political Science 711, 724-28.

Throughput legitimacy covers, according to Vivien A. Schmidt, 'everything that transpires between the input and the output, encompassing issues of accountability, transparency, inclusiveness and openness', while, in contrast, 'throughput via corruption, incompetence or exclusion could be disastrous'.[74] Throughput in one sense concerns the conditions under which the will of the people makes its way through the institutions and is finally converted into effective action without being distorted. It is similar to, and may even be regarded as a kind of input-legitimacy. But it focuses more on *how* input becomes effective. What is at stake is the trust of the people in their institutions and, therefore, the proper functioning of the political system.

In respect of the multilevel structure of the EU, this trust, as fundamental for its legitimacy as it may be, is threatened by the complexity and opaqueness of the processes and the multiplicity of actors participating in the decision-making at the national and European levels. This multiplicity is not a problem in itself, but it frustrates attempts to ensure democratic control and, ultimately, political accountability. Here is the question of where and how the internet can offer a remedy to existing deficiencies so as to enhance *throughput legitimacy*. Any solution has to keep in mind that the EU system of governance, established by the Treaties, encompasses the citizens, the Member States —and their respective local and regional communities— as well as the institutions of the European Union.

A. *Transparency of decision-making processes*

Openness and transparency in the processes of decision-making, as has already been mentioned, seem to be an initial step forward by the internet in offering the public better understanding and control. The abovementioned provisions providing for electronic access to information and files, transparency in decision-making processes at specific websites, the public streaming of political debates, and openness on the part of the institutions in entering into a dialogue with the citizens and in consulting with the interested public, serve to reduce the complexity. In particular, the creation of interactive websites by the institutions to explain their objectives, giving an account of participating actors and their respective input and influ-

74 Schmidt (n 18) 286.

ence and stating at what stage the decision-making process actually is, but also giving interested citizens and civil society at large a meaningful opportunity to make their voice heard, are a first step towards more *throughput* legitimacy.

To take this a step further, there should be direct access, via electronic links, to the relevant files of the Commission, to the documents and work of the European Parliament, including protocols and archives of streams of the debates in committees and of the plenary, but also to any relevant documents relating to the meetings of the Council and the positions of the Member States. Openness and transparency cannot be limited to legislative processes though; this kind of openness is particularly important with regard to the European Council, the institution defining the 'general political directions and priorities' in accordance with Article 15 § 1 TEU. How can 'the open method of cooperation',[75] where decisions are taken at the highest political level, with the greatest impact upon the Member States and their internal policies and, in particular, on economic and financial policies, be confidential? Can we accept that these decisions are taken behind closed doors, excluding any parliamentary or public control? Even if these questions are regarded as 'matters concerning the European Union', to use the terms of the German Basic Law (Article 23 § 2 and 3), which provides for consultation of the Parliament before the government decides on the position it will defend at the Councils or European Council, how can a parliament control what the chancellor or prime minister really says during the deliberations of the institution, as long as the deliberations remain private? There are certainly matters that need to be kept confidential, but on the other hand there seems to be great potential for more transparency. This transparency can be provided through the internet and so help building trust in, and the legitimacy of, the Union and its policies.

75 Even if the conclusions or decisions taken within this framework are not legally binding, they are most relevant for the policy orientation of the Union; for more detail see: B Braams, *Koordinierung als Kompetenzkategorie* (Tübingen, Mohr & Siebeck, 2013) 9-76, 215-16, with proposals for enhancing transparency (ibid, pp 244-46).

B. Networks for parliamentary, administrative and judicial cooperation

Another example of an area where the internet already plays an important role, and where openness for the public could add to transparency and thus enhance trust and legitimacy, is the diverse networks of parliamentary, administrative and judicial cooperation established among the Member States, in which the Commission is more or less involved. To name but a few of these networks:

- the Interparliamentary Cooperation involving the European Parliament and the national Parliaments, as stipulated by Articles 9 and 10 of Protocol 1 to the Treaty of Lisbon, with COSAC and other Interparliamentary Conferences like that on CFSP, that established under Article 13 of the Fiscal Compact or the new Joint Parliamentary Scrutiny Group;[76] all this cooperation is supported by the Interparliamentary EU Information Exchange (IPEX).[77]
- the European Union Network for the Implementation and Enforcement of Environmental Law (IMPEL), which has been created for ensuring a better and harmonised implementation of European environmental directives throughout the Union;[78]
- the European Competition Network (ECN), which creates an effective mechanism to counter companies which engage in cross-border practices restricting competition through mutual information and cooperation of the competent national authorities.[79]
- the Body of European Regulators for Electronic Communications (BEREC) established by Regulation (EC) No 1211/2009 with the aim of contributing to the development and better functioning of the internal market for electronic communications networks and services.[80]

---

76 The Group was established under Article 51 of Regulation (EU) 2016/794 of 11 May 2016 on the European Union Agency for Law Enforcement Cooperation (Europol), OJ L 135/53, based upon and implementing Article 88 (2) TFEU. For a profound analysis of the practice of interparliamentary cooperation so far see: I Cooper, The Emerging Order of Interparliamentary Cooperation in the Post-Lisbon EU, in: D Jancic (ed.), *National Parliaments after the Lisbon Treaty and the Euro Crisis. Resilience or Resignation?* (OUP 2017) 227-46.

77 The platform for EU Interparliamentary Exchange (IPEX), see: http://www.ipex.eu/IPEXL-WEB/home/home.do.

78 www.impel.eu/.

79 www.ec.europa.eu/competition/ecn/index_en.html.

80 www.berec.europa.eu/eng/about_berec/what_is_berec/.

Smooth cooperation within these networks and the provision of public information about their existence, structure, tasks and actual policies are facilitated by the internet. Developing their openness for interactive communication with civil society, interested citizens and academics could allow the decisions taken at EU level to be considered part of the self-rule of the citizens in a transparent system of European governance. As European regulatory networks generally seem to be playing an increasing role in the formulation, deliberation, and implementation of EU policies,[81] it is important to explore in greater depth the possible applications of the internet with a view to ensuring more transparency in this field too.

C. *Public discourse on subsidiarity as a case of throughput legitimacy*

Last but not least, mention should be made of the attempts to ensure subsidiarity within the EU, in accordance with Article 5 TEU, and the application of the early warning system under Article 8 of the Subsidiarity Protocol (no. 2) to the Treaty of Lisbon. While this system, at first sight, looks like an instrument for defending the Member States and their regions against excessive action at the European level, it also triggers parliamentary and public debate within the Member States on the Commissions' legislative proposals, raises public awareness of the political questions involved and thus prevents any surprises being sprung on the citizens potentially affected by the measure in question. It is part of what the Commission presents, on its website, as the attempt to ensure 'better regulation', where it also invites the public to participate in making EU legislation more effective and less burdensome.[82] What is still missing, however, is transparency of the work of the institutions at the national level in this regard. As national parliaments play a crucial role in controlling and legitimising European legislation (Article 10 § 2 subpara 2 TEU and Protocol 1 on the role of national parliaments in the European Union), greater trans-

81 See the study by M Blauberger and B Rittberger, 'Conceptualizing and Theorizing EU Regulatory Networks' (2015) 9 *Regulation & Governance* 367.

82 European Commission, Better Regulation, www.ec.europa.eu/smart-regulation/better_regulation/key_docs_en.htm: 'The Commission would like to hear your views on how to make EU laws more effective and efficient via an online contact form. Your suggestions will be examined by the Commission and may be used to identify actions for simplification and burden reduction within the REFIT programme. The Commission publishes relevant contributions and feedback.'.

parency of their debates, hearings and positions on particular legislative proposals of the Commission, made public through the internet, would contribute considerably to increasing trust in, and the legitimacy of, the Union's policies.

Conclusions

If Article 1 § 2 TEU requires that within the EU decisions are taken as closely as possible to the citizen, this is not only a matter of strictly observing the principle of subsidiarity. This issue may also be considered from the point of view of the openness and transparency of the diverse decision-making processes of the Union, at all levels. Input, throughput and output are legitimising factors of the EU when the citizens are taken seriously and understand themselves to be the owners of the Union. The internet and thus methods of e-government and e-democracy seem to offer considerable opportunities for the inclusion of the citizens and civil society through tools offering easier information, transparency and participation.

If 'full e-democracy' means 'changing the operating system of the State', as Kai von Lewinski pointed out in 2005,[83] many developments at EU level can be viewed as steps aimed at making the most of ICT for the Union's operating system. It is time, nevertheless, to elaborate a systemic perspective of the diverse initiatives and innovations that are taking place. Similarly, time has come to reflect on a more proactive use of digital technologies to help bridge the gap between the citizen and the public authorities in the European Union. Both could contribute to the debates on a more democratic future of the European Union. This is what the present paper aims to initiate.

Taking such an initiative does not ignore the manifold problems that remain to be solved at a technical, legal and political level in order to allow the internet to develop its full potential for the benefit of democratic legitimacy. As recent experience shows, there are at least three fundamental conditions for the internet to provide such beneficial opportunities:

83 See K von Lewinski, 'Downstream of Information and Upstream of Signals: E-Democracy in Germany beyond E-Voting' in S Flogiatis et al (eds), *E-Government and E-Democracy. E-Gouvernement et E-Démocratie* (London, Esperia Publications, 2006) 205, 217-18.

- First, there is a need for a functioning internet and a proper system of internet governance. This is a global challenge and invites us to consider new forms of international or global ruling.
- Second, easy and effective internet access for everybody is necessary; it must be based upon the principle of net neutrality and allow all citizens effectively to take part online in European governance and politics.
- Third, provision must be made for a safe and trustworthy internet through effective regulation and technical provisions for data protection, as well as for cyber security at a global level.

After the Snowdon revelations and other recent discoveries of mass surveillance and spying activities by intelligence services, re-building trust in the internet[84] is crucial, and establishing a trust-building constitutional framework for global regulation[85] may be decisive if further progress is to be made towards overcoming the legitimacy deficits of the European Union.

84 For an attempt to achieve a new balance between trust and distrust, with regard to internet governance, see: J Hofmann, 'Constellations of Trust and Distrust in Internet Governance' in European Commission, *Report of the Expert Group 'Risks of Eroding Trust – Foresight on the Medium-Term Implications for European Research and Innovation Policies (TRUSTFORESIGHT)'* (Brussels, 2015), available at www.ssrn.com/abstract=2608414.

85 See I Pernice, 'Global Constitutionalism and The Internet', in: R Hofmann & S Kadelbach (eds.), *Law beyond the State. Past and Futures* (Campus Frankfurt am Main, 2016) p. 151-206.

Part Four
Re-organising Legitimacy in the European Union: Lessons Learned from the Financial Crisis

13 Institutional Reforms in the EU: Rethinking the Relation between the European Council and the Council

Federico Fabbrini

Abstract

This chapter discusses ideas for a new institutional relation between the European Council and the Council in the light of the ongoing debates about reforming the constitutional architecture of the EMU. The Lisbon Treaty formally recognised the European Council as a new EU institution, marking its separation from the Council. However, the integration between these two bodies remains strong. In fact, the Council suffers from several dysfunctionalities, since it is a single institution but meets in multiple configurations, some of which are de facto more important than others. As a result, the European Council has recurrently been asked to remedy the Council's shortcomings, often acting as a quasi-legislator. As this chapter suggests, an option that would be worth considering for the future is to revise the EU Treaties, by explicitly making the European Council, rather than the Council, the upper legislative house of the EU. Transforming the European Council into a kind of EU Senate would have a positive effect on the functioning of the EU, since it would make clear to citizens the dual nature of the EU. Reforming the relation between the European Council and the Council, however, requires efforts to redefine also the locus of executive power in the EU.

Introduction

The Euro crisis and the responses to it have prompted a new discussion about the institutional architecture of the European Union (EU). Although the constitutional set-up of the EU had been subjected to important changes by the Lisbon Treaty, which entered into force in December 2009, the almost simultaneous outbreak of the Euro crisis, and the swath of legal and institutional measures adopted to address it, have forced academics and policy-makers to restart the debate about institutional reforms in the EU.[1] In particular, institutional proposals driven by the aim to deepen and complete the European Economic and Monetary Union (EMU) have been considered in a report written in 2012 by the President of the European Council, jointly with the Presidents of the European Commission, the Eurogroup and the European Central Bank (ECB),[2] and more recently in June 2015 in a report prepared by the President of the European Commission, in cooperation with the Presidents of the European Council, the Eurogroup, the ECB and the European Parliament.[3]

The purpose of this chapter is to contribute to this ongoing debate by analysing the relation between the European Council and the Council, and presenting some thoughts on its possible development in the future.[4] As is well known, the Lisbon Treaty gave for the first time explicit recognition to the European Council in EU primary law. Moreover, the Lisbon Treaty took steps to separate the European Council from the Council. While in the past the presidency of the European Council was assigned to the Member State holding the six-month presidency of the Council,[5] the Lisbon Treaty created a new figure of semi-permanent European Council President, charged with providing direction and continuity in the institution's work.[6] At the same time, the Lisbon Treaty formally distinguished the functions of the European Council and the Council:[7] while the latter was tasked to exercise legislative and budgetary powers, together with the coordinating functions provided in the Treaties,[8] the former was vested with the responsibility to 'provide the Union with the necessary impetus for its

1 See, eg Ingolf Pernice et al, *A Democratic Solution to the Crisis* (Baden-Baden, Nomos, 2012); Franz Mayer, 'Eine Reform der institutionellen Architektur Europas?' in Stefan Kadelbach (ed), *Die Europäische Union am Scheideweg: Mehr oder weniger Europa?* (Baden-Baden, Nomos, 2015) 187.
2 President of the European Council, Final Report 'Towards a Genuine EMU', 5 December 2012.
3 President of the European Commission, Report, 'Completing Europe's EMU', 22 June 2015.
4 See also Federico Fabbrini, 'Arguments in Favor of an EU Senate' (2016) 22 *European Public Law* 485.
5 See Art 146 TEC.
6 See Art 15(6) TEU.
7 See Art 13 TEU.
8 See Art 16 TEU.

development and [to] define the general political direction and priorities thereof'[9] —with the explicit caveat that it 'shall not exercise legislative functions'.[10]

As this chapter maintains, however, notwithstanding the Lisbon Treaty's efforts to separate the European Council and the Council, these two institutions have remained closely interlinked. In fact, the European Council has increasingly come to play the role of a stop-gap for the deficiencies of the Council. As is again well known, the Council is one institution, but it works in different configurations.[11] The Council groups together the representatives of the governments of the EU Member States,[12] but its composition always varies, because national ministers change depending on the items to be discussed: e.g. agriculture, foreign affairs, finance or social affairs etc. While the design of the Council follows a functional logic, the lack of unity has also created problems: some compositions of the Council have become more important than others, producing imbalances in the policy-mix of the EU. Moreover, because representatives of the EU Member States in the various Council formations are not the same, it has become more difficult for states to reach agreement on legislation. Given this state of affairs, the European Council has frequently been called upon to step in, coordinating the work of the sectorial Councils, and striking package deals on legislative files which are beyond the reach of any single Council formation.

In the light of this, this chapter outlines a possible EU institutional reform aimed at reconfiguring the relation between the European Council and the Council for the future: as I propose, the European Council should absorb the legislative functions of the Council, leaving to the latter only administrative tasks (in the coordination of state policies), and preparatory duties (in instructing which files should be discussed by the European Council). As the chapter suggests, some important advantages would follow this institutional reform. First, the European Council, as a unitary body bringing together the heads of state and government of the EU Member States, would have the institutional capacity and political capital to strike deals among different legislative files, ensuring greater balance in the EU law-making process than that which currently exists due to the

9 Art 15(1) TEU.

10 Art 15(1) TEU.

11 See Art 16(6) TEU.

12 See Art 16(2) TEU.

fragmentation of the Council's formations. Second, the European Council, acting as a kind of upper house representing the EU Member States, would legislate on a par with the European Parliament, which would act as a lower house representing the EU's citizens —thus providing greater clarity on how the EU functions, and securing enhanced legitimacy for the laws adopted by the EU.

Needless to say, a reconfiguration of the European Council into a sort of EU Senate, vested with key legislative functions (to be exercised on a par with the European Parliament), would entail a rethinking of the locus of executive power in the EU.[13] In fact, today the European Council mainly considers itself as the chief executive organ of the EU.[14] However, the performance of the European Council as a collective executive has been meagre,[15] and for this reason I have argued elsewhere that the EU executive should be reformed by improving the powers and legitimacy of the President of the European Council, so as to make it the President of the EU as a whole:[16] as I have claimed, this new President of the EU should be endowed with appropriate executive powers of his own, and elected through a pan-European electoral process backing these new powers with adequate democratic legitimacy. Seen in this perspective, the reallocation of tasks between the European Council and the Council, with the attribution of legislative powers to the former in lieu of the latter, would also be a way to compensate the European Council for the loss of its executive powers —and thus should be seen as part and parcel of a broader package of constitutional reforms to put the EU institutional system on a more solid basis.[17]

---

13 See also Paul Craig, 'The Locus and Accountability of the Executive in the European Union' in Paul Craig and Adam Tomkins (eds), *The Executive and Public Law: Power and Accountability in Comparative Perspective* (Oxford, Oxford University Press, 2006), 315.

14 See also Deirdre Curtin, *Executive Power of the European Union: Law, Practices and the Living Constitution* (Oxford, Oxford University Press, 2009).

15 See also Hauke Brunkhorst, 'Collective Bonapartism – Democracy in the European Crisis' (2014) 15 *German Law Journal* 1177.

16 Federico Fabbrini, 'Austerity, the European Council and the Institutional Future of the EU' (2015) 22 *Indiana Journal of Global Legal Studies* 269.

17 For an analysis of a comprehensive overhaul of the EU constitutional architecture, of which the proposal advanced in this chapter is a part, see further Federico Fabbrini, *Economic Governance in Europe* (Oxford, Oxford University Press, 2016).

In sum, this chapter maintains that the relation between the European Council and the Council represents a critical juncture of the EU institutional architecture, and suggests that redefining the spheres of responsibility of these two institutions may constitute a positive step towards improving the functioning of tomorrow's EU. As such, the chapter is structured as follows. Section I underlines the shortcomings which are currently associated with the Council's fragmented work in legislative affairs, and outlines several unsuccessful attempts to address these. Section II then explains how, as a result of the shortcomings of the Council, the European Council has increasingly been dragged into the business of legislating, and articulates the proposal to codify this state of affairs by amending the Treaties so as to shift the legislative power from the Council to the European Council. Section III, finally, concludes by emphasising how the changes in the relations between the European Council and the Council could and should be part of a broader package of constitutional overhauls of the EU system of government.

I. The Council and its shortcomings in EU legislation

Since the foundation of the EU, the Council has been a central institution in the governance of the EU.[18] The Council plays multiple roles:[19] while performing administrative functions, for example by coordinating the policies of the Member States via the Open Method of Coordination (OMC),[20] and even some quasi-judicial functions, for instance in the enforcement of the Stability and Growth Pact,[21] one of its main tasks is the adoption of EU legislation[22] —a power it now shares with the European Parliament.[23] However, the action of the Council in the area of legislation

18 See Joseph HH Weiler, 'The Transformation of Europe' (1991) 100 *Yale Law Journal* 2403.

19 See Fiona Hayes-Renshaw, 'The Council of Ministers' in John Peterson and Michael Shackleton (eds), *The Institutions of the European Union*, 2nd edn (Oxford, Oxford University Press, 2012), 68.

20 See Art 121 TFEU.

21 See Art 126(11) TFEU.

22 See Helen Wallace et al, *Policy-Making in the European Union* (Oxford, Oxford University Press, 2010).

23 See Art 14 TEU.

has been an increasing subject of concern.[24] Although the Council is one institution, representing the governments of the EU Member States at ministerial level, it meets in different compositions: depending on the issue to be deliberated, national governments dispatch to Brussels the minister in charge of that specific portfolio at domestic level. The original logic of this solution was a functional one:[25] rather than simply having ministers of foreign affairs deliberate, states realised that it was more productive if negotiations in the Council were held between the competent line ministers. As a result of this, the configurations of the Council have grown over time, following the expansion of the legislative competences of the EU.[26] Yet, the multiplication of the Council formations has led to an inevitable problem of fragmentation.

Two downsides are associated with the lack of unity in the Council. Firstly, the work of the Council is repeatedly described as lacking consistency, since the various Council formations operate in parallel to each other, and with only very limited coordination between them.[27] Hence, even in files which are clearly overlapping —e.g. economic policy and social policy— the ability of the various formations of the Council to take into account each other's work is negligible. Secondly, some of the Council's formations have acquired more weight than others, creating relevant imbalances in the policy-mix of the EU. While the Foreign Affairs Council —grouping together the foreign affairs ministers of the Member States, now under the chairmanship of the High Representative for Foreign Affairs[28] —has a reserved role in EU foreign policy, the Economic and Financial Affairs (ECOFIN) Council —the formation grouping together the

24 The focus of this chapter is on the institutional shortcomings connected with the functioning of the Council, not on the substantive problems triggered by the exercise of legislative powers by the EU. On this see Sasha Garben, 'Confronting the Competence Conundrum: Democratising the European Union through an Expansion of its Legislative Powers' (2015) 35 *Oxford Journal of Legal Studies* 55.

25 See Pierre Pescatore, *Le droit de l'intégration*, reprinted ed (Bruxelles, Bruylant, 2005).

26 See Fiona Hayes-Renschaw and Helen Wallace, *The Council of Ministers* (Basingstoke, Palgrave Macmillan, 1997).

27 See already European Commission, Communication 'European Governance: A White Paper', 25 July 2001, COM (2001) 428 final, 25 (stating that the Council 'has lost its capacity to give political guidance and arbitrate between sectoral interests.').

28 See Art 18(3) TEU.

finance ministers— has emerged as the most senior Council configuration.[29] At the same time, since 1997 the ECOFIN Council has been complemented by the creation of the Eurogroup, a body which brings together the finance ministers of the Eurozone states.[30] The Eurogroup, which is now officially recognised by the Treaty and is also endowed with a semi-permanent president, has no legislative functions.[31] Nevertheless, it effectively works as a powerful sub-committee of the ECOFIN, setting most of the policy initiatives that are adopted by it.[32]

Scholars of EU law and governance have repeatedly emphasised how the EU tends to be more concerned about economic than social issues.[33] During the Euro crisis, furthermore, the EU social deficit has arguably been dramatised through the promotion of budgetary policies of fiscal consolidation which have heavily affected the functioning of the welfare state.[34] As Uwe Puetter has emphasised, however, the weakness of social policy in the EU is also the result of an imbalance between Council formations: the Employment, Social Policy, Health and Consumer Affairs (EPSCO) Council, which is nowadays in charge of social affairs, is much less prominent than the ECOFIN Council, with the result that the latter has more power to shape the EU agenda than the former.[35] In fact, in the non-legislative context of the European Semester, a framework in which the EU Member States coordinate their economic policies with the aim of en-

29 See also Uwe Puetter, *The European Council and the Council: New Intergovernmentalism and Institutional Change* (Oxford, Oxford University Press, 2014) 155.

30 See European Council Conclusions, Luxembourg, 12-13 December 1997, para 44.

31 See Protocol No. 14 on the Eurogroup.

32 See Uwe Puetter, *The Eurogroup* (Manchester, Manchester University Press, 2006).

33 See, eg Stefano Giubboni, *Social Rights and Market Freedoms in the European Constitution: A Labour Law Perspective* (Cambridge, Cambridge University Press, 2009).

34 See Claire Kilpatrick and Bruno De Witte (eds), 'Social Rights in Times of Crisis in the Eurozone', European University Institute Department of Law Working Paper No. 5/2014.

35 Uwe Puetter, 'European Council and Council Leadership in EU Socio-Economic Governance: Asymmetric Institutional Development and the Problem of Cross-Sectorial Policy Coordination', paper presented at the workshop 'The European Semester and the New Architecture of EU Socio-Economic Governance', UvA, Amsterdam, 11 April 2014 (on file with author).

suring greater EMU convergence,[36] the Employment and Social Protection Committees —two EPSCO preparatory committees— have complained that EU policy-making 'needs to work in a more balanced way'[37] and claimed that 'the EPSCO and ECOFIN Council formations must have primary responsibility for its implementation on the basis of an equitable partnership'.[38]

To address the challenge of unity in the work of the Council, the Member States have attempted to adopt a number of reforms. A first strategy has been to progressively reduce the number of Council configurations.[39] While at its maximum in 1996 the Council had 22 formations, the Rules of Procedure adopted by the Council in 2000 brought this number down to sixteen,[40] and in 2002 the heads of state and government of the EU Member States meeting in the European Council reduced it further to nine.[41] Today, the Rules of Procedure adopted by the Council in 2009 list ten official configurations of the Council;[42] and pursuant to Article 16(6) TEU the European Council may adopt a decision modifying this list.[43] Neverthe-

---

36 See Francesco Costamagna, 'The Impact of Stronger Economic Policy Co-Ordination on the European Social Dimension: Issues of Legitimacy' in Federico Fabbrini et al (eds), *The Constitutionalization of European Budgetary Constraints* (Oxford, Hart Publishing, 2014) 359.

37 Employment and Social Protection Committees, Joint Opinion 'Europe 2020 Strategy: Mid-term Review, Including the Evaluation of the European Semester', 3 October 2014, Doc. 13809/14, para 17.

38 Ibid, para 18.

39 See Bernard Steunenberg, 'Coordinating Sectoral Policymaking: Searching for Countervailing Mechanisms in the EU Legislative Process', CESifo Working Paper No. 888/2003.

40 Council Decision 2000/396/EC, ECSC, Euratom of 5 June 2000 adopting the Council's Rules of Procedure OJ 2000 L 149.

41 European Council Conclusions, Seville, 21-22 June 2002, SN 200/02.

42 Council Decision 2009/937/EU of 1 December 2009 adopting the Council's Rules of Procedure, OJ 2009 L 325/35, Annex 1 (listing the following 10 Council configurations: 1. General Affairs, 2. Foreign Affairs, 3. Economic and Financial Affairs, 4. Justice and Home Affairs, 5. Employment, social policy, health and consumer affairs, 6. Competitiveness – internal market, industry, and research, 7. Transport, telecommunication and energy, 8. Agriculture and Fisheries, 9. Environment, 10. Education, youth and culture).

43 See European Council Decision 2010/594/EU of 16 September 2010 amending the list of Council configurations OJ 2010 L 263/12 (reaffirming the list of Council configurations set in the Council Rules of Procedure, but changing the name of two compositions as follows: 6. Competitiveness – internal market, industry, research and space; 10. Education, youth, culture and sport).

less, the reduction of the Council configurations has not really worked as expected. To begin with, the recognition of a limited number of Council configurations has meant that some formations effectively continue to operate with sub-formations, since the breadth of the policy fields covered still requires the involvement of different line ministers, with well-known coordination problems.[44] In particular, the EPSCO Council is a mega-formation with three areas of responsibility: employment, social affairs, and equal opportunity. So even if technically the EPSCO Council is one, the ministers meeting in it depend on the file to be discussed, and are rarely the same.[45] As a result of the creation of heterogeneous Council formations, the disparity between configurations has continued, with cohesive formations such as ECOFIN playing a greater role than dis-homogenous ones such as EPSCO.[46]

A second strategy embraced by the EU Member States to address the challenge of unity has been to strengthen the role of the General Affairs Council (GAC).[47] In the run-up to the Lisbon Treaty, Member States decided to entrust to it a key coordinating task.[48] In fact, the GAC is one of the few Council configurations explicitly recognised in the text of the Treaty. Pursuant to Article 16(6) TEU, the GAC 'shall ensure consistency in the work of the different Council configurations. It shall prepare and ensure the follow-up to meetings of the European Council.' And, according to the current Rules of Procedure of the Council, the GAC 'shall be responsible for overall coordination of policies, institutional and administrative questions, horizontal dossiers which affect several of the [EU]'s policies [...] and any dossier entrusted to it by the European Council, having regard to operating rules for the [EMU].'[49] Nevertheless, as has been ob-

44 Puetter (n 35) 22.

45 Ibid, 23.

46 Ibid, 25.

47 See already European Council Conclusions, Helsinki, 10-11 December 1999, Annex III (stating that GAC's 'central responsibility for general horizontal issues, including overall policy coordination, means that it will have to manage an increasingly complex external and internal agenda, dealing with major multidisciplinary and interpillar dossiers.'.).

48 See Jean-Claude Piris, *The Lisbon Treaty: A Legal and Political Analysis* (Cambridge, Cambridge University Press, 2010) 209.

49 Art 2(2) Council Rules of Procedure.

served, the GAC has failed to fulfil its mandate.[50] A possible explanation for this has to do with its composition: in principle, the GAC should bring together the EU Affairs Ministers of the Member States, but often these are junior ministers in national governments. Moreover, because the GAC does not debate substantive issues, but simply assesses the activities of the other Council formations, ministers have limited incentives to attend, and frequently dispatch permanent representatives (i.e. state ambassadors based in Brussels). As a result of this, the GAC has very limited political weight. Hence, even after the entry into force of the Lisbon Treaty, the Council continues to face a challenge of unity.[51]

In order to address this state of affairs, a third bold strategy had been advanced at the time of the European Constitutional Convention.[52] Following a proposal articulated by the Vice-President of the Convention Giuliano Amato, it was suggested that a special composition of the Council, exclusively dedicated to the job of legislating, ought to be created.[53] The essence of the proposal was that, while different Council configurations could remain in place for subject-specific policy-coordination, only a Legislative Affairs Council —grouping the delegates of the national governments in charge of EU affairs— would be empowered to pass bills jointly with the European Parliament.[54] This idea would have effectively solved the challenge of unity, with its related problems of incoherence and imbalance between the Council's configurations. It would have created an upper legislative chamber in which the representatives of the EU Member States could secure coordination between the various legislative files, balance the issues at stake in different substantive areas, and strike deals.[55] And it would have increased the ability of national parliaments to control the action of national representatives in the Council, by centralising ac-

50 See Ignacio Molina, 'The Role of the General Affairs Council Revisited in Light of the Experience of 18 Months with the Lisbon Treaty', Real Instituto Elcano Working Paper No. 105/2011.

51 Ibid.

52 See Jean-Claude Piris, *The Constitution for Europe: A Legal Analysis* (Cambridge, Cambridge University Press, 2006) 109.

53 See also Ben Crum, 'Tailoring Representative Democracy in the European Union: Does the European Constitution Reduce the Democratic Deficit?' (2005) 11 *European Law Journal* 452, 461.

54 See Art 23 Draft Treaty Establishing a Constitution for Europe, 18 July 2003.

55 I am grateful to Giuliano Amato for making this point clear to me.

countability within a single person charged to vote on EU legislation on behalf of the state.[56]

Nevertheless, the proposal of a Legislative Affairs Council advanced by the Convention was rejected by the Member States at the ensuing intergovernmental conference.[57] While the main opposition to the proposal came (unsurprisingly) from national ministers, the heads of state and government of the EU also disliked the idea of an institution which would concentrate significant law-making power.[58] Because, according to the proposal, the Legislative Affairs Council would have been composed of ministers specialised in EU affairs, prime ministers and presidents feared that these ministers would come to wield significant autonomy from them; and ultimately, that they could become a threat to their power and status at the domestic level.[59] Scholars, in fact, have pointed out how national ministers sitting in the Council are progressively Europeanised:[60] ministers develop personal bonds with each other, and strategically seek to mutually support each other —also vis-à-vis their national colleagues and constituencies. Often decisions reached by competent ministers in Brussels are then presented in national capitals as fait accompli, with limited or no leeway for prime ministers, or the ministers of other portfolios, to re-open the negotiations. This is particularly true for the ECOFIN Council, and finance ministers have become prominent players at the domestic level — often in competition with the prime minister— due to their involvement in decision-making at EU level on the key national deficit and debt targets.[61]

In the settlement reached by the Lisbon Treaty, therefore, the heads of state and government of the EU Member States worked to reaffirm their

56 See Crum (n 53) 461.

57 See Paolo Ponzano, 'Les institutions de l'Union' in Giuliano Amato et al (eds), *Genesis and Destiny of the European Constitution* (Bruxelles, Bruylant, 2007) 439, 459.

58 See Crum (n 53) 462.

59 See Piris (n 52) 110.

60 See eg Christopher Bickerton, *European Integration: From Nation States to Member States* (Oxford, Oxford University Press, 2012).

61 An example of this state of affairs is provided by the repeated tensions which emerged in the system of government of Italy in the decade from 2003 to 2013 between the Prime Minister and the Minister of Finance, on the design of budgetary policy. See on this Tommaso Giupponi, 'Il governo nel sistema bipolare' in Augusto Barbera and Tommaso Giupponi (eds), *La prassi degli organi costituzionali* (Bologna, Bononia University Press, 2008) 51.

preeminence in the EU decision-making system[62] —and while they set aside the proposal for a Legislative Affairs Council, they entrenched their seniority vis-à-vis their ministers who meet in the various Council configurations. According to Article 15 TEU, the European Council 'shall define the general political directions and priorities' of the EU, and, based on Article 16 TEU, the Council is tasked to follow up on the European Council's requests. Moreover, at the height of the Euro crisis the heads of state and government of the Eurozone states took steps to affirm their position also in the governance of EMU, reining in the autonomy of the ECOFIN Council, and of the Eurogroup.[63] In particular, the Fiscal Compact created a new forum, the Euro Summit, endowed with a semi-permanent President, in which the heads of state and government would meet, jointly with the President of the Commission and the President of the ECB.[64] And it clearly established a vertical hierarchy between the Euro Summit (grouping prime ministers and presidents) and the Eurogroup (grouping finance ministers) by stating that '[t]he body charged with the preparation and follow up to the Euro Summit meetings shall be the Eurogroup and its President may be invited to attend such meetings for that purpose.'[65]

In sum, while often scholars criticising the EU legislative process have focused on the shortcomings of the European Parliament,[66] this chapter has emphasised how the Council also suffers from a significant dysfunctionality. Because the Lisbon Treaty has not successfully tackled the fragmentation of the Council's compositions, a challenge of unity continues to affect the work of the EU upper legislative house.

62 See also Frederic Eggermont, *The Changing Role of the European Council in the Institutional Framework of the European Union* (Cambridge, Intersentia, 2012) (tracking the growing role of the EU heads of state and government).

63 See Dermot Hodson, *Governing the Euro Area in Good Times and Bad* (Oxford, Oxford University Press, 2011) ch 3.

64 See Christian Calliess, 'The Governance Framework of the Eurozone and the Need for a Treaty Reform' in Federico Fabbrini et al (eds), *What Form of Government for the European Union and the Eurozone?* (Oxford, Hart Publishing, 2015) 37.

65 Art 12(4) Fiscal Compact.

66 See further Federico Fabbrini, 'Representation in the European Parliament: Of False Problems and Real Challenges' (2015) 75 *Zeitschrift für ausländisches öffentliches Recht und Völkerrecht* 823.

II. The European Council and its potential in EU legislation

As was pointed out in the previous section, the challenge of unity traditionally burdening the Council has so far remained unanswered. Because of the fragmentation between the Council's configurations, the ability of the various formations to coordinate their work —and the possibility of ministers striking compromises through horse-trading, where a vote in support of a bill in a given policy area is rewarded with future support in another policy area— remains limited.[67] Moreover, by establishing the European Council as the top forum for decision-making, the Lisbon Treaty created strong incentives for national ministers to send complex legislative files upwards to the table of the EU heads of state and government. Because of the high political salience of some of the legislative files that the Council debates, national ministers prefer to refer the matter to the European Council, especially when agreement is difficult.[68] In fact, on some issues the Treaties explicitly foresee this possibility.[69] As a result, an ironic development has occurred: as mentioned in the Introduction, Article 15(1) TEU officially proclaims that the European Council 'shall not exercise legislative functions' —with the aim of making the European Council an executive body. Yet, as Jörg Monar has pointed out, in reality the European Council has increasingly been dragged into the business of legislating, coming to play the role of a 'quasi legislator'.[70]

---

67 See Bernard Steunenberg, 'Deciding Among Equals: the Sectoral Councils of the European Union and their Reform' in Manfred Holler et al (eds), *European Governance* (Tübingen, Mohr Siebeck, 2003) 1.

68 The fact that the Council always seeks to decide by consensus, even when QMV would be possible, has increased the number of occasions on which the Council has preferred to move controversial files upward to the European Council. See on the use of QMV in the Council Stefan van den Bogaert, 'Qualified Majority Voting in the Council: First Reflections on the New Rules' (2008) 15 *Maastricht Journal of European & Comparative Law* 97.

69 See Arts 82(3) and 83(3) TFEU (allowing a Member State to request that a draft directive in the field of criminal procedural law and the approximation of substantive criminal law be referred to the European Council), and Art 48 TFEU (allowing a Member State to request that a draft measure in the field of social security be referred to the European Council if it affects important aspects of its social security system).

70 Jörg Monar, 'The European Union's Institutional Balance of Power after the Treaty of Lisbon' in *The European Union after the Treaty of Lisbon* (Luxembourg, Publication Office of the EU, 2011) 60, 75.

As the challenge of unity continues to affect the Council, the European Council has turned for parts of its activities into a kind of upper legislative chamber, in which heads of state and government ensure consistency between the files discussed by the various Council configurations and strike package deals which are beyond the reach of the separate Council formations. The example of the EU regulation on patent protection,[71] or more recently, the deliberation surrounding the adoption of an EU legislative response to the challenge of international migration,[72] attest to the extent to which the European Council has been getting involved in the details of legislative drafting that should formally be a responsibility of the Council. Otherwise, although the Lisbon Treaty sought to institutionally separate the Council and the European Council,[73] the integration between these two bodies has remained extremely strong —a fact which is perhaps inevitable considering that the same people (i.e. members of national governments) staff the two institutions.[74] Significantly, the European Council and the Council do not even have separate websites,[75] and the Legal Service of the Council acts as the counsellor also of the European Council in judicial proceedings.[76]

Given this state of affairs, it may be wondered whether a future treaty reform should not simply take stock of this fact and institutionalise the role of the European Council as that of a high legislative body, on a par with the EP. While the fragmentation of the Council compositions undermines the coherence of EU action, and creates imbalances in the EU policy-mix, the European Council, as a single institution, would constitute a

71 See Franklin Dehousse, 'The Unified Court on Patents: The New Oxymoron of European Law', Egmont Royal Institute for International Relations Paper No. 60/2013, 25 (explaining the recurrent interventions by the European Council in the drafting of detailed aspects of the EU regulations and related agreement on the creation of a unitary patent system).

72 See European Council Conclusions, 26 June 2015, EUCO 22/15 (formalising a very detailed agreement between the Member States in the field of immigration, setting measures for the relocation and resettlement of third country nationals which had been proposed by the European Commission pursuant to Art 78(3) TFEU).

73 See Art 13 TEU (listing the European Council and the Council as separate institutions).

74 I am grateful to Andy Moravcsik for making this point clear to me.

75 See www.consilium.europa.eu/en/home/ (last visited 2 July 2015).

76 See Case C-370/12 *Pringle v Government of Ireland*, judgment of 27 November 2012, nyr.

suitable forum in which the Member States could strike deals and reach a compromise on important legislative initiatives. As this chapter suggests, in other words, the European Council has the potential to play a positive role in EU legislation *as an EU Senate* of a sort. Needless to say, the Council could continue to ensure preparatory work for the European Council, and it would retain administrative powers, especially in the coordination of Member States' policies under the framework of the OMC. Moreover, the European Council could still delegate tasks to the Council, including the adoption of implementing (regulatory) acts. But the Council would be deprived of legislative powers, with this competence now being officially entrusted to the European Council through a formal amendment of the EU Treaties.[77]

From a comparative constitutional point of view, the solution I am envisaging here would make the EU system somehow institutionally similar to that of Germany. As is well known, in the German architecture for law-making a lower house, the Bundestag, directly representing the German citizens, coexists with an upper house, the Bundesrat, which directly represents the executives of the 16 Länder that compose the German Federal Republic.[78] Article 51 of the German Basic Law does not specify who exactly represents each of the Länder within the Bundesrat, since this is to be determined by the constitution of each Land: but in general it is the Minister-Presidents of the various Länder, that is, the chiefs of the Länder governments, who lead each Land's delegation, and directly participate in the voting.[79] Of course, the German example is not truly analogous to what is being proposed here: in the German system the Bundesrat is not involved in the approval of every bill,[80] and on some issues the Bundestag enjoys

77 The institutional reform proposed here only affects the allocation of powers between the European Council and the Council, so is without prejudice to the competences of the Commission, on which see John Peterson, 'The College of Commissioners', in John Peterson and Michael Shackleton (eds), *The Institutions of the European Union*, 2nd edn (Oxford, Oxford University Press, 2012) 96.

78 See Arthur Gunlicks, *The Länder and German Federalism* (Manchester, Manchester University Press, 2003).

79 See also BVerfG 2 BvF 1/02, judgment of 18 December 2002 (upholding the practice according to which the Prime Ministers of the Länder lead the vote in the Bundesrat, casting the vote of that Land together and uniformly).

80 See Art 77 Basic L. Germ. (setting rules on the legislative procedure and distinguishing situations when the approval of legislation by the Bundesrat is required from situations in which it is not).

supremacy over the Bundesrat.[81] In the EU, on the other hand, the parity between the two houses of the legislature would have to be absolute. In fact, it may even be conceivable that the European Council should play a greater role than the European Parliament —just as in the United States the Senate (the upper house) has more competences than the House of Representatives (the lower house), e.g. in foreign affairs.[82] Yet the institutional logic which inspires the composition of the Bundesrat could be replicated in the EU: the European Council, as the body representing the top executives of the Member States, would be directly involved in approving legislation for the EU, together with the European Parliament.[83]

The proposal to vest in the European Council, rather than in the Council, the function of passing bills jointly with the European Parliament would have several advantages. First, it would assign to each institution the powers that, comparatively, it can exercise best: as Neil Komesar has argued from a law and economics perspective, functions should be attributed among different institutions based on their capacity to perform a given task comparatively better than others.[84] From this point of view, while the fragmented composition of the Council has weighed negatively on its legislative role, the unitary nature of the European Council makes it better placed to exercise legislative powers. At the same time, while the collective nature of the European Council makes it unsuitable for performing executive functions in the EU, the collegial nature of this body renders it an ideal candidate to act as an upper legislative house.[85] In fact, both lawyers and political scientists have pointed out how the role of the European Council as an EU executive has produced multiple dilemmas of ef-

---

81 See also Arthur Gunlicks, 'Legislative Competences, Budgetary Constraints and the Reform of Federalism in Germany' in Michael Burgess and Alan Tarr (eds), *Constitutional Dynamics in Federal Systems* (Montreal, McGill-Queen's University Press, 2012) 61.

82 See Art II, Sec 2, cl 2 US Const. (subjecting the presidential power to make treaties to the approval by two thirds of the senators).

83 See also Robert Schütze, *From Dual to Cooperative Federalism* (Oxford, Oxford University Press, 2009) (defending the possibility of comparing institutional design in the EU with fully-fledged federal systems like the US and Germany).

84 Neil Komesar, *Imperfect Alternatives: Choosing Institutions in Law, Economics and Public Policy* (Chicago, Chicago University Press, 1994).

85 See *ceteris paribus* Paul Craig, *The Treaty of Lisbon* (Oxford, Oxford University Press, 2010), 93 (claiming that the decision to maintain one commissioner per member state has made the Commission, with a college of 28 members, unfit to act as an effective executive authority).

fectiveness,[86] and raised major problems of legitimacy.[87] As a congress of 28 state presidents and prime ministers, however, the European Council could provide a valuable forum to deliberate on legislation, in the form of an EU Senate.

Second, the proposal to transform the European Council into the upper legislative house of the EU would play a valuable role in making clear to the people the dual nature of our Union of states and citizens,[88] and improving the separation of powers in the EU.[89] A serious and recurrent concern is that the functioning of the EU is too complicated for the people to understand.[90] The reform proposed here, however, would help to address this state of affairs, making it clearer to the people how the EU functions. On the one hand, the reform proposed in this chapter would entrench bicameralism and vest EU legislation with the special democratic imprimatur deriving from its explicit approval, not only by (a majority of) MEPs in the European Parliament, but also by (a qualified majority of) national leaders in the European Council. On the other hand, the reform proposed here would more clearly separate the realm of legislation (where the European Council and the European Parliament would be involved) from that of administration and policy coordination (which would be left to the Council and the Commission). If combined with a reform of the EU executive power,[91] therefore, the transformation of the European Council into an EU Senate would simplify the organisation of public authority in the EU constitutional system.

All in all, therefore, the re-definition of the relation between the European Council and the Council would have a positive effect on the legiti-

---

86 See Sergio Fabbrini, 'Intergovernmentalism and Its Limits: Assessing the European Union's Answer to the Euro Crisis' (2013) 46 *Comparative Political Studies* 1003.

87 See Deirdre Curtin, 'Challenging Executive Dominance in European Democracy' (2014) 77 *Modern Law Review* 1.

88 See also Walter Van Gerven, *The European Union: A Polity of States and Peoples* (Oxford, Hart Publishing, 2005) 362 (emphasising the dual nature of legitimacy in the EU).

89 See also Christoph Möllers, *The Three Branches: A Comparative Model of Separation of Powers* (Oxford, Oxford University Press, 2013) 169-71 (discussing the blurred recognition of the principle of separation of powers in the EU).

90 See also Laeken Declaration, 15 December 2001, SN 273/01 (stating that 'the European institutions must be brought closer to its citizens' so as to address the democratic challenge facing the EU).

91 See below the text accompanying n 106.

macy of the EU system of governance. If it is true that the simplicity of a constitutional system is the prerequisite for its success, the clarity of the EU institutional architecture has to be improved.[92] For better or for worse, heads of state and governments have acquired growing visibility in the national democratic processes[93] —a dynamic fuelled by European integration.[94] Since action by heads of state and government —including at EU level— attracts the attention of most of the citizens,[95] transferring to them a share of the EU legislative authority would enhance the accountability and the transparency of EU law-making, as the exercise of legislative power by the European Council would be the object of greater public scrutiny than is the case for the Council. At the same time, by simplifying the EU governance system, and by assigning different functions to different institutions, the reform proposed here would improve the responsibility of each actor, and the clarity of the EU constitutional architecture.

The proposal to attribute to the European Council the role of an upper legislative house, however, must be defended against several criticisms. Leaving aside the fact that the reform envisaged here would require a treaty change —with the connected problem of unanimity[96]—, a first criticism that can be made from a policy perspective against the proposal advanced here is that heads of state and government are too busy in running their Member States to take on this job.[97] However, there are arguments to overcome this concern. On the one hand, according to the proposal made in this chapter, ministers in the various Council configurations (and permanent representatives within COREPER) would continue to undertake preparatory work for the European Council. In fact, the idea of entrusting legislative powers to the European Council follows the logic which in-

---

92 See Eoin Carolan, *The New Separation of Powers* (Oxford, Oxford University Press, 2010).

93 See Thomas Poguntke & Paul Webb, *The Presidentialization of Politics* (Oxford, Oxford University Press, 2005).

94 See Karl Magnus Johansson & Jonas Tallberg. 'Explaining Chief Executive Empowerment: EU Summitry and Domestic Institutional Change' (2010) 33 *West European Politics* 208.

95 See Alicia Hinarejos, *The Euro Area Crisis in Constitutional Perspective* (Oxford, Oxford University Press, 2015) Ch 6 (analysing the action of head of states and government at the European level, and their oversight at the national level, in the context of the Euro-crisis).

96 See Art 48 TEU.

97 I am grateful to Paul Craig for making this point clear to me.

spired the idea of a Legislative Affairs Council,[98] but also takes stock of the fact that only heads of state and government have the political weight to take salient decisions and, if need be, strike compromises between the files discussed by sectorial ministers.[99] On the other hand, the reality of Euro crisis management has revealed how the leaders of the EU Member States now meet with great frequency, sometimes as often as every other week.[100] Considering that the EU is recurrently criticised for being over-regulatory, and for enacting too many bills, regular monthly meetings by the European Council would appear to be a reasonable time-frame for the adoption of EU legislation.[101]

A second criticism that could be made against the proposal to empower the European Council with the legislative function (on a par with the European Parliament) is that this could paradoxically increase the degree of technocratic governance in the EU.[102] Because —as has just been emphasised— heads of state and government are mainly concerned with running their respective Member States, there is a risk that they may devote too little attention to their new responsibility as EU legislators, thus leaving EU bureaucrats with more room for making decisions. However, this risk should not be over-estimated. On the one hand, even today technocrats already play a major role in the work of the Council: although political scientists debate about the exact percentage, there is little doubt that many EU legislative measures are agreed upon by lower-level officials and simply rubberstamped by the Council.[103] On the other hand, although bureaucrats would probably continue to play a relevant role even if the European Council were to become the EU upper legislative house, it is

98 See the above text accompanying nn 52-65.

99 See also Luuk van Middelaar, *The Passage to Europe* (New Heaven, Yale University Press, 2013) (suggesting that the expansion of EU competences in high salience areas has required a greater involvement of the European Council, as opposed to the Council).

100 See also Dieter Smeets and Marco Zimmerman, 'Did the EU Summits Succeed in Convincing the Markets during the Recent Crisis?' (2013) 51 *Journal of Common Market Studies* 1158.

101 See also European Commission, Communication on 'Regulatory Fitness and Performance Programme (REFIT): State of Play and Outlook', 18 June 2014, COM (2014) 368 final (pledging to fight over-regulation).

102 I am grateful to Jean-Victor Louis for making this point clear to me.

103 See Frank Häge, 'Who Decides in the Council of the European Union?' (2008) 46 *Journal of Common Market Studies* 533 (discussing the impact of preparatory bodies on the work of the Council itself).

plausible that their activity would only focus on questions of low politics, while legislation on questions of high politics would directly trigger the attention of the members of the European Council.[104] With the support of preparatory bodies, prime ministers and presidents could focus their negotiations and deliberations only on major outstanding issues.

In sum, this section has proposed reconfiguring the relation between the Council and the European Council by shifting to the latter the legislative powers of the former. While the Council has been hampered by its fragmentation, the European Council as a unitary body could perform a potentially positive role as an upper legislative house, vested with legislative powers on a par with the European Parliament.

III. Conclusion

In a recent article Jürgen Habermas has restated the case in favour of the development of a transnational democracy in the EU, and identified a number of obstacles, which must be addressed on the road towards democracy in Europe.[105] Building on his previous criticism of the intergovernmental activity of the European Council, which he had defined as a form of 'post-democratic executive federalism',[106] Habermas also emphasised the need to reconfigure the relation between the European Council and the Council.[107] The aim of this chapter has been to analyse the relation between the European Council and the Council and to consider some possible developments for the future. Given the growing debate at the highest political level about the future of the EU's constitutional architecture — with the possible revision of the EU founding treaties, notably in the field of EMU—, this chapter has attempted to address a critical juncture in the institutional system of the EU. While the European Council was only recognised as an official institution of the EU by the Lisbon Treaty, which

104 See Ben Rosamond, *Theories of European Integration* (Basingstoke, Palgrave Macmillan, 2000) (explaining theories of integration and the distinction between high politics and low politics).

105 See Jürgen Habermas, 'Democracy in Europe: Why the Development of the EU into a Transnational Democracy is Necessary and How it is Possible' (2015) 21 *European Law Journal* 546.

106 See Jürgen Habermas, *The Crisis of the European Union* (Cambridge, Polity Press, 2012) 12.

107 See Habermas (n 106) 555.

entered into force in 2009, a few years of practical experience revealed the need to reconsider the relation between the European Council and the Council, identify its weaknesses, and propose possible options for reform in the future.

As was explained in this chapter, the Council, in the exercise of its legislative powers, suffers from a serious dysfunctionality. The fragmentation between the various Council formations —which derives from the fact that the Council is one institution but meets in different compositions — has produced a major lack of coordination among legislative files, and the seniority of several of the Council's configurations vis-à-vis others has generated relevant imbalances in the policy-mix of the EU. At the same time, both the efforts to reduce the number of the Council's formations, and the attempt to strengthen the role of the GAC as a clearing-house for the activities of the Council, have failed to achieve their desired goal. A more audacious idea —the creation of a Legislative Affairs Council— was discarded at the time of the European Convention as a potential threat to the standing of the EU heads of state and government. As a result of that, however, the European Council has increasingly been called upon to perform quasi-legislative functions. While only the European Council has the political clout to decide on a number of legislative files, the fragmentation between the Council configurations hampers the capacity of state ministers to reach trans-sectorial compromises, making the European Council the real body in which states can strike package deals on legislation.

Given this state of affairs, in this chapter it has been proposed that a shift of legislative power from the Council to the European Council should be institutionalised by amending the Treaties to this end. While the Council would retain coordinating tasks in the OMC, the European Council would act as the EU upper legislative house, passing legislation on a par with the European Parliament. It goes without saying that the proposal advanced in this chapter would also imply a significant conceptual reconfiguration of the constitutional architecture of the EU as far as the executive power is concerned. EU heads of state and government meeting in the European Council today mainly perceive themselves as the executive branch of the EU. But in my view their performance as a collective government has been meagre, and full of shortcomings. In fact, elsewhere I have made the case for an EU constitutional reform strengthening the power and the legitimacy of the President of the European Council, with the aim of transforming this institution into the presidency of the Union.[108] The idea of formalising the role of the European Council as a kind of EU Senate should therefore be seen as part of a broader programme of constitutional reforms aimed at creating an effective and accountable executive power in the EU:[109] while the European Council would lose executive power to a European President, it would gain the legislative power from the Council.

In conclusion, the proposal advanced in this chapter outlines an ambitious program of treaty revisions for the EU, which seeks to complement the ideas already advanced in the debate about completing EMU. In fact, the proposal to rethink the relation between the European Council and the Council goes beyond the simple realm of economic governance and affects the overall functioning of the EU as a political project: as such it could be considered in the context of the window of opportunity that Brexit —the withdrawal of the United Kingdom from the EU following the June 2016 referendum— creates for future institutional reforms in the EU.[110]

108 Fabbrini (n 16).

109 See also French Minister of the Economy Emmanuel Macron and German Minister of the Economy Sigmar Gabriel, Op-Ed, "Europe Cannot Wait Any Longer", The Guardian, 3 June 2015 (stating that "to make its institutions work [...] Europe will need to address its democratic deficit as well as its executive one.")

110 See further Federico Fabbrini, 'How Brexit Opens a Window of Opportunity for Treaty Reform in the EI' Bertelsmann Stiftung paper1/2016.

14 A Roadmap to Exit the Crisis: Democracy and Justice in Europe

Miguel Poiares Maduro

Introduction

The crisis of the Euro is a European crisis. It is so not only, or even predominantly, because of the importance of the Euro in the context of European integration or the extent to which a failure of the Euro might impact on other areas of European integration. The reason why the Euro crisis highlights a deeper crisis of Europe is twofold. First, as I will try to make clear in the following pages, what explains the fiscal crisis and its impact on the Euro are different democratic malfunctions that the States and the Union have not properly addressed. Second, the EU's poor reaction to the crisis is simply a symptom of a much deeper existential malaise in the process of European integration and the nature of its authority.

The paper is a first attempt at identifying these issues and a roadmap to address them. My core thesis is that the level of interdependence in Europe is such that it can only be effectively and legitimately governed with a European polity but that the latter can only legitimately organise its democratic authority if it is supported in a European political space and embedded in a theory of justice.

I argue that the future governance of the EU must depart from a revised justification of the project of European integration. A justification that focuses on the democratic and social challenges faced by the States and the EU value in answering them. The EU should not be constructed as a challenge to national democracy but, instead, as offering renewed possibilities for democracy and social justice where States can no longer offer them. In this context, it is fundamental for democracy to be linked to a theory of justice in the EU. Citizens should be able to understand the benefits flowing from the process of European integration but also why those benefits come with certain duties towards others. Rights must be complemented by political empowerment and civic solidarity for the Union to be able to develop a really legitimate form of economic and political governance.

I start by providing a democratic explanation for the crisis and the Union's failure in successfully addressing it so far. The origin of the crisis can be found in the democratic failures of some states and the externalities they imposed on others but also in the incapacity of national democracies to control excessive cross-border capital flows. The Union's failure to solve the crisis is, instead, imputable to the diffuse character of its political authority and its excessive reliance on national politics. The latter are incapable of internalising the consequences of the interdependence generated by the Euro and integrated markets. As a consequence the Union can't, de facto, govern and its policies are a prisoner of national politics. The real EU democratic deficit is the absence of European politics.

The second part discusses two models of governance for the Euro area as I review some of the proposals put forward so far. One model has at its core the Stability Compact. The other complements the discipline enshrined in such a compact with instruments of financial solidarity and debt mutualisation. Either through the ESM or jointly issued bonds, for example, states insure each other's debt. For reasons I detail below I have serious reservations that such models can work. Their dependence on a permanent negotiation with national democracies (and the multitude of actors therein) will prevent them from providing the certainty that markets require. As to democracy, they are bound to put national democracies on a collision course. Some states will perceive themselves as supporting others (and their moral hazard) while these others will feel that they are being governed by the former. A key finding is that financial solidarity in the EU must be detached from transfers between states and related, instead, to the wealth generated by the process of European economic integration.

My alternative proposal departs from the previous idea. It requires an EU budget capable of providing the Union with the necessary financial muscle to address and prevent future crises. Such a budget will dispense with national democracies and their citizens insuring each other. Their liability will be limited to the contributions to the EU budget resulting from the EU's own resources. These resources are, in turn, linked to EU-generated wealth: economic activities that the EU makes possible and have mostly benefited from the internal market. The legitimacy of these resources is further enhanced by linking them to forms of revenue that have made use of increased economic mobility to lower their tax burden at a national level. The proposal suggests using the enhanced EU budget for two fundamental purposes: a stability fund providing collateral to state-issued debt when necessary and subject to an adjustment program; new EU policies aimed at addressing asymmetries in the economic and monetary union. In addition, I argue that the Union needs more than simply new policies. It needs to change the nature of its policies so as to improve how they 'communicate' with citizens and increase their capacity to induce real systemic reforms in the States. These changes will also allow the Union to complement the increase of discipline it can impose on states with positive incentives. The final pillar of the model proposed addresses political integration. More than institutions my focus is on politics. It's by transforming the character of politics at EU level that we will be able to infuse its institutional system with real democratic potential. I try to explain how to do this.

I. Two Narratives and Democracy

When the Euro was created it was presented as a big achievement of European integration but the rationale behind it was never fully articulated before European citizens. It was perhaps thought that any attempt to do so would engulf it in endless political debates about the nature of European integration and the impact of the single currency on national sovereignty. Instead, the Euro seemed an ideal way to deepen European integration in the usual way: as a technocratic regime disciplining (but not replacing) national democracies. The governance regime emphasised this technocratic dimension of the project with a focus on the role of the European Central Bank and its insulation from political pressures. Economic and fiscal politics were left to the states which were deprived of its role in monetary policy but, for the rest, were supposed to comply with certain limited rules that proved to be too weak to prevent the current crisis. The hope was that the model could protect both national and EU different legitimacies by a strict separation between the technocratic and political dimensions. The price to be paid for it was leaving outside the Euro governance fundamental dimensions of economic and fiscal policy impacting on a monetary Union. This was necessary in order to preserve the space for national politics.

This separation has failed. We have found out that it is not possible to have a European Monetary Union fundamentally dependent on national politics. Yet, though many now recognise the political dimension of the Euro project and call the present crisis a political crisis, we are far from articulating what exactly that means and its consequences. In order to think correctly about the future democratic governance of the EU we have to clearly understand the political and democratic dimension of the current crisis.

There are two narratives of the current crisis. The first is the dominant narrative. It puts most of the blame for the crisis on some states and their irresponsible fiscal policies and lack of economic competitiveness. Capital flight from those states is a simple consequence of those irresponsible fiscal policies and underlying economic problems. But, in the meantime, the interdependence generated by the Euro led to the financial problems of those states becoming a problem for all. This can be presented as a democratic problem since the interests of the latter states are not taken into account in the former state democratic process (the EU can, in many respects, be presented precisely as expanding the scope of interests to be taken into account in national democracies). What happened is that there were no effective mechanisms to ensure that the fiscal policies of a state in the Eurozone would take into account the interests of the other member states.

This is a democratic externality that is favoured by deeper integration and the interdependence it creates. The crisis makes clear our interdependence but also our failure to internalise its consequences. This failure is a democratic failure. But it is a democratic failure of the states and one that extends beyond Euro-related issues. It is sufficient to remember the circumstances in which a wrong assessment made by the health authorities of a state on the risk of a particular vegetable led to high losses for farmers all over Europe. Many such externalities are also not a product of economic integration but independent from it. The Euro crisis is, in part, a product of such a type of democratic failure that the Euro governance regime was not structured well enough to correct.

The second narrative does not see markets sanctioning the mismanagement of States but, instead, as the main causes of the crisis. The crisis is a product of unfettered capital flows. After the creation of the Euro there was an excessive influx of capital from the northern banks to several European states, particularly in the south. Those banks benefited from the Euro to inject liquidity in other states in search of increased profits. This artificially lowered interest rates in those states, creating a credit bubble. This narrative is, in fact, very similar to the dominant narrative of the American financial crisis, presented as a creditor-generated problem rather than a debtor responsibility. In this narrative, some States became the victims of what Dani Rodrik described as a phenomenon similar to a run on the banks but at the level of states.[1] Moreover, deprived of the possibility to devaluate their currencies or reinstate currency controls, those States can no longer respond to those capital flows and their consequences.

This narrative can (and ought) also to be presented in democratic terms. It is a form of transnational democratic externalities imposed on states. Or, in other words, capital movements can be presented as having a profound impact inside a state without being subject to its democratic control.

In fact, the stronger normative justification for the Euro might be the opportunity it offers to Europe to address the democratic challenges posed by capital flows. The latter, while also bringing, as mentioned, many advantages, challenge two dimensions of democracy: policy autonomy and distributive justice. They do so because they offer exit and entry possibilities to particular economic actors from the deliberative settlements reached in the democratic process. The Euro offers an opportunity to address those risks both by providing a new deliberative space for those issues at the European level and empowering Europe to protect them at the global level. For this, however, the right governance model needs to be adopted.

Understanding this second democratic challenge is also crucial to understand why it is wrong to present the current crisis as involving a trade-off between democracy and economic catastrophe. Many are assessing this crisis and the different alternatives to address it under this paradigm. But, for the reasons given above, this is simply wrong. Giving up the Euro will not, in itself, protect national democracies. The challenges to national democracy arise from economic integration and, in this particular context, unhindered capital mobility at the European and global levels. If the Euro has failed so far it is because it has not been effective in protecting democracy from these challenges, not because it is itself the source of those challenges. The Euro may well be the only effective way to ensure, at the European level, the conditions necessary for the policy autonomy and distributive justice that any democracy requires.

1 Dani Rodrik, The Globalization Paradox – Democracy and The Future of the World Economy (New York, Norton, 2011), p 93.

II. EU Failings in Addressing the Crisis and Democracy

To fully understand the nature of the democratic challenges facing Europe and what to do to address them it is also important to make sense of EU (in)action in the aftermath of the crisis. The perceived incapacity of the EU political process to solve the crisis is a simple continuation of the national democratic failure to internalise the consequences of interdependence. National democracies can't correct their mutually imposed externalities nor effectively regulate the transnational forms of power that evade their control. But because European regulation of these phenomena is too deeply dependent on national politics it too has proved incapable of addressing them effectively.

In fact, the failure of the EU political process to successfully address the current crisis has, at its core, a political gap: the scope and level of politics has not followed the scope and level of political problems in Europe. This is our most important democratic deficit.

European integration generates a deep interdependence between national policies that has, however, never translated itself into European politics. But if national politics are not able to incorporate the existing European interdependence on certain issues then it will not provide the correct political incentives for the necessary and democratic legitimate solutions to those issues. This has consequences on what decisions the EU takes but also on how they are interpreted since they are both the product of the political incentives originating in national political processes and then, again, appropriated by the latter. In other words, political actors at EU level are predominantly responsive before national constituencies that are not able to internalise the consequences of interdependence. As a consequence, European decisions suffer from the democratic failure to which those national political spaces are subject to. But they are further affected by the fact that, when adopted, they are then subject to different (and often opposite) interpretations by those national political spaces.

This failure to internalise interdependence is aggravated by what many perceive as the erosion of solidarity within the EU. In fact, it is more the reverse. More than being the product of the absence of a European cultural or social identity, the lack of European solidarity is the result of the lack of internalisation of the consequences of interdependence: this time, of the benefits it generates. The bedrock of European solidarity will not be a pre-existing cultural or social identity. It will be an awareness of the benefits of European integration and that such benefits must come with duties too.

In other words, the easier (and more legitimate) path to European solidarity comes by establishing a link between the wealth generated by European integration and the requirement to distribute it fairly.

Finally, this excessive dependence of the EU political process on national politics has another negative consequence: political authority is too diffuse in Europe. We have often in the past been concerned with the democratic risks involved in the concentration of political power. But the opposite may also amount to a democratic problem. There's only self-government if there is government. When political power is too diffuse then democracy becomes ineffective or dominated by minorities.

Europe's answer to this problem has often been to try to side-step democracy itself. The EU's recurring preference for technocratic solutions is, in many instances, a simple consequence of the ineffectiveness of its political process. Since European democracy can't effectively address some of the current issues, the solution has been to take those issues out of politics. It is true that democracy also needs editing and discipline and that this may require insulating certain questions from the politics of the day.[2] But this cannot be taken too far otherwise it becomes a challenge to democracy itself. This highlights a conundrum faced by European integration in its relationship with politics; it seems to be faced with a choice between either too much politics or no politics at all. The answer passes by a reorganisation of European political spaces, including the emergence of a real European political space.

III. Conditions for a democratic and just EU governance

Any form of EU governance that is developed to answer challenges of the current crisis will have to fulfil certain conditions in order to be both effective and legitimate. What follows is a list of such conditions. The proposals that are put forward later must be understood in the light of these conditions. These conditions are also closely interrelated.

1) We need political authority. Any successful model of governance will have to make clear that there is political authority behind the Euro and the EU. It is the absence of this political authority that undermines the ef-

2 That is one of the functions of constitutions.

fectiveness and credibility of the Union's governance of the Euro and its capacity to govern financial markets instead of being governed by them.

2) We need accountability. The diffuse nature of the EU's political authority leads both to a lack of accountability and misplaced accountability. The current crisis is a primary example of the need for accountability. Who should citizens hold accountable for the results of the adjustment programs 'imposed' on some states: their national governments or the EU? And if the EU, does that mean the Commission, the ECB, the Council, or some states within the Council? The diffuse character of the EU's political authority makes accountability virtually impossible and favours its manipulation by political actors: national political actors can use the nature of intergovernmental bargaining to transfer political costs to the EU. But, increasingly, the EU institutions might use the fact that its policy choices will have to be enforced by national governments to evade accountability too. Clearer political authority will be a necessary (but not sufficient) condition for accountability in Europe.

3) We need to re-establish mutual trust between states and between citizens. This has been severely affected by the crisis. The risk is real. In order to prevent it we do not simply need a contract linking solidarity with conditionality. We need both the rules and solidarity to be traced back to a theory of justice for the EU. To collective goods shared by all and criteria of distributive justice for the redistributive impacts of European integration. In other words, they must be linked to the broader purposes of European integration and the fair distribution of its costs and benefits.

4) We need to render both the benefits and the democratic consequences of interdependence visible before the citizens. This will never be achieved by information campaigns, no matter how well designed. The real source of communication of a political authority with its citizens is through the policies that it enacts and how they impact and are perceived by citizens. The benefits and costs of the European Union are only properly internalised by citizens if they are inherent in the character of the EU policies, including its revenues.

5) We need to legitimate financial solidarity by relating it to the wealth generated by European integration and not the wealth of some states. The idea that the EU is an instrument to transfer the wealth of some states to other states is the poisonous tree that undermines any form of solidarity within the Union. We must detach financial solidarity from financial transfers between states. Financial solidarity must be a product of the wealth that the process of European integration, itself, generates and be guided by

the goal of a fair distribution of the benefits of integration among all European citizens.

6) We need political integration to support the increased transfer of powers to the Union and its financial solidarity. The starting point for such political integration must be a European political space. Any form of political integration based only on national political spaces will, for the reasons described above, lack political authority and be incapable of internalising the democratic consequences of interdependence. Ideally, such a form of political integration would also include a reform of the institutions so as to guarantee that its processes of decision-making more closely fit ideals of representation and participation in the context of multi-level polities. The proposals I put forward here depart, however, from what is possible with the current Treaties.

Before presenting my proposals I want, however, to discuss the two alternatives that, in my view, have dominated the terms of the debate so far.

A. Union of Rules

The first alternative would limit itself to building upon the Stability Compact and the revised legislative framework on excessive deficits and macro-economic imbalances, as resulting from the adoption of the 'six-pack' in 2011. The thesis is that what failed with the Euro was appropriate supervision of the fiscal policies of states. If the EU were in a position to effectively guarantee compliance by the Member States with its fiscal discipline, the markets' trust would be restored, the crisis would ultimately be overcome and the credibility of the Euro strengthened. The overwhelming majority of the steps taken so far regarding the governance of the Euro have followed this approach. The Stability Compact embodies this approach. It could be incorporated into the Treaties in the context of a broader reform that would further enhance the powers of the Union with respect to Member States' fiscal policies. The proposal to create an EU Treasury Minister fits in this model. The same could be said of the suggestion to grant more powers to the Court of Justice, beyond what is already in the Stability Compact.

This approach is also presented as being reconcilable with democracy. The Union is not perceived as intruding in national democracies but simply guaranteeing the rule of law in the Euro area. It would be a European constitutionalisation of fiscal discipline similar to that already in place in some Member States. Member States have democratically bound themselves to these rules and the Union is simply enforcing them, preventing some from having a free ride at the expense of others. This thesis endorses only the first of the two narratives on the crisis identified above. In doing so, it underestimates the extent of the democratic challenges faced by Europe. It also underestimates the democratic consequences of the powers being transferred to the Union.

Whatever our view on the benefits and costs of constitutionalising fiscal discipline, there are two things that are clear in the current EU context: such discipline is a necessity, if not to reestablish market trust, certainly to reestablish trust between the Member States; but such discipline is also insufficient to address the current crisis.

It is insufficient for economic and democratic reasons. It starts by ignoring the fact that the fiscal situation of a state is closely dependent on its underlying economic situation. Several of the states, now in a profound fiscal crisis, were, until recently, fully compliant with the Maastricht criteria. The reasons for their fiscal crisis should be sought in deeper economic problems that rapidly turned into a fiscal crisis. This has two consequences. First, it is artificial to assume that the EMU will magically function in such a way that all its states will have permanent trade surpluses. There will always have to be financial transfers; the question is how and under which conditions? Second, we need to take seriously the economic part of the Economic and Monetary Union. A Fiscal Union requires more than fiscal discipline and coordination of the economic policies of the states. It requires an EU economic policy, albeit limited to the correction of the asymmetries emerging in a monetary union.

But a Union only of rules and discipline will also be democratically unacceptable. Budgetary and fiscal policies are at the core of democracy. A regime that relies exclusively on fiscal discipline being enforced by the EU will undermine the already limited political and social legitimacy of the Union: either national political processes will preserve autonomy and the effectiveness of the rules will be put into question or the disciplining of national political processes by a non-political space will put democracy itself in question.

B. Union of National democracies

It is always attractive to talk about a Union or Federation of national democracies. It seems to reconcile the irreconcilable and as a label it works. It also seems to be the path preferentially explored in the report presented by President Rompuy to the Council. It reflects many of the proposals being put forward regarding forms of debt mutualisation and further political integration.

The idea is to complement the fiscal discipline regime embodied in the Fiscal Compact with forms of fiscal solidarity between states and enhanced democratic legitimacy (preferably through national democracies). Fiscal solidarity will take the form of either a limited mutualisation of the debt (in the form of jointly issued EU bonds or some form of ECB intervention) or loans to be provided by the ESM. We could describe this system as one where states provide insurance for other states' debt but such insurance is limited and dependent on a case-by-case political assessment. Democratic legitimacy will be provided by the participation of a broader set of national political actors in such decisions. National Parliaments and courts will be involved by, for example, reviewing the assumption of any new financial liabilities by their state.

I have serious reservations regarding the feasibility and legitimacy of such a model. Financially, it is doubtful that such an approach will be sufficient to restore confidence in the common currency and in the political will supporting it. To make the governance of the Euro dependent on a permanent 'negotiation' with national democracies will leave intact the uncertainty over the extent of financial and political support underlying the common currency. It is this uncertainty that feeds market fears and speculation.

It can be argued that a model that would make EU political authority and democracy wholly or fundamentally dependent on national democracies is destined to fail. It will suffer from the fundamental problem of relying too much on national political processes incapable of internalising the consequences of interdependence. Furthermore, a model that will require constant bargaining on how much some states ought to pay to others, and in which the latter states are subject to the policies imposed by the former, will erode rather than support European integration. The paying states will think they are carrying the other states on their backs and rewarding moral hazard. Those being 'disciplined' will see themselves as being governed by those lending the money.

C. Europe's Semi-Federalism

There is an alternative. I have advanced above the necessary conditions for a successful model of governance of the EU and the Euro. It is now time to render concrete the forms through which those conditions may be fulfilled and how and why they may be politically feasible.

There are three pillars in my proposal: an increased EU budget supported by real EU revenue sources; new EU policies and a different kind of policies; and more effective political authority supported by a European political space.

1. A Budget and Resources for Stability and Democracy

Currently the Union's budget is 1% of EU GDP. Though I cannot go into further detail here, I estimate that an increase in the EU budget to at least 3% of the GDP (an amount foreseen at earlier stages of European integration and also when the Euro was created) should provide the Union with the firepower necessary to play two fundamental roles in the context of a Monetary Union. First, introducing policies capable of addressing the asymmetries affecting the smooth operation of the monetary union. Second, using the EU budget to address financial emergencies like the one that the Union is currently experiencing.

I want to highlight a particular advantage of such a proposal. In the ESM, for example, funds are guaranteed by the participating states. This limits its firepower but also undermines the social and democratic legitimacy of the Union. The citizens of States which, at a particular moment in time, will be net contributors under the ESM will tend to construct it as a transfer of their own funds to cover risks assumed by other states. The use of the EU budget would prevent that direct link from being established. It would also make clear to citizens, in all states, that their financial solidarity will be limited to their obligations towards the EU budget and is the price to be paid for the general benefits and costs of being part of the EU.

The legitimacy of this form of financial solidarity will also be made stronger by changing the character and origin of EU revenues. The argument I want to put forward next is that what will make an increased EU budget possible, new own resources, can actually also serve to legitimate the Union. A polity, including the political authority exercised therein and the necessary solidarity between its members, must be rendered meaningful and intelligible to its citizens not only in the way it represents itself but also by what it does. One fundamental aspect is certainly how revenues are collected and taxes organised. These are not simply a source of revenue. They are also a way of making the reasons for solidarity clear to the members of the polity. EU revenues should not be determined on a pragmatic basis of how much is required to fund the Union budget. Instead, the sources of EU revenues should be determined by what makes the Union more legitimate to its citizens by making visible the reasons for the Union's existence and linking its revenues to the benefits and costs that different social groups obtain from European integration.

If conceived in this way, the new EU own resources will not only provide it with the funds necessary to support the proposed budget increase but will contribute to a clearer justification of the project of European integration. Furthermore, only in this way will we be able to legitimate on any meaningful and lasting basis solidarity within the Union. It is essential that the Union is seen as redistributing the Union's wealth overall and not the wealth of a certain number of states alone. It is equally important for such solidarity to be related to the different degree to which different social groups benefit from European integration and, in particular, the internal market. In a recent report to the European Parliament I put forward some specific proposals on what those resources could be.

2. *New and Reformed EU Policies*

Union policies also need to be rethought in the light of what justifies European integration. The European Union can increase its democratic legitimacy by more closely aligning its policy priorities to the problems that, given the ineffectiveness of Member State solutions, it should address.

The problem with current policies is visible in the clear gap between what EU citizens expect from the Union (as expressed in Eurobarometer surveys) and what the Union can do. The Euro is a dramatic example of the EU's policy gap. One of the most important instruments of correction of economic and fiscal asymmetries in a monetary union is the mobility of the work force. But the free movement of persons remains the most underdeveloped of all free movement provisions. And the Union also does not have any active policies regarding training, employment or social security. The same could be said of the financial services market. How can we correct the underlying economic asymmetries in the Euro area when companies compete under profoundly different conditions in accessing credit depending on their state of origin?

This requires new policies. Among those to be considered, two priorities must be a European employment agency (that could coordinate and facilitate the exchange of job offers and demand among the different member states) and a job training and mobility program that could focus on structural unemployment.

But the problem with EU policies has to do with more than having the right policies. The structure and character of EU policies also needs to be rethought. It is unrealistic (and also wrong) to eliminate inter-governmental bargaining from EU policy-making. But EU decisions, whatever the bargaining before they are made, should be designed along EU citizenship and not nationality lines and conform to universality criteria. This would require a higher percentage of the expenditure of the Union to be allocated to policies structured around citizen entitlements instead of funds allocated along national quotas.

This reform of EU policies should also transform the way in which the EU interacts with national polities and policies and its role in reforming them. EU structural policies, in particular, should be more closely linked to domestic institutional reforms. In other words, the EU should use its purse to promote deeper institutional reforms at the national level. One example will, hopefully, render this idea more concrete: in the area of education and research, instead of defining research subjects on the basis of which the Union selects research projects deemed worthy of funding, the EU could easily use those funds to have a real systemic impact on higher education and research in Europe. It could, for example, make the award of those funds conditional on certain institutional criteria defined so as to reform national higher education and research in a more meritocratic and international direction (in order to access these funds, institutions would have to fulfil or commit to criteria regarding academic mobility, internationalisation of faculty and student bodies etc.).

Increasing the power of the purse and linking it with institutional reforms is also essential in the light of the number of regulatory and supervisory powers that the EU exercises with respect to the States and that have expanded further with the on-going Euro reforms. In the context of the extended powers being attributed to the EU in national economies, the Union cannot be limited to using a 'stick'. It must also provide positive incentives. This comes in the form of new policies but also by rethinking how

EU policies may be adjusted to further national reforms with systemic impact.

3. A European political space

One hears endlessly about the European democracy deficit, real and imagined. But, as I tried to explain at the start of this report, Europe's real democratic deficit is to be found in its excessive reliance on national politics that have not internalised the consequences of European and global interdependence. Europe can certainly improve its forms of democratic representation and participation but without European politics other democratic developments will either be ineffective or even harmful in legitimacy terms. For example, without proxy politics (organised around transnational and not national lines) any further moves towards a more majoritarian and proportional representation in the Union will simply be perceived as larger states imposing their will on smaller states. All this is only rendered more urgent by the powers being transferred to the Union.

The democratic problem of the Union is also one of effectiveness. A democracy that cannot effectively govern is no democracy. As stated earlier, there is no self-government without government.

The need for European politics is also founded in the increased redistributive effects of its policies. The expanded scope of EU policies and the predominantly majoritarian character of its decision-making no longer allow us to conceive of the Union simply as a regulatory authority. Its policies and forms of decision-making produce redistributive effects that require more than technocratic legitimacy and a different kind of politics than inter-governmental politics. The deliberative and institutional system of the EU should favour proxy politics (where majorities constructed along national lines are progressively replaced by cross-national ideological majorities). Any future institutional amendments should also prevent the emergence of permanent and insulated minorities (*net losers*), the development of rigid and insulated majorities or minorities and the creation of pivotal players. It is this that will be capable of securing citizens' loyalty to Union decisions. It assures them that their voice is not limited to the voice of their State and that, even if one day they find themselves in the minority, on another they may be part of the majority. Securing these conditions might require additional institutional reforms. But, as stated earlier, my proposals focus on what can be done even in the absence of

Treaty amendments. In any case, any institutional reforms, to be effective in enhancing the Union's legitimacy, must be done together with or preceded by changes in the nature of EU politics.

My fundamental proposal is to 'transform' the elections to the European Parliament into an electoral competition for the government of Europe. The most important step in this direction would be for the different European political groups to present competing candidates for the role of President of the Commission before the next election to the EP.[3] The Treaties attribute to the European Council the power to propose the President of the European Commission but its subjection to approval by the European Parliament, and the electoral focus on the choice of a President, will ensure that the 'winner' of the elections would be the selected President. This is similar to the situation in several member states where the head of government is appointed by the head of state but following the result of the parliamentary elections.

The cohesion of the Commission will also be reinforced by the fact that the President-elect will have much stronger bargaining power vis-à-vis the member states in the selection of the other members of the Commission. One may even consider the question whether the Commission should not fully reflect the political majority in the EP following the elections. Even if the Treaty on European Union states that the list of other members of the Commission to be proposed by the Council to the Parliament is based on suggestions by national governments (Article 17, para. 7, second subparagraph TEU), nothing in the Treaties requires or even suggests that they have to be affiliated or related to the political parties in power at national level.

A first consequence of the transformation of EP elections into an electoral competition for the government of Europe will be the promotion of transnational politics. Once each European political group selects a candidate for President of the Commission they must also come up with a political platform or government program. It is obvious that such political platforms, in order to be agreed within that political group and to be successful in all member states, will have to focus on genuinely European issues. Issues where citizens are not divided along national lines but across them. The simple need to come up with such European political platforms is

3 This proposal has notably been developed in a book by Simon Hix, *What's Wrong With the European Union and How to Fix It* (Cambridge, Polity Press 1998).

bound to generate European politics. The election itself will finally be focused on European issues framed by the competing candidates and their alternative political platforms.

The Commission and its President would not simply gain a stronger legitimacy. They would gain political capital. The political authority of the EU would also be reinforced. The link established between the election and a specific political platform would provide the Commission and Parliament with a strong political claim in the pursuit of the proposals contained in that platform. I am not arguing that national governments and the Council will become irrelevant in the politics of EU decision-making. Far from it, and they shouldn't. But the current proposal would balance the politics and political authority of Europe. It would promote what we could coin 'semi-federalism'.

15 United in Fear – The Loss of Heimat and the Crises of Europe

J.H.H. Weiler

I

Legitimacy is a notoriously underspecified concept in social science and political theory. I am going to use it in this essay in a specific way – as a resource, a social and political "credit", which is nice to have when the going is good, but indispensable when the going is not so good, when democratic leaders cannot turn to opinion polls and immediate electoral prospects but hard decisions, of the Statesman genre, at times unpopular, have to be taken.

Fear and loss of Heimat are the interpretative keys I will employ in this brief essay.

The only thing, or at least the principal thing, that unites Europeans today, seems to be fear. By "Europeans" I mean citizens but also States, governments and the Union and its institutions alike. At times fear can be productive, but in the current circumstance the consequences, intended and unintended, are mostly pathological accentuating the underlying set of crises which produces the fear in multiple forms.

It is, I hope, apparent from the title of this essay that in trying to understand the current European circumstance I eschew the immediate and monolithic – not crisis but crises, not 2008 as the turning point but long term processes going back to WWII and the origins of our Union. In particular I eschew one such quite common monolithic explanation, which seeks to find the root (and, thus, also the solution) of crisis in the material needs of human existence – primarily the unacceptable condition of unemployment and the uneven distribution of material deserts of globalization within our Member States and among our Member States. I do not at all dismiss such, but, I believe, that there is much more and one ought to explore as well psycho-social and spiritual factors in addition to the material. Not on bread alone does man liveth (Deut. 8:3).

The German word *Heimat* -- captures, I believe, better than *home*, or *hogar*, or *casa*, or *maison* (and even *chez moi*) as well as homeland or patria one idea I am trying to convey. *Heimat* is not limited to the material or the spatial. It represents, too, a state of being, a zone of comfort. It represents both, home and homeland, a mental landscape, a state of the mind. You can live in the same house and the same village and the same country and still lament the loss of *heimat*. It is often spoken of with nostalgia (and in the German context embarrassed irony or cynicism). Loss of *Heimat* – in any of the senses described above – is second only to loss of life or family. It can be disorienting in profound ways. It leads to vulnerability. It is open to exploitation.

I will proceed in three steps. I will first suggest some long term processes which in different ways lead to this condition – multifaceted – of loss of *heimat*. I do not claim that this is the only way to describe and understand the current circumstance but I hope to persuade the reader that it offers some insight that the purely economic or even political prism lack.

Then, drawing on earlier work, I will explain the depletion of legitimacy resources of Europe and the Union, which aggravate the challenge of leadership in addressing the crises.

Finally, I will use Brexit and especially the response thereto as a prism to examine the reaction to the crisis. Having spent a lifetime as a student of the European Construct, and still firm in my belief that it represents a unique and noble achievement – on par with the French Revolution – of European civilization, I will stake out some markers, which I believe would be necessary to arrest its decline and even possible demise.

II

I want to describe now three processes which began as reactions to the Second World War and have progressed over the last decades and I believe help explain the current circumstance in the terms I described above.

The First Process: For reasons that are quite understandable, the very word "patriotism" became "unprintable" after the WWII notably in Western Europe. Fascist regimes (among others), by abusing the word and the concept, had "burned" it from our collective consciousness. And in many ways this has been a positive thing. But we also pay a high price for having banished this word—and the sentiment it expresses—from our psycho-political vocabulary. Since patriotism also has a noble side: the discipline of love, the duty to take care of one's homeland and people, of accepting our civic responsibility toward the collective. In reality, true patriotism is the opposite of Fascism: "We do not belong to the State, it's the State that belongs to us." This kind of patriotism is an integral part of the republican form of democracy.

Today, we may call ourselves the Italian or French "Republic," but our democracies are no longer truly republican. There's the State, there's the government, and then there's "us". Ours have become democracies who are as remote as shareholders of a large enterprise. If the directorate of this enterprise called "the Republic" does not produce political and material dividends, we change managers with a vote during a meeting of shareholders called "elections." If there is anything that does not work in our society, we go to the "directors"—as we do, for example, when our internet connection isn't working: "We paid (our taxes), and look at the terrible service they're giving us…" The State is always the one responsible. Never us. It's a clientelistic democracy that not only takes away our responsibility toward our society, toward our country, but also removes responsibility from our very human condition. It does more: There is not only no responsibility – there is no control in this non-Republican form of democracy. The possibility of replacing the government in elections is indispensable for democracy, but it is a minimal form of control over one's destiny and that of one's family, one's neighbors. Changing the gardener is a far cry of tending one's garden. Schumpeter famously extoled this form of material "democracy". Normatively I find it deplorable. But democracy in this context is not just a system of governance. It is a foundational *heimat* of the post WWII generations. When our democracy becomes 'hollowed out' in the accurate and damning term used by the late and unforgettable Peter Mair, the loss of faith in democratic institutions and democratic processes is fast to follow, and with it that security which democracy as mental and spiritual *heimat* promise shatters. Deep fear sets in, exploitable by even worse forms of 'democracy' such as the oxymoronic 'illiberal' democracy.

The second process which helps to explain what happened to Europe comes, once again, as a reaction to the War, and is paradoxical. We've accepted, both at the national and international levels, a serious and irreversible obligation rooted in our Constitutions to protect the fundamental rights of individuals, even against the political tyranny of the majority. At a more general level, our political-juridical vocabulary has become a discourse of rights. The rights of an Italian citizen are protected by our Courts, and, above all, by the Constitutional Court – but also by the Court of Justice of the EU in Luxembourg, and—again—by the European Court of Human Rights in Strasbourg, and in different variants this just about in all our Member States. It's enough to make your head spin.

Just think about how common it has become, in the political discourse of today, to speak more and more about "rights." It's enormously important. I would never want to live in a country in which fundamental rights are not effectively defended. And we lawyers in particular celebrate such as the crowning achievement of our legal systems and legal culture. We are the Rights Generation. But here too—as with the banishment of patriotism—we pay a dear price. Actually, we pay two prices.

First and foremost, the noble culture of rights does as we proudly proclaim put the individual at the center, but little by little, almost without realizing it, it turns him or her into a self-centered individual. It is always a discourse of entitlement, rarely of civic duties. It is always what we deserve, the deserts owed us, rarely, if you discount taxes, what we civically owe.

There is, however, a second effect to this "culture of rights"—which is a framework all Europeans have in common— a kind of flattening of political and cultural specificity, of one's own unique national identity. To explain this I need to digress to and present my understanding of the most fundamental of all rights, the one that features first and foremost in so many of our constitutional documents – human dignity.

The notion of human dignity—the fact that we have been created in the image of God (or the secular equivalent) —contains, at one and the same time, two facets. On the one hand, it means that we are all equal in our fundamental human dignity: Men and women, rich and poor, Italians and Germans, Muslims, Christians and Jews. On the other hand, recognizing human dignity means accepting that each of us is an entire universe, distinct and different from any other person. We are not fungible. Our uniqueness is, on this understanding, as essential to our dignity as our equality. When either of these elements of diversity is diminished or derided, we rebel. It is easy to understand the rebellion when our equality is violated. But the failure or refusal to recognize and respect our uniqueness is, normatively, equally offensive and psychologically equally humiliating. It offends our dignity. The uniqueness facet of our dignity plays an important role to our very sense of existential meaning which, I believe, we are hard wired desperately to seek. We all ask, explicitly or otherwise, what is the meaning of our being, of our existence. Of course, it is up to each of us, through our actions and emotions to give meanings to our lives. But if we lose our uniqueness, that meaning is diminished. Does it make a difference to a flock of birds if there is one more or less? It makes all the difference to the universe we occupy if there is one or more less. That is, indeed, why we privilege human dignity above all.

As human we are social beings. The social is the context in which we live our lives be it family, tribe, or the modern liberal (non racial, multicultural) nation. The two facets of dignity play out also in the context of the social, which brings us back to the culture of rights. The culture of rights – universal, pan-European – are the values we share, across family, tribe, nation and State. At the same time, the ubiquity and celebration of such cannot but help flatten the uniqueness of collective identities, a flattening which is aggravated because normatively, let us admit it, the only form of patriotism permitted is 'constitutional patriotism' – everything else is suspect for the reasons I outlined above. Let me somewhat polemically argue that the only thing we may unashamedly take pride in our State and nation is our football team. The essential balance of dignity – the universal and the unique – in our social context has been seriously skewed – and if I am right about the metaphysical significance of dignity (personal and collective) this is not a trivial loss. Here is another disorienting lost *heimat* grist to the mill of atavists and crypto-fascists.

The third process that explains what has happened to Europe is secularization. Let me be clear: this observation is not an evangelical rebuke. I do not judge a person based on his or her faith or lack thereof. And even though, for me, it's impossible to imagine the world without the Lord—The Holy Blessed Be He—I also know many religious people who are odious and many atheists of the highest moral character.

The social and political importance of secularism is in the fact that a voice which was at one time universal and ubiquitous, a voice in which the emphasis was on duty and not only rights, on personal responsibility in the face of what happens to us, our neighbors, our society and not the instinctive appeal to public institutions, has all but disappeared from social praxis.

This process also began with World War II. Who among us, after having seen the mountains of shoes from millions of assassinated children at Auschwitz, didn't ask the question: God, where were you? I think it is not far fetched to characterize this process too as loss of *heimat.*

It has taken decades for these three processes to mature and produce now their "sour grapes" (Is. 5:2). We see the impact everywhere, not least in matters regarding the European Union.

III

I turn now to Legitimacy. Typically European legitimacy discourse employs two principal concepts: Input (process) legitimacy (or input and throughput in the felicitous and illuminating construction of Vivian Schmidt) and Output (result) legitimacy. I will add a third, less explored, but in my view central legitimating feature of Europe – Political Messianism. I will explore, in turn, each of these forms of legitimacy in their European context, and in relation to each show why, in my view, they are exhausted, inoperable in the current circumstance.

There are two basic genres – languages, vocabularies – of Legitimacy: Normative and Social. The vocabulary of normative legitimacy is moral, ethical and it is informed by political theory. It is an objective measure even though there will be obvious ideological differences as to what should be considered as legitimate governance. Social legitimacy is empirical, assessed or measured with the tools of social science. It is a subjective measure, reflecting social attitudes. It is not a measurement of popularity, but of a deeper form of acceptance of the political regime.

The two types of legitimacy often inform each other and may even conflate, but not necessarily so. A series of examples will clarify. By our liberal pluralist normative yardstick, German national socialism of the 30s and 40s was a horrible aberration, the negation of legitimate governance. Yet, socially and empirically, for most Germans almost until the defeat in 1945 it was not only popular but considered deeply legitimate leadership. By contrast, Weimer Democracy would pass our normative test of legitimate government, yet for a very large number of Germans it was not merely unpopular, but considered illegitimate leadership, a betrayal of Germany.

However, in less extreme situations we do expect some measure of conflation between the two. One hopes that if a regime is normatively legitimate, because, say, it practices constitutional democracy, it will enjoy widespread social legitimacy, and that the opposite will be true too: In a regime which fails the normative tests, one hopes that the social legitimacy will be low too. One can imagine complicated permutations of these parameters.

Legitimacy, normative or social, should not be conflated with legality. Forbidding blacks to sit in the front of the bus was perfectly legal, but would fail many a test of normative legitimacy, and with time lose its social legitimacy as well. There are illegal measures which are considered, normatively and/or socially as legitimate, and legal measures which are considered illegitimate.

For the purpose of this essay, it is worth exploring briefly the relationship between popularity and legitimacy. If I am a life long adherent of the Labor party in the UK, I might be appalled by the election of the Tories and abhor every single measure adopted by the Government of the Tory Prime Minister. But it would never enter my mind to consider such measures as "illegitimate." In fact, and this is critical for one of the principal propositions of this essay, the deeper the legitimacy resources of a regime, the better able it is to adopt *unpopular* measures critical in the time of crisis where exactly such measures may be necessary.

Moving from the genres of legitimacy to a typology I would like to suggest the three most important types or forms of legitimacy which have been central to the discussion of European integration. As noted, the most ubiquitous have been various variations on the theme of input and output legitimacy.

> Process (or input) Legitimacy – which in the current circumstance can be, with some simplification, be synonymized with democracy. It is easier put in the negative: To the extent that the European mode of governance departs from the habits and practices of democracy as understood in the Member States, its legitimacy, in this case both normative and social will be compromised.
>
> Result (or output) Legitimacy – which, again simplifying somewhat, would be all modern versions of Bread and Circus. As long as the Union delivers "the goods" – prosperity, stability, security – it will enjoy a legitimacy that derives from a subtle combination of success *per se*, of success in realizing its objectives and of contentment with those results. There is no better way to legitimate a war than win it. This variant of legitimacy is part of the very ethos of the Commission.
>
> Telos Legitimacy or Political Messianism whereby legitimacy is gained neither by process nor output but by promise, the promise of an attractive Promised Land. I will elaborate on this below.

I will now try and illustrate the collapse of all three forms of legitimacy in the current European circumstance.

a. As regards process legitimacy, there is the persistent, chronic, troubling Democracy Deficit, which cannot be talked away.

First, although the "No Demos" thesis seems to have receded in recent discourse, its relevance is suddenly more acute than ever. The difficulties, as will be seen, of constructing all manner of "fiscal union" type solutions for the Euro crisis are in no small measure the result of – yes, "no demos" – a lack of transcendent responsibility for the lot of one's fellow citizens and nationals. Germans and Dutch and Finns are not saying: 'A Bailout is the wrong policy." Many of them are are saying, why should we, Germans, or Dutch, or Finns, help those lazy Italians or Portuguese or Greeks who in the shameful words of one Euro leader were busy spending their money on women and wine: A very visibile manifestation of the No-Demos thesis of Europe's democracy crisis.

Second, there are failures of democracy which simply make it difficult to speak of governance by and of the people. The manifestations of the so-called democracy deficit are persistent and no endless repetition of the powers of the European Parliament will remove them. In essence it is the inability of the Union to develop structures and processes which adequately replicate or, 'translate,' at the Union level even the imperfect habits of governmental control, parliamentary accountability and administrative responsibility that are practiced with different modalities in the various Member States. Make no mistake: It is perfectly understood that the Union is not a State. But it is in the business of governance and has taken over extensive areas previously in the hands of the Member States. In some critical areas, such as the interface of the Union with the international trading system, the competences of the Union are exclusive. In others they are dominant. Democracy is not about States. Democracy is about the exercise of public power – and the Union exercises a huge amount of public power. We live by the credo that any exercise of public power has to be legitimated democratically and it is exactly here that process legitimacy fails.

In essence, the two primordial features of any functioning democracy are missing – the grand principles of accountability and representation.

As regards accountability, even the basic condition of representative democracy that at election time the citizens "…can throw the scoundrels out" – that is replace the Government – does not operate in Europe. The form of European governance, governance without Government, is, and will remain for considerable time, perhaps forever such that there is no "Government" to throw out. Dismissing the Commission by Parliament (or approving the appointment of the Commission President) is not quite the same, not even remotely so.

Startlingly, but not surprisingly, political accountability of Europe is remarkably weak. There have been some spectacular political failures of European governance. If we look well before the current crisis, the embarrassing Copenhagen climate fiasco; the weak (at best) realization of the much touted Lisbon Agenda (aka Lisbon Strategy or Lisbon Process), the very story of the defunct "Constitution" to mention but three. It is hard to point in these instances to any measure of political accountability, of someone paying a political price as would be the case in national politics. In fact it is difficult to point to a single instance of accountability for political failure as distinct from personal accountability for misconduct in the annals of European integration. This is not, decidedly not, a story of corruption or malfeasance. My argument is that this failure is rooted in the very structure of European governance. It is not designed for political accountability. In similar vein, it is impossible to link in any meaningful way the results of elections to the European Parliament to the performance of the Political Groups within the preceding parliamentary session, in the way that is part of the mainstay of political accountability within the Member States. Structurally, dissatisfaction with "Europe" when it exists has no channel to affect, at the European level, the agents of European governance.

Likewise, at the most primitive level of democracy, there is simply no moment in the civic calendar of Europe where the citizen can influence directly the outcome of any policy choice facing the Community and Union in the way that citizens can when choosing between parties which offer sharply distinct programs at the national level. The political colour of the European Parliament only very weakly gets translated into the legislative and administrative output of the Union.

The Political Deficit, to use the felicitous phrase of Renaud Dehousse is at the core of the Democracy Deficit. The Commission, by its self-understanding linked to its very ontology, cannot be 'partisan' in a right-left sense, neither can the Council, by virtue of the haphazard political nature of its composition. This of course does not mean that the Commission is politically "neutral". Such neutrality is impossible. So any decision is obviously ideologically laden. But it is always below the surface. It is not openly and accountably a policy at the service of an ideological commitment. Democracy normally must have some meaningful mechanism for expression of voter preference predicated on choice among options, typically informed by stronger or weaker ideological orientation. That is an indispensable component of politics. Democracy without Politics is an oxymoron. And yet that is not only Europe, but it is a feature of Europe – the "non-partisan" nature of the Commission – which is celebrated. The stock phrase found in endless student text books and the like, that the Supranational Commission vindicates the European Interest, whereas the intergovernmental Council is a clearing house for Member State interest, is, at best, naïve. Does the "European Interest" not necessarily involve political and ideological choices? At times explicit, but always implicit?

Thus the two most primordial norms of democracy, the principle of accountability and the principle of representation are compromised in the very structure and process of the Union. It often serves governments (the executive branch) to play the game of European ideological neutrality, thus getting 'cover' from Brussels for politics which would be unacceptable in national politics.

Two deeper and longer-term trends give expression to the above. The first is the extraordinary decline in voter participation in elections for the European Parliament. In Europe as a whole the rate of participation is below 45 per cent, with several countries, notably in the East, with a rate below 30 per cent. The correct comparison is, of course, with political elections to national parliaments where the numbers are considerably higher. What is striking about these figures is that the decline coincides with a continuous shift in powers to the European Parliament, which today is a veritable co-legislator with the Council. The more powers the European Parliament, supposedly the *Vox Populi*, has gained, the greater popular indifference to it seems to have developed. It is sobering but not surprising to note the absence of the European Parliament as a major player in the current crisis. But the Institutional crisis runs deeper.

b. In analyzing the legitimacy (and mobilizing force) of the European Union, in particular against the background of its persistent democracy deficit, political and social science has indeed long used the distinction between process legitimacy and outcome legitimacy (aka input/output, process/result etc). The legitimacy of the Union more generally and the Commission more specifically, even if suffering from deficiencies in the state democratic sense, are said to rest on the results achieved – in the economic, social and, ultimately, political realms. The idea hearkens back to the most classic functionalist and neo-functionalist theories.

I do not want to take issue with the implied normativity of this position – a latter day *Panem et circenses* approach to democracy, which at some level at least could be considered quite troubling. It is with its empirical reality that I want to take some issue. I do not think that outcome legitimacy explains all or perhaps even most of the mobilizing force of the European construct. But whatever role it played it is dependent on the Panem. Rightly or wrongly, the economic woes of Europe, which are manifest in the Euro crisis are attributed to the European construct. So when there suddenly is no Bread, and certainly no cake, we are treated to a different kind of circus whereby the citizens' growing indifference is turning to hostility and the ability of Europe to act as a political mobilizing force seems not only spent, but even reversed. The worst way to legitimate a war is to lose it, and Europe is suddenly seen not as an icon of success but as an emblem of austerity, thus in terms of its promise of prosperity, failure. If success breeds legitimacy, failure, even if wrongly allocated, leads to the opposite.

Thus, not surprisingly there is a seemingly contagious spread of 'Anti-Europeanism' in national politics. What was once in the province of fringe parties on the far right and left has inched its way to more central political forces. The "Question of Europe" as a central issue in political discourse was for long regarded as an 'English disease.' There is a growing contagion in Member States in North and South, East and West, where political capital is to be made among non-fringe parties by anti-European advocacy. The spill-over effect of this phenomenon is the shift of mainstream parties in this direction as a way of countering the gains at their flanks. If we are surprised by this it is only because we seem to have air brushed out of our historical consciousness the rejection of the so-called European Constitution, an understandable amnesia since it represented a defeat of the collective political class in Europe by the *vox populi*, albeit not speaking through, but instead giving a slap in the face to, the European Institutions.

At some level the same could have been said ten and even twenty years ago. The Democracy Deficit is not new – it is enduring. And how did Europe legitimate itself before it scored its great successes of the first decades?

c. As I hinted above, at the conceptual level there is a third type of legitimation which, in my view, played for a long time a much larger role than is currently acknowledged. In fact, in my view, it has been decisive to the legitimacy of Europe and to the positive response of both the political class and citizens at large. I will also argue that it is a key to a crucial element in the Union's political culture. It is a legitimacy rooted in the '*politically messianic*'.

In political 'messianism', the justification for action and its mobilizing force, derive not from process, as in classical democracy, or from result and success, but from the ideal pursued, the destiny to be achieved, the 'Promised Land' waiting at the end of the road. Indeed, in messianic visions the end always trumps the means.

Mark Mazower, in his brilliant and original history and historiography of 20th-century Europe -- Dark Continent-- insightfully shows how the Europe of monarchs and emperors which entered World War I was often rooted in a political messianic narrative in various states (in Germany, and Italy, and Russia and even Britain and France). It then oscillated after the War towards new democratic orders, that is to process legitimacy, which then oscillated back into new forms of political messianism in fascism and communism. As the tale is usually told, after World War II Europe of the West, was said to oscillate back to democracy and process legitimacy. It is here that I want to point to an interesting quirk, not often noted.

On the one hand, the Western states, which were later to become the member states of the European Union, became resolutely democratic, their patriotism rooted in their new constitutional values, narratives of glory abandoned and even ridiculed, and messianic notions of the State losing all appeal. Famously, former empires, once defended with repression and blood, were now abandoned with zeal.

And yet, their common venture, European integration, was in my reading a political messianic venture *par excellence,* the messianic becoming a central feature of its original and enduring political culture. The mobilizing force and principle legitimating feature was the vision offered, the dream dreamt, the promise of a better future. Unlike output democracy, which is measured by concrete results, Messianism is built on a dream, and one often couched in metaphysical goods rather than material ones. It is this feature, which explains not only the persistent mobilizing force (especially among elites and youth) but also key structural and institutional choices made. It will also give more depth to explanations of the current circumstance of Europe.

Since, unlike the democracy deficit, which has been discussed and debated *ad nauseam* and *ad tedium*, Political Messianism is a feature of European legitimacy, which has received less attention, I think it may be justified if I pay to it some more attention.

The Schuman declaration is somewhat akin to Europe's "Declaration of Independence" in its combination of vision and blueprint. Notably, much of its text found its way into the preamble of the Treaty of Paris, the substance of which was informed by its ideas. It is interesting to re-read the declaration through the conceptual prism of political messianism. The hallmarks are easily detected as we would expect in its constitutive, magisterial document. It is manifest in what is in the Declaration and, no less importantly, in what is not therein. *Nota bene*: European integration is nothing like its European messianic predecessors – that of monarchies and empire and later fascism and communism. It is liberal and noble, but politically messianic it is nonetheless.

The messianic feature is notable in both its rhetoric and substance. Note, first, the language used – ceremonial and "sermonial" with plenty of pathos (and bathos).

> World peace cannot be safeguarded without the making of creative efforts proportionate to the dangers which threaten it....
>
> The contribution which an organised and living Europe can bring to civilization is indispensable ...
>
> ...a first step in the federation of Europe [which] will change the destinies of those regions which have long been devoted to the manufacture of munitions of war...
>
> [A]ny war between France and Germany becomes not merely unthinkable, but materially impossible.
>
> This production will be offered to the world as a whole without distinction or exception...
>
> [I]t may be the leaven from which may grow a wider and deeper community between countries long opposed to one another by sanguinary divisions.

It is grand, inspiring, Churchillian one might even say with a tad of irony. Some old habits, such as the White Man's Burden and the missionary tradition, die hard:

> *With increased resources Europe will be able to pursue the achievement of one of its essential tasks, namely, the development of the African continent.*

But it is not just the rhetoric. The substance itself is messianic: A compelling vision which has animated now at least three generations of European idealists where the 'ever closer union among the people of Europe', with peace and prosperity an icing on the cake, constituting the beckoning promised land.

It is worth exploring further the mobilizing force of this new plan for Europe. At the level of the surface language it is its straightforward pragmatic objective of consolidating peace and reconstructing European prosperity. But there is much more within the deep structure of the Plan.

Peace, at all times an attractive desideratum, would have had its appeal in purely utilitarian terms. But it is readily apparent that in the historical context in which the Schumann Plan was put forward the notion of peace as an ideal probes a far deeper stratum than simple Swords into Ploughshares, Sitting under ones' Vines and Fig Trees, Lambs and Wolves -- the classic Biblical metaphor for peace. The dilemma posed was an acute example of the alleged tension between Grace and Justice which has taxed philosophers and theologians through the ages -- from William of Ockham (pre-modern), Friedrich Nietzsche (modernist) and the repugnant but profound Martin Heidegger (post-modern).

These were, after all, the early 50s with the horrors of War still fresh in the mind and, in particular, the memory of the unspeakable savagery of German occupation. It would take many years for the hatred in countries such as The Netherlands, Denmark or France to subside fully. The idea, then, in 1950, of a Community of Equals as providing the structural underpinning for long-term peace among yesterday's enemies, represented more than the wise counsel of experienced statesmen.

It was, first, a "peace of the brave" requiring courage and audacity. At a deeper level it managed to tap into the two civilizational pillars of Europe: The Enlightenment and the heritage of the French Revolution and the European Christian tradition.

Liberty was already achieved with the defeat of Nazi Germany – and Germans (like their Austrian bretheren-in-crime) embraced with zeal the notion that they, too, were liberated from National Socialism. But here was a Project, encapsulated in the Schuman Declaration, which added to the transnational level both Equality and Fraternity. The Post WWI Versailles version of Peace was to take yesterday's enemy, diminish him and keep his neck firmly under one's heel, with, of course, disastrous results. Here, instead was a vision in which yesteryear's enemy was regarded as an equal – Germany was to be treated as a full and equal partner in the venture – and engaged in a fraternal inter-dependent lock that, indeed, the thought of resolving future disputes would become unthinkable. This was, in fact, the project of the enlightenment taken to the international level as Kant himself had dreamt. To embrace the Schuman Plan was to tap into one of the most powerful idealistic seams in Europe's civilizational mines.

The Schuman Plan was also a call for forgiveness, a challenge to overcome an understandable hatred. In that particular historical context the Schumannian notion of Peace resonated with, was evocative of, the distinct teaching, imagery and values of the Christian call for forgiving one's enemies, for Love, for Grace – values so recently consecrated in their wholesale breach. The Schuman plan was in this sense, evocative of both Confession and Expiation, and redolent with the Christian belief in the power of repentance and renewal and the ultimate goodness of humankind. This evocation is not particularly astonishing given the personal backgrounds of the Founding Fathers -- Adenauer, De Gaspari, Schumann, Monnet himself – all seriously committed Catholics.

The mobilizing force, especially among elites, the Political Classes who felt more directly responsible for the calamities of which Europe was just exiting, is not surprising given the remarkable subterranean appeal to the two most potent visions of the idyllic "Kingdom" -- the humanist and religious combined in one Project. This also explains how, for the most part, both Right and Left, conservative and progressive, could embrace the project.

It is the messianic model, which explains (in part) why for so long the Union could operate without a veritable commitment to the principles it demanded of its aspiring members – democracy and human rights. Aspirant States had to become members of the European Convention of Human Rights, but the Union itself did not. They had to prove their democratic credentials, but the Union itself did not – two anomalies, which hardly raised eyebrows.

Note however, that its messianic features are reflected not only in the flowery rhetoric. In its original and unedited version the declaration is quite elaborate in operational detail. But you will find neither the word democracy nor human rights, a thunderous silence. It's a 'Lets-Just-Do-It' type of program animated by great idealism (and a goodly measure of good old state interest, as a whole generation of historians such as Alan Milward and Charles Maier among others have demonstrated).

The European double helix has from its inception been Commission and Council: an international (supposedly) a-political transnational administration/executive (the Commission) collaborating not, as we habitually say, with the member states (Council) but with the governments, the executive branch of the member states, which for years and years had a forum that escaped in day-to-day matters the scrutiny of any parliament, European or national. Democracy is simply not part of the original vision of European integration.

This observation is hardly shocking or even radical. Is it altogether fanciful to tell the narrative of Europe as one in which 'doers and believers' (notably the most original of its institutions, the Commission, coupled with an empowered executive branch of the member states in the guise of the Council and COREPER), an elitist (if well-paid) vanguard, were the self-appointed leaders from whom grudgingly, over decades, power had to be arrested by the European Parliament? And even the European Parliament has been a strange *vox populi*. For hasn't it been, for most of its life, a champion of European integration, so that to the extent that, inevitably, when the Union and European integration inspired fear and caution among citizens, (only natural in such a radical transformation of European politics) the European Parliament did not feel the place citizens would go to express those fears and concerns?

The political messianic was offered not only for the sake of conceptual clarification but also as an explanation of the formidable past success of European integration in mobilizing support. They produced a culture of praxis, achievement, ever expanding agendas. Given the noble dimensions of European integration one ought to see and acknowledge their virtuous facets.

But that is only part of the story. They also explain some of the story of decline in European legitimacy and mobilizing pull, which is so obvious in the current circumstance. *Part of the very phenomenology of political messianism is that it always collapses as a mechanism for mobilization and legitimation.* It obviously collapses when the messianic project fails. When the revolution does not come. But interestingly, and more germane to the narrative of European Integration, even when successful it sows its seeds of collapse. At one level the collapse is inevitable, part of the very phenomenology of messianic project. Reality is always more complicated, challenging, banal and ultimately less satisfying than the dream, which preceded it. The result is not only absence of mobilization and legitimation, but actual rancor. When, as we saw, output and input legitimacy are in shreds too, the collapse is a veritable *debelatio*.

Democracy was not part of the original DNA of European Integration. It still feels like a foreign implant. With the collapse of its original political messianism, the alienation we are now witnessing is only to be expected. And thus, when failure hits as in the Euro crisis, when the Panem is gone, all sources of legitimacy suddenly, simultaneously collapse.

This collapse comes at an inopportune moment, at the very moment when Europe of the Union would need all its legitimacy resources. The problems are European and the solution has to be at the European level.

IV

There has been yet a fourth, fear inducing loss of *heimat* – the zone of comfort of Union leadership, habituated for decades to consistently high Eurobarometer ratings and with all the difficulties, an on track integration project. All that has changed, and as just noted, the legitimacy credit is depleted. What then has been the reaction? United in fear. The response to Brexit will serve as illustration.

The kneejerk reaction from the usual suspects has been More Europe and a retreat to the self-defeating search for projects to mobilize support. Bread and Circus yet again. Whereas there has been sensible talk of financial governance, there is in my view a total failure to appreciate the long term unresolved problem of input and throughput legitimacy. A political Europe which is the only viable solution to such, would require leadership and courage. It is not even on the agenda. But most telling is the reaction to Brexit.

Of course, we know better than to be shooting at each other; but the post June 23rd relationship between the UK and the EU is woefully bellicose and increasingly so. In tone and mood, diplomatic niceties are barely maintained and in content positions seem to be hardening. I will readily accept that the UK leadership bears considerable responsibility for the bellicosity and the escalating lawfare. Yet, the inequality of arms so strikingly favors the Union that its attitude and policies should not be driven by emotional pique and issues of 'honor' but by mature responsibility for the future of the Union, Europe and, indeed, world stability. Let the UK play *L'enfant terrible*; Europe can afford a certain magnanimous disregard of British ongoing provocations. Yet fear dominates.

It is easy to understand European Union frustration with the UK. When Cameron called for a renegotiation followed by a referendum he had no clue what it is he wanted and needed to renegotiate. It also became abundantly clear that the UK went into the referendum without any strategic – political and legal – plan in the event of, well, Brexit. One did not know what the Brits wanted ahead of the referendum and one still is not clear what they want in its wake. Any fair-minded observer would agree that Juncker and other European leaders bent over backwards to accommodate the UK. The anger at the decision, so damaging to Europe (and the UK) is understandable and even the barely disguised sentiment of needing to 'punish' them.

Still, setting aside this kind of emotional state as the basis for, or even influencing, a Brexit strategy is well overdue.

I take it as axiomatic that it is in the interest of the Union – economic, strategic (not least security) and even social to have as amicable open and cooperative a relationship with a post Brexit UK as possible. One cannot very justly express alarm and disapproval at the protectionist winds blowing from the White House and then not accept that even if outside the Union it is in our interest to keep as open a marketplace and cordial a relationship with such an important contiguous economy and polity as the UK. Or not to realize that with the end of the Pax Americana, how damaging it would be for Europe in finally beginning to take its security responsibilities seriously not to be able to count on a robust participation of the UK. And beyond the money power matrices, the UK has to remain a firm ally in the defense of liberal democracy under attack.

What, then, from the Union's side – at the policy rather than the emotional side -- seems to explain the bellicosity? There are two interconnected arguments which are presented to justify the rhetoric of a "hard" Brexit, 'first the money, then trade negotiations' etc.

The first is that one cannot compromise the conceptual and practical coherence of the Single Market of which free movement of workers is an indispensable and non-negotiable principle. It is. And since the UK insists that it can no longer accept free movement, it cannot both have its cake and eat it. You cannot be in the Single Market without accepting its cardinal principles.

The second – interconnected -- reason for the tough rhetoric is the "discourage the others" argument. If the UK gets too comfortable a deal – i.e. is not made to pay a heavy price for Brexit – it might tempt other Member States to seek the same thereby bringing about a weakening or even disintegration of the Union.

I think the first argument is based on a misunderstanding and the second argument is self-defeating for the future of the Union.

It is clear that if the UK leaves the Union and rejects free movement it cannot be a full participant in the Single Market. But, it is worth making, again and again, the obvious distinction between *being part* of the Single Market and *having access* to the Single Market.

For decades it has been European policy that granting access to the Single Market to partners all over the world was an important objective beneficial both to the Union and dozens of external trading partners. The recent conclusion of CETA is just the last if very visible manifestation of such a policy. The Union has countless agreements of this nature – the common denominator of which is the granting of access to the Single Market not only without requiring free movement of workers but specifically excluding such. It is true that for the most part the agreements relate to goods rather than services but the access is extensive nonetheless. These agreements have their autonomous mechanisms for dispute settlement, thus sidelining the issue of reference to the European Court.

The Union should announce, unilaterally, that it would be its desire that the UK would at a minimum have an agreement granting it access to the Single Market on terms no less favorable than any of its existing reciprocal agreements with third parties. I could see several distinct advantages of such a declaration. Of course the UK may wish for more. Still, it would change the existing damaging bellicose atmosphere and mood, which are not auspicious for an amicable divorce. Second, it would not compromise any European interest from a commercial perspective. And third it would allow that aspect of the negotiations to be handed over to the technocrats while allowing the political level to deal with the more sensitive issues such as financial services, passporting and the like.

In the same vein, just about all Member States of the Union have bilateral investment treaties with third parties, which typically give extensive access to company directors etc. Is it thinkable that the UK should not have similar privileges? Why should the same "most favored" principle not be extended as regards these privileges accorded third parties?

And finally, there can be a unilateral declaration of a willingness in principle to accord permanence to all UK nationals established in the Union on condition of reciprocity.

The current strategy of insisting on first settling the terms of the divorce (how much Britain owes etc.) before any trade negotiations can begin, rather than run the two agendas simultaneously would receive an F (failure) in any negotiating workshop in any school of governance. It is a lose-lose strategy. You never want your partner to a deal to feel blackmailed. You prevent 'horse trading' between the two agendas, thus reducing the chances of optimal outcomes and you only achieve false finality on the first agenda which will inevitably be reviewed in the light of the results in the second, inviting a subsequent renegotiation. Above all you raise the risk of overall failure, surely an outcome in the interest of none.

What then of the "discourage the others" argument?

The truly catastrophic damage to the Union of Brexit was to grievously damage the slow transformation of the European Construct from a community of convenience (concrete achievements leading to de facto solidarity – in the language of the Schuman Declaration) to a Community of Fate. Our Member States are communities of fate – even those with multinational populations. There may be deep social and political divisions, but it is commonly understood that they will find resolution with the framework of the nation and State. We have, after all, come a long way from the ethnic purity of post World War I and understand the civilizing effect of settling differences rather than turning one's back and seceding. The Union was reaching that point. The Exit option of the Lisbon Treaty, a nod towards the residual sovereignty of the Member States was always to remain the arm you never use. Cameron used this nuclear weapon to the detriment of all. Brexit discourse, spilling over from the UK debate to the whole of Europe, regressed the Union back to a contingent, on-going project, the viability of which may be challenged at any moment, depending on a material balance of costs and benefits. Unwittingly, in an almost panicky knee jerk reaction, European discourse became one of "we have to come up with projects which will prove to the peoples of Europe that it is in their interest to maintain the Union. Even if successful in finding such projects, this is a self-defeating approach, because of its contingent, cost-benefit logic, on which the future of the Union is now to rest. The "discourage the others" argument in the current post Brexit approach belongs to the same genus.

Does one really want the future of European integration to rest on a support driven by scaring our peoples by setting up the UK as a reminder of the bad fate, which awaits the heretics?

So, think now the unthinkable – an approach which would afford the UK as comfortable a status as possible, even perhaps a form of Associate Membership.

If a UK status is appealing to this or that Member State, let it be. Those States would not in any event be helpful in a Union which needs some brave and decisive fixes to its structure and processes, not least in the fiscal and governance areas. For those who remain, most if not all, it will be a moment of willed re-commitment rather than scared, coerced, resentful and contingent inertia.

Dialogical Epilogue

J.H.H. Weiler

In this Epilogue I assume the role of 'Consul of the Reader'. I try to raise with several of the authors the kind of questions which, to the best of my ability, an attentive and critical reader might wish to raise as regards the various contributions. The last word, naturally, goes to the authors.

On Chapter 1: George Gerapetritis

Thank you for your illuminating chapter. Here are some questions that come to mind.

1. You (re)present – and advocate – quite categorically and robustly the much discussed Deliberative model of democracy in the context of the legitimacy debate of the European construct. Your presentation is categorical in the following sense: Deliberativeness is presented as a conditio-sine-qua-non for democratic legitimacy. Here is a representative quote:

Although there are significant conceptual varieties of the doctrine [of Deliberativeness], deliberative democracy stands for the process of opinion convergence thorugh wide and equal participation and the reasoned and elaborate exchange of arguments so as to produce legitimate outcomes, i.e. ethical and justifiable grounds for regular obedience to power. Accordingly, no judgment can claim correctness and validity unless it constitutes the product of a deliberative process that makes it justified and reasoned. (My emphasis.)

Your presentation is robust in that it presents a very definite set of criteria which, in turn, are a condition-sine-qua-non to satisfy the requirements of deliberativeness. (Your categories of A-E).

I think it would be fair to say that only by a considerable stretch, a stretch which would eviscerate your very own criteria (in A-E) could any of the democratic structures and processes in all of our Member States be said to satisfy even remotely your conditions for deliberativeness.

Would not then the inevitable conclusion be that in all of our Member States (leaving aside European Union governance) public power as exercised by national parliaments and national executives is illegitimate and lacks ethical and justifiable ground for obedience? Are you really willing to stand behind this apparent implication of your analysis?

2. You place a lot of stock in the 'external deliberative techniques such as polls and referenda which can 'assist and substantiate' the deliberative internal (institutional) deliberative process. To an innocent reader Brexit would appear to be a textbook example that follows your very own prescriptions for such an external deliberative technique, as would, for example, the Swiss referendum on the building of mosques. I imagine that you would argue that in the conduct of the campaign some of your criteria were compromised. If this is the case, could you not only explain which criteria were compromised, but try and give a thick description of how the Brexit process should have taken place in order to be truly deliberative. My hunch is that once you pile up all the conditions in this concrete situation it might well call into doubt the practicability of this external technique and might confirm the intuition that a referendum is almost by definition a non-deliberative mechanism. Even more puzzling is your reference to 'polls' as a deliberative technique. Can you explain how 'polls' fit into your legitimation scheme? I raise the issue of Brexit as an indication of a more general unease with the paper: There is a marked discrepancy, in length and detail between the first (long and detailed) part of the paper which sets out the concept and the model and the second (short and approximate) where you give some indications of how the model could actually be actuated in the reality of European governance. I think many readers will share my view that this very discrepancy is telling and that despite your declared intention, the operationalization of deliberativeness advocated by you does not really break away from the conceptual and the model. No operationalization of any model of democracy is perfect which is why we speak of imperfect democracies, but it is hard to gauge from your paper what meaning could be given to 'imperfect deliberativeness'. It almost seems an oxymoron.

3. When it comes to the European Union, when talking about the horizontal dimension of deliberativeness to characterize the Commission as the Executive and the Parliament and Council as the Legislative branches of the Union. I would argue that this is simply wrong in a profound way. The Commission exercises extensive autonomous legislative functions and is part of the legislative procedure and the Council in its various derivations (from Comitology to the European Council) exercises extensive executive functions and most importantly missing from this picture is the

primary role which national administrations play as the executive arm of the Union. Do you disagree? If I am right, what does this do to your whole concept as to how deliberativeness should be grafted on to European governance?

4. In most of our democracies (I insist on calling them democracies, your critique notwithstanding) courts play a role in ensuring that the other branches of government respect the primordial rules of democratic process through a variety of doctrines such as respect for essential procedural requirements as a ground for reviewing both legislative and administrative exercise of power. Your paper is essentially silent on this. My difficulty is in trying to imagine how courts could be effective guardians even of the core of your conditions for deliberativeness in A-E. In your scheme, would the procedures and process of deliberativeness not be subject to judicial review? Is this consistent with our contemporary notions of the Rule of Law?

Reply of George Gerapetritis

1. Deliberative democracy basically refers to a *decision-making process*. Thus, deliberativeness provides legitimacy to a decision that has followed specific methodological steps and abides by certain conditions. Orthodox deliberative theory suggests that a decision taken by a competent authority may well be formally legitimate and legal but can lack substantive legitimacy due to a lack of deliberative processes. Thus, substantive legitimacy stemming from deliberative techniques neither refers to nor substitutes formal legitimacy, which is the exclusive forum of representation in the context of conventional representative democracy. Deliberative democracy is the type of formal democracy that enhances the deliberative decision-making process. From this viewpoint, it constitutes an additional asset to formal democracy and operates as an antidote to the deficiencies of wide-scale formal democracies where the mere role of the electorate is exhausted once the election process is over. Accordingly, EU Member States can hardly be qualified as employing deliberative processes. This applies *par excellence* to the EU constitutional order due to the democratic deficit so well exemplified in the literature, which directly calls for legitimacy upgrade. However, this assertion does not lead us to the conclusion that all legal orders are illegitimate and lack ethical and justifiable grounds for obedience, since there is a formal standpoint of legitimacy (more so in na-

tional states). There is no doubt that European regimes are genuine democracies; what remains strongly questionable is whether they can qualify as *deliberative* democracies. The prevalence of majoritarian parliamentarism seems to substantiate this allegation.

2. Polls, juries and assemblies constitute significant means of deliberative democracy subject to the following observations:

First, they are not the only practical means of deliberativism. Given that this theory suggests a specific technique of decision-making processes, any procedure before a collective body (e.g. the parliament, the council of ministers, a court) can qualify as deliberative.

Second, a referendum, although admittedly a participatory process and, thus, a technique of participatory democracy, does not per se constitute a deliberative technique. In order to establish the deliberative quality of a referendum all set criteria must operate cumulatively, i.e. inclusiveness, endorsement, evidence, interplay and fair play and transparency. Unfortunately, nationwide referenda only rarely reflect the criteria of deliberativeness, since not all related evidence is adduced and numerous totally false statements are set in place (in violation of the evidence requirement), the opposing views are expressed in a dogmatic manner that does not allow any space for retraction on the basis of a rational choice approach (in violation of the endorsement requirement) and there is no genuine and on an equal footing exchange of argumentation (in violation of the interplay and fair play requirement). This is particularly true in the case of the Bremain/ Brexit referendum where a lot of inaccurate information was set forth and, at the same time, the key political actors were so polarised that, in fact, no evidence whatsoever, irrespective of its conclusiveness, could even remotely result in a change of view to support another option.

Third, any decision-making process applies within a particular institutional context. There is no subjective veil of ignorance or objective *tabula rasa* when it comes to a decision of a state organ. A decision ought to be taken pursuant to the rules of division of competences and within the state of legality, as enshrined in the hierarchy of norms. Thus, in a legal environment a decision ought to be both legitimate and legal. Any policy choice, such as the question of whether to construct a mosque or not, is placed within the institutional context of the constitutional protection of religious liberty and of the secular state. An unconstitutional/illegal decision cannot be valid within a rule-of-law regime, irrespective of whether it has been achieved through deliberative processes. This is why human rights issues, which are by definition set to protect individuals and to overlook the opposing majority, may not be subject to referenda. Still, legal interpretation can also be subject to deliberative techniques which cater to conclusions based on reason and reject the idea of a single and dogmatic truth.

Fourth, the set criteria for deliberativeness constitute an amalgam of objective and subjective conditions. It is true that deliberative democracy relies heavily on the latter, i.e. a different culture of decision-making that, in turn, presupposes a different human mentality in collective decision-making and bargaining that is currently missing, as proved by the rising level of populism, extremism and xenophobia. In that, it seems that a lot ought to be done with respect to deliberative education. However, 'imperfectness' is presumably not an inherent default of deliberativism but merely a symptom of our era, otherwise one must accept that there is no rational human interaction at any level. Deliberative democracy cannot be a panacea; but it is not a utopia either.

3. Due to the complexity and the uniqueness of the EU structures, there can be no effective and accurate correspondence to state architecture. This is particularly true with regard to the Commission, which exercises multilayer competences touching upon the executive, the legislature and the (pre-)judiciary. Although significant steps were taken through the Lisbon Treaty to bring EU structures closer to a Westminster-type parliamentarism, the Commission still suffers from a relatively low level of deliberation (in terms of decision-making) and accountability (in terms of responsibility). When it comes to deliberation, the Commission procedures seem to fail significantly in relation to inclusiveness (by often failing to address all stakeholders in a particular setting), interplay and fair play (by lacking processes of dialogue based on an equal footing) and transparency (mainly due to widespread comitology). By way of contrast, the Commissions show more satisfactory results in relation to the subjective criterion of endorsement, especially vis-à-vis the Parliament, where solid party politics seem to apply more and more, in the sense that it appears at times more ready to amend or overturn specific policies and stereotypes. Of course, this process of adjustment is not always the product of a genuine retraction predilection but mostly of a realistic approach in order to achieve more desirable results. Still, it seems that when compared to member states' executives and/or legislatures, the Commission seems to lack the objective standards of deliberativeness more than the subjective.

4. Deliberative democracy, as any other model of democracy, mostly operates on a normative level. It essentially serves to improve the actual

functioning of democratic processes and optimise the results thereof. Specific aspects associated with deliberativeness are already part of the judicial control of administrative action: *audi alteram partem*, the obligation to provide reasons for individual executive decisions, prior hearing and publication. Still, deliberative democracy as an overall project cannot altogether become a justiciable issue. It is mostly used as a yardstick to assess the quality of democratic governance without judicial sanctions altogether. This is not inconsistent with the rudiments of the rule of law: very many features that one might reasonably argue as falling within the core of democracy and constitutionalism escape judicial control, such as the parliamentary *interna corporis*, the acts of governments or political questions. This does not result in a curtailment of the level of the rule of law because, at the end of the day, it is the electorate itself that will approve or disapprove of an applicable model of democracy.

On Chapter 2: Lina Papadopoulou

Thank you for your illuminating chapter. Here are some questions that come to mind.

You make a valid and important point in indicating that normative preferences as to the telos and shape of the European construct condition the various proposals for reform of the institutional and other governance arrangements of the Union aimed at enhancing its democratic legitimacy. You also rightly point out that rarely do authors explicitly and capaciously discuss thesis teleological normative preference which underlie their empirical, social science based, advocacy. The reader thus expects that you yourself would be explicit and capacious in outlining your own normative preferences and biases which underline your own analysis and advocacy. But I, and I expect some other readers, was unable to find in your text that kind of explicit and capacious self-examination which, by employing the very methodology which you inveigh, would be necessary critically to evaluate your own take on the current circumstance of Europe and your empirical advocacy. Could you succinctly and transparently set this out?

I think many readers would find useful the conceptual clarification of moving from double to triple legitimations through States, peoples and citizens (in their capacity as individuals rather than national communities. But at the same time I think many would have my difficulty in understanding why, in accordance with this scheme, the European Parliament is not already an institutional vehicle for representing citizens. To be sure, this aspect would be enhanced by the creation of pan-European parties and some of the other devices you critically examine and advocate in the context of Treaty/Constitutional amendment. But is it the conclusion to be drawn from the paper that Europe already enjoys such triple legitimation and the only issue is to enhance it further by some fine tuning of existing arrangement, and greater loyalty to provisions which already exist?

I have, I believe, a serious disagreement with your definition of political legitimacy. I quote (omitting footnotes):

Legitimacy is 'the belief that authorities, institutions, and social arrangements are appropriate, proper and just' (cite to Tyler). Legitimacy facilitates the exercise of power by enhancing the probability that certain or all commands will be obeyed by a given group of persons. The internalization of specific justification by the people allows a political system, its legal texts and its personal authorities, to be viewed 'as normatively or morally appropriate by the people within the system'(id.). As a result, 'control by others is replaced by self-control, as social norms and values are internalized and become part of the individual's own desires concerning how to behave'. (cite to Hoffman).

This is social science (here, social psychology) without political theory and a very problematic foundation on which to build your conceptual and pragmatic edifice. In general I am usually dismissive of 'reductio ad Hitlerum' arguments, but in this case it begs to made. The National Socialist regime in Germany would seem to me to satisfy amply your definition of legitimacy. Would you call that regime legitimate? By the criteria you propose one would, in my view, be obliged to come to this conclusion. One can think of some other historical examples of such. This extreme example is not a mere 'debating point' a way of picking holes but goes to what I think is a deep problem of the paper. Of course I am not suggesting, as you will readily understand and accept, that you harbor even the slightest affinity to even the smallest part of Nazi ideology. But I am arguing that the normative force of your tripartite conceptualization and the pragmatic incremental steps that you suggest are considerably weakened by this foundation. Because, shorn of an underlying political theory of legitimacy, as one reads through the paper it increasingly resembles the kind of analysis that a marketing firm might give a corporation on the steps to be taken in order to enhance consumer attachment to a product being sold. It is not about a vision of a normatively legitimate construction of polity and governance, but rather a mechanism for enhancing citizen compliance. Here is a representative quote which comes right at the beginning of the section entitled Enhancing the Citizens' Europe:

The direct participation and involvement of citizens in the decision-making process is likely to enhance their trust in the outcomes and enhance their readiness to comply.

Res ipsa loquitur. This goes back to my first question to you. Unless one is clearer about the underlying vision of Europe we may legitimately question whether mechanisms designed to enhance the readiness to comply are from a political theory perspective rather than a social science perspective desirable and hence legitimacy enhancing. If citizens participate and are involved in a project which substantively is nefarious – like slavery in the South of the United States – the outcome will be nefarious. A democracy of vile persons will be a vile democracy, even if very 'legitimate' because considered 'appropriate' by its citizens who participate and are involved, perhaps even with relish, in the decision making process.

Reply of Lina Papadopoulou

1. Dear Professor Weiler, you are right to point out that my own teleological normative preference is not outlined clearly enough. The main phrase that indicates such a preference is admittedly the following:

> The point of departure for the present paper is the adoption of the Habermasian political scheme for Europe, according to which, '…the challenge before us is not to invent anything but to conserve the great democratic achievements of the European nation-state, beyond its own limits'. [1]

Having adopted the 'Habermasian political scheme' for Europe and assumed that it would be familiar to the readers, I myself failed to repeat its caveats. I still think it would be wiser and more useful for any reader to go back to the original works of Habermas,[2] according to whom the main normative preferences are:

1 J Habermas, 'Why Europe Needs a Constitution' (2001) 11 *New Left Review* 5: 6, id., 'Democracy in Europe: Why the Development of the EU into a Transnational Democracy Is Necessary and How It Is Possible', 21 (2015) *European Law Journal* 546 (553).

2 See, for example, *The Crisis of the European Union: A Response*, Cambridge, Polity Press 2012.

a. 'to conserve the great democratic achievements', which include 'not only formal guarantees of civil rights, but levels of social welfare, education and leisure that are the precondition of both an effective private autonomy and of democratic citizenship'.[3]
b. to invent 'a form of democracy that is at once supranational and situated above the organisational level of a state' (Habermas 2015, 546).
c. to manage 'a shift to solidarity-based policies for mastering the continuing crisis', which will not be possible 'without transferring additional sovereignty rights to the European level' (Habermas 2015, 550).

I would add to that point my own normative preference, which pervades the whole of my paper, to place citizen-based legitimacy on the same footing as that stemming from states and peoples, as introduced by Tsatsos.

2. The answer is 'yes but…'. Normatively, one may find provisions in the Treaties allowing Europe to enjoy triple legitimacy. However, I have two observations here. First of all, the normative content of these Treaties has not yet been deployed. Secondly, as a matter of degree, while one may find some institutional tools to enhance the politicisation of European citizenship, more such tools could and —according to my normative preference as outlined above— should be inserted in the Treaties (e.g. the election of the Union's President by the European citizens on a 'one-wo/man-one-vote' basis).

At the same time, the triple legitimacy theory seeks to underline the fact that the tendency to equate (European) peoples with (European) citizens that is common in the academic debate and present in the Treaty (see e.g. article 10[2] TEU), is both analytically and institutionally flawed. In this context, the European Parliament cannot really be considered to directly represent the citizens as long as there are neither pan-European parties nor a single pan-European electoral system and elections are only considered as a formal poll for national parties with national agendas. In this context,

> [t]his theoretical approach aims both to describe the 'state-of-the-legal-art' of the Union today and serve as a normative yardstick for future developments. It is also a critique of procedures that either preserve or enhance only the intergovernmental legitimacy pillar, thus justifying accusations speaking of an 'executive federalism'.[4]

---

3 J Habermas, 'Why Europe Needs a Constitution' (2001) 11 *New Left Review* 5: 6.

4 J Habermas, *The Crisis of the European Union: A Response* (Cambridge, Polity Press, 2012) 12.

3. Dear Prof. Weiler, this is indeed a very powerful, deeply political question, but I am not sure to what extent it conceals an underlying disagreement. First of all, the Nazi regime, despite gaining power through elections, neither empowered citizens nor enhanced their participation. Neither, for that matter, did it allow for free parties and elections. On the contrary, it gained social and popular legitimacy through the *Führer Prinzip*, and rejected the 'rational form' of legitimacy and all the values I embrace as fundamental in my paper.

In contrast to the above historical paradigm, European citizens should be invited to participate within the value system that is outlined in Part II.C of my paper, where the underlying vision of Europe is (or should be) considered, from a political theory point of view, to be comprised by:

> personal autonomy and dignity (enshrined in civil rights and protecting minorities), political equality (enshrined in the political rights of free and equal citizens participating in a democratically governed polity) and solidarity (aiming at social equalisation, reflected in the social state's ethos and enshrined in social rights)." ... "These values are common to both the European and national constitutional settings. Thus, the value triplet functions as 'roadmap' for the EU's policies and as a criterion for its political legitimacy. The European Union also draws its legitimacy from the belief that unification is necessary in order to safeguard these values —maybe the concomitant of what Weiler[5] calls 'political messianism'.

Coming back to your first question, and combining my normative preferences with my deep longing that Europe's citizens might develop a sense of trust and devotion in —or even, why not, achieve a state of complianee with— the Union, its integration process and underlying values, I can only add that this longing is due to my (not expressly stated) belief that nationalism —as opposed to European patriotism— will not only fail to preserve the *acquis* of the political and constitutional culture of post-WWII Europe but even lead to a new bloody adventure. That's why I conclude my paper by saying that

> Fighting this kind of false patriotism, namely nationalism, requires the construction of a European political identity.

In this sense I think the kind of legitimacy for Europe I propose is not only at a far remove from the type adopted and promoted by Hitler but it is ex-

5 JJH Weiler, 'The political and legal culture of European integration: An exploratory essay' (2011) 9 *International Journal of Constitutional Law* 678, 682.

actly the opposite, even if they both share, as all regimes do, I suppose, a necessity to guarantee the citizens' consent, trust and compliance.

On Chapter 3: Giacinto della Cananea

Thank you for your illuminating chapter.

I have great sympathy with the argument made in your paper. On May 2, 1998 I published in El Pais an article entitled *No a la representación sin impuestos* which, far more superficially than you do, made the case. Among many others there are two fundamental emphases in your paper: One is the nexus between this circumstance and the rights-duties issue. The second regards the power distribution among the political stakeholder in the Union and most importantly the reduced role of the European Parliament degraded as you felicitously put it to a spending authority.

My comments are less in the nature of a challenge to your analysis with which as I mentioned I find myself clearly in your camp, but rather some clarification and enhancements on which you may wish to comment.

1. The absence of robust European fiscal competences – in effect means that the Union remains on the periphery of one of the most central dimensions of democracy – as Gian Domenico Majone has been persuasively arguing for decades – and social justice, namely redistributive politics. It is one of the central issues in democratic politics in all liberal democracies. One can disagree – as the Right and Left disagree on this sharply – on the extent and circumstances of redistributive politics. But there is no modern democracy, certainly not in Europe, which does not have significant redistributive policies in place. Because the Union does, by contrast, have robust monetary competences, it is not only that it cannot itself, even in times of crisis with severe human and social costs, engage in redistributive policies except in a paltry way, but its monetary disciplines chill the ability of Member States, notably in the Eurozone, to do such with serious implications to the central theme of this volume – legitimacy, both in the empirical social science sense and in the normative sense. What kind of polity is it, that exercises serious monetary discipline but, structurally and constitutionally, is unable to mitigate such with fiscal and redistributive measures?

This absence also militates against one of the most frequently mentioned – and abused – values of the Union, Solidarity. I wish to illustrate such with a little morality tale. In the 80 Texas underwent what was called the Savings and Loans crisis which resembled very much the Irish circumstance in the recent 2008 crisis in Europe: The risk of massive failure of banks over exposed to bad loans in the private sector. Not surprisingly there was a live and serious debate on the appropriate reactions with many similarities to the current debates in Europe: Bail them out with the specter of moral hazard not holding irresponsible bankers to account for foolhardy loans? Let them fail with very considerable social cost to many savers who could not be seriously held responsible for the follies of the banks. (The actual 'bankers' were naturally well cushioned unlike the savers whose money they irresponsibly loaned out). The big difference between the current European debates and the American debate in the 80s was the following. You did not hear hardly at all in the USA the very common European argument 'why should we in, say, California or New York, spend our hard earned tax money on those 'louts' in Texas. This was not simply because of the longevity of American citizenship as the primary identity reference in the United States. It was mostly because any money spent on any bailout would be American, federal money rather than Californian or New York.

The absence of serious Union resources that would only be available with a meaningful fiscal competence, militates against the development of that kind of solidarity as was much in evidence in the last half decade. One could still have disagreement as to whether at all, and under what conditions, one should or should not bail out. But it would not be Germany or Finland or the Netherlands who would be bailing out (if that were the decision) but the polity of European citizens. Put differently, taxation is not only about providing the Union with the means necessary to achieve its objective but goes to the heart of the European construct understood as a community of fate.

I wonder if you would agree with me that in examining the institutional implications it would be useful to engage in some form of disaggregation. It is not, as you seem to argue simply EP v Member States although it is that too. Since the funding of Europe remains as you say squarely in the hands of the Member States, it produces, as we have seen, huge Orwellian type empowerment and disempowerment effects as between Member States ripping apart the careful equilibria which the institutional rules on voting in the Council is meant to preserve. All are, within those rules, equal, but suddenly some are far more equal than others – another blow at the heart of the European construct.

Finally, I think it may be more clarifying, in this context, to speak not of the rights-duties effect but the rights-responsibility effect. This, in my view, is not a lexical point. Citizens in the European Union are not bereft of duties. But these duties are of a peculiar kind – which, too, are at the center of so many contributions to this volume: The duty to obey the Law of the Union – supreme and often of direct effect. But given the structure of governance in Europe, and its persistent political democratic deficits, they cannot in good conscience be held responsible for such and in effect are reduced to subjects of the law (and the concomitant duty of obedience) rather its subjects. Your paper explains convincingly why representation without taxation enhances this culture of non-responsibility for the direction and fate of the Union.

Reply of Giacinto della Cananea

First and foremost, I would like to thank you not only for your very careful review of my paper and for the ensuing comments, but also for drawing my attention to your 1998 study on representation and taxation in the EU. Instead of embarking on a radical revision of the paper, I have made an attempt to take all your comments into account in the following pages, addressing them sequentially. And I believe the argumentation presented in my paper has been significantly improved, not only for the readers but also for myself and for the enriching dialogue that takes place within the ECLN.

Regarding your comments:

1. There is, as you observed in 1998, a fundamental contradiction in the institutional design of the Union. On the one hand, its legislative powers have grown considerably over time. Whether the prophecy attributed to Jacques Delors, according to which 'in ten years 80 per cent of the legislation related to economics, maybe also to taxes, will be of Community origin' has been fulfilled, is an open question, which should be ascertained on the basis of scientific methods. However, there is no doubt that the Union's exercise of its legislative powers has a strong impact on national constituencies, for example by providing EU citizens with access to social benefits. This impact is even stronger in the light of the limits imposed on national budgets since Maastricht. On the other hand, the EU cannot mitigate the consequences of such limits because it is not vested with fully-fledged fiscal powers. Indeed, there is no redistributive taxation. Nor is

there any capacity to borrow money, not even for capital investment, a point to which I will return later (in § 2).

A twofold consequence follows from this, for the comparative analysis of federal and quasi-federal institutions and, more practically, for redistributive purposes. Comparatively, several scholars and statists have asserted that the EU is a quasi-federation. This may hold true in some respects, for example with regard to the judicial power. But it does not hold true as far as the power of the purse is concerned. Consider, for instance, the US Constitution. Following James Madison's argument that only the legislative department could have 'access to the pockets of the people', Article I, section 8, of the Constitution vested the power of the purse squarely in Congress. By contrast, in the 1970's the drafters of the new financial framework deliberately divided government by making national ministers the competent authority for obtaining money and for compulsory expenditure, while the European Parliament could decide on the rest of expenditure. The least that can be said, therefore, is that the EP differs not only from its national counterparts, but also from those of the American federation. The widespread rhetoric on the role of representation, also in view of the 'democratic deficit', should confront this basic fact.

I am aware there are some statists and scholars who disagree with the critical approach that Weiler and I share with regard to redistributive policies. In its essence, their argument is that nothing prevents the Union and its Parliament from making redistributive policies, through expenditure. But this is not a convincing argument for two reasons. First, as observed earlier, there is no redistributive taxation and this leaves the Union with only one arm. Second, the remaining arm, the expenditure side, is severely limited.

2. The absence of serious Union resources is all the more important in view of two distinctive and genetic features of the European Community: diversity and the promise of solidarity. James Madison's analysis is, again, quite helpful. In Federalist No. 10, he argued that the greatest source of factions had always been the various and unequal distribution of property. 'Factions', from his viewpoint, were groups of citizens united by some common passion or interest that conflicted with the rights of other citizens.

Now consider diversity within the Union. Economic diversity between the Member States was evident when the Treaty of Rome was signed. It has not diminished across the years, with the accession of several Central and Eastern European countries. Social and religious diversity has increased, too. The Union is characterised by a variety of languages, religions, and political beliefs. This might have led to a higher level of redistribution. In other words, the higher the diversity of interests in the electorate, the more justified the necessity of redistribution. But the absence of serious Union resources has undermined any significant step in this direction. Consequently, the Union's measures, for example, in favour of better living and working conditions as well as of social mobility, are essentially legislative measures. It is in this sense that Majone's characterisation of the Union as a sort of 'regulatory State' has its strength. It is in this sense, moreover, that we can see the distance between the emphasis that the constitutive documents of the Union assign to solidarity, from the Schumann plan to the Lisbon treaty, and the effective dimension that solidarity has.

Arguably, there is more in the assertion that 'taxation is not only about providing the Union with the means necessary to achieve its objective but goes to the heart of the European construct understood as a community of fate' than the discourse about bailing out shows. Consider, again, Madison's acknowledgement of the 'unequal distribution of property' as the greatest source of factions. This awareness did not make of him a predecessor of socialism. Indeed, Madison was an advocate of a system based on individual freedom and the pursuit of happiness. He then thought that a free government could tolerate the unequal distribution of wealth especially if the wealth of the nation increased. It is important to focus on Madison's characterisation of the common good in terms of economic expansion, as distinct from redistribution of wealth, because this provides a key to understanding how the absence of redistributive taxation is worsened by the absence of borrowing, even for capital investment in material infrastructure. It is frequently noted that, whatever their intrinsic appeal, such policies have a sort of low profile, precisely as a result of their being favourable to the whole of society and in the medium or long term. But it is precisely the fact that investment policies maintain consistency across the years that makes them particularly suitable to increase the common wealth, with advantages for all.

In conclusion, the absence of serious Union resources does not only weaken the capacity of its institutions to devote resources to redistribution from the viewpoint of social justice. It also weakens their role from the viewpoint of the idea of fundamental fairness, à la Rawls and even from that of the 'classic' theory of public finances, according to which public authorities must promote infrastructure.

3. This remark sounds convincing. The absence of serious Union resources has two institutional consequences that are related, but distinct. First, the fact that the Member States are the only holders of the power to tax limits the role of the European Parliament. Meanwhile, the role of national parliaments is weakened precisely in the area where historically it had grown; that is, the control of taxation, because a regulation enacted by the Council of Ministers pre-empts national legislation and thus impinges on the role of national parliaments.

Second, it can be said that any increase of the Union's own resources lies in the hands of the Member States, considered as a whole. But any proposal to increase such resources can be seen through the lens of the distinction between those who are to spend and those who are to pay or, what is even worse for the Union, through the lens of inter-governmental transfers of money. This not only undermines the formal equality between the Member States and the balance of powers that rules on voting in the Council are meant to preserve, but it also shapes discourses about revising the own resources, because such transfers must be justified. One way to do so is to argue that such transfers are needed to redress the gap that stems from the different degrees to which the Member States gain from market integration. Another, and more controversial, ground to justify transfers is to argue that they are needed in the interest of equity or 'cohesion'. In both cases, the reverse side of the coin is that the rulers of more efficient political and administrative systems may argue that less efficient ones must carry out certain reforms. This produces two consequences that have emerged in the first two decades of the 21st century: the 'economic' logic of conditional funding and the 'moral' (or, better, moralistic) approach that tends to identify debt with 'culpable' attitudes, thus distorting the idea of solidarity.

4. The heart of my argument is that, whatever the institutional consequences of constitutional rules governing taxation and expenditure, both historically and systematically such rules have a crucial importance for any legal theory about rights and duties in the public sphere. In this respect, there is no need to engage in the discussion between two consolidated schools of thought. The first, and increasingly less appealing, school of thought asserts the priority of duties over rights, in the sense that the latter can only be identified with reference to the former and thus argues that someone has a right if someone else has some kind of duty towards him. The second school of thought, which is by far more fashionable in our epoch, asserts the priority of rights over duties, at least in the sense that it

is only if certain rights are recognised and protected that there is adequate ground for duties. The reason why we do not need to engage in this debate is, first and foremost, that the Union's lack of power to tax disconnects the dimension of rights from the dimension of duties. This is evident not only if one thinks that rights cannot be recognised in an abstract manner, but exist in a specific institutional context, in relation to a given social group or set of social groups (a viewpoint closer to the Union, considered as a res publica composita), but also if one accepts some kind of correlativity between rights and duties. Even for those who believe that rights can generate new duties, the question that arises is that of who should bear such duties; that is, a matter of defining and attributing a responsibility, and ultimately of value judgements. It is hard to see how a sound theory of rights can be based on a framework that does not promote a culture of responsibility, but its opposite; that is, a culture of irresponsibility, and not simply of a fiscal type. In fact, in the more recent period of European integration, this culture of irresponsibility has developed together with the lack of awareness or sensibility for the impact of the Union's rules on the ability of Member States to cope with social issues. It is not easy to understand how the protection of rights can be secured within such a culture.

On Chapter 4: Tom Eisbouts

Thank you for your illuminating chapter. Here are some questions that come to mind.

I am not sure how effective your 'debunking' of the No-Demos myth really is. There are several reasons for my doubts. Let me list them and then explain each in some greater detail. First, I do not think you accurately or fully present and explain the No-Demos critique (in your view a 'myth') of European democracy. There are different strands to it, and each of these strands is multilayered. So it is not clear to which of these strands and/or layers your critique relates.

I think you present a caricature of the German Constitutional Court Lisbon Decision. There can be a fundamental critique of one premise in that judgment but, once corrected, there is much to praise to in that decision. I don't think academic discourse is particularly advanced by dismissing two doctoral dissertations as "epigones" or labeling scholarship "epigonism" (in a clearly pejorative sense) simply because they follow, or are influenced by, a strand of constitutional reasoning with which you disagree. I admire many things you have written and it has helped my thinking on several issues. Does that make me your 'epigon'? Am I guilty of epigonism? If so, I am a serial epigoinist and see nothing wrong in such.

I think your claim that the reference to "peoples" in the iconic "Ever Closer Union among the Peoples of Europe" to include national communities outside those of the Member States is powerful, plausible (oops, epigonism) and, so far as I know, original. The work it does for your argument is to remind us that even in the Treaties, the same word, e.g. peoples. May have more than one meaning. Indeed. You second distinction between people in a Volkish or 'traditional' sense (more on this below) and people in a 'political' sense as 'electorate' is far more problematic. For two reasons. At least once you conflate between the 'political' people – the electorate – and citizens. There are a large number of citizens, all those below voting age, which are not part of the electorate but are certainly citizens and part of the people. This is not a debating point; a 'caught you' statement. It is actually of significance to the issue. Because so much of what happens in politics, including voting, is about the future of the people, the future of these citizens which are not part of the electorate but are in our mind when we do politics. The distinction you try to draw is not nearly as sharp and hermetic as you present it. I believe that for the purpose of democratic theory and practice the 'traditional' and 'political' are inextricably linked. Be that as it may, the real problem with this distinction, persuasive or otherwise, is that, as I shall explain below, it does not actually do much work for what is the central point of your contribution to this volume, namely the No-demos thesis.

Finally, and in my eyes most importantly, the heart of the matter become transparent in your 'few last words' where you advance two propositions:

> 1. "it is not entirely wrong [you write] to claim that some historical, social and/or cultural unity, or consensus mostly underpins a democracy. But the democracies of Belgium, Switzerland, India, to name but a few, demonstrate the measure of diversity in language, culture, religion etc. that such democratic unity may contain."

This statement is correct; but how does that debunk the demos or the no-demos thesis? At best it debunks a particular strand of the no-demos thesis (more apparent in the German Constitutional Court Maastricht Decision and hardly at all in the Lisbon Decision) that insists on homogeneity – ethnic, cultural religious etc -- as an essential characteristic of demos. But that has been debunked again and again and again both normatively and empirically by the very examples you give, and many others. So demos may be influenced but is not dependent on any one of those markers. But nonetheless, as you say, "some kind of … unity" underpins democracy. It is a strong word – underpins. And I share your view: But that puts you squarely in the 'no-demos' camp. You need "some kind of … unity" to underpin a democracy. That 'kind of … unity' (however it is established) is what in contemporary political theory and praxis we call demos. What you are debunking is not the 'no demos' theory, but a particular version of it. Quite frankly, if that is what your critique amounts to – it is true but it has, I fear, been made more than once before including in the context of European integration.

What is more surprising is the second proposition in your last words which follows directly from the passage I just quoted.

> 2. "To reflect this, if you want to use the word 'demos' reasonably, in a political sense, you might accept the following: whenever and wherever groups of people can live together for a longer [sic] time in a single territory and in freedom, without making civil war, there you have a demos. This is the situation the peoples of Europe are in, seventy years after the end of the last world war."

I do not feel that this paragraph reflects at all the one that preceded it, I do not think it 'reasonably' defines demos, in a political or any other sense, it rests on a non-sequitur (i.e. presuming that which it tries to prove) and most of all it demonstrates in my view a profound misunderstanding of the use of the word demos in the context of democratic discourse.

So now let me elaborate somewhat on each point in a friendly invitation to you to clarify that which I think at least some readers might find problematic.

The Demos Thesis in Democratic Theory

The demos thesis kicks in, so to speak, not when groups of people, in a "single territory" (whatever that means) live together (whatever that means) without making civil war (civil war of course begs the question since classically it presumes a state or nation (otherwise it is not defined as civil war) – as do, for example the Canadians and Americans or the Norwegians and the Swedes. It kicks in only within a polity which claims the basic democratic discipline of the majority having a legitimate claim to impose its will, through law, on the minority. The demos thesis makes an empirical (social science) and a normative (political theory) claim that this basic democratic discipline operates only within a demos. The ability of the majority to demand compliance will be contested (empirically) and not be justified (normatively) – so the demos thesis claims – outside the framework of a demos. This is a very concise explanation to your very own claim of a 'unity' which 'underpins' democracy. I think that is what is meant by that rather strong word 'underpin' and in this basic sense you seem to accept the demos thesis. It is, indeed, very difficult to speak intelligibly about democracy – which encapsulates the word demos – without this basic understanding. Indeed, in the examples I gave, they live peaceably together precisely because, say, neither the Americans, nor the Swedes, claim that they enjoy a democratic coercive power over the Canadians or Norwegians respectively.

It would seem, thus, that your debunking does not challenge the foundational claim of the demos thesis but the second step, so to speak, which is – how to understand or define demos so that it could become operational (empirically and normatively) in any given polity. As hinted above, you seem to conflate the no-demos thesis with one strand, for long out of favor, of this second step, which insists that the only acceptable and operational definition of demos is one that insists on homogeneity – often of an ethnic nature i.e. demos as ethnos. I think it is possible to read the Maastricht Decision of the German Constitutional Court as founded on this Schmittian notion, contested even at the time by, say, Heller. I do not think it is fair to characterize the Lisbon decision in this way. Most modern democracies, and practically all European ones are in one way or another multicultural and have abandoned, as has modern democratic theory, this notion of homogeneity as necessary for an operational demos. Indeed, it is doubtful if it were ever true. If that is what your debunking amounts to, you are flogging a dead horse.

So what does constitute demos under the non homogeneity version? It can be different combinations of the cultural elements you mention such as language (but not necessarily so), religion (but not necessarily) so et cetera etcetera. Ultimately there is, in the notion of demos a strong subjective feeling of the individuals of belonging to the same demos, that subjective element essential to both the empirical and normative facets of the demos thesis. As you yourself point out, the Swiss speak four languages but none the less have a very strong sense of belonging to the same demos, and Italian speaking Swiss, though sharing a language with their neighbors to the South and living peaceably along side them for centuries, do not at all feel as being Italian, or belonging to the Italian demos. One of the striking and most original contributions of Ernst-Wolfgang Böckenförde (now finally translated into English and accessible to non-German speakers) was to point out that what differentiates different demoi are not only those cultural indicators but different understandings within different demoi of what constitutes demos, as a legitimating condition for democratic discipline – an illumination which underscores the subjective element in the notion of demos. Brubaker in his classic (though in some respects erroneous) analysis explained thus the difference between French (community of values) and German (organic) sense of nationality.

I think your endorsement of the 'underpinning' element combined with your trenchant critique of the homogeneity version of demos, still position you comfortably within the demos thesis as explicated so far.

Now things get deliciously interesting when one turns to the demos (or no demos) thesis in the context of European integration.

There is a claim, even among those (just about everyone except the extreme right) who reject the homogeneity version of demos as a condition for democracy, who claim that even if one accepts that there can be a multicultural demos, one cannot simultaneously belong to two (or more) demoi – see for example all those states – even in Europe -- who do not allow double nationality. In the context of European integration this claim translates to the proposition that since in Europe (ever closer union among the peoplessss of Europe) as distinct from, say, the United States (one nation under God) which is premised on the existence of sovereign Member States (albeit pooling their sovereignty) and distinct peoplessss, there simply cannot be a European demos, since such would mean the need to abandon the distinct demoi of the Member States. This version of the demos (or no demos) thesis has also been 'debunked' convincingly in my view by many, not least Nicolaidis in her felicitous thesis of demoicracy. The argument is that just as someone can be Protestant and German (i.e. having a strong sense of belonging to two groups differently defined) one can be German and European and have a strong sense of belongingness to both. I think you (and I) would still find ourselves together in belonging to the demos thesis. I once called this the multiple demoi thesis.

However, in the context of democratic theory and its foundational claim that demos is indispensable, empirically and normatively in order to underpin democracy, the sense of belonging to the European Union would have to be sufficiently thick in order to underpin a democratic discipline claim (majority can compel minority) within the European polity.

And now we get to the last strain of the argument, which, at is simplest, does not claim that there is a conceptual or empirical impossibility for the existence of a European demos (along side vibrant national demoi) as underpinning European democracy, but makes a more modest claim that in the état de choses this condition does not prevail, or is very weak, which makes the current claim of European democracy fragile normatively and unstable empirically – as the recent resurgence in Euroskepticism seems to give evidence. And, surprise surprise, even on this issue you seem to be on board when you write:

> „I agree that the legal creation of an EU-wide electorate in the form of EU citizenship with voting rights is not catching on as expected, in terms of political allegiance and unity",

the very unity which earlier you indicated, a titre juste, was necessary to underpin democracy. Welcome, Tom, as a solid card-carrying member, to the No Demos Thesis (myth?) club.

The only difference which remains among the honorable members of the club is between those who say – give it time (it took a hundred years and a civil war for the American demos to coalesce) and those who say that in the 21st century it is intolerable to go on expecting democratic discipline in a polity which after 70 years still lacks one of the primordial conditions for such discipline (coupled with a host of other defects in the institutional arrangements of its democracy).

My final two points can, thankfully, be much briefer.

1. Your definition of demos

I think that your very loose and permissive definition of demos is actually contradicted by your own analysis. It is contradicted by your own acknowledgment just before that definition (despite the word 'mostly') that some sense of unity is necessary to underpin democracy and is further contradicted at the end of your essay by adding to unity the need not only for unity but political allegiance. Your loose definition may be valid for many purposes but not for the purpose for which the concept of demos is used in democratic theory.

2. The German Constitutional Court and its Lisbon Decision

It was predictable and both sad and funny to see the speed and ferocity with which those belonging to the Church of European Integration ganged on the German Constitutional Court's heresy in that decision. Within hours (!) of the publication of the decision, cyberspace was awash with denunciations the result of careless reading and, in my view, careless thinking. The 'fast food' dimension of instant blogging has that effect – the race to get out there as soon as possible. I don't think it is possible fairly to accuse the Court in the Lisbon decision of espousing a Volkish notion of demos. The only valid critique, in my view, of the German Court in this regard is that they had not internalized the Böckenförde insight that modern democracies understand the very notion of demos in different ways. They seemed to be insisting that a European demos would have to conform to the German understanding of the concept which, as I said before, is certainly not a Volkish concept. In the concept of the Union even the German Court has to accept that one cannot expect and/or demand that the Union self understanding of demos who have to conform to that of a particular Member State. It is a serious defect, but not a fatal defect of the Judgment.

For the rest, I find that Judgment admirable. It was the only constitutional organ (among which I include national parliaments) which openly and rigorously was willing to examine and then point out the obvious – that the Lisbon Treaty did not cure the European Union from the very serious and persistent democratic defects in the structure and process of its governance. Kudos to them. And I happily regard myself in this respect as their epigone.

Reply of Tom Eijsbouts

Dear Professor Weiler,

what an honour for me to be taken so thoughtfully and seriously by you. To be complimented for an original and powerful claim regarding the iconic 'Peoples of Europe'. And, in spite of attempts at debunking the EU No Demos Thesis, to be offered membership of the No Demos Society. Thank you! Will I accept? Maybe not.

To be sure, it is good to be handed, by a leading member of the Society, a single authoritative definition of the *Demos* in its sophisticated version:

> 'Ultimately there is, in the notion of demos a strong subjective feeling of the individuals of belonging to the same demos, that subjective element being essential to both the empirical and normative facets of the demos thesis.' (above)

And a single fatality of the lack of this Demos in the EU (the No Demos Thesis):

> 'However, in the context of democratic theory and its foundational claim that demos is indispensable, empirically and normatively in order to underpin democracy, the sense of belonging to the European Union would have to be sufficiently thick in order to underpin a democratic discipline claim (majority can compel minority) within the European polity.'

Why do I not yet accept membership? Because 'strong subjective feelings' and 'a sense of belonging' to me are no solid basis for anything empirical nor for anything normative, demos or other. The *empirical* needs to find support in stable data or fact. Feelings and senses of belonging are fickle and whimsical; they coincide only passingly when whipped up into a common emotion: not the most reliable or definable, let alone desirable state. The *normative* needs to arise from the actual, historical fact of agreement among those concerned. No normative reality can draw directly on feelings or senses.

So if feelings and senses are what the ultimate Demos claims to be based on, I don't trust the notion either empirically or normatively. Nothing wrong with using it in common parlance, as we use other notions, in spite of its uncertain basis and varying significance, but not empirically and certainly not normatively. In both spheres, empirical and normative, you need stability, consistency and precision; in the normative sphere, on top of these, you need historicity (date, place of foundation, actors).

How can the notion claim that there is, among *the* (=all) members of any existing democratic state population, this 'strong subjective feeling of belonging to the same demos'? Would it not be extremely coincidental if all the citizens of an existing state shared precisely this feeling of belonging? And belonging to what? I have feelings of belonging to different communities, including those of my Dutch countrymen, the co-inhabitants of Amsterdam and, not least, the European Constitutional Law Network. But can I be held to have a strong feeling of belonging to the Kingdom of the Netherlands, the state? And can all my countrymen?

If it is a tall order for each and every person in this peaceful and prosperous country to feel a strong belonging to his or her state, how can it ever be asked, or surmised, of every citizen of every democratic state? So how can it be asked of every EU citizen? I indeed wrote, as you quote, 'it is *not entirely wrong* to claim that *some* historical, social and/or cultural unity, or consensus *mostly* underpins a democracy.' (my emphasis) But that is nothing like claiming the need of any defined demos for a democracy.

In communities there are two ways of belonging. Either the community membership is voluntary and the feeling of belonging can be assumed for all, as with the ECLN. Or membership is not voluntary and the *feeling of* belonging, even if often present, cannot be assumed nor decisive. The facts and the law of belonging come in to back the feeling, or take over when it turns sour. So it is with political communities such as our states *and* the EU. Surely the law should not go too strongly against the feeling. But it doesn't in the EU, does it, whose law and feelings of citizenship are equally thin and weak. We academics should not elevate feelings over fact and law, and certainly not if we are lawyers and the feelings of belonging are those presumed to be lacking in others.

As for the political Demos, I would advise against trying a uniform definition, because every political community does that for itself, and authoritatively, in its own different way and under its own name, as you write yourself referring to Böckenförde. The German democracy calls its people the *Volk*; the French democracy calls the people *La Nation*. The EU calls the people of its democracy by their status of *EU citizens* (and it includes that of a member state citizenship). Why superimpose a singular uniform notion for such different things, with the only effect of discounting the EU citizenry as falling short?

The democracy of the EU and its citizenship are thin, indeed. But they exist. If they were presumptuous and arrogant, if they seriously affected the member states' democracies and citizenships, I would agree with you about putting them seriously to task for raising 'intolerable' expectations, lacking 'the primordial conditions' and having a 'host of other [institutional] defects'. But they are not and they do not. The Union is not a presumptive full successor to the member states' democracies, as the Bundesverfassungsgericht stubbornly fails to see. The EU's democracy is an original and hopeful, if prim and fledgling, democratic addition to the member states' democracies. Its citizens, when asked in polls, *feel* generally not more unhappy with it than they feel about their home state and government. No reason then to use powerful negatives for the EU such as No Demos!

Dear Joseph, I cannot thank you enough for your invitation to the No Demos Club and for your elaborate, keen and clarifying criticism, even though I hesitate to accept either. Yours, in admiration and inspiration,

Tom

P.S. *epigonism* of the Bundesverfassungstericht, as I use it, is not just using or following it, but 'the tendency for a pupil to follow a master with a true belief, dropping the latter's reserve and context and topping the master's claim with a disciple's fervour' (second page of my paper). A sort of sorcerer's apprenticeship *light*.

On Chapter 6: Karavokyris

Thank you for your illuminating chapter. Here are some questions that come to mind.

1. In your introduction you seem to posit a dichotomy between "liberalism" and "democracy" – a relationship of either conflict or consent and, if I understood correctly granting judicial organs a certain superiority in resolving this conflict or assuring consent. I hope I have understood you correctly, but if not I suspect that many readers will have come to the same conclusion. In any event the actual phrase you employ is as follows:

> "In fact, the courts-legislators relation captures, in legal terms, the conflict or consent between liberalism and democracy and thus results in the identification of the legal organ which is actually being granted, within the existing legal and political framework, the most significant role."

You go on to write, following from the same passage the following:

> "In other words, the dialogue between the two major actors of contemporary legal systems, the judge and the legislator, should finally be understood as a matter of sovereignty." (footnote omitted).

It may be useful if you were to clarify some issues. Why (or at least in what sense) are democracy and liberalism postulated as dichotomous and in conflict? We understand many of our democracies as liberal democracies, the two going hand in hand (as opposed to some new trends in some Member State of so called illiberal democracy). Is that tension inevitable rather than contingent, and, indeed, from what follows in your peace it is never clear why the cases you discuss, whether the courts are "activist" or "self-restrained" exemplify a conflict between democracy and liberalism.

Furthermore, as a general question of concept and theory of relationship between courts and legislators, since liberalism is a distinct manifestation of a particular political and moral philosophy, you seem to squeeze out of the equation the possibility of socialist or communist or any other non-liberal political philosophy.

2. There is another tension between this opening statement and your very own subsequent analysis. Though, and you explain this with finesse it is in some ways the Courts who have the final word (in most cases, I should add) in interpreting the constitution, in fact your analysis demonstrates, again with finesse, that the more profound the crisis, the more reticent will be the Courts to intervene with legislative choices, so that, except in a formal, positive sense (which you rightly reject) it is hard to speak of the Courts playing the "more significant part".

3. It might be worth giving the reader a better understanding of what you meant when you say that the relationship between courts and legislators in contemporary legal systems should be understood as "a matter of sovereignty". What alternative understanding are you rejecting? Is this not inherent in a system which allows for judicial review of constitutionality?

4. A lot of your analysis seems to ride on the distinction of activism and restraint – trying both to describe and analyze when and why in the context of the Greek crisis the courts (including the ECtHR) veered in one direction or another. But given that your own analysis so powerfully (and persuasively) adopted a non formalist but rather a realist approach to this jurisprudence in which the assessment of the courts of the factual matrix seemed determinative – does the notion of 'activism' make any sense at all? Surely (or so I believe) refraining from intervening would appear (depending on one's set of moral and political convictions) no less activist – some have used the expression 'passive activism'. When you do not do something which you should do, it can hardly come under the soothing category of 'restraint' – just as in psychology we use the term passive-aggressive. One could defend a formal distinction and say that when the court does not restrict the legislator it is doing something different from intervening. But your very analysis militates against this formal distinction.

5. A critical tone creeps into your analysis of the use of proportionality by the Courts when in the situation of extreme crisis it prefers the general interest over the individual interest. You use the term 'plastic application of proportionality'. Why this characterization? Does proportionality mean that in every case as between the collective good and the individual liberty

the outcome has to be a, say, 4-3, and that if it is 5-0 – this becomes a 'plastic application of proportionality?

6. Finally, by way of both comment and question: You contribution describes how in relation to the First Memorandum the appreciation of the Courts of the depth of the crisis was such, that they gave a free hand to the legislator, but in relation to the Second Memorandum, they judged the most severe aspects of the crisis to have abated and thus were willing to exercise control (for example over pensions) that hitherto they did not. Would that mean that had the government introduced the pension reforms which the court rejected the second time round, in the first crisis, they would have been accepted by the courts?

Reply of George Karavokyris

1. My analysis of the relation between courts and legislators is based firstly on a normative level and secondly on a specific definition of democracy as a political regime where decisions rest on the political sovereignty of the people (I am referring to the famous Lincoln formula, according to which democracy is a government 'of the people, by the people, and for the people'), essentially linked to the concept of representation. Granted that the courts are non-elected bodies, which are also supposed to express the general will, and that their normative competence tends to acknowledge them as the organs holding the ultimate word on the interpretation of the constitution and therefore on the meaning of the constitution, there is, in my view, a profound tension, not only legal or normative, but equally political, within the principle of the separation of powers. In other words, (especially) the constitutional courts seem to alter the traditional meaning of democracy because their normative impact is the one that illustrates the post-World War II continental perception of constitutional/liberal democracy and the Rule of Law/État de droit/Rechstaat doctrine/regime. Instead of confusing liberalism and democracy, constitutional justice emerges as one of the normative and political criteria that indicate the evolution from a volitional model of democracy (the people's will) to a more rationalistic one (the general will as a result of a synthesis between the Parliament and the Courts, the so-called 'shared-authority' thesis). In fact, modern liberal democracies are mixed regimes and national/popular sovereignty is formed from distinct elected and non-elected organs. In this framework, normatively speaking, the tension is unavoidable, regardless of the activist

position of the Courts, and the conflict between democracy and liberalism exists per se. Nevertheless, on an hermeneutical and political ground, the courts eventual consent to the Parliament's will exemplifies the political weight of the traditional democratic form of government (based on the idea of elections and legitimacy) within liberalism and indicates that the matter of sovereignty is not only a normative one (from a pure positivist thesis) but also a pragmatic and political issue. So, I am suggesting that we should not hesitate to reflect on the very concept of liberal democracy and its inherent antinomies or contradictions, such as the tension surrounding the authority principle and I do not intend to exclude non-liberal political or legal thinking or socialist or communist democracies (such as the radical left tradition or contemporary democratic constitutionalism which seem to highlight a certain need for strengthening political representation) but, on the contrary and indirectly, I intend to include them as democratic possibilities and theories, even if it is true that I do not essentially embrace their epistemic, methodological and political foundations. In other terms, my view remains mostly a democratic critical point inside the liberal democracy scheme.

2. There is a certain contradiction here that nevertheless stems from my —I believe exact— methodological choice of a two-sided approach to the authority (courts-legislators) scheme: the normative and the hermeneutical. According to the former, the courts seem (in most cases and legal orders) to have the final word and to play the 'more significant part', but when it comes to the latter, the real exercise of sovereignty, the example of the Greek crisis shows that the political relation between the authorities is far more complicated.

3. I am suggesting that the matter of sovereignty should not be undermined, granted that in most contemporary constitutional or political theories the relation between courts and legislators is a fundamental element of the Rule of Law and is believed to be a complementary one, as the (rational) courts are widely supposed to be controlling the (arbitrary) politics.

4. I agree with you that, from a realist standpoint, the distinction between activism and self-restraint is normatively inaccurate and I also share the conviction that the notion of self-restraint is a pure paradox (i.e. Hobbes argues that self-restraint is simply something that we want to do and that no one is bound by oneself). On the other hand, I think it is a pragmatological/factual and not a formal or substantial distinction, which allows us to interpret and explain the courts' position and overcome some

inevitable fallacies of the realist thesis (and most of all its auto-referential formalism).

5. My aim is to highlight the fact that the use of the proportionality principle has facilitated the courts' task of dealing with the extreme pressure of the financial crisis on constitutional rights. In other words, it has helped the courts to normatively enlarge the interpretative horizon of the constitution. On the other hand, this 'plastic' application of the principle can lead in extremis to the normalisation of the violation of standard human rights protection.

6. The critical point here is the factual appreciation by the courts, which is linked, in my opinion, to a certain political idea about the extent and timing of the crisis. Bearing in mind that in the first phase of the crisis the imminent danger of bankruptcy seems to have affected the intensity of the judicial review, I believe that you are suggesting a very strong possibility.

On Chapter 7: Jean Victor Louis

Thank you for your illuminating chapter. Here are some comments and questions that come to mind.

1. The analysis of the case, with its detailed and nuanced comparison of AG and Court, is exemplary in all respects. Hence my questions to the author seek his reflection and wisdom on two issues which go beyond the actual decision.

I share the view, that both legally and 'diplomatically', the approach adopted by the Court in relation to the Preliminary Reference, relying on its long standing jurisprudence of not questioning, except in extremis, the request for a Preliminary Ruling was the wiser one. The author notes that several governments as well as Institutions – Commission, Parliament and the ECB itself – were opposed to the admissibility of the substantive questions themselves. Earlier there is justly a reference to Draghi's famous "whatever it takes" speech, the impact of which cannot be overstated. Words from Central Bankers are "speech acts' par excellence – and depend on their efficacy on the authority and credibility of those who utter them. They are often as important as measures actually adopted. Is there not a danger, the positive outcome of OMT notwithstanding, that this power will henceforth be compromised: Whatever it takes, provided the European Court agrees. And though the test was not overly onerous, it went beyond simply given a statement of reasons. I do not mean this as a criticism of the Court because declaring the questions as inadmissible rather than addressing in detail the various objections of the German Constitutional Court would not only kill the beginning of a veritable dialogue (artless as the framing of the German questions were) but also be an invitation for the German Court to go its own way. But the result might simply be tragic, a result of 'damned if you do (answer) and damned if you do not (answer). The ECB emerges strengthened in that the logic behind OMT has been sanctioned, but perhaps somewhat weakened by having now the sword of judicial review over its head in future crises?

2. Though this was a sideline, and the analysis of the Advocate General was particularly powerful in this regard, one might wonder what role, in the preservation of both Constitutional identity and national identity, national courts can and should play. Is it to be limited to expressing concerns and considerations in the reference to the European Court and then waiting its assessment? The comparison to the old saga of human rights (So lange etc) comes to mind, but the comparison is problematic. It is far more easy to accept that within the legal order of the Union, the ECJ could and should assert the fundamental rights to be asserted even if these differ, one way or another, more or less exigent, than those applying within purely national contexts. But Constitutional and/or national identity is a different beast. By its very nature I would argue, it does not lend itself to that kind of uniform standard and the claim of national courts to be custodians of such is much stronger. Has the Union shot itself in the foot by legitimating this consideration at all, or are we here, again, in the face of a conceptually insoluble dilemma condemned, if it is to be taken seriously, to muddle through with the questionable help of the various theories of constitutional pluralism.

Reply of Jean-Victor Louis

The *first question* could be summed up as follows: Could the view be sustained that the decision of the Court of Justice in favour of the admissibility of the German Constitutional Court's request for a preliminary ruling and its positive answer on the legality of the OMT have at the same time a positive and a potentially negative effect on the autonomy of the ECB in adopting non-conventional monetary policy decisions in times of crisis?

Referring to the famous 'whatever it takes speech' of President Draghi in July 2012, Prof. Weiler asks himself if we should in the future read it as 'whatever it takes, provided the Court agrees'? And should we add: isn't the ECB in a less comfortable position than its counterparts in turbulent periods?

The president of the ECB was well aware when he pronounced the famous sentence that the ECB was limited in its action. The sentence started with the words: 'Within our mandate, the ECB is ready to do…'.

In the second paragraph of my contribution it was my intention to recall why the rule of law and the role of the Court of Justice have a non-negligible role in the ECB statutes. It was conceived as an element of legitimation of the organ in charge of monetary policy, acting like a form of compensation for the weak powers of the legislative power, certainly weaker than those of the US Congress, which has the power of changing the Federal Reserve Act, as it has intended in recent years and perhaps will do in the next few years.

Legal control granting a significant degree of discretion to the ECB in its choice of instruments, such as that shown by the Court in the Gauweiler case, appears to be the counterpart to the large degree of independence that the ECB has been recognised as having.

The *second question* relates to the ongoing debate between the Court and the Constitutional Courts about their respective role in the control of the respect of constitutional and national identity.

I will limit myself to some brief comments on this subject, which is at the centre of an abundant literature.

I am very receptive to the strong reservations expressed by the Advocate General in his conclusions on the Gauweiler case against the use by the EU Member States of arguments based on their constitutional identity in order to oppose a provision of Union law.

In theory, one can support the view that in such a context, it could appear problematic to apply a 'uniform standard' but, as a matter of fact, I am not the first to suggest that the values recognised by EU constitutional provisions and the national values of the Member States tend to coincide.

In the rare EU case law on the matter, it is well known that the Court was able to link questions related to national or constitutional identity to general principles of EU law, like the prohibition of discrimination, and the respect of human dignity.

The control by the Court of Justice of the proportionality of the national measure to the pursued national objective when it conflicts with a Union principle appears anyway to be fully justified.

On Chapter 9: Antonis Manitakis

Thank you for your illuminating chapter. Here are some questions that come to mind.

1. You begin and end your essay with a certain adulation to the "impressive resilience" of the Greek constitutional order in the face of an incredibly challenging political, social and economic context. What is more, one of the key elements of your analysis is that this resilience has not been bought through the extensive use of emergency power or suspension of the constitution. But I am sure that at least some readers whilst in no way challenging your description and analysis will take issue with your normativity and wonder how impressive the resilience has really been.

You cite with approval the foresight of the constitutional drafters in the privileged position they give international norms in Article 28 (2) and (3) of the Constitution. These provisions have created, to use your own words,

A broad and welcoming gateway for the incorporation of European and international law into the Greek legal order (emphasis in the original)

but what is more remarkable is that this incorporation is of a constitutional nature and may amount to modification and amendment of the Constitution itself. Thus

> "through simple decisions of Parliament to *automatically adapt itself* to every decision or act of the EU bodies, even those of intergovernmental character, such as the acts and decisions of the European Council of Heads of State and Government. And all this has been achieved without engaging in the arduous and time consuming process of reforming a rigid Constitution. (emphasis in the original).

And make no mistake: We are not dealing with arcana or trivia but has a "bearing on sensitive and key areas of the State."

Now, the process of constitutional amendment differs from State to State, in some relatively easier (Germany) in others arduous and difficult (USA; European Union). But I am unaware of any State where the Constitution can be amended in sensitive and key areas of the State, by a simple act of Parliament, and notably where the source for that is the decision of the representatives of the Executive Branches of the Member States (the European Council) the decisions of which from a legal point of view have no constitutional standing in any of the Member States and not even, without any more, in the European Union itself. Does it not seem that the resilience you praise is achieved at the price of removing what is normally understood by referring to constitutional norms?

2. On some occasions the resilience has been achieved by resort to extraordinary powers that under the constitution can be exercised by the President (under extraordinary circumstances of an urgent and unforeseeable need). But here again you yourself say, that what is meant to be extraordinary has been so inflationized as to become normal – once again at least to some extent emptying constitutionalism from its meaning where the exception – government by Presidential decree – become norm rather than exception?

3. Finally, when it comes to the function of judicial review, a critical component of modern constitutionalism, whether in the supervision of the executive or legislative branches, once again your words are eloquent and worth citing in extensu:

You mention that the Council of State, which has in your words the function of a constitutional court, regularly judges the constitutionality of measures restricting and potentially violating individual and social rights with the classical tools of proportionality and public interest. But, through the crisis it would appear that in the cases that have been tried during the period of crisis, judges have restricted themselves to carrying out a legal evaluation and assessment of the 'factual circumstances' … and have confined themselves to ascertaining whether the public interest grounds have played an 'actual' role or not in each cases, without assessing or weighing up further the suitability, the expediency, or the proportionality and balance between the violation of a right and the pursued aim.

It is hard to imagine a weaker form of review. The conclusion you draw is that Greek Constitutional reality is – unlike the political and economic realities – displaying signs of an impressive resilience and adaptation to the new European and globalized reality (emphasis in the original). I find myself more impressed by the political and economic resilience then by the Constitutional reality which you describe.

Reply of Antonis Manitakis

1. One of the most crucial issues that Greek constitutional reality and theory have faced is, indeed —as Prof. Weiler correctly observes in his comment— the extent to which the state of exceptional circumstances, which during the endless crisis in Greece has justified the taking of exceptional legislative measures, has constituted an *exception from the constitutional rule*, that is to say, a singular form of *état d'exception*, or, on the other

hand, has gradually established a new constitutional normativity within the existing constitutional legality. I supported the latter view.

This exceptional normativity has not been entirely disputed. On the contrary, it has been considered justified due to the exceptional circumstances that the country has gone through. In fact, gradually, through its application over a long period and its common acceptance, it has come to *acquire a normality that has stripped it of its exceptional character*. Indeed, the moment it was considered justified by jurisprudence, by the judges exercising a judicial review of legislation, *this singular form of exceptional legislative reality also acquired legitimacy.* And this was because it aimed to serve the public interest, it did not violate the principle of proportionality and it found formal support in the Constitution itself.

Its legitimisation in the constitutional consciousness of the citizens *strengthened the normative resilience of the Constitution* vis-à-vis the political and social upheavals caused by the economic crisis. Thus the following strange thing has happened: instead of constitutional legality being shaken by the effects of the economic crisis, it has in fact been strengthened due to the *remarkable adaptability* shown by the Constitution in the course of its application by the legislator and the judge, who have assisted this process by interpreting the Constitution in a flexible and realistic manner.

Moreover, the self-restraint which the judges have imposed on themselves in their judicial review of the exceptional legislative measures has not merely given an institutional precedence to the legislative power; it has also, at the same time, recognised that *the political and legislative power have a wide field of action and a very broad scope for formulating public policies.* This does not mean, however, that the rule of law has made any concessions to politics, since the judicial protection of human rights and freedoms has not been jeopardised by the tough legislative measures.

What have suffered —it is true— are social rights, and what has suffered the most devastating blow is, without doubt, the social state. This has clearly proved what some constitutional theorists have been stressing for some time: the insufficient regulatory binding nature of social rights and the total inability of the judge of constitutionality to protect those rights.

2. And now I come to the apt —and catalytic for my study— observation by Prof. Weiler concerning my final conclusion. His observation obliges me to correct, or rather add a necessary clarification to my conclu-

sion. I quote, for the sake of accuracy, the phrase singled out for comment in my conclusion, together with Prof. Weiler's catalytic observation:

> Our Constitutional reality is —unlike the political and economic realities— displaying signs of an *impressive resilience and adaptation to the new European and globalised reality*. (The emphasis is in my original text.)

'I find myself more impressed', observed Prof. Weiler in his comment, 'by the political and economic resilience than by the Constitutional reality which you describe.'

Prof. Weiler is right to connect the resilience of the Constitution with the political system since the latter is based on the former and is regulated by it. It is just that when I refer to the resilience of the Constitution, I do not mean merely formal constitutional legality —what we usually call the 'formal' Constitution— but also the constitutional-political institutions, that is to say, the parliamentary system, the principle of popular sovereignty, parliamentary elections and the democratic alternation of parties in power. I therefore also include the democratic regime. The term 'Constitution' on its own also implies what in Greek is called the constitutional 'regime' (*politeuma*), in contradistinction to what is commonly called the political system. (The term *politeuma* is usually rendered in other languages by the term 'political regime', *which is not the same*.)

To supplement my conclusion, therefore, I would say that the resilience of the Constitution has been accompanied by a truly remarkable resilience on the part of the democratic regime, a smooth operation of the parliamentary system (i.e. one achieved in accordance with the Constitution), and also a respect for the constitutional rules of the democratic game.

The frequent recourse to parliamentary elections and the smooth alternation of parties in power have lent a necessary democratic legitimacy to the political power, enabling it to adopt and implement exceptional legislative measures, while giving the judiciary the necessary justification to be able to exercise self-restraint in its judicial review of legislation.

In a word, both democracy and the rule of law, along with the Constitution, have stood firm and proved flexible while the economy has collapsed, and both have resisted the discrediting and ethico-political fragmentation of the political system.

On Chapter 10: Anna Maria Guerra Martins

Thank you for your illuminating chapter. Here are some questions that come to mind.

1. I am among those who consider Opinion 2/13 problematic and unsound on legal grounds as well as its erroneous underlying assumptions about the nature of the European Union and its constitutional order. Having said that I am agnostic about the utility of the multilevel constitutional paradigm as an alternative route to a different outcome.

My agnosticism is in part fed by what seems to a central artifact of your reasoning – which I find no less problematic than the reasoning of the Court. The following seems to be foundational to your entire reasoning. In your opinion

> a multilevel constitutional system should achieve a higher standard of protection and enforcement of fundamental rights than that achieved by any single constitutional layer on its own.

This assertion is grounded in what appears to be both an axiomatic notion of political theory and moral philosophy but also as an empirical social science observation of individual acceptance of the constitutional order:

> [T]he EU and the ECHR can only be understood and accepted by individuals, as long as they add something to the effectiveness of the protection of fundamental rights and, from there, draw legitimacy.

I think the two statements taken together are frequently meaningless or wrong or both.

You present the notion of higher standards of protection (I leave enforcement aside for now) as unproblematic. But although it is used frequently both in official texts such as the famous Articles 53 and in the literature, it is conceptually at times incoherent and almost invariably not without normative and socially empirical problems.

The easiest demonstration is, of course, in the growing number of cases where we oppose human rights not as between an individual and a public authority but among individual actors. This seems to be a la mode, to judge for the growing number of cases of this nature to reach judicial instances. So, which is the higher standard in, say, a case of abortion: The State which protects the unborn child at the expense of the mother, or the State which protects the mother at the expense of the fetus. And imaging this situation, which is a reality in Europe, how is the multilevel constitution system going to achieve a higher level of protection? It is a zero sum game. Or what about gender equality and freedom of religion – which pose a similar zero sum game? Or freedom of expression and the right to privacy? And the list goes on. And moving from the conceptual to the social and empirical, any attempt of the multilevel constitution to enhance the standard of protection of one of these private interests, will meet with cheers from some and howls from others.

Now, it could be argued that this (individual) right v (individual) right is atypical, and that the majority of cases still involve the pitching of an individual liberty compromised by a public authority – this indeed is the more typical case. And that in these circumstances it is meaningful to refer to higher standards and that in this case everyone would be more cheerful if the multilevel constitution enhanced the level of protection achieved by any single state.

In my opinion, wrong again. For even in this situation there is a failure to grasp that the phenomenology of protecting human rights is, except in extremis, a balancing of competing goods, and that people would absolutely not automatically cheer for a higher standard of protecting individual liberty.

It is easiest to illustrate this with another example. Imagine hypothetically that the protection of private property in Germany is 'higher' than that in Italy in the simple sense that the circumstances under which public authorities may interfere or even confiscate private property in Germany are more limited than they are in Italy. Or, another example, imagine that in the Ireland there is a higher level of protection of individual freedom of speech than, say, in France in the simple sense that the circumstances in which the State may restrict speech in the Ireland is more limited than that in France. And finally imagine that the protection of the privacy of communication between lawyers and clients receives higher protection in the UK than it does, say, in Greece.

According to the theorem advocated in your paper the multilevel constitutional order should aim to give a higher standard of protection to private property in Italy, to speech in France and to legal clients in Greece. After all you argue that the multilevel constitutional system should achieve a higher standard of protection than that achieved by any single constitutional layer, and that this would be the only basis of its legitimacy.

Now let us go back to our hypothetical (or not so hypothetical) examples. Imagine that under the German system of private property Graf von X is the owner for centuries of a marvelous estate on the outskirts of Munich. Would it not be wonderful if it could be taken over (with due compensation of course) and made available for the enjoyment of the public at large. But the high standard of protection of private property in Germany does not allow such. Whereas in Italy, with a system of human rights with a more lefty social sensibility, the glorious villa of the Contessa San Severina on the outskirts of Florence could be seized so that the thousands of inhabitants of Florence, suffocating in the heat of the Summer would have a nice place to spend their weekends, and that this were permitted under the 'lower' standard of protection in Italy. Are we so sure that the Italians, one and all, would be happy for the multilevel constitutional system to 'upgrade' their standard of protection of private property? Or imagine that in Ireland, as is actually the case in the USA, a band of racist homophobes may march in the center of Dublin banners and all, exercising their enhanced standard of freedom of expression. Are we so sure that the French, where hypothetically, such marchers would be promptly arrested, would welcome an upgrade of their standard of freedom of expression? And if fraud on public finance is, hypothetically, rife in Greece and often involves collusion between lawyers and clients, would the Greeks welcome an upgrade of their right to private communication with lawyers if such impedes effective detection and prosecution of such fraud?

For the simple truth is that in the phenomenology of protection of fundamental individual liberties and collective public goods, the value is in the balance, and there is no automatic value preference for standards which ensure maximum liberty to the individual at the expense of the collective public good.

2. Let me add one more consideration which feeds my agnosticism as regards multilevel constitutionalism in the area of human rights as presented by you. I think there is value in a multilevel system which valorizes different balances as between the public good and the private liberty at different levels. I do not think the EU should always adopt the highest standard from its Member States to be the prevailing standard in the EU (indeed, this is the reality – the standard of protection against search and seizure in commercial premises is lower in the EU than in some of the Member States – I see nothing wrong in that). But would not the logic of your premise – though you do not explicitly say so – lead to a flattening of this diversity robbing different states and levels of their constitutional identity? Think of the Italian example mentioned above. Once the notion of higher standards is problematized in the way I have done, the entire edifice seems to be resting on somewhat shifting sands.

3. Finally I want to add something on more effective enforcement. In principle I do believe, as you do, that all and sundry would want to see more effective enforcement of whatever rights they coalesce around. But far more problematic is the notion that transnational institutions achieve such. There is a double problem: Decisions of such bodies do not always enjoy the same level of acceptance as do those of bodies which are part of the organic body politic, and then, sadly, the time delays at say the ECHR are far from an enhancement in effective enforcement.

Reply of Ana Maria Guerra Martins

1. As far as I can understand, the first two points of Joseph Weiler's comments on my article are based on the following premises (a) the principle of the higher protection of fundamental rights is the only pillar of my reasoning; (b) this principle cannot overcome a casuistic approach; (c) I do not take into account other principles, such as the principle of constitutional identities, and (d) a multilevel constitutional paradigm would be useless in this context.

a. First of all, points 1 and 2 of Joseph Weiler's comments on my article are based on two sentences of my article, which, as he said, are fundamental to my reasoning. I would say that they are one of the bases of my reasoning, not the only one. There are three other principles: the existence of common values among EU members, the EU, the Council of Europe and its Member States: the cooperative judicial dialogue and the sincere cooperation and mutual trust which play in multilevel constitutionalism a role as important as that of the higher protection of fundamental rights. That means my reasoning and conclusions could survive without the principle of higher protection. Anyway, although Joseph Weiler said that some of the statements I make are wrong or meaningless or both, I will try to convince my readers of my reasons.
b. The use of the casuistic approach in order to 'destroy' the principle of a higher protection of fundamental rights is perfect. I would agree, at the end of the day, this is always a question of balance, which leads to a zero-sum game. But in my opinion this reasoning would fit like a glove if a court —of whatever kind— is challenged by a judicial review, i.e. the court decides a case between A and B, public or private (it does not matter). However, this casuistic approach is not appropriate

when we assess *Opinion 2/13*, because the Court of Justice could never have adopted this casuistic approach. *Opinion 2/13* was taken under an abstract and a priori judicial control, and not in a concrete case and in those procedures the reasoning is much more abstract and generalist. That means the legal orders are assessed in general. And what did the Court say? The EU legal order should prevail, independently of the protection of fundamental rights. Full stop.

c. Concerning Joseph Weiler's implicit comment that I have to take other principles into account, such as the principle of the constitutional identities of the Member States. I would say *touché*. In fact, it is true that I made brief mention of this topic, but, of course, it deserves more space in a multilevel constitutional context. However, I am not sure that this principle or the principle of primacy could have played a significant role in a decision such as Opinion 2/13.

d. Above all, let me draw attention to the fact that Joseph Weiler has always been sceptical about 'multilevel constitutional paradigms', and I greatly respect his scepticism. However, for me, the 'multilevel constitutional paradigm', in the way I have applied it to the ECHR-level, allows us to conceptualise the protection of fundamental rights at the national, the EU and the (international) ECHR levels not in isolation but as components of one system striving to make the protection of these rights as effective as possible. It allows meaning to be given to Article 52 (1) and (3) and Article 53 of the Charter of Fundamental Rights by defining the Charter with a view to the protection of fundamental rights under the national constitutions and the protection of human rights by the ECHR in a complementary and additional way, and not as a substitute or restriction. The clear intention of these provisions, understood as part of a multilevel system, to make sure generally that people enjoy, in any given case, the highest possible protection of their rights, allows us to accept it as an important pillar of the legitimacy of the EU at large.

2. Point 3 of Joseph Weiler's comment relates to the enforcement of fundamental rights. I could agree that the decisions of international courts do not always enjoy the same level of acceptance, as do those of national courts. Yet, the ECHR system was created as a result of the experience that states, in some cases, fail to ensure a sufficient level of protection of human rights. The high number of cases demonstrate that people trust the Strasbourg Court as an *ultima ratio* remedy to this failure, and, thus, they

demonstrate that there is a considerable level of acceptance. Time delays are the result of this success, of which the ECtHR itself became the first victim.

On Chapter 12: Ingolf Pernice

Thank you for your illuminating chapter. Here are some questions and comments that come to mind.

Your contribution is most timely and important since the role cyberspace and the internet may play in the governance of Europe is a topic, which has not received sufficient attention so far.

There are some issues in your contribution on which I think readers would profit from your further thoughts.

1. The first issue, prevalent in the 'legitimacy literature' on the European Union, goes to the normative core of our commitment to democracy and transparency. Our democracies are not value free in that we shackle them with a commitment to pluralism and respect of fundamental rights which even parliamentary majorities might not compromise. But beyond that, both the concepts themselves (democracy, transparency etc.) and our position as scholars critically reviewing and evaluating the democratic lacunae of government and governance are meant to be neutral, driven by our adherence to the democratic method, rather than this or that outcome. Herein lies my first question to you.

You open your contribution with the following statements:

> Euroscepticism is spreading around the 28 Member States. People seem to be more and more disappointed with the European Union….There is an increasing gap between the institutions and the individual, and people seem to be abandoning their hope that European integration would be the solution for many of their problems; indeed, more and more people see the EU itself as the problem.
>
> …
>
> The present chapter focuses on the activities of the EU related to the internet and strives to identify and further develop aspects that may have a positive impact on the relationship between the citizen of the Union and the institutions.

I see several problematic issues in framing your project in this way. First, to take it on its own terms, throughout the chapter there is an assumption, sometime explicit and sometimes implicit, that enhanced transparency in both the input, throughput and output aspects of European governance will indeed result in an enhanced positive impact on the relationship between the citizen of the Union and its institutions. It is a problematic proposition. It is reminiscent of the reactions from the European Institutions in the face of the referenda results on the European Constitution in The Netherlands and France: 'We did not explain ourselves well enough'. The assumption there was that the citizens who voted No in those referenda simply did not understand. If they were better informed they would have voted differently. I have seen the same said as regards the outcome of the Brexit referendum. The underlying approach of those reactions, and to some degree the underlying approach of your Chapter, hearken back to the old Marxist notion of False Consciousness. Euroscepticism is growing? Lets use all the (internet) tools available to enhance knowledge through transparency as a way of combatting such.

Is it not quite possible that the high level of support which the Union enjoyed in a pre-internet era and with far greater lacunae of transparency was in part due to its much commented character as an elite driven project, and to citizen indifference. And that growing Euroscepticism is the result of enhanced interest and transparency. That citizen know what they feel they ought to know and do not like what they see? Can I be even more provocative, based on my knowledge and experience of the throughput process of European governance and suggest, in contrast with your optimism, that the more transparent this process becomes, it is quite possible that citizens will like it even less? I see no evidence in your paper, apart from an optimistic belief, that increased transparency of the throughput will have achieve the result for which you are advocating such, namely creating '… a positive impact on the relationship'.

But my critique goes even further. Like you I regard the European construct as noble, the European Union as a bold and historically successful experiment in inter State and inter human relations, apart from its positive impact on aggregate prosperity. But I find rather problematic the normative framing of the project in the following sense: You are committed to the potentialities of the internet and consequently "… strive to identify and further develop aspects that may have a positive impact on the relationship between the citizen of the Union and the institutions."

There may, indeed, be aspects of enhanced transparency and enhanced democracy that the internet may, as you advocate at times persuasively, be able to deliver. But what if these do not have a positive impact on the relationship between the citizen and the Union and the institutions, but have the opposite effect? The more I know, the less I like it, may be quite a possible reaction by some or many. Your framing and your rather extensive and uncritical citation of several self-celebratory statements and instruments of the Commission (all of which are not without some serious problems) give the impression that the underlying interest of the approach your contribution represents is not a real and neutral interest in transparency and democracy as collective goods in and of themselves, but only as tools to shore up support for the Union and its Institutions.

2. Your contribution is prudent in that it mentions from time to time some of the problems which cyberspace poses. It is summarized in the final conclusions when you write, and I agree with this, that certain conditions would have to be fulfilled for the internet to provide its potentially beneficial opportunities. In some ways these three conditions claw back much or at least some of what preceded them. You write:

First there is a need for a functioning internet and a proper system of internet governance.

Presumably we do not have that in place yet, nor does the paper actually outline what such a "proper" system will look like. Do you believe that the proposals of von Lewinski whom you cite satisfy that condition? And what does one do until that or some similar system is in place as regards the piecemeal proposals already adopted and some which you propose? Is there not a danger that ad hoc measures in the absence of an overall 'proper' system might distort democracy, by empowering certain stake holders and not others?

Your second condition is framed thus:

> [E]asy and effective internet access for everybody is necessary; it must be based upon the principle of net neutrality and allow all citizens effectively to take part online in European governance and politics.

A similar question emerges here. I think no one would quibble that governance would be more effective and user-friendly if Union deliverables were, when possible, available also on line. Though I should add that the examples you gave would pertain mostly to economic operators (e.g. enterprises providing cross boundary services etc) rather than natural individuals and might even increase the perception, only partially true, of a Union of businessmen. But when it comes to governance – input and throughput – would not the current state of internet access which is far from allowing "all citizens effectively to take part online in European governance and politics' frustrate much of what is being advocated. Is there not here, too, the risk of empowerment and disempowerment?

Finally, your third condition:

> [P]rovision must be made for a safe and trustworthy internet though effective regulation and technical provisions for data protections as well as for cyber security at a global level.

Would you not say that we are not only further away than ever in achieving this condition but that recent experiences suggest that the potential for dangerous subversion of democracy is at least as great as the potential for beneficial effects you discuss?

3. My final question goes to an aspect of internet governance and democracy which you mention only obliquely (when for example you wonder whether there is a virtue in having people actually get up and go physically to the polling booth) but which I think merits some reflection. There are a myriad of cyberspace features which even if all your three conditions were satisfied might call for considerable prudence and quite a mixed judgment on the potential impact of the internet on our civic and democratic culture. The internet does create communities, but their internal organization in terms of hierarchy and control or often quite problematic. The internet often atomizes and fragments a sense of collective community and demos in the sense we use this word in the context of 'deoscracy'. It also has the potential to by-pass and undermine our traditional democratic institutions such as parliaments – one feature of our contemporary crisis of democracy being precisely that. And, last but not least, the worrying phenomenon of fake news, even if somewhat exaggerated, is real and gets most of its traction from and within cyberspace.

This is not an invitation to you to address all of these here and now, but if I go back to the title of your paper I think that in the current state of things a more appropriate title would indicate the problematic nature of this tool which like fire can both warm and burn. Maybe a question mark at the end of the title would have struck an appropriate note of caution.

Reply of Ingolf Pernice

1. The first issue to discuss is my attempt to address the gap between the citizens and the institutions of the Union as a problem of democratic legitimacy and transparency. Striving to be as neutral as possible, my under-

standing is that the democratic method could not work without a minimum of understanding of the system and a minimum of information about the political processes, the positions of the actors, the actual debates and also the decisions taken by the institutions. This is what transparency is about, and without this transparency there can be no democratic control, nor can there be accountability. Without transparency and access to information, I submit, people would remain distant and would not care about nor take ownership of the Union and, as a result, would not even be able to take responsibility for the policies led by the institutions. Admittedly, transparency may be ambivalent in real life. If people see and understand what the Union really is and does, they might like it and participate, or they might not be happy with it and turn away. Knowing about the impact of the EU's policies on their conditions of life, they would not remain indifferent; rather, they would get involved, either in an attempt to abolish the EU, or in an attempt to develop it so that it can become what it should be. This is what democracy is about. It is difficult to see, thus, how the EU could function properly without understanding and an open and continuing public discourse not only on specific political issues but also on its constitutional foundations, structures and procedures. Transparency and reliable information on the objectives, institutions and processes are essential for this discourse, and my proposition is that the internet has a potential to facilitate it. The outcome of democratic processes based upon transparency through the internet is not foreseeable, but in spite of the risks posed by filter bubbles[6] and emerging practices like fake news,[7] social bots,[8] manipulative use of big data analysis and micro-targeting,[9] I am confident

6 Eli Pariser, *The Filter Bubble* (London, Penguin Books, 2011).

7 See Fabian Reinbold, 'Deutschland fürchtet die Lügenschleudern', in Spiegel Online of 14 December 2016 at: http://www.spiegel.de/netzwelt/web/fake-news-in-deutschland-was-wir-ueber-das-phaenomen-wissen-a-1125498.html (accessed 7 February 2017).

8 See Justus Bender & Marvin Oppong, 'Frauke Petry und die Bots', in: faz-net of 7 February 2017, at: http://www.faz.net/aktuell/politik/digitaler-wahlkampf-frauke-petry-und-die-bots-14863763.html.

9 See Hannes Grasegger & Miael Krogerus, 'Ich habe nur gezeigt, dass es die Bombe gibt', in *Das Magazin,* No 48, 3 December 2016, at: https://www.dasmagazin.ch/2016/12/03/ich-habe-nur-gezeigt-dass-es-die-bombe-gibt/, for later comments and critique see Patrick Beuth, 'Big Data allein entscheidet keine Wahl' in Zeit Online of 6 December 2016, at: http://www.zeit.de/digital/internet/2016-12/us-wahl-donald-trump-facebook-big-data-cambridge-analytica (both accessed 10 February 2017).

that people will see the benefits of the EU not only as a guarantor of peace, freedom and prosperity in our countries but also for our active participation in shaping globalisation according to our common values. But this, again, needs information, education and transparency as well as a close dialogue between people and institutions as it is facilitated by the internet. The 'self-celebratory statements and instruments of the Commission' you say I am quoting in my chapter, though problematic in part and insufficient, serve as examples of what is already being done —or is on the agenda— to initiate and promote this dialogue, through the introduction of participative procedures about to bring the EU institutions and the citizens closer together.

2. The second issue is the conditions I briefly mentioned that are necessary for the internet to bring about benefits for the legitimacy of the EU and its policies. Yes, they are far from being met, and while we are still striving to achieve a proper system of internet governance, equal and open access for everybody and sufficient data protection and cyber-security as a basis of trust, the benefits for the citizens and for legitimacy may not yet be achieved. In my chapter I basically focus on the opportunities and the aim is to show why it is worthwhile developing further the diverse positive applications of the internet in particular with a view to encouraging citizens' participation in the EU while at the same time emphasising that this objective will not be met without strong efforts to make sure that the three conditions mentioned are met as soon as possible. Both go hand in hand, and one will not be achieved without the other.

3. The third issue is very deep and fundamental: 'Changing the operating system of the state' is not necessarily what we really want; it is full of risks. We have not yet sufficiently studied the impact the internet and —in a broader sense— the information technologies including the internet of things, big data analysis, artificial intelligence, and machine learning will have not only on our societies, business and markets, sciences and work, social relations and many other areas, but also on our systems of governance in a broad sense at all levels, from local to global. This includes a change of the notion and role of states, of supranational organisations like the EU and of international organisations, as well as the emergence of other forms or practices of governance like ICANN or the Internet Governance Forum in the specific field of the internet. Even the internal structures and procedures of public administration are already undergoing fundamental changes, and we have little idea where these processes will lead. You mention a number of risks and issues that need to be considered.

There is a vast field of interdisciplinary research to be undertaken rapidly and seriously, in order to contribute to providing some basis for responsible policies regarding the development, regulation and applications of the internet. My hope is to give a small contribution in this direction, driven by some optimism, I admit, but aiming at opening a discussion on a subject that has not yet been sufficiently discussed.

Many thanks for your comments indicating many important issues for further reflection and research. And I have already put a question mark after the title of my chapter, as you suggested, in order to underline the problematic nature of the internet in this context.

List of Authors

Giacinto della Cananea is full professor of Administrative law and EU administrative law, University of Rome "Tor Vergata". He has tought in the universities of Yale, Duke and Frankfurt. He's is the founding editor, *Italian Journal of Public Law* (2009-) and has been the chairman, panel for the assessment of research output in Italian law schools (2011/13). His last work is "D*ue Process of Law Beyond the State*" (Oxford University Press, 2016, forthcoming).

Tom Eijsbouts is professor of European Constitutional Law at UvA since 2000 and was professor of EU law in Leiden from 2010 to 2015. He is a founding editor of the European Constitutional Law Review. Also has taught philosophy. Before becoming a university teacher in 1986 he made a career as a journalist. Still writes columns and op-eds. Studies: Leiden University, LLM (1969) and PhD (1989, on Law and Chance); Graduate Institute Geneva (DEA).

Federico Fabbrini is Full Professor of European Law at the School of Law & Government of the Dublin City University. He holds a B.A. in "European & Transnational Legal Studies" from the University of Trento (2006), a J.D. in "International Law" from the University of Bologna (2008) and Ph.D. in "Law" from the European University Institute (2012. Before moving to Dublin, he was Associate Professor of "European & International Law" at iCourts, Law Faculty, University of Copenhagen in Danmark and Assistant Professor of "European & Comparative Constitutional Law" at Tilburg Law School, in the Netherlands, where he was awarded tenure. He has published two monographs with OUP and edited several volumes on EU law.

George Gerapetritis is associate professor of constitutional law at the Faculty of Law of the University of Athens. He studied in Athens (LL.B.), Edinburgh (LL.M.) and Oxford (D.Phil), has been a visiting fellow at the University of Oxford and at the University of London and has taught European and comparative constitutional law and history in many universities. He has also been a Fellow of the State Scholarships Foundation of

Greece, of the British Council, of the US German Marshall Fund and of the French Council of State. He is practicing law before the Greek Council of State, the Court of the European Union and the European Court of Human Rights.

George Karavokyris was born in Athens in 1977, he studied law at Aristotle University of Thessaloniki and at University Paris II (Panthéon-Assas), where he completed his Ph.D. in public law. His doctoral thesis is entitled «Personal Autonomy in French Public Law» (ed. Bruylant, 2013, 778 p., in french). He is teaching constitutional law and sociology of law as an adjunct lecturer at the Law School of Democritus University of Thrace. He is also a member of the Athens Bar Association.

Anna-Maria Konsta is a Lecturer at the School of Law of Aristotle University of Thessaloniki, and an Associate Researcher at the Institute for Research in European, International and Comparative Law (IRDEIC) of the University of Toulouse 1 Capitole. She holds a law degree from the Aristotle University, an LL.M. from the College of Europe in Bruges, and is a Doctor of Laws of the European University Institute in Florence. She has worked for the Council of Europe in Strasbourg, the European Commission in Brussels, as a professor in European politics and law at the American College of Thessaloniki, as a Research Associate in the Department of Politics of the University of Leicester, and has taught as a visiting lecturer at the Hellenic National Centre of Public Administration, the Greek National School of Judges, and the European University Centre at Peking University. She has been a visiting scholar at the China University of Political Science and Law in Beijing, and a research fellow at the School of Law of the University of California at Berkeley. She has published in the field of Comparative and European Social Law.

Mattias Kumm is the Inge Rennert Professor of Law and has joined NYU in 2000. He is also Research Professor for "Global Public Law" and is Managing Director of the Center for Global Constitutionalism at the WZB Social Science Research Center in Berlin as well as Professor of Law at Humboldt University.His research and teaching focuses on basic issues and contemporary challenges in Global, European and Comparative Public Law. He has taught at leading universities wordwide, and has held professorial appointments at Harvard, Yale, and the EUI. He is on the Board of various International Journals and Professional Societies and is Founding

Co-Editor in Chief of "Global Constitutionalism" (CUP). Kumm holds a JSDmfrom Harvard Law School and has pursued studies in law, philosophy and political sciences at the Christian Albrechts University of Kiel, Paris I Pantheon Sorbonne and Harvard University before he joined NYU.

Jean-Victor Louis is Hon. Professor at the Université libre de Bruxelles (ULB) (1971-2003); he was legal advisor (1972-1980) and general counsel of the National Bank of Belgium (1980-1998). He is a former president of the Institute of European Studies of the ULB (1980-1992) General Editor of the Cahiers de droit européen since 2001. He was Visiting scholar at the Woodrow Wilson Center for International Scholars, Washington D.C. (September 1988), Visiting Professor at the Columbia University (December 2011-February 2012), and invited professor in a number of Universities, in particular, Universities of Paris I (1986-1987 and from 1995-1996 to 2002-2003), Paris II, (2002-2003). Louis was also Part time Professor at the European University Institute, Florence (1998-2002). He was decorated as Docteur honoris causa of the University of Paris II (Panthéon-Assas), in 2001, and he was Titular of a Belgian Francqui chair at the University of Ghent (Belgium), from 2007 to 2008.

Miguel Poiares Maduro is Professor at the Robert Schuman Centre of the European University Institute where he was the Founding Director of the Global Governance Programme (from 2010 to 2013). From 2013 to 2015 he was Minister Deputy to the Prime Minister and Minister for Regional Development in Portugal. Until 2009 he was Advocate General at the European Court of Justice. He has been a regular Visiting Professor at Yale Law School, the College of Europe and Universidades Católica and Nova in Portugal. He has also taught at the London School of Economics, the Centro de Estudios Constitucionales (Madrid) and Chicago Law School. He is a Doctor of Laws by the European University Institute (Florence) and was the first winner of the Rowe and Maw Prize and winner of the Prize Obiettivo Europa (for the best PhD thesis at the EUI). He has been Fulbright Visiting Research Scholar at Harvard Law School. He is Co-Director of the Academy of International Trade Law (Macao). He belongs to the editorial or advisory board of several law journals, including the European Law Journal and the Common Market Law Review. He has been honoured by the President of the Portuguese Republic with the Order of Sant'Iago da Espada for literary, scientific and artistic merit. In 2010 he was awarded the Gulbenkian Science Prize.

Antonis Manitakis is Emeritus Professor of Constitutional Law, Aristotle University of Thessaloniki (AUTh), Greece; Dean, honoris causa, Law Faculty, Neapolis University, Cyprus; Ex-Minister of Interior and Administrative Reform (May 2012- June 2013, Sept.2015). He holds a PhD in Law, "Université Libre de Bruxelles" (1973) and has been a full-tenured Professor of Constitutional Law (1982-2011) at the Aristotle University of Thessaloniki. He has taught as visiting Professor at the Universities of Montpellier, Saint-Etienne, Paris X, Rome "La Sapienza" and has been a Visiting research-fellow in Princeton University (1998-99). Manitakis has served as Dean of the Law Faculty (AUTh) (1989-1991) and Director of the Post-graduate Department of the Law Faculty of the Thessaloniki (2004-2011). He has also served as Vice President of the Radio and Television National Council (Independent Public Authority, 1997-1999), President and vice- President of the National Committee of Human Rights (2011-2012, member since 1999).

Ana Maria Guerra Martins is Associated Professor at the Law Faculty of Lisbon University, where she read for her PhD and for her Aggregation. Justice at the Portuguese Constitutional Court between 2007 and 2016, she is an expert in EU Law, Constitutional Law and International Law, areas in which she develops her teaching and her researching activities. In her academic path, she was Invited Researcher at the Max-Planck-Institut in Heidelberg and Invited Professor of the Jean Monnet Faculty of the University of Paris XI. She is also a member of the European Public Law Organization and the European Constitutional Law Network. She has published many books, articles and commentaries in various languages on EU **Law** in general, International and European Union Human Rights Law, Procedural Law of the EU, Equality and Non-discrimination in EU Law, European Citizenship and Fundamental Rights, the Treaty of Lisbon and, more recently, Judicial Dialogue between Constitutional Courts and European Courts, Portuguese Constitution and EU Integration, and Portuguese Constitutional Court and Social Rights.

Lina Papadopoulou is an associate professor of constitutional law and holder of a Jean Monnet Chair for European Constitutional Law and Culture at the Aristotle University of Thessaloniki (AUTh), Greece. She studied Law at AUTh (Bachelor 1993), Trier (LLM 1994) and Hannover (PhD 1998) and Political Theory at the London School of Economics (LSE, MSc 1999). She was a Post-doc '*Marie Curie*' Fellow at the LSE (2000-2001) and A.U.Th. (2001/02). Her primary areas of expertise include Greek, comparative and European constitutional issues and human rights, especially equality and non-discrimination, religion and the state, political parties and referenda, and bioethical issues.

Ingolf Pernice served at the European Commission before he became Professor for Public, European and International Law at the Johann Wolfgang Goethe-Universität, Frankfurt and, from 1996 to 2015, at the Humboldt-Universität of Berlin. He founded the Walter Hallstein-Institut for European Constitutional Law and was director of it until spring 2016. He was visiting professor at Paris II (Panthéon-Assas) in 1998. He created the DFG-financed junior research program „Multilevel Constitutionalism – European Experiences and Global Perspectives“ and directed it from 2006 to 2015. In 2008/9 he was invited as a LAPA-fellow to the Woodrow Wilson School for Public and International Affaires and to teach as a Visiting Professor at the Princeton University. In 2011 he established, together with three colleagues, the Alexander von Humboldt Institute for Internet and Society at the Humboldt-University of Berlin and is co-director responsible for the research area "global constitutionalism and the internet".

Joseph H. H. Weiler is Joseph Straus Professor of Law, European Union Jean Monnet Chaired Professor, Co-Director, Jean Monnet Center for International and Regional Economic Law and Justice at NYU. He studied law (LLB and LLM) in the United Kingdom (Sussex and Cambridge) and at the European University Institute in Florence, Italy (PhD), where he later served as professor of law, head of the Department of Law, and most recently as President. In the United States, prior to his appointment at NYU School of Law, he served as professor of law at the University of Michigan and as a chaired professor at Harvard Law School. His research and teaching focus on international law, the law of the European Union and the WTO, and the interface between religion and law. Among his noted books are The Constitution of Europe, Un Europa Cristiana, and a novella, Der Fall Steinmann etc.

Jiri Zemánek is Justice of the Constitutional Court of the Czech Republic and Jean Monnet Professor at the Charles University in Prague Law Faculty. His primary interests are European constitutional law and comparative research of 'European' doctrines of national constitutional courts. He is fellow of Alexander von Humboldt-Stiftung and member of European Constitutional Law Network. His main visiting positions has been Europa-Kolleg Hamburg, HU Berlin and University of Regensburg. His non-academic consulting included membership of the Council for Legislation of the Czech Government, advisory activities for the Senate of the Parliament and for the Representative of the Czech Government in the European Convention on Constitutional Treaty. He was the President of the Czech branches of the International Law Association and of the European Community Studies Association. He is the member of the advisory board of European Constitutional Law Review.